POLICE IN AFI

JAN BEEK
MIRCO GÖPFERT
OLLY OWEN
JONNY STEINBERG
(*Eds.*)

Police in Africa

The Street-Level View

HURST & COMPANY, LONDON

First published in the United Kingdom in 2017 by
C. Hurst & Co. (Publishers) Ltd.,
41 Great Russell Street, London, WC1B 3PL
© Jan Beek and Mirco Göpfert and Olly Owen and Jonny Steinberg,
and the Contributors, 2017
Printed in India

The right of Jan Beek, Mirco Göpfert, Olly Owen, Jonny Steinberg,
and the Contributors to be identified as the authors of this publication
is asserted by them in accordance with the Copyright, Designs and
Patents Act, 1988.

A Cataloguing-in-Publication data record for this book
is available from the British Library.

ISBN: 978-1-84904-577-3 *paperback*

This book is printed using paper from registered sustainable
and managed sources.

www.hurstpublishers.com

CONTENTS

Acknowledgments   vii

Contributors   ix

Foreword: Towards What Kind of Global Policing Studies?
                                           Ian Loader   xiii

Introduction: Policing in Africa Reconsidered
        Jan Beek, Mirco Göpfert, Olly Owen and *Jonny Steinberg*   1

PART I
WHAT IS THE POLICE IN CONTEMPORARY AFRICA?

1. Policing Africa: Structures and Pathways   *Klaus Schlichte*   19

2. What is the Concept of Professionalization Good for? An Argument
   from Late Colonialism   *Joël Glasman*   27

3. The Colonial Subtext of British-led Police Reform in Sierra Leone
                                      Erlend Grøner Krogstad   39

4. Policing During and After Apartheid: A New Perspective on
   Continuity and Change   *Jonny Steinberg*   61

5. Historicising Vigilante Policing in Plateau State, Nigeria
                                              Jimam Lar   79

PART II
WHO ARE THE POLICE IN AFRICA

6. Who are the Police in Africa?   *Thomas Bierschenk*   103

7. Somewhere between Green and Blue: A Special Police Unit
   in the DR Congo   *Laura Thurmann*   121

CONTENTS

8. Moonlighting: Crossing the Public-Private Policing Divide in
   Durban, South Africa   *Tessa Diphoorn*   135
9. Risk and Motivation in Police Work in Nigeria   *Olly Owen*   149
10. Fighting for Respect: Violence, Masculinity and Legitimacy
    in the South African Police Service   *Andrew Faull*   171

PART III
HOW ARE THE POLICE DOING THEIR WORK?

11. Policing Boundaries: The Cultural Work of African Policing
         David Pratten   193
12. The Belly of the Police   *Julia Hornberger*   199
13. Inside the Police Stations in Maputo City: Between Legality and
    Legitimacy   *Helene Maria Kyed*   213
14. Money, Morals and Law: The Legitimacy of Police Traffic Checks
    in Ghana   *Jan Beek*   231
15. Soft Law Enforcement in the Nigerien Gendarmerie: How a Case
    is Born   *Mirco Göpfert*   249
Epilogue   *Alice Hills*   263

Notes   269
Bibliography   329
Index   359

ACKNOWLEDGEMENTS

The idea of this book started with two workshops we held in 2013: one in Oxford (Reconsidering Policing in Africa) and one in Mainz (Just Police Work: Ethnographic Research on the Police in Africa). Already then, the idea of this book was long overdue. Realising this project was, of course, only possible with the relentless support of many friends, colleagues and supporting bodies. Unfortunately we can mention only a few. We would like to express our sincere gratitude to the African Studies Centre and St. Antony's College at the University of Oxford, the Department of Anthropology and African Studies of the Johannes Gutenberg University Mainz, the British Academy's International Partnership and Mobility Scheme, the German Research Foundation (DFG) and the Institute for Advanced Study Konstanz for their assistance and financial support that made the two initial workshops and the preparation of this book possible. For critical comments and guidance, we are grateful to Thomas G. Kirsch, Carola Lentz, as well as the other participants, writers and discussants in our two workshops. In Mainz, Lisa Peth, Mamoudou Sy, Agnès Badou, Sarah Biecker and Julia Eckert, with organisational support from Sven Mietzsch and Cornelia Steudner; and in Oxford Maria Eriksson-Baaz, Andrew Faull, Kemi Rotimi, Bruce Baker, Laurent Fourchard, Bob Arnot, Innocent Chukwuma and Kemi Okenyodo, and discussants Andrea Purdekova, Ben Bradford, Chris Giacomantonio and Bea Jauregui, with support from Susanne Verheul. Above all, we are deeply grateful to the gendarmes and police officers who have accepted us and helped us to understand a little of their world.

CONTRIBUTORS

Jan Beek is Postdoctoral Research Fellow at the AFRASO research programme, Goethe University Frankfurt. He finished his DPhil at the Department of Social Anthropology and African Studies at the University of Mainz in 2014. Based on extensive fieldwork in Ghana, India, Niger and Germany, he has published a book *Producing Stateness: Police Work in Ghana*, (2016) and several articles on everyday police work, state bureaucracies, cybercrime, transregional connections and collaborative research methods.

Thomas Bierschenk is Professor of Anthropology and Modern African Studies at Gutenberg University Mainz, Germany. In his research, he has focused on African public services and civil servants, the ethnography of public policies as well as of the local state in West Africa. He has published, together with Jean-Pierre Olivier de Sardan, *States at Work: Dynamics of African Bureaucracies* (Brill 2014); recently, he authored the chapter 'Police and the State,' in *The Handbook of Global Policing* (Sage 2016).

Tessa Diphoorn is Assistant Professor at the Department of Cultural Anthropology at Utrecht University. In January 2017, she will start on a new NWO-funded (Veni) research project: 'Policing the Police in Kenya: Analysing State Authority from Within'. Previously she conducted extensive ethnographic research about private security in South Africa and her book, *Twilight Policing. Private Security and Violence in Urban South Africa*, has been published with the University of California Press (2016). She also worked as a post-doctoral researcher at the University of Amsterdam, where she conducted research on public-private security assemblages in Kenya, Israel, and Jamaica.

Andrew Faull is a senior researcher at the University of Cape Town's Centre of Criminology, and Editor of the journal South African Crime Quarterly. He is author of the books *Behind the Badge: the untold stories of South Africa's Police Service members*, and *Police Work and Identity: A South African Ethnography*.

Joël Glasman is a lecturer in African History at Humboldt University Berlin. He published a monograph on colonial and post-colonial police forces in Togo (*Les Corps habillés au Togo. Genèse coloniale des métiers de police*, Karthala 2015), as well as several articles on the comparative history and sociology of police forces in Africa (in *History in Africa*, *The Journal of African History*, *Politique Africaine*, and *Genèses*).

Mirco Göpfert is a lecturer in Social and Cultural Anthropology at the University of Konstanz, Germany. While working on this book he was a Fellow at the Institute for Advanced Study, Konstanz. He has published numerous articles on security, police work, and bureaucracy in Niger.

Alice Hills is Professor of Conflict Studies in the School of Government and International Affairs, Durham University. Her current research, which is supported by the European Commission's Horizon 2020 programme, focuses on police-community engagement in Mogadishu, Somaliland and Kenya.

Julia Hornberger is Senior Lecturer in the Department of Anthropology at the University of the Witwatersrand, South Africa. She has worked extensively on questions of policing and human rights in Africa, resulting in the book *Human Rights and Policing: The Meaning of Violence and Justice in the Everyday Policing of Johannesburg* (Routledge 2011). Her current research interest lies in how health, security and market forces intersect around the figure of the pharmaceutical company, globally and in South Africa.

Erlend Grøner Krogstad is Senior Adviser in the Norwegian Ministry of Climate and Environment where he works on supporting climate action in developing countries. His DPhil from Oxford explored how reinterpretations of sovereignty, security and statehood affected British-led strategies of state-building in Sierra Leone from 1945–1961 and 1998–2007.

Helene Maria Kyed is an anthropologist and Senior Researcher at the Danish Institute for International Studies. Her research focuses on the politics of everyday justice and security provision, including extensive ethnographic fieldwork on the state police, civilian community policing groups and traditional authorities in Mozambique and Swaziland. Her latest edited book is *Policing and the Politics of Order Making* (2015, Routledge).

Jimam Lar is Lecturer in History at the University of Jos, Nigeria; he has done extensive research on the history of plural policing and inter-group relations in central Nigeria. He is currently researching the role of non-state actors in conflict management and peacebuilding in selected central Nigerian conflict theatres.

Ian Loader is Professor of Criminology at the University of Oxford, UK. He is editor (with Ben Bradford, Bea Jauregui and Jonny Steinberg) of the *SAGE Handbook of Global Policing* (2016).

Olly Owen is a Research Fellow at Oxford University's Department of International Development. His interests centre on political anthropology and political economy in West Africa. His doctoral study was an ethnography of policing in Nigeria; both this and his current research on taxation and social contract in Nigeria were funded by the UK's Economic and Social Research Council.

David Pratten is Associate Professor at the African Studies Centre and Institute of Social and Cultural Anthropology, Oxford University, UK. He is author of *The Man-Leopard Murders: History and Society in Nigeria* (2007) and co-edited *AFRICA: The Journal of the International African Institute* (2010–16). His research focuses on youth, vigilantism and masking in Nigeria.

Klaus Schlichte is Professor of International Relations, University of Bremen. With an interest in global political sociology, Klaus Schlichte has carried out research in Senegal, Mali, Serbia, France and Uganda. His main publications include *In the Shadow of Violence: The Politics of Armed Groups* (Frankfurt/ Main; Chicago 2009) and *The Dynamics of States. The Formation and Crises of State Domination* (Routledge; Aldershot, UK).

Jonny Steinberg is Professor of African Studies at Oxford University. His books include *A Man of Good Hope* which explores the aftermath of the Somali civil war, undocumented migration in the Horn of Africa and xenophobia in South Africa; and *Thin Blue*, which examines policing after apartheid.

Laura Thurmann studied Social Anthropology at Johannes Gutenberg University, Mainz. For her Bachelor thesis on a special police unit in Kinshasa, she conducted field research on police and security issues in the DR Congo (2012), followed by a field study on police, media and counter-terrorism measures in Niamey, Niger (2013). She received an M.A. degree with an empirical study on gender and security issues in anthropological fieldwork in 2016.

FOREWORD

TOWARDS WHAT KIND OF GLOBAL POLICING STUDIES?

Ian Loader

The social scientific study of policing is now over more than half a century old. Since the pioneering work of William Westley in the 1950s and Michael Banton in the 1960s, scholarly research and reflection on policing has mushroomed into an established sub-field of the social sciences. Such research now takes place in universities, think-tanks, government agencies and inside police departments. A great deal has been learned about the police mandate, styles and effectiveness, about the use and social and spatial distribution of coercive force, about the training of officers and cultures of police organizations, about racist and sexist practices, about governance and accountability, and about cultural representations of policing and the symbolic power of state police. Yet notwithstanding these accomplishments, and the plurality of theoretical perspectives and methodological approaches that have generated them, the field has tended to coalesce around certain features. The study of policing remains dominated by US scholarship and weighted towards Anglo-American police institutions (in part because these institutions have become relatively open to accountability via research, something that cannot really be said of their counterparts in, say, continental or post-communist Europe). The field tends to be focused on police organizations and working practices in ways that lift those organizations from the social, cultural and political contexts that structure policing and which are, in part, structured by policing. We thus know a lot about 'police culture' but still rather less about what I once termed 'policing cultures'—the amalgam of institutions, practices and policies, myths, memories, meanings, and values that, at any given time, constitute the idea of policing within particular societies.[1] Finally, the field has developed a proximity to its object of enquiry that undoubtedly brings many benefits but which also places it at constant risk of addressing official problematics—and thereby prioritizing questions of instrumental effectiveness (does this or that police tactic work?) over those of sociological curiosity (why did this happen? what is its meaning and significance?) and philosophical import (can this be justified?). As Murphy puts it: 'Local police studies are primarily aimed at refining established police techniques, organization and operations'.[2]

There have in recent years been several indications that policing studies is shedding such parochialism—becoming, one might say, more 'global' in outlook. In the policing context, however, this slippery term can signify a range of orientations. It can be taken, firstly, to refer to the growth of studies of police organizations beyond the Anglo-American 'core' and to the related development of comparative enquiries into policing models and the formation and functioning of different national police institutions. As a consequence, we now know much at a descriptive level about policing across the world. Secondly, a global orientation can signal the increased movement across borders of policy formulas, rhetorics and motifs and the paying of closer attention to the manner and directions in which police practices do or do not 'travel'. Some police scholars have become engaged as 'policy entrepreneurs' in these processes of circulation, whether in respect of community policing, zero tolerance, intelligence-led policing or nodal governance. Others have remained observers and critics—attuned to and often sharply critical of what they see as the uncritical marketing and import of 'Western' policing models and a traffic flow which remains overwhelmingly from the North to the 'global South'. A global outlook has, thirdly, come to mean attending to the expansion of forms of cross-border police cooperation and to the development of new international or transnational policing institutions. Research here has focused on the way in which cross-border policing practices have emerged in response to such matters as organized crime, terrorism, mega-events, political protest and cybercrime; on the formation and work of international police units in peace-keeping operations and post-conflict reconstruction, and on the part that agencies such as Europol and Frontex are playing in shaping contemporary

Europe and defending its borders. Finally, one might point to successive bids for hegemony made by coalitions of police actors and researchers proselytizing on behalf of particular conceptions of policing and an attendant mission for police research. For many years, police activists and scholars have lobbied in these terms to spread the wisdom of community or problem-solving policing. Today, a bid for global reach and influence is being actively made by the 'evidence-based policing movement' in support of a particular vision of 'what works' in policing and its preferred model and set of methods for conducting police research.

In light of these developments there is value just now in taking time to reflect on the various paths that an emergent field of global policing studies might take. Given the competing possibilities at play, it is also worth thinking hard about how to shape the global study of policing so that it is informed by a diverse range of theoretical resources and disciplinary traditions, methodologically pluralist, intellectually curious, and socially engaged. One has to think, furthermore, about the conditions for that field to become genuinely cosmopolitan in orientation, open to having the social analysis and understanding of police forms influenced by experiences of policing, and of being policed, beyond the parameters of hitherto dominant Anglo-American models.

Set against this backdrop, this volume is to be greatly welcomed—both for its contributors and its contributions. The former merit a mention because, taken together, they constitute a group of young scholars from different jurisdictions bringing energy and insight to the study of policing in Africa from a range of disciplinary perspectives—history, political science and perhaps especially anthropology.[3] In terms of its substance, three particular themes are worthy of note, not only in terms of their contribution to understanding the dynamics of police institutions in Africa, but also in respect of the wider question of what they might bring to the prospective field of global policing studies.

The first issue concerns the way in which the studies collected in this volume contribute to what may amount to an ethnographic turn in policing studies. As is well known, the pioneering work in police sociology in the 1970s largely involved immersive participant observation of officers at work or encounters between the police and the policed. Much of what has become part of the stock of common knowledge in the field of policing—whether in respect of police culture, or selective law enforcement, or the use of discretion—began as ethnographic discoveries, social facts about police work that were often greeted initially by official denial. Over recent decades, for reasons ranging from the dominance of policy concerns to the altered conditions of academic knowledge production, ethnographic enquiry has shifted from the centre to the margins of policing studies—albeit those methodological margins continue to produce some exemplary studies. Its central place in the studies collected in this volume is thus a welcome development. In the present case, ethnographic fieldwork generates the kinds of fine-grained knowledge of the social world that deepens our understanding of state policing across Africa. But it also bodes well for the formation of a field of global policing that is intellectually curious and methodologically pluralistic. It is a common misconception that globalizing processes necessitate a turn away from 'the situated' and 'the local' towards the large-scale mapping of flows and networks and efforts at grand theorizing. This book does a great deal to demonstrate that this need not—and should not—be the case. Global policing studies needs to make ample room for the close observation of 'local' forms—in the full knowledge, well evidenced in this volume, that local policing is shaped by legacies of the past and criss-crossed and in part constituted by trans-local and trans-national actors and processes.

A second contribution lies in the emphasis—or, one ought to say, re-emphasis—on practice. As John-Paul Brodeur pointed out in his last book,[4] the prevailing instrumentalism of policing studies has resulted in the question of 'what works?' elbowing out consideration of the prior, more basic matter of 'what happens?'. The studies collected in this volume offer a much needed corrective to this tendency. They refocus our collective attention on questions of what the police do and who the police are. They make central the issue of what it means and feels like to be a police officer working in often precarious institutional contexts and socio-political settings—conditions in which officers are variously shown to be managing multiple risks, searching for respect, procuring food and drink, or simply trying to scrape together a living. The research reported here also returns us—in new settings—to some old and sometimes neglected thematics of police studies. These studies demonstrate that policing is about much more than something called crime: it is always also about violence, negotiation, trading, morality, sociality, and the control and constitution of populations. They highlight the limitations of some currently in-vogue notions, such as professionalism. They remind us that 'cases' are produced rather than discovered and that 'Law' is a resource that officers deploy, not a set of sovereign proclamations that the police enforce. This refocusing of enquiry around the part that police practices play in the constitution and regulation of everyday life offers one route through which knowledge might productively travel (back) from South to North.

Thirdly, and finally, this volume testifies to the value of studying police organizations in ways that acknowledge and investigate how these organizations condition, and are conditioned by, the socio-political contexts within which they operate. This volume joins a relatively small but important body of scholarship on policing in Africa. However, the editors argue, previous research has tended to take the failings of state policing institutions as a given and explore instead the alternative, non-state means through which Africans conceive of and seek security. The aim of this volume, by contrast is to re-centre—and in so doing re-consider—state police forces. This re-centring is accomplished in ways that do not merely shed light on the practices of these institutions, as mentioned. Full and close attention is also paid to the intimate entanglement of state policing with the question of how 'community', 'governance' and 'political order' are made and imagined, and with processes of continuity and change in respect of these larger entities. Via a series of detailed engagements with particular African police forces and the close analysis of how these forces interact with their 'outside', we are once again reminded that policing is inseparably part of struggles over the meaning of social and political order and an important determinant—for better and for worse—of the well-being of those living under that order. Global policing studies that are neglectful of these lessons are not going to be worth building on.

INTRODUCTION

POLICING IN AFRICA RECONSIDERED

Jan Beek, Mirco Göpfert, Olly Owen and *Jonny Steinberg*

Ethnographic work on public police bureaucracies in Africa is just beginning. There are reasons for this. That Africanist scholarship, voluminous and wide-ranging, has until recently taken next to no interest in public police forces is no coincidence. When introducing the work contained in this volume, we need to account for what has sparked it, and why the spark has come so late.

The spectacle of public institutions unravelling, of state formation in reverse, as it were, is something to behold. Scholarship on Africa spent a good quarter of a century fixated upon it. And quite understandably, for a series of processes both dramatic and tragic did indeed engulf many African states in the late twentieth century. We are talking, of course, of the oil shocks of the 1970s, of the endemic indebtedness that ensued, the structural adjustment programmes, the drama of state institutions shrinking, corroding, and, in some instances, disappearing; of everyday life adjusting to new absences. In his panoramic book, *Africans: The History of a Continent*, John Iliffe describes aspects of this corrosion in forensic detail:

> Ghana's real per capita public expenditure on health fell by 60 per cent between 1974 and 1984; eight years later the country had some 50,000 cases of yaws, a disease of poverty supposedly eradicated before independence, and its childhood

1

mortality had risen. Tuberculosis, cholera and yellow fever became more prevalent in sub-Saharan Africa, while each year an estimated 20,000 to 25,000 victim contracted sleeping sickness ... Access to effective medicine depended increasingly on wealth, so that infant mortality rates varied more widely with income in cities like Abidjan than they had in nineteenth-century Europe.[1]

As for education:

Between 1960 and 1983, primary school education in Black Africa roughly quadrupled, secondary school places multiplied six-fold, and the number of university places increased twenty-fold. It was one of the great successes of independence... Thereafter, however, state education faltered as the ever-expanding child population outran resources. During the 1980s, primary school enrolment dropped from 70 to 77 per cent of the age group. Good education often became a privilege of the elite who could pay for it...[2]

Public security and justice also fell subject to the same logics. As informal livelihoods supplemented and supplanted formal employment, 'grey' and criminal economies also grew, increasingly penetrating state institutions whose sovereignty became a tradeable asset even implicating the criminalisation of the state itself.[3] At the same time, state capacity for law enforcement and justice was continually reduced, contributing to the holistic failure of state systems, and sometimes dissolving into instability and conflict.

It is no exaggeration to say that in the last quarter of the twentieth century, almost everything written on Africa that has come to be regarded as seminal has in some way documented, or borrowed its spirit from, the spectacle of decline. To name just a handful of works: in anthropology, there is James Ferguson's celebrated ethnography of the Zambian copperbelt in which expectations of modernity live on after its prospects have disappeared, creating the eerie sense that Zambia has been cut adrift from the world.[4] In political science, there has been something of an intellectual celebration of the functionality of disorder, of informality, of shadow systems concealed behind the façade of formal systems, of elites who prosper not in spite, but because of the ruin of public institutions.[5]

Others have taken the spirit of decline that pervaded late twentieth-century Africa and used it to project a story into the past, tracing continuities that would have puzzled and offended the generation of Africans who celebrated independence. There is Jean-Francois Bayart's famous thesis on 'extraversion', in which he argues that African elites have since long before colonial times used the very weakness of their institutions in the international system to leverage the power of external forces.[6] There is Jeffrey Herbst's influential argument that from pre-colonial times right through to the present, states in Africa have always struggled to project power; whether in regard to early eighteenth-century Kumasi or late twentieth-century Accra, he argues, a person who walks far enough from the capital city will inevitably find themselves on land where questions of sovereignty and authority are murky and grey.[7] And there is Jackson and Rosberg's seminal thesis that Africa's postcolonial states were established juridically, in other words, by international agreement, rather than empirically, that is, through an endogenous monopolisation of legitimate violence, suggesting that African states were flimsily assembled at the very beginning and liable to fall over or buckle.[8]

The list goes on: the most enduring ethnographies of commercial life in late twentieth-century African cities are on economies that manage to flourish or endure in the absence of well-functioning state institutions;[9] while scholarly work on youth has focused on the absence of the state bureaucracies that once provided careers by which middle-class Africans defined adulthood.[10]

But preoccupations are beginning to shift, fashions to change. Processes that have long been invisible to scholars have come into view. In part it is because sub-Saharan Africa has just experienced its first uninterrupted decade of economic growth since the 1960s; in part because a long resource boom has made African states more visible in the international system. Whatever the causes, and they are surely many, in recent times, attention has begun slowly to settle, not on bureaucratic absences, but on presences, not on projects abandoned, but on projects that endure. In what Ricardo Soares de Oliveira and his colleagues have called Africa's new illiberal states—Ethiopia, Rwanda, Angola, Sudan—scholarship has begun to grasp the powerful presence of state institutions in everyday African life, the purposes that animate them and the people that staff them.[11] To cite just a couple of examples, recent scholarship has shown the extraordinary dexterity to which the Ethiopian state reached into the everyday lives of youths on the margins of Addis Ababa in the wake of urban disturbances in 2005.[12] In Angola, attention is now being paid to the ambitions of the state to exhibit signs of its permanence in the form of grand infrastructure and design projects. In Rwanda, the ubiquity of state security organs in the most intimate spheres of common life is now well documented.

More benign examples abound. There is currently a project underway documenting the extraordinarily rapid rise of non-contributory welfare transfers in several sub-Saharan African countries.[13] In medical scholarship, attention is focusing on the public institutions in sub-Saharan Africa responsible for administering anti-retroviral treatment to several million people. The best of this scholarship is by no stretch of the imagination a facile, good news story about Africa rising. It is born, rather of the analytical recognition that African states have a presence in African life, a presence that has been neglected for many years and that needs to be better understood.

Policing scholarship has been slow to register these new preoccupations. This is in part because the spirit of decline that marked Africanist scholarship for so long rendered the very idea of studying state police organisations odd. Until recently, scholarly works on formal policing institutions in Africa were few and far between, despite the fact that in countries like Nigeria, South Africa, Ghana and others, there are very large public police bureaucracies with long histories. Africanist scholars who did turn their attention to questions of coercion in the recent past have on the whole written about the multitude of informal processes that fill the vacuum in which a professional, public policing bureaucracy ought to have stood. A great deal of attention has also been paid to state actors who co-opt or manipulate informal organs like vigilante groups and urban gangs to disorganise and disrupt their opponents.[14] But throughout, state police forces have stood as a silent 'offstage' other, assumed to be either barely present or not relevant. If scholars mentioned the police, they reproduced the powerful and unambiguous imaginaries that also circulate in Africa: of corrupt, politically influenced, brutal and overall dysfunctional organisations treating citizens as their captives rather than their wards. The police, considered from this aspect, were not a symbol of security but of the various insecurities that dictated the lives of Africans.

This book gathers together some of the work that we like to think constitutes the beginning of a renaissance. Most of the scholars whose essays follow are ethnographers. All have spent considerable time on the ground with African police personnel, observing the quotidian dimensions of their work. This everydayness is new: it has been a long time since scholarship in Africa paid any serious attention to the rhythms and mentalities of what one author in the volume refers to as 'bureaucrats in uniform'.[15]

Re-focusing on the state

Globally, the state is the expected final arbiter of security and resolver of security challenges, normatively cast in that capacity by citizens and by the international system alike. Police are central to that, ordinarily delegated the monopoly of legitimate violence at the core of statehood itself. This remains a constant and durable fact in the way we imagine security, even in a world where some states have partially re-oriented away from directly providing it, to authorising or regulating others who do.[16] In Africa, as that capacity, legitimacy and monopoly was stretched to—and in some cases, past—breaking point in the 1990s, non-state actors supplanted many of those functions. In the subsequent decade of regrowth, a number of African states have moved to re-occupy this space, or to link with and control those who now do, especially where the growth of such alternative founts of security and sovereignty pose a threat to party-states such as Ethiopia which aspire to omniscience over society.[17] This re-occupation is not a uniform trend and varies immensely from region to region, as developments in northern Mali or Nigeria show. Still, Ethiopia or Rwanda have shown that African states operate within a new set of possibilities, including the expansion of state control and authority.

Study of the African state has unsurprisingly been the domain of political scientists, who have largely engaged in systemic analyses, assumptions about the state as a total formation. Yet this ignores something which requires problematising, something Ralph Miliband neatly captures as 'the fact that the "state" is not a thing, *that it does not, as such, exist*'.[18] The state is an abstract, a system of institutions, people, buildings, uniforms, documents and above all, practices and the imaginaries they produce, bound together by ideology, constitution and/or simple mass collusion. Abrams notes that we often confound ourselves at the outset by taking the political imagining at its word and studying an abstracted state rather than what its component parts and agencies actually do.[19] Instead of treating the state as an entity, it can often more productively be understood as state-ness, a quality of persons or organisations, to link social imaginations and practices.

So perhaps we are overdue a closer look at states in terms of those institutions, people, and practices. This is an emergent field in the social sciences. One way is through the models constructed in schools of public administration. Another is qualitative studies of actual state practices, which began with a realisation of the importance of the state as imaginary in everyday life. Examinations of how people interact with or imagine the state from outside— how it is construed through and in practice—have often been influenced by Akhil Gupta's work on discourses of corruption seen through the offices of village bureaucrats in north India, itself a development of a regional school of looking at politics from below.[20] In Africa, Janet Roitman and Brenda Chalfin have similarly examined gatekeeper institutions, as customs agents, traders, smugglers, reformers, entrepreneurs and others negotiate the powers and perks of the state, defining the contours of the public sphere at the borders of nations.[21] Blundo and Olivier de Sardan began to cross the outside/inside boundary in what they called 'a socio-anthropology of African public spaces'.[22] The works here are part of a closer examination taken further inside state institutions themselves. As such, these essays form part of a wider movement. The collaborative European-African States at Work project has been influential in bringing many scholars with such interests together, and has prompted parallel studies of 'bureaucrats in uniform' across a variety of African state agencies.[23] Still, other researchers have come to the same subject via other paths, through studies of change processes, histories and anthropologies of security and control, awareness of the deficiencies of existing paradigms, and above all, the simple salience of the issues around state policing in the lived experience of African public spaces, all of which have led to the same fundamental enquiry: what are state police forces, and what do they really do?

This question is all the more important because dominant disciplines dealing with the security sector—politics, peace studies, and the burgeoning policy-oriented security-sector reform—all tend to assume either the mechanistic functioning or inherent dysfunction of state security institutions, without examining what they really do and how they really do it. Policing practices inform public expectations, shape responses and spawn imitators in their own image: informal institutions and their practices are equally influenced by the state as a fount of juridical legitimacy—vigilance groups and others speak 'languages of state-ness' as part of their claims to status.[24] Beyond this, policing practices and procedures structure public life in the sense of creating meaning, in the lived existence of stateness as experienced by their citizens. What we see here is not an externally-imposed state teetering on top of traditional African society, two spheres always doomed to collision and contention; nor do we see state bureaucracies continually disembowelled by their 'shadows'.[25] Instead, we see state institutions, the people who staff them, and the people who interact with them engaged in practices which continually fuse and reshape, while remaining path-dependent. In these studies, we see policing practices which incorporate both colonial pasts and communitarian models of justice, as well as the 'sedimentation' of successive waves of reforms and readjustments in daily arbitrations of justice and order.[26]

Furthermore, many of these studies should point us back to an object hiding in plain sight—the state institution as part of society. Perhaps due to their restricted abilities to mobilise politically, the human presence of police officers in the social and political landscape remains generally less visible than other organised sectors of state employees such as teachers, civil servants and others.

Yet police forces are huge social formations—encompassing hundreds of thousands of officers and their dependents across the African continent—which lay totalising claims on their members, dictating residence, career paths, economic and social status and mobility, professional and personal values and often political positions. Police remain a somewhat exotic object even within the realm of studying the state, and this volume is a contribution towards rendering them more visible.

Ethnography and police work in comparative perspective

Ethnographic research, a somewhat intimate empirical endeavour that stretches out over a long period of time, is a privileged way to make sense of any human occupation, not least police work. Since the 1960s, many sociologists and criminologists have conducted ethnographic studies of police. One of the most prominent is Egon Bittner.[27] Other pioneers are Michael Banton who worked with police in Scotland and the USA,[28] William Westley on police occupational culture,[29] Simon Holdaway, a policeman-turned-sociologist, who conducted a covert ethnography of police work in Britain, and his policeman-turned-anthropologist contemporary Malcolm Young,[30] Peter Manning who writes of the 'drama' of police work,[31] and Dominique Monjardet who studied the police in France.[32]

But police in Africa, along with most other postcolonial state institutions on the continent, have rarely been studied with ethnographic methods until quite recently.[33] Otwin Marenin was about the first empirical researcher to focus on police in Africa, albeit from a non-ethnographic political science perspective.[34] Apart from the work of historians like Tamuno, Anderson and Killingray, Rotimi[35] and more recently the contributors in the volume *Maintenir l'ordre colonial* edited by Jean-Pierre Bat and Nicolas Courtin,[36] police in Africa was almost exclusively studied by political scientists. Alice Hills' *Policing Africa* is one of the most influential works in that respect.[37]

Since the 2000s, more and more scholars have focused on everyday modes of public security provision in Africa; but they have been mostly interested in non-state policing by vigilante organisations or other alternative policing actors.[38] With the growing interest in state institutions by anthropologists and ethnographers, ethnographic research on state police is finally beginning to emerge. Each of the authors assembled in this volume has contributed to this rapidly expanding field of ethnographic research on police organisations in Africa.[39] There are, of course, others who have contributed and still are contributing significantly in this respect, such as Sarah Bieker and Klaus Schlichte on policing arrangements in Uganda,[40] Jean and John Comaroff with their work on police work in South Africa,[41] and Gernot Klantschnig with his work on policing narcotic drugs in Nigeria.[42] In-depth ethnographic approaches toward police work have also multiplied beyond Africa: Julia Eckert's and Beatrice Jauregui's studies in India,[43] Didier Fassin's research in France,[44] and Jeffrey Martin's work on police work in Taiwan,[45] to name but a few.

What does ethnography bring to the study of police work in Africa? First, it opens a window onto the banality of everyday police work in Africa. As surprising—or as obvious—as this statement may seem, police work in Africa is as workaday as it is anywhere, a fact often overlooked by the customary debates about violence and corruption that consume scholarly writing about police in Africa. Observing from close range the social practice of police officers' daily work, sometimes even participating in it, reveals that police officers in DR Congo, Ghana, Mozambique, Niger, Nigeria, Sierra Leone, South Africa and Togo control traffic, patrol streets, maintain public order, investigate petty crimes and produce bureaucratic documents, just like police anywhere. And so, ethnography shifts focus, as it were, and allows us to change the subject to the everyday.

Second, ethnographic research, when substantiated by historical and sociological knowledge, allows for what Didier Fassin calls 'bringing into perspective different perspectives about the world'—a critical perspectivism.[46] It makes accessible the police officers' point of view, situates it among other local views on what the police do or should do, and thus enables us to question problematic blanket terms such as 'corruption' and 'police violence'. And here, once again perhaps to the surprise of many, one learns that many police officers in Africa also want to be fair and just in what they do and are caught in paradoxes generated by the ways in which they do it.

Third, and perhaps most importantly, ethnography allows for close comparison. The fieldwork reflected in this volume was conducted in different police organizations in various African countries, ranging from the Gendarmerie in Niger to the South African Police Service. Despite obvious differences between these countries, many of the practices and interactions depicted in this volume are similar enough to withstand fruitful comparison. The chapters that follow also implicitly make global comparisons, for all of them are in dialogue with police research from non-African countries, using scholarship from around the world to make sense of their own findings in the field. At first glance, the usefulness of concepts developed on the basis of research on police in the Global North seems questionable. For instance, how germane are the concepts Bittner developed while working on skid row in the 1960s for contemporary Africa? We are convinced that such ideas can success-fully travel, as long as the journey is conducted with scholarly care. The con-tributors to this volume share the fundamental assumption that African and non-African police organisations are comparable with one another. Instead of searching for stark contrasts—or marked similarities—this allows us to con-template such comparisons based on ethnographic material.[47] Comparative research in that sense means sharing questions, not conclusions.[48] It also allows for a fruitful dialogue between African and other police scholars, opening up possibilities for police scholarship in general to move in new directions.

However, the approach presented here also has certain limitations. For example, case studies from East Africa could have enlarged this volume. Their absence makes apparent that ethnographic police research in Africa is a newly emerging field, with many possible areas for future research. Another limita-tion derives from the distribution of this book's case studies. Indeed, this book attempts to enable comparisons of very different bureaucracies in hugely different contexts, including cases from Sierra Leone and the DR Congo with arguably rather fragile policing arrangements, but mostly drawing from rela-tively democratic or consolidating countries. This selection was shaped in part by access; while ethnographic police research enables a more in-depth view of police organisations, the risk this implies for senior officers and politicians makes access for researchers highly improbable in non-democratic political systems. Thus, while earlier studies might have overemphasised insecurities in Africa, our approach perhaps overlooks some of these state-sponsored inse-curities or highly politicised conceptions of crime and order that still deter-mine the lives of many Africans; policing in a *de facto* party state may look as different to its liberal neighbour as the East and West Berlin police forces depicted by Glaeser,[49] and different again in places where the concept of state authority itself is precarious, such as Somalia.[50] Still, the selection of demo-cratic countries and countries in which the police organizations are being rebuilt also reflects real historical transformations. The democratization pro-cesses of the 1990s, reconstruction processes in post-conflict states, and the growth of an international police reform apparatus have changed police work in sub-Saharan Africa, and thereby enabled and channelled the contributors' research access.[51] What this book can offer, however, is an anti-exoticist view on state policing in Africa and bring it into dialogue with other forms of policing worldwide.

Police work in Africa is not essentially different, but that does mean that there is nothing distinctive about African state police. What differentiates it are specific features that mark its context: the historical sedimentation of unique colonial and post-colonial experiences, the particular localised geometry of security challenges, competing state and non-state policing organisations, weak police legitimacy, a multitude of transnationally circulating police models, plural public notions of fairness and justice, formal under-regulation, limited resources and improvised equipment. This context and particular historicity brings to the fore specifics of police work that are not as visible and obvious, but nevertheless present, in other police organisations. Particular arrays of security challenges are undoubtedly common in many contemporary African states, whereby mundane crime against property and persons is joined by organised banditry, gang violence, insecurity generated by the state itself, political or communal violence, and not least sustained existential challenges with effects in the field of security. But such 'radical insecurity' is not limited to, or even typical of, African states as much as it is resonant with other developed and developing-world contexts (see the ethnographies mentioned above). Key issues that can be explored in research of the police in Africa— fragile legitimacy, competing violence specialists and transnational influences—are central to the understanding of the police and the state everywhere, but in African countries these questions can be developed more explicitly. Thus social scientists in Africa are in a position to contribute to police research at large, as well as to broader debates on social order in contemporary societies. This is what Jean and John Comaroff hope to achieve with their book *Theory from the South*, when they insist that the 'Global South' ought to be a source rather than an object of theory.[52]

Contributions of this volume

Police research in Africa is an interdisciplinary endeavour; this book brings together young researchers and established scholars from social anthropology, political science, peace and conflict studies, and history; from both within and outside the continent. They explore ethnographically the mundane, everyday dimension of police work in Africa. The case studies here use ethnographies of police work to reflect on questions relating to the nature of legal norms, the political dimension of police work, questions of state, stateness and bureaucracy, and the complex relationship of crime and punishment in—but also beyond—police organisations, in—but also beyond—Africa. The studies here depict state institutions at work in wider society, both entities interpenetrating and structuring each other. Public cultures, public demands, and notions of legitimacy and justice condition what Schlichte (in this volume) calls the connected history of policing, a recognisable global model applied everywhere with innumerable local nuances; whether rooted in local forms and ideas, derived from a sense of professional identity, influenced by transnational currents, or by other influential state agencies such as militaries.

This volume is organised into three parts, each headed by an introductory discussion and containing four chapters. The first part asks *What is the police in contemporary Africa?* Adopting a historical perspective, the contributors here retrace the pathways of police organisations (and one vigilante movement) in Africa. A contribution by Klaus Schlichte sets the framework. From a well-informed vantage point of a historical sociology of the police and a broad comparative perspective, he argues that policing in Africa should be situated in a globally connected history. Specific policing practices and organisational models were exported from Europe and then creatively adapted; other practices and models emerged in different places simultaneously and were re-connected through ex-post classification (as under the label 'community policing'). The central question he evokes is: if the global history of policing is indeed a connected history, of what do these connections consist and how do they change over time?

One essential moment in this connected history is the notion of 'professionalization'. Joël Glasman, drawing on archival material and oral sources from his historical research on the Togolese police, argues that the notion of professionalization, until now a hidden passenger of police studies, is not a useful analytical category to make sense of police organisations. Like many of the notions used in police support and Security Sector Reform projects, it is both teleological and Eurocentric, and as such creates analytical problems. The underlying presupposition is that African police are still not professional enough; and professionalisation is often equated with adherence to strict bureaucratic standards. Yet Glasman shows that the bureaucratisation of late colonial Togolese police was also perfectly in line with a rise in police violence and the neglect of legal norms.

Erlend Grøner Krogstad examines the role of memories of Sierra Leone's British colonial past in shaping policing practices in the wake of a long civil war. Sierra Leonean powerholders mobilise this history nostalgically to build international alliances, ensure continued funding and as an insurance against coups. This is a particularly complex exemplar of Schlichte's 'connections', for the connections here are as much to the past as to the present, and as much to Sierra Leone itself as to Europe.

Jonny Steinberg addresses the question of historical continuity and change within one particular police organisation, namely the South African Police Service after the end of apartheid. The prevalent interest in continuity between apartheid and post-apartheid policing is understandable, as Steinberg concedes, but it 'risks blinding scholarship to what has changed'. At the heart of this change lies the relationship between policing and political order, between politics and state coercion. Whereas during apartheid the police was primarily driven by the fight against insurgency, the police in democratic South Africa is primarily tasked with managing the conflicts of the ruling ANC. Steinberg's piece is essentially an investigation into the causal connections between past and present. He argues that instruments, institutions and mentalities from the past survive insofar as they are useful to agents in the present. This is not dissimilar to the conclusions Krogstad draws in regards to Sierra Leone's relationship to its colonial past. Reading Krogstad's and Steinberg's pieces together is a good example of the power of comparison; for, on the surface, Sierra Leone and South Africa could not be more different.

Starting from the premise that in studying contemporary policing practices in Africa one needs to also acknowledge the role of non-state policing actors, Jimam Lar explores the historicity of community policing groups, or, more pejoratively, vigilante movements, in Plateau State, Nigeria. He establishes a link between the plural policing landscapes of colonial and postcolonial Nigeria, and finally takes the Vigilante Group of Nigeria as a case study to highlight contemporary features and characteristics of this plurality. One of its features is, perhaps ironically, not the absence, retreat or weakness, but rather the extension of the state.

The second part asks *Who are the police in Africa?* It adopts the 'inside view' from within the police and is interested in police organisations as social institutions consisting of individuals struggling with their jobs. Thomas Bierschenk provides a broad introduction to this part, asking whether police in Africa is even a useful category. Developing three comparative dimensions, Bierschenk highlights the particular context of police work in Africa at a specific historical moment. In Africa, police organisations are characterised by a high degree of internal norm pluralism, organisational opacity and a large gap between everyday practices and bureaucratic ideals, set amid wider societies marked by uncertainty and precariousness. Police officers respond to these conditions with improvisation and 'bricolage' in a 'twilight zone' between public and the private. Tessa Diphoorn focuses on that twilight zone in her study of police officers' 'moonlighting' in South Africa. Working in security-related fields outside their police job, as bouncers or in private security companies, police officers engage in a space between public and private policing. She shows not only that state and non-state policing practices influence one another, but that each contains an element of the other. Moonlighting is a continuous boundary-crossing between public and private, between state and non-state.

In the following chapter, Laura Thurman explores a different kind of twilight zone: she describes the ambivalent self-perception of the officers in a recently created special police unit in DR Congo. Even though the police reforms since 2009 have aimed at a demilitarized Congolese police, the organization and structure of this special unit, tasked with the fight against organised crime in Kinshasa, is remarkably similar to military forces. She argues that these officers are ambivalent about whether they are soldiers or police personnel.

Olly Owen also accentuates police officers' self-perception and sets it in relation with the organisational conditions in which officers work. His contribution focuses on risk and motivation in the lives of police officers in Nigeria. He argues that officers perceive risk, especially career risk, as a result of the everyday contingencies of their job including the hierarchy of their institution. The strategies they employ to deal with this risk, particularly evasion and dissembling, have palpable effects on the whole organisation, and ultimately on the character of the Nigerian state.

Masculinity is an often-cited element of what has frequently been described as a distinct police professional culture, a heavily criticised notion. Andrew Faull explores police masculinity in a much more nuanced way. He analyses the discourses and practices in South African police stations on violence and authority, particularly during the months following a police massacre of striking platinum miners at Marikana. Police officers who were not present at the shooting instinctively defended their colleagues from external criticism. Faull suggests that members of the South African Police Service believe that the use of violent force in the performance of their duties is necessary to gain the respect of the communities they serve, which is also linked to constructions of masculinity.

Part Three asks *How are the police doing their work?* Close observations and thick descriptions allow for a detailed study of police practices and police officers' engagements with the public in the face of legal, economic, and moral constraints and ambitions. David Pratten's introduction to this part starts from his research on vigilantism and informal justice in Nigeria. He looks at policing practices in the light of their links to wider practices and repertoires of legitimacy, visibility, knowledge, and punishment used in controlling crime and social deviance and resolving disputes in Africa. These practices include both long-established cultural framings of rectitude and popular legitimacy and practices which appropriate 'state-ness', as demonstrated by vigilante groups with whom police forces share a public space.

The first thing that comes to mind when thinking about how 'African police' work is the accusation of being corrupt. Julia Hornberger adopts a nuanced view of this accusation, particularly with regards to what is often called 'petty corruption'. In the chapter entitled 'The Belly of the Police' she takes Jean-François Bayart's metaphor of the stomach seriously. She argues that giving food to police officers is a serious form of corruption, as it creates reciprocal obligations that are more meaningful than the exchange of money. Food fundamentally structures police work, determining how officials interact with each other and with citizens.

The accusation of corruption often goes hand in hand with the assumption that African police officers work more informally than formally. Helene Maria Kyed shows that this has only limited explanatory value with regards to everyday police work. She studies how police officers in Maputo, Mozambique, deal with everyday cases. She reflects how police officers draw on a large and flexible repertoire of measures when handling cases, some of them formal, others informal. Their choice is often shaped by the competition for legitimacy they find themselves in with communities and private actors.

Legitimacy is also what Jan Beek examines in his case study on traffic checks conducted by police officers in Ghana. He describes how they use specific choreographies, tools and rhetorics, which Beek conceptualises as registers that evoke different moral orders: violence, law, social order, sociability, and the market. The chapter explores how police officers attempt to render their actions more legitimate by selecting and deselecting specific registers. In this view, stateness is not a substantial essence but a quality of the police that emerges out of this interplay of registers in everyday interactions.

Notwithstanding the aspiration for popular legitimacy, Mirco Göpfert explores how gendarmes try to justify their actions, not to others, but to themselves. His case study is the Nigerien gendarmerie. Civilians bring the stories of their problems to the gendarmes' attention in the form of complaints. Whether a complaint turns into a case, and thus whether the gendarmes become active, depends on their appreciation of the complainant's story and whether their 'vocational ear' is attuned to this story; and their vocational ear functions much more in terms of the material and moral gravity of the alleged offence, not in terms of the law.

Despite the wide range of case studies and issues, this volume can of course not offer a complete picture of all forms of police work in Africa; and it is mostly composed of non-African perspectives. This is partly due to the relative unpopularity of ethnography in postcolonial African universities, but more due to the forms in which research funding is available on the continent, being often driven by the knowledge demands of development programmes. There is in fact a fair amount of work on African policing conducted by African scholars, mainly individual consultants or civil society organisations, which is not published or classified under the (sometimes unfairly named) category of 'grey' literature. This work is however often conducted outside of African universities and does not find its way into academic journals, in part because of more policy-oriented research aims. We hope that these limitations allow the reader to map possible new fields of research and spark new approaches to policing in Africa.

Together, we hope that the research presented here allows a fuller, better, deeper understanding of the realities and perspectives of police institutions in contemporary Africa, and in doing so renders these people of the state and their work visible again.

PART I

WHAT IS THE POLICE
IN CONTEMPORARY AFRICA?

1

POLICING AFRICA

STRUCTURES AND PATHWAYS

Klaus Schlichte

Police and the history of government

Why is there police? This question has been answered quite differently in the
scholarly literature on police forces. Most, if not all of these answers have been
developed on the basis of the historical experience of Europe and North
America. African police forces constitute particularly interesting instances for
discussing the question anew and delving into surrounding questions of the
social and political rule of police forces once they are established.

Three basic explanations can be distinguished when it comes to the formation of police forces in general. The first of these three views combines ideas
of liberal political theory and functionalism: the police, according to this view,
is a functional requirement in modern or modernizing societies as older forms
of social control disintegrate in the course of urbanization and other large
scale processes. New institutions are required to keep social anomie under
control.[1] As similar processes take place throughout the world, we observe a

global tendency of isomorphism of police institutions as well: while idiosyncrasies may persist for a long time, police models and police practices become ever more similar over time. Current political science has taken over this view, stressing mechanisms of global convergence and diffusion of institutions, often seeing Europe as the hotbed for such innovations.[2] African police forces would then just be another field of cases in which we see such adaptations of external standards at work.

A second, more critical tradition of explaining police forces would stress the conflictive history of modern capitalism as a framework in which the emergence, persistence and change of police forces can be accounted for. In this view, states' armed forces have predominantly the function to defend a given order of property rights. Pretty much still in the understanding of the Marxist state theory, the police is part of the state as a 'committee of the bourgeoisie' by which the owning class defends its position.[3] It is this strand of police literature that stresses the repressive function of policing the most.

A third view would draw on institutional theory, this time on the ideas of Max Weber on bureaucratic organizations. The spread of national and international policing would then be interpreted as a semi-autonomous movement of bureaucracies that once created, develop their own momentum.[4] In a similar vein, the Europeanization and internationalization of police institutions could then be seen as such a dynamic of self-interested institutions and their personnel. Often this perspective is combined with Foucauldian ideas about the 'politics of unease', arguing that regimes feed popular fears and animosities in order to secure tight measures of rule.[5]

African police forces fit, to some extent, into these schemes of explanation, and to some extent, they defy them. While our knowledge of African police is still rather limited, recent research, including the contributions in this volume, will hopefully trigger a new round of reflection on why the police is there, what it does and how it changes.

A first observation on police in Africa confirms what we know already from the study of police forces elsewhere: none is like the other. Each single force has its own historical trajectory, which is molded by a specific political history, social constellations and institutional path-decisions. In continental Europe centralized police forces with a strong conservative bias dominated, securing the 'fortress' of the state,[6] while England and the United States had a much more localized organization of policing. While a general understanding of what police forces are and should do might be spread together with an idealized understanding of the state,[7] the actual setting of its organization, the institutional structure of security forces and their internal functioning continue to differ a lot, in Africa and elsewhere. Even colonial imprints have a much longer life than presumed. This raises doubts about the thesis of growing institutional isomorphism.

It is equally doubtful whether the functions of police can be reduced to the repression of political opposition and the 'dangerous classes'.[8] This image of policing is based on the experiences with police in nineteenth-century Europe, later totalitarian states and military regimes in Latin America. The repressive function of police forces, their tendency to secure the status quo is beyond question. The origin of most African police forces is to be found, of course, in measures to secure the colonial regime by coercive means. But most if not all single case analysis that really delve into the everyday practices of police forces shows that another older sense of police, the element of 'care' never vanishes totally, as paternalist it might be. This Janus face of police forces, repression and the paternalist care, can be found in contemporary police forces in Uganda[9] and probably many other African cases as well.

There is also evidence that African police forces show elements of bureaucratic self-interest and internal organizational dynamics. This is particularly evident in current internationalized efforts to govern 'uncovered spaces'[10] and of 'state-building' missions, of efforts of 'capacity-building' and 'security sector reforms'. These forms of internationalization are remindful of the Europeanization of police forces within the EU. The long international history of African police forces with their numerous importations, adaptations and appropriations of models and techniques is thus perhaps even the forerunner of internationalized organizational dynamics that we now see at work in other places as well.

It is thus the irritating 'otherness' and 'sameness' of African police forces that turns them into telling cases for current debates on the sociology of organization, on international politics and, last but not least, research on police. Based on the contributions in this section, three issues—among other possible ones—might be highlighted to illustrate this point a bit more: the practices and problems of colonial policing; the intricate relation between police forces and their 'subject'—the population; and finally the internationalization of policing and its bureaucratic element.

Colonial policing—a still largely unexploited field of research

Colonial police is just one element of a global history of policing that still waits to be written. Such a history might reveal that a number of distinctions that we think to be fundamental in social and political theory might be abolished or replaced by others.

First, our idea of nationally distinct and unconnected institutions for which cooperation is always a problem no longer seems to be appropriate. As Erlend G. Krogstad shows in his contribution to this volume, the colonial past still informs relationships, even fifty years after formal independence. Whereas the multitude of these special relationships have been described for the case of French-African relations and even labeled as '*la Françafrique*', we do not yet possess similar studies on British, Portuguese and Spanish relations with former colonies in Africa. Studying the long shadow of colonial African policing, as the contributions in the following sections show, has the potential to produce a number of new insights which can innovate our understanding of the history of political institutions and of global history altogether.

Second, these historical investigations are relevant for our analysis of current affairs. Colonial history, be it of police forces or other institutions, can be understood as a major phase of the internationalization of politics of which we currently observe another phase. Under the heading of 'humanitarianism'[11] we see a new wave of institutionalizations and of constructions of relationships for which the historicity of international ties seems to play a decisive role, as the contribution of Krogstad illustrates. The present is built upon the past, and the asymmetry that is usually ascribed to these relations is not as unambiguous as we tend to assume. Krogstad argues quite convincingly that the 'extraversion' as a main trait of Africa's social and political history plays out again here: what a naïve leftist critique denounces as oppression and dependency is in fact also a very subtle and complex game of mutual manipulation. All actors involved develop an interest in the maintenance of the relationship of 'aid', and what can be seen here for police forces will apply to other forms of technologies of rule as well, be it technical infrastructure, technologies of teaching or other forms of guiding and 'policing' people.

Third, the study of colonial policing enlarges our view on constellations of policing which still exist but are largely understudied. It informs us that the centralization of the use of force in the hands of a government is rather the historical exception. It might drive us to revise images of colonial rule as well. Colonial policing often rested upon vigilantism and other forms of social control, as Jinam Lar shows in his contribution. It is generally erroneous to consider such forms and weakly institutionalized agencies as opposites of the state.

Furthermore, this revision might force us to pay closer attention to precolonial settings. Jinam Lar argues convincingly that colonial policing differed along the line that separated centralized from acephalous pre-colonial political organization. It is not the colonial scheme alone that decides about the institutional outcome. Local social and political structures co-determine and might even decide what form of organization will result from colonial encounters. Much like today, colonial settings might better be understood as overlapping political orders in which the fight between centripetal and centrifugal forces continued, as in the case of European or American police forces. Vigilantism, it seems, is rather a reaction against the centralizing forces of governments, and it uses something that could be called 'public morality' as a source of legitimacy, as precarious as this often may look.

Institutionalized ambiguity: police forces and 'the people'

The phenomenon of vigilantism discussed in Lar's contribution is remindful of another characteristic of state policing: police forces always and everywhere depend on the population that it shall control and govern. Without at least the partial collaboration of citizens, police work is impossible. Any investigation and any attempt to structure the social space depend on the willingness within a given society to deliver information and to collaborate in the efforts of the police forces proper. The precondition for this collaboration is that police forces are seen as acting within the boundaries of public morality, an idea that has become an essential part of modern political thinking, at least since Hegel's philosophy of law.

This complex moral dimension is however not the only tie between police forces and their social environment. Police forces are generally examples of a 'state in society':[12] much more than military force, police depend on a certain intimacy of its personnel with its social environment. There are endless stories about the tensions between this need for a close relationship to the social space which is the object of policing—and the need for a distance that shall ensure 'discipline', the ultimate orientation of police work towards the supposed ends of the state.

As Jonny Steinberg's contribution shows, the popularity of police forces often stands in direct contradiction to what the political embedding of police forces produces. His analysis shows that even a very repressive and unpopular force can, after a period of transition, become a public institution that is 'demanded' in the sense that local people appropriate it and make use of it for their own purposes. At the same time, police forces in South Africa became a battleground for internal regime competition. This shows how contradictory the imperatives often are that work on police forces as organisations.

So while it is still true that no police work is possible that utterly contradicts public morality, African cases show the persistence of legal pluralism and an often contradictory simultaneity of different orders. What looks like an exception on first sight, especially in continental Europe where the illusion of legal homogeneity is particularly strong, is in fact a reminder of social truths: even the seemingly most homogeneous political spaces are in fact subject to sometimes concomitant, sometimes juxtaposed and sometimes openly contradictory legal orders.

A connected history—the internationalization of policing

At first sight, it looks as if the history of African police forces is a show-case of how European models of political and social orders have been exported and applied elsewhere. This is the traditional view on the 'imported state'[13] that still dominates a huge segment of political science and sociology. African police forces, in this view, are just another case of the diffusion and isomorphism of institutions that we observe globally. Meanwhile, after lengthy discussions about varieties of capitalism and multiple modernities, other approaches have emerged which give more room to differences and see less hierarchical patterns at work. The first contributions we have on the global history of policing clearly confirm this scepticism about an assumed hierarchy by indicating how important the colonial experience was for the formation and development of policing in the metropoles as well.[14] The concept of a 'connected history', as suggested by Gurminder Bhambra[15] and others, is therefore a more appropriate way of thinking about the global history of policing. It allows for giving room to differences while accepting the connectivity of research on spatially distant dynamics.

As it stands now, the history of policing in Africa is a clear instance of a connected history. One major feature by which this becomes more evident is the comparative view on the role of bureaucracies in African police forces. At first sight, the astonishing presence of bureaucratic elements indicates indeed a tendency towards isomorphism of police institutions. A closer look reveals, however, as Joel Glasman's contribution to this section shows, and with him a number of other studies, that behind the screen of filling forms and writing reports, there is quite a manifoldness of practices and meanings which cannot easily be subsumed to the same theoretical understanding. 'Professionalization' and bureaucratization of police work are just processes in which formal elements appear more often and develop another internal dynamic. Bureaucratic rule, however, does not imply that government as such becomes more 'rational' in the full sense of the word.[16] The study of African police forces has already shown that the logic of paperwork there can be quite different from one case to the other. And often, there are multiple logics at work even in one single office. 'Professionalisation' and bureaucratization can thus be used as concepts to study both the degree of convergence and connections between dynamics at different places.

What we know about colonial policing and its post-colonial afterlife is however important beyond the case of African police forces. This research might inform other, more recent fields of internationalized policing that is part of contemporary interventions. The analysis of the African police forces' history and present will help us to disentangle what happens when Canadian police forces train police in Haiti, and when German police do the same in Afghanistan. The connected history of policing is not over, it might just have entered a new state. And there is the danger that the discourse on the globalization of policing and surveillance[17] glosses over important differences as it seems all too easy to follow the established matrix of 'global dangers', namely organized crime, transnational terrorism, and 'state failure'.

Conclusions

In these introductory remarks I have tried to show that the study of African policing is a particularly prolific interdisciplinary field of research in the social sciences. This research is still relatively young and will most certainly produce a lot of further insight, both on the trajectories of single cases and in a more general perspective. In order to preserve its particular value, namely to speak to different social sciences at the same time, a reminder might be in order.

Speaking in a historical perspective, policing is a name for a broad variety of practices and ideas about social order. In our times, policing is still thought of as mainly a state affair. Such state police forces are at the same time both the result and an indicator of conflicts about state power. Police forces are therefore an excellent subject of study for an improved understanding of how states and rival social orders develop and are related to each other. We know now that this does not need to be a zero-sum game, nor can political orders be reduced to state institutions. They consist of concomitant social orders as well. Studying police forces is a privileged way of understanding currently emerging orders in which the divide between public and private is redefined and in which new forms of international connections seem to elapse our established views. Of course, political science might look like the first place to locate these insights within the broad range of social sciences. Luckily, research on police forces in Africa so far has not cared much about such disciplinary demarcations. It has been able to speak to different disciplinary discourses at the same time. While the production of new empirical insights will guarantee such attention beyond disciplinary boundaries certainly for another extended period, it will become ever more important to link the study of police forces to greater debates, not least to the more general theoretical reflection in the social sciences, such as social theory. My assumption is that such a theoretical reference will allow the study of police to fully exploit its great potential.

2

WHAT IS THE CONCEPT
OF PROFESSIONALIZATION GOOD FOR?

AN ARGUMENT FROM LATE COLONIALISM

Joël Glasman

The idea of professionalization is the hidden passenger of police studies. This notion is used in key documents of the security sector reform, as well as in the growing literature on police history and sociology in Africa.[1] It is used both in a normative way, to make suggestions for the future (the police institution should professionalize) and in a descriptive way, to characterize a historical process (over time, police forces became more and more professional). The concept of police professionalization appears in two different bodies of litera-ture—the grey literature of development agencies on one side, and, on the other, scholarly literature on police history.[2] These two bodies of literature mostly do not refer explicitly to one other, and the idea of professionalization is often mentioned, yet rarely discussed. Nevertheless, this concept silently links together our representations of the past and the future. The idea of pro-fessionalization is sometimes an explicit part of a larger argument, but, in many cases, it is used as a self-evident term for a process not worth further

27

investigation. It is so widely used that it has become exactly the kind of unquestioned truth of which social scientists should be particularly wary. The reasons for its success are probably manifold. The concept of professionalization bears both the apparent authority of scientific discourse—since it has hijacked the terminology of the well-established sociology of professions—and the straightforward simplicity of common sense, with its correlation of the history of an institution with the trajectory of a single person becoming more and more professional over time through training and experience. It is an all-encompassing concept which encapsulates the concomitant changes occurring within the police, including the bureaucratization of police work, the separation of the police institution from the military, the specialization of police work on crime control and the defence of public order, the rationalization of procedures, the improvement of police efficiency, etc. It takes part of its strength from its untold collusion with modernization theories, used as shorthand for comparisons between Europe and Africa as well as between police and other institutions.

This chapter—which borrows its title from the famous article by Frederick Cooper on another topic[3]—argues that 'professionalization' is not a useful analytical category for police studies. Being ultimately both teleological and Eurocentric, it creates more analytical problems than it solves. As it is used in some programmatic documents of SSR, it brings with it the notion that the professionalization of African police forces is not yet complete, implying that this is the reason for the inefficiency of security institutions on the continent. Thus, professionalization is an emic native category used by developers, politicians and bureaucrats, but should be abandoned as a conceptual tool.

This piece draws on evidence from Togo, where I conducted my research. As an historian, I spent most of my time in archives, but my doubts about the concept of professionalization came from oral sources.[4] While collecting the life stories of former members of the police force in that country, I was surprised by the fact that these men had very different ways of presenting themselves or their colleagues as professionals. The ideal portrait of the 'good cop' that these stories evoked was at times linked to the ability to write good police reports, or to listen to the demands of the public, at others to mastering the skill of wearing the uniform in the correct way, or to the ideal size or body proportions, and at others still to the ability to understand orders, or to obey them in the proper way. I talked only to a tiny fraction of the police, but even a small group of men mobilized a wide range of arguments and very diverse professional repertoires which they used to legitimize their actions and prove their ability to serve.

Not only did they give different definitions of what professionalism could mean, they also made very clear that these definitions were often incompatible with one another. Those who were described as good report writers were the same ones who were characterized as lacking discipline. Similarly, those who took the best care of their uniform were also thought to lack writing and reading skills. In a very schematic way, it was possible to formalize the different repertoires used by the interviewees as standing in a twofold opposition to one another. On a first axis, professionalism could be described either as a matter of discipline (understanding orders, ability to read ranks on uniforms, knowing the unwritten rules of life in military camps, etc.) or of autonomy (reactivity, ability to make independent decisions, to give leeway, etc.). On a second axis, professionalism could be understood in terms of a policeman's proximity to the population, with some arguing in favour of close interaction with the population (understanding local languages, having good relations with local informants, being polite and accessible, etc.), and others favouring an intimate knowledge of written rules (good writing skills, knowledge of formal procedures, etc.). This twofold opposition (discipline/autonomy and remote control of/direct interaction with the public) seemed to offer a good overview of the different positions adopted by these agents.

But whatever possibility there may have been to reconcile these different poles, the policemen made clear that the question 'what is professionalism?' allowed for several answers. It is not the aim of this paper to make a plea for a structural analysis of the discourse of professionalism, even though this could prove useful for further research on police studies. Rather, it is an invitation to explore what happens with the definition of professionalism when a major reform of the security forces is at stake.

There have been several moments in the history of West Africa in which those in political power have attempted to improve the quality of its security forces via a betterment of its policemen. The Security Sector Reform is simply the last in a series of more or less ambitious police reforms. It is important to remember that, just like the prison as described by Michel Foucault, the police is an institution that is perpetually being reformed.[5] In Togo, for instance, the beginning of the French mandate—when the French administrators claimed that they would do better than their German predecessors—or the early 1930s—when the French administrators created a Service de Sûreté—were important historical junctures.[6] But the moment under scrutiny here is the 1950s, when the French administration attempted to bureaucratize its security institutions. This period of late colonialism was a period of major changes for security institutions which as a consequence saw the emergence of a new definition of police professionalism. As I will argue, returning to such historical moments can inform our understanding of the present changes currently occurring in security matters, arguably more than an idealized vision of professionalization could ever do.

Reforming security forces in late colonial Togo

The maintenance of order in the French colonies of Africa was based on a wide range of disparate though closely linked institutions. There were the Gardes cercles (district guards), Gardes indigènes (indigenous guards), Gardes frontières (frontier guards), Gardiens de routes (road guards), Gendarmes, Goumiers (auxiliary soldiers), Spahis (mounted cavalry soldiers), Tirailleurs, etc. Even in the small territory of Togo alone, order enforcement was ensured by the official Troupes coloniales (1914–25), a Milice (1928–44), a Bataillon Autonome du Dahomey Togo (1944–1958), a Compagnie d'Infanterie (1958–61), a Garde Indigène (1922–52—later renamed Corps des Gardes, 1952-7), a Détachement de Police (1920–33), a Service de Police et de Sûreté (1933–60), and a Détachement de Gendarmerie AOF (1942–60). Forest guards, hygiene guards and road guards should also be added to this list.

Although these institutions had different juridical bases, they formed a common professional field. The number of Togolese staff in uniform was very limited: around 500 men in the inter-war years-mandate territory, barely a thousand at the end of the trusteeship period. Whatever institution they belonged to, these men had to observe similar hierarchies and had the same French commanding officers. At the top of the hierarchy was the Commandant des forces de police in Lomé. At the local level, orders were eventually issued by the Commandants de cercle (district officer). In spite of the multiple institutional labels, African members of the security police were trained together, they lived together in military camps, and they received their orders from the same superiors. In many cases—investigations, patrols, crowd control—they had to work together. In emergencies, for instance during riots, all forces—guards, militia members, policemen or soldiers—intervened together in joint operations.

The result was that members of the security forces frequently changed their official institution of affiliation. One could be recruited as a Tirailleur, transferred to the Milice, then be deployed at district level as a Garde cercle before being eventually dispatched to the civil police or becoming a forest guard or a gendarme. The circulation of African staff within security institutions was made possible by the system of similar ranks and by a shared professional culture comprising languages of discipline and of uniform, values of colonial masculinity, discourses on 'martial races', etc. They also shared similar material conditions, for instance comparable salaries. African employees were linked by their specific position in colonial society. Since they earned less than African clerks and bureaucrats, they had a paradoxical status: they were both dominant in relation to the colonized society and dominated in relation to the bureaucratic field.

Their place of residence, the military camps, exemplified this specific situation, located as they were both at the centre of colonial power—in Lomé and in the district capitals—and at the periphery of the colonial city. The camp defined a space which was protected from the hazards affecting the rest of the colonial society (food supply, hygiene and sanitation, schooling and medical care), as they were supported by the state. At the same time, however, these camps were sites of surveillance and control, conceived to avoid the merging of the security forces' interests with those of the urban notables.

After World War II, French officials had to rethink their vision of colonial order. The most important decision taken was the bureaucratization of both the monitoring of agents and their daily work. This was not the first attempt to strengthen bureaucratic tools in police work. The French administration had made a first attempt to do so in the early 1930s—but this had been a long shot.[7] The 1940s and 1950s was a period of rapid population growth and urbanization. Political parties and trade unions were founded, changing the form and intensity of anti-colonial opposition. The international context also changed during this period. Togo, previously a mandate territory of the League of Nations, became a United Nations trusteeship territory, which gave the UN stronger means of control over French politics. It could now deploy observation missions on the ground. Togo was turned into a showcase for French colonial policy; the territory was declared a 'pilote nation' for the advancement of administrative reforms. It would become an autonomous republic within the French Union in 1956 (and eventually became independent in 1960 under the leadership of Sylvanus Olympio).

Faced with these changes, the French administration started what it considered to be a modernization of the colonial apparatus. The colonial state in Togo grew quickly, in both financial and personnel terms, making the move towards bureaucratization apparent. Within the colonial state, the bureaucratic staff grew more quickly than the military staff. In 1929, security forces made up 43.2 per cent of all African employees of the state in Togo, compared with only 35.4 per cent in 1952. Within the security forces, the bureaucratic segment—the civil police—expanded more quickly than the military one— the Native Guard and troops.[8] At the end of the 1950s, policemen represented almost one quarter of all security personnel.

The will of the administration to shift towards a more bureaucratic means of policing was even plainer. Officials felt the need to improve surveillance at a distance with the compilation and storage of information files and statistics. Towards the end of the French Empire, the idea that native or district guards embodied an old-fashioned style of colonial order made headway and these became increasingly associated with forced labour and the arbitrary power of district officers. A civil police department came to be seen as a more modern way of controlling the city than the military-trained Native Guard.[9] The police were to become less visible—the red fez worn by the guards was increasingly perceived as invasive—but better informed. New tasks were allocated to security forces: political intelligence, investigations and accumulation of data were to be pushed. Colonial policing, administrators thought, was to become less about being seen, and more about seeing. The production of written documents increased rapidly. Within twelve years, the number of annually produced crime reports ('procès verbaux de crimes') multiplied by 6.5, the number of civil information reports ('procès verbaux de renseignement') by 23, and the number of juridical information reports ('procès verbaux de renseignement judiciaire') by 49.[10]

During the 1950s, the Service de sûreté—originally created in 1933— became the nodal point of police work. The intelligence section produced notes and reports on political, economic and juridical issues. The immigration section monitored the circulation of persons and issued passports and travel documents, as well as statistics on emigration and foreigners living in the territory. One section was devoted to the storage and management of judiciary material (such as court records, identification files with fingerprints, or reports coming from the central national security office in Paris). A last section specialized in the production of anthropometric measures—a technique of identifying individuals based on the measurement of different body parts (head, little finger, foot, etc.).

It was not only procedures at police headquarters that became more sophisticated; in the day-to-day running of local police stations bureaucratic procedures also became more important. Reports had to be sent to the office next up in the chain of command, to the justice administration office or other institutions, and even interaction with the public had to be documented. Police stations filed annual, biannual as well as daily reports. They wrote minutes for different activities: investigations, crimes, minor offences, nocturnal noise disturbance, public disorder and so on. Police stations were also in charge of issuing all kinds of official papers for the population (certificates of good conduct, residence certificates, life certificates, certificates of losses, etc.). They managed the receipts of collected taxes (taxes on the market, butchers' taxes, petrol pump taxes, court fines, etc.), distributed notifications and warrants. They archived files on topics such as prostitution, vagrancy and accidents; they supervised inmate files, folders on customary justice as well as on European justice. They managed the correspondence with the prosecutor, the prison governor and the mayor. Moreover, in a context of rapid alphabetization, Togolese citizens increasingly sent written complaints to the police— about bad debtors, dangerous neighbours, etc. There were also the piles of flyers, brochures, posters and articles produced by political parties, trade unions and the press.

For several decades, security forces in Togo had managed to keep most bureaucratic duties in the hands of European officials. After the Second World War, this was no longer possible. The bureaucratization of police work logically led to a rethinking of how policemen should be recruited.

The exacerbation of professional competition

The bureaucratization of the late colonial state might have been a headache for the police station staff of the time, but it is a blessing for today's historians. Since the administrators started collecting information on their own employees, we have much more valuable information on African employees of the post-World War II period than on the previous period. The personnel files of Togolese employees are stored at the Archives du Ministère du Travail et de la Fonction Publique du Togo (AMFP). They give a unique insight into the day-to-day life of state employees as well as into their sociological profile.[11]

The first insight from these files is that African policemen did not have very secure jobs. In spite of public representations of policemen as a strong occupational group, archival evidence makes a strong case for arguing that it was not such a stable occupation. Only one third of policemen worked in their corps until retirement. One fifth died before retirement (most of them whilst off duty), and one tenth resigned beforehand. Most importantly, between one quarter and one third of the policemen were dismissed, either for political, administrative, medical or juridical reasons.[12] As a consequence, the average career span in the police was not very long: only one third of staff worked in the police for more than fifteen years. One third stayed in the police for less than five years. Interestingly, in 15 per cent of cases, policemen resigned or were dismissed less than one year after being recruited. The late colonial and early postcolonial periods were times of rapid reforms and rapid political changes, which paved the ground for career uncertainty. This meant that the policemen could not be certain about keeping on a straight career path for very long.

The files show clearly that careers were often chaotic. Some staff would be hired in the police, would resign or be dismissed, and then would try to return to the corps a few years later. The police was a new institution, so almost all staff started their professional lives in another occupation. Amongst the policemen, one finds former peasants, fishers, workers, dockers, soldiers, drivers, teachers, clerks and unemployed men. Most police staff regarded their work in the police as another occupation within the security sector. More than three quarters of the policemen served in at least one of the other institutions of law enforcement (Native Guard, Milice, colonial troops, gendarmerie, etc.). Some of them gained work experience in four or even five different security institutions.[13]

In fact, even the staff that stayed for many years in the police institution had experience in several occupations. Take for instance Gnabodé A., a 1918-born Togolese man who worked in the police for eighteen years. Prior to being a policeman, he worked as a farmer with his father, then as a weaver, before enlisting in the army for three years during World War II. After the war, he came back to Lomé, where he worked successively as a labourer, a train-driver, a mechanic, before eventually starting a career in the police in 1950.[14] Like his fellow comrades, Gnabodé A. had to rethink his career strategy several times. His renewed attempts to find different opportunities clearly reflect the rapidly changing context of the late colonial period and the uncertainties inherent to the job market of that time. Even for the very small minority of the population of French West Africa who were employed on wage labour basis (in 1950, less than 2 per cent of the population of French West Africa (16 million inhabitants) worked as wage labourers),[15] which included policemen, the work situation was precarious.

The civil police was one of the institutions in which the bureaucratization of the late colonial state was the most visible. It was thought to be a modern and urban institution able to face the challenges to come—quite the opposite of the Native Guard which, in the eyes of both colonial administrators and anti-colonial parties, was regarded as a reminder of interwar colonialism. The new African Corps police force was organized into two groups: the officers (commissioners, inspectors, police assistants) and the rank and file (warrant officers, sergeants, police agents).[16]

The personnel files of members of the police corps reveal a very heterogeneous staff. In the 1950s, some policemen (around a quarter of the corps) held a school degree, others (another quarter) could read and write but did not hold a degree, and others (one third of the group) could neither read nor write.[17] Unsurprisingly, the most educated policemen were the high-ranking officers (commissioners, inspectors, police assistants). But within the rest of the police staff, the degree of formal education remained very heterogeneous. Adjutants (warrant officers) were equally divided into literate and illiterate employees. The two lower ranks—brigadiers (sergeants) and agents (police agents)—were equally divided into holders of a school qualification, literate and illiterate individuals. In other words, well-educated police commissioners and inspectors gave orders to warrant officers, who were quite often uneducated or illiterate and who themselves gave orders to sergeants and police agents of all levels of education.

In this context, the bureaucratization of the state did not, despite Max Weber's optimistic prevision, reduce uncertainty. Quite the opposite: for many police agents, the policy of bureaucratization was another source of destabilization of the occupational structure. Of course, the growing importance of the bureaucratic sphere opened up new opportunities for literate staff, and even more so for staff with educational qualifications. But on the other hand, this also meant that opportunities for non-literate staff dwindled.

Virtually all non-literate policemen had earned their position due to their military experience. As the files show, around a quarter of the policemen had no military experience, around two-fifths had military experience of one to five years, and around a third had extensive military experience, that is, over five years of military duty with, for some of them, direct war experience (in Europe during World War II or in Indochina and Algeria). The best-educated policemen—among them commissioners, inspectors and police assistants— were true bureaucrats who lacked military experience. But NCOs were very heterogeneous in this respect: almost all warrant officers had military experience, while only around half of the sergeants and agents were former soldiers. In other words, in the 1950s, police officers who had never been in the army gave orders to warrant officers who were former soldiers, and in turn gave orders themselves to sergeants and agents who had very diverse military experience, some having spent most of their career in the army, whilst others had no knowledge of this institution.

Military and academic skills barely overlapped. Illiterate police staff had almost always been in the army (9 out of 10) while, conversely, only a small number of employees with educational qualifications had been soldiers (8 out of 10 had no military experience). Thus, the police microcosm was structured around an unequal distribution of skills: on the one hand cultural competence (formal education, fluency in French, typing skills, etc.), acquired typically at the colonial or missionary school, and on the other hand, martial or military skills (physical strength, discipline, fighting and shooting skills, etc.), acquired in the army.

In this context, the bureaucratization of police work led to tensions. A new generation of police agents, better educated than their NCOs but recruited in the lowest ranks of the institution, exposed a structural conflict. As a policeman with educational qualifications explains, 'The older policemen could neither write nor read. When we used a word that they did not understand, they would punish us. Relations were bad.... They were deeply mistrustful of us [the educated agents]'.[18] This line of tension did not only structure the police institution, but went through all fields of security. As a former (literate) soldier explains:

> The NCO avoided asking me questions because he was illiterate. If I spoke to him in good French using correct vocabulary and grammar, he would not understand. I am only a simple soldier. He is an NCO, he is my superior. He cannot ask me to explain.... I am of a lower grade than them but in vocabulary, I dominate them. In eloquence, I dominate them.[19]

Even though most policemen would agree that education and bureaucratic skills are important for being a good cop, many of them argue that they are by far not enough, and might not even be the most important qualities to qualify as a good agent. Policemen lacking formal education and school degrees are particularly willing to stress the importance of 'knowing the field', being able to 'do the dirty tasks', to 'apply order' and 'being disciplined'. As one of the interviewees stated, to be a respected police agent, the way you wore your uniform was crucial:

> It is said that a well-dressed agent is very popular. The shoes are well waxed, the hair well cut. Before you talk with this agent, you know that he is respectable. But an agent, I'm sorry, who has a very dirty uniform, whose clothes are wrinkled, who has a tired face, you know he has...not alcohol but...you know he is a drunkard, you

know that this is someone who does not control himself. But if someone is well dressed... Even if he does not speak French well... French is not our language. Vocabulary, grammar, are something different.[20]

In the narratives of men in uniform, the division between the values of the army and the values of education play a prominent role. Talking about their daily work, they often emphasize the different behaviour of *lettrés* (literate) and *illétrés* (illiterate) employees. Some criticize the ignorance of employees who are *illétrés*, *ignorants* (ignorant), *Akawe* (a military term to designate illiterate agents), the *moi y'a dit* (an expression which designates a lack of grammatical skills) or *Coulibaly*. This latter expression, a Bambara name implicitly referring to former Tirailleurs (who were quite often recruited from Bambara society), is associated with both a lack of education as well as military experience. One interviewee says *Coulibaly parle charabia* (Coulibaly speaks gibberish) or *Coulibaly ne connaît pas papier* (Coulibaly cannot do paper work). Conversely, other agents mock the lack of military competence shown by *intellectuels* (intellectuals), *bacheliers* (graduates), and those who are *indisciplinés* (undisciplined). Another interviewee says *'intellectuel n'a pas de discipline'* (intellectuals have no discipline), *'intellectuel ne sait pas tirer'* (intellectuals cannot shoot).

In the 1950s, the policy of bureaucratization led to the devaluation of military skills within the security forces. Until then, access to the profession remained open. It was possible for men lacking formal education to carve out a successful career in the police. By the end of the 1950s, however, military capital had been strongly devalued. Between 1945 and 1955, more than 8 out of 10 agents had no school diploma. Between 1955 and 1963, these numbered only 5 out of 10. It became more and more difficult for men lacking education to enter the police.

This evolution did not only concern the civil police, but eventually transformed all security institutions. In the Milice, the Gendarmerie and even the Native Guard, a working knowledge of French became a condition of recruitment. More and more institutions—including security institutions—would introduce written entrance exams for the corps. In the 1930s, the only security units concerned with written exams were the African and inspectors corps. At the end of the 1950s, written exams were compulsory even in the lower ranks of the police. A few weeks before independence in 1960, a new cohort of police agents, gendarmes and custom officers was recruited on the basis of a written examination.

Conclusion

The 1950s was a decade of reform within the Togolese police services. The accumulation of legal norms and bureaucratic procedures radically transformed the everyday work of policemen. Of course, this does not mean that colonial policing became less violent—bureaucratization is by no means the opposite of violence. In fact, the bureaucratization of the police was perfectly in line with the systematization of raids on the private homes of anti-colonial leaders. Brutal arrests, beatings and the dispersion of demonstrations with the use of force, including shooting with real ammunition, were another well-documented aspect of the late colonial state.[21]

Neither did the policy of bureaucratization lead to a more professional police force. It did, though, change the everyday work of police agents, increasingly requiring of them the ability to read documents and to produce written reports. The value of military skills decreased, and the importance of formal education was reinforced. Both the administration and policemen themselves tended to evaluate the professionalism of policemen in terms of their bureaucratic skills. The production of good police reports (*PV bien propres, bien soignés*) became proof of professional competence. However, many policemen would not interpret this evolution as a positive move towards a more efficient police force. In fact, many of them maintained that a good police force was more than just a bureaucratic police force.

3

THE COLONIAL SUBTEXT OF BRITISH-LED
POLICE REFORM IN SIERRA LEONE

Erlend Grøner Krogstad

It has become common to criticize policy doctrines on post-conflict reconstruction and security sector reform (SSR) for being 'ahistorical' and insensitive to local conditions.[1] Firstly, such doctrines are accused of neglecting how
and why specific military and police forces achieved their character and function, offering generic advice that does not address real challenges. Secondly,
they are built on overly ambitious ideas of rapid reform that are not supported
by historical evidence.[2] Because foreign donors use templates which do not
enable them to understand the institution they are trying to reform, the argument goes, reforms are often ineffective.

The criticism of inadequate models and doctrines is persuasive, but it cannot explain why some reforms seem to be more successful than others. Clearly,
there are a number of other factors besides policy doctrines that influence
outcomes, such as the level of violence and political tension and the amount
of time and resources devoted to reform of a particular institution. Then there
is also the deceptively simple question: do foreign reformers and their local
counterparts get on? This question is particularly pronounced with respect to

39

reforms in the security sector because elites there are said to be 'in the main, skeptical and resistant to reform'.[3] 'Even more than most institutions', argue Gordon Peake and Otwin Marenin, 'the police are characterized as distrustful of outsiders and prone to traditions and conventionality'.[4]

Focusing on British-led reform of the Sierra Leone Police (SLP) in the late 1990s and early 2000s, this paper argues that what we might call 'reconstruction relationships' are critical to how reforms play out. While everyone would agree that a degree of mutual trust between foreigners and locals is an important determinant of whether reforms will succeed or not, little attention has been paid to why some reconstruction relationships appear to work better than others. This is partly because of a tendency to talk about 'donors' in the abstract as promoters of universal models, failing to discriminate who the donors are and where the models come from. Donors, however, are not perceived locally as interchangeable representatives of the 'West'; they are assessed and approached according to their historical ties with the country in question. In many cases this tie will be strongly coloured by the history of colonialism.

The first argument advanced in this paper is that representations of colonialism informed personal relationships and professional perceptions in a way that greatly buttressed the (re-)introduction of a British-style policing model in Sierra Leone. One interpretation of this seemingly successful transfer would be that the British reformers exploited their position as representatives of the largest donor to force through large-scale institutional change. However, the image of imposition fits the Sierra Leonean case poorly. There were many in and outside the SLP who were familiar with, and wished for, the same model. This wish was not coincidental, but stemmed from an identity as professionals belonging to an organization recognized to have British origins. The paper attempts to show how this 'subtext' of reform was rooted in a broader popular narrative that associated British influence with order and prosperity.

The second and more theoretical argument concerns how the historical relationship between Britain and Sierra Leone shaped their bilateral relations during post-conflict reconstruction. It is argued that sovereignty was not primarily an attribute (of autonomy) that the Sierra Leonean executive guarded against foreign influence, but a medium through which it sought to integrate its former colonizer into domestic politics. Contrary to what we would expect from the image of sovereignty as a shield the weak use to protect themselves from the strong,[5] the Sierra Leonean government seemed less anxious to comply with notions of sovereignty than its British counterpart. In other words, the colonial subtext could be mobilized by the Sierra Leonean executive for purposes quite different than the introduction of a particular policing model. Prolonging direct British involvement in the security sector for as long as possible was both a way for the Sierra Leonean government to ensure continued funding and an insurance policy against coups. The activation of the colonial past, both rhetorically and through the reproduction of a colonial authority structure, therefore offered opportunities to the weaker as well as to the stronger party. I use this dynamic to substantiate Bayart's concept of 'extraversion' whereby 'sovereignty in Africa is exercised through the creation and management of dependence'.[6]

The paper starts with a short description of the root-and-branch reform of the SLP between 1998 and 2005. A striking feature of the reform was that a British national, Keith Biddle, maintained operational control of the SLP during the reform period. Using examples from other countries, the paper goes on to develop the idea of the colonial past as a social subtext with a direct bearing on reforms in the present. In order to place the analysis of the SLP reform in its proper context, the narratives on colonialism and independence in Sierra Leone are described as manifested in newspaper debates on the celebration of independence. The focus, in other words, is on the nature of 'reconstruction relationships' rather than on the workings of policing itself. Finally, the paper offers some ideas on how historical understandings might shed light on police reform and international interventions in general.

Reviving the SLP

Post-conflict reconstruction in Sierra Leone following its 1991–2002 civil war is widely regarded as successful, and the British-led reform of the SLP has been singled out as a 'test bed' for present donor thinking on police reform policy and practice in other post-conflict countries.[7] Indeed, reforms started from a very low point. 'On its knees', 'spent' or even 'non-existent' are typical terms used to describe the state of the SLP as the first members of the Commonwealth police reform team arrived in Sierra Leone in the summer of 1998.[8] During the 1991–2002 war, the force shrank from 9,317 to 6,600, with some 900 officers killed and a considerable number suffering amputation.[9] Basic equipment was missing, most police stations were torched, training had virtually stopped and the leadership had fled. A survey done by the British reform team in 1998 showed that 100 per cent of respondents thought the SLP were corrupt and 83.3 per cent viewed them as generally 'bad'.[10]

After being evacuated from Freetown twice, a reconstituted British-led reform team were given extensive freedom by the Sierra Leonean executive to rebuild the SLP. The team were funded by DfID, whom they also reported to. Following President Ahmed Tejan Kabbah's express wishes for a foreign candidate, British national Keith Biddle was sworn in as Inspector General of the SLP in 1999. In the following years, an unprecedented amount of funding was poured into the SLP via the Africa Conflict Prevention Pool.[11] Between 2002 and 2005, the UK government spent just over £27 million on the SLP,[12] restoring a decimated force to some 9,500 officers. Through Biddle and his team, the United Kingdom retained operational control of the SLP until Biddle stepped down in 2003.

Early on, the British reform team devised a 'Local Needs Policing' model that promised deep changes in the country's policing culture. The mainstay of the model was decentralization and increased community input through so-called 'Local Policing Partnership Boards'. In a context where the boundaries between police and military power had broken down, it was considered essential to instil in the SLP a sense of civilian duties. Pride of place was given to ensuring behavioural change 'of all police officers together with a critical shift in the management culture of the organization'.[13] 'Merely supplying material' would not work, it was claimed, what was needed was a 'managerial approach to resourcing and operating a police service in a modern democracy'.[14]

The effectiveness of these reforms remains in question. Bruce Baker found in 2006 that 'the government of Sierra Leone still does not exert effective control over, nor is it able to deliver state policing services to, significant parts of the territory',[15] an impression confirmed in later studies.[16] Furthermore, the reform deviated quite strongly from original plans. In a striking turnaround of initial working assumptions about an unarmed SLP, the armed wing of the SLP was renamed and supplied with more than £1m worth of weapons and munitions. Indeed, from making up about a fifth of the force[17] at the time the British started their work with the police in the late 1990s, the British left an armed wing making up about a third of the force in 2005.[18]

While it remains questionable whether reforms were successful in making the SLP honor the slogan chosen by their British mentors, 'A force for good', it is striking that the British reform team retained strong support in both government and police circles throughout. Observers noted 'powerful and consistent buy-in' to the idea of heavy British influence over national security institutions among elites.[19] Given that internationally led security sector reforms elsewhere are often characterized by discord and mutual suspicion, the sources of this 'buy-in' in Sierra Leone deserves further attention. This requires an investigation which goes beyond the security sector.

The subtext of colonialism

Sierra Leone is occasionally noted in academic literature for the exceptional 'nostalgia with which much of the population regarded colonial rule'.[20] However, the character and significance of this nostalgia is rarely elaborated on. Directly or indirectly, the significance of the colonial relationship was recognized in interviews conducted by this author with British and Sierra Leonean respondents alike. 'I never thought in my life that I would end up in Africa doing a colonial police chief's job', admitted Keith Biddle.[21] 'We handed over sovereignty to them and it went to shambles', another British adviser told me. 'People remember the British fondly, with rose-tinted glasses.... As a white British male, when I worked for the High Commission, we were regarded as the father of the nation'.[22] Prompted about the period of British predominance in his organization, a senior SLP officer put the matter in perspective: 'I would say: if this is colonialism, you have to judge it against the period before'.[23] The former vice president, who chaired the Police Council, explained the nature of police reform in no uncertain terms: 'The only model we knew was the British model.... So everything was British, and the aim was to come back to that'.[24]

Little guidance can be found in the substantial scholarship on post-conflict reconstruction about the significance of such views for how reforms play out. While it is understandable that the grey literature is thin on colonial history, this line of inquiry has rarely been pursued in scholarship on intervention either. This is in large part due to the strong politicization of terms like empire and imperialism.[25] As Simon Chesterman has argued, the mere attempt at comparing current interventions with colonial practices is often taken as a charge of neo-colonialism or imperialism.[26] This does not mean that everyone has shunned such comparisons. However, the most sophisticated attempts have focused on the philosophical affinities between current intervention and imperialism, and not on actor-level understandings of such connections.[27] On this view, modern-day state building, peace building or post-conflict reconstruction were united with imperialism by a civilizing spirit deeply ingrained in the enterprise of Western-led social engineering.

This understanding has lent itself to images of essential continuity. According to Rita Abrahamsen, it has been common to interpret post-Cold War interventions as yet more evidence that the situation of contemporary Africa, and most other ex-colonies 'is one of neo-colonialism, imperialism, and continued subservience in the international system'.[28] Oliver Richmond has described the 'liberal peace' as 'a model through which Western-led agency, epistemology, and institutions, have attempted to unite the world under a hegemonic system'.[29] My purpose here is not to disprove Richmond's diagnosis that many supposed beneficiaries of the liberal peace find it 'ethically bankrupt, subject to double standards, coercive and conditional, acultural... and insensitive towards its subjects'.[30] However, these grievances do not sum up how interventions were perceived by those at the receiving end, and more positive receptions have received little analytical attention.

It is sometimes noted, but rarely appreciated analytically, that 'hosts' and 'partners' in international interventions were often embedded in an international social structure which itself has roots in the history of colonialism. Two international relations scholars have argued that 'Great Powers are widely acknowledged to have special prerogatives in their "spheres of influence" to help "manage" the international system [that are] recognized as legitimate by international society as a whole'. A strong exercise of such influence would amount to what they call informal empires; 'transnational structures of de facto political authority in which members are juridically sovereign states'.[31] A recent article comparing Spain, France and Britain found that 'relationships between European powers and their former colonies are more important and enduring than explanations based on conventional, objective national interests would predict', and that 'historically conditioned notions of collective, familial relations motivate the European powers to maintain distinctive types of relations with their former colonies'.[32] The British military intervention in Sierra Leone, the authors argued, would have been 'unimaginable without the historical relationship of Empire and Commonwealth'.[33]

Such findings suggest that the category of 'Western' dominance is too coarse, and that what I have termed subtext may be crucial to understand how they play out. I understand 'subtext' to be a tacit structure of identities and authority resulting from a history of previous interaction. The analytical purchase of this loose definition, I believe, is to call attention to the historically constituted sympathy, skepticism, indifference or animosity that characterized the relations among local 'hosts' and foreign 'partners' during an international intervention. An advisor to the Sierra Leone army indicated that this factor accounted for the UK's achievements in the country: 'This is a great success story, the greatest in the Blair era. You don't need troops here anymore, what you need is advice and influence—soft power. And soft power is generated here quite well'.[34] Even in countries that are culturally very close to one another, such as Sierra Leone and Liberia, the conditions for such soft power are different. An adviser in the ONS illustrated this:

Many people here see a special relationship because of a shared history. Not because of domination, but...they see a cultural affinity. I think it is one of the positives, when you compare with Liberia and others, it is a British focus, and we can't help translating our British approach into practical advice. Maybe that's a strength. In Liberia the military would complain that different international advisors told them to salute in different ways. Sierra Leone hasn't had that confusion.[35]

Afghanistan presents a different example where the subtext was characterized by the absence of a colonial relationship: 'Afghans have a significant amount of pride because Afghanistan has never been colonized'.[36] Historical relations nevertheless shaped the allocation of responsibilities in the early phase of the ongoing intervention. Thus, Germany, which provided police assistance to the country as early as the 1930s, was given responsibility to reform the Afghan National Police at the start of the 2001 intervention.[37]

These scattered examples are insufficient to generalize about how the colonial subtext shaped links between ex-colonies and ex-colonizers after independence. Yet there is evidence to suggest that colonial histories influenced patterns of aid. Between 1970 and 1997, British aid to the Commonwealth ranged between 69 and 84 per cent of its total official development assistance, whereas the OECD average to the Commonwealth in the same period ranged between 24 and 26 per cent.[38] A similar pattern was found in the case of Spain and France and their respective ex-colonies.[39]

The next section describes the narrative about colonialism in Sierra Leone as it appeared in debates about the celebration of independence. This will also provide necessary context for our analysis of the elite strategic mobilization of colonial nostalgia that makes up the bulk of this paper.

The disappointment of independence

On 27 April 2011, Sierra Leone celebrated 50 years of independence. As on previous occasions, this jubilant moment was also a time for sobering reflections on what independence had meant for the country. As the *Sierra Leone Telegraph* noted before the forth-ninth celebration, 'the question of whether Sierra Leoneans should celebrate the country's independence from colonial rule, is one that has become a hot topic of debate at each anniversary, with emotions running high'.[40] An editorial in *Awareness Times* entitled 'Celebrating 50 years of what?' suggested why: the country was 'still under colonialism, politically and economically'.[41] It was ironical, some argued, that no one seemed devoted to earning actual independence in a time where the country relied on foreigners for its most basic services: 'We have come a long way but we sadly have nothing to show after fifty years'.[42] The lavish budget allocated to the fiftieth celebration was a particular point of contention, leading many commentators to ask what expensive fireworks would do for hungry people. The sacking of the Independence Celebration Committee's leader over financial mismanagement further fueled the argument that the day should be spent pondering what could be done to root out the country's ills. Others were more upbeat, arguing that the country had cause to celebrate the end of the war, two successive peaceful elections and religious tolerance.[43]

One thing was remarkable about this debate; colonialism was never invoked to explain Sierra Leone's problems. Instead, both those who spoke in favor of and against celebrating independence tended to identify the end of colonialism as the origin of the country's problems: 'It seems our problems as a nation begun with the declaration of independence, for since then our experiences have been negative [and] retrogressive, with government officials of various denominations taking the law into their hands and doing everything with impunity'.[44] Another commentator asked rhetorically: 'We became independent in 1961. Kindly research the history of Sierra Leone—has that country progressed, stayed the same, or has it deteriorated?'[45] The impression of a fall from grace was reinforced in a letter from one Billy Bridges who witnessed Independence Day in 1961: 'the Duke of Kent took out a white handkerchief from his jacket pocket and wiped his eyes. He wept. Not because another colony had shred [sic] its yoke of colonialism but, I presume, he had foreseen the untold sufferings that were ahead of us'.[46]

These opinions testified to a strong narrative, also expressed by SLP officers, where independence had become associated with violence and decay. Colonialism, although rarely described in any detail, represented what had been lost with independence; whether a decent standard of living, impartial authorities, or functioning schools, roads, and hospitals. This loss was symbolized in a lyric by the Mende folksinger Salia Koroma in which he asked the British to 'please come back, watch over me and free me from my woes' because 'this thing called "independence" has become like an albatross around the neck of my people'.[47] This narrative thus centered on dishonesty and ineptitude of the country's leaders and could in fact accommodate diverse attitudes to foreign influence. While some romantically portrayed the colonial power as benign and far-sighted custodians, others appealed to reclaim the country's economic and political independence.

However, after the British intervened militarily in May 2000, their popularity soared. A Sierra Leonean analyst writing at the height of British influence placed this popularity in the context of colonial nostalgia, which now took on significance for a new generation:

> There has always been a soft spot for the British among Sierra Leoneans. That feeling has now come into full play, with public demands for the Brits to stay for as long as necessary, because of the helpless condition of the country... [T]his welcoming feeling for the British has extended to the youth who never experienced the era for which their parents nourish such nostalgic yearnings.[48]

Apparently, however, the colonial past was also in the minds of British envoys, and Independence Day was again the occasion that brought it to the surface. In a highly unusual move, British troops stationed in Freetown marched through the city to celebrate the fortieth independence anniversary of its former colony. The next day, a British newspaper reported that Whitehall had actually 'politely rejected' a Sierra Leonean request for an even more impressive show of British forces. Major Debbie Noble explained why:

> They wanted several British battalions, fighter jets and parachutists to take part, including a fly-over by the Red Arrows plane formation, but we thought it would be better to take the back seat in this. More troops in the parade would have sent the wrong message and given people the hope that Britain will take them on again as a colony.[49]

The British view that a ritual display of sovereign power in a former colony had to be curtailed—not because it would offend Sierra Leoneans but because it would give them hope that they were being recolonized—broke cleanly with standard narratives on decolonization and independence. However, the eagerness to see British troops in Freetown is just as likely explained by the fact that they were perceived in the country as a neutral party in the ongoing conflict. Whereas Sierra Leonean pundits later conceded that there were 'many in Sierra Leone including senior government ministers who welcome the return of British government control', they also argued that 'most Sierra Leoneans would find rather unsettling...the idea of a partnership not led by the elected government of Sierra Leone, but by the former colonial power'.[50] The analyst observing the flourishing of colonial nostalgia in 2000, for example, took pains to argue that these sentiments did not mean that Sierra Leoneans were ready to surrender their independence. The 'feelings of nostalgia for British colonial rule', the author held, were 'not really borne out of conviction. Far from that! Rather, they are the product of the accumulation of so many years of frustration and the total lack of confidence in the politicians and the political system that has been in operation ever since the mid 1960s'.[51] In other words, the 'soft spot' Sierra Leoneans felt for the British and which manifested itself in public demand that they stay for as long as possible was not evidence of a wish to be re-colonized, but a wish for respite from their own politicians.

The picture emerging from this brief survey is that colonial nostalgia was recognized as a powerful and politically significant factor both by Sierra Leonean and British observers in the aftermath of the British military intervention, and that it continues to be part of the country's political debate. However, it also shows that the bittersweet talk of 'the good old days' cannot be reduced to a longing for renewed colonialism. This ambiguity is supported by ethnographic work on Sierra Leone, which sees memories of colonialism embedded in diverse rituals invoking not one past but many.[52]

Having outlined the complexities of colonial nostalgia in Sierra Leone, the remainder of this paper is concerned with how it could be mobilized by Sierra Leonean and British elites to reap opportunities offered in the context of Sierra Leone's lingering conflict. In order to do this I will draw on the concept of extraversion.

Extraversion and sovereignty as dependence management

The chief idea behind extraversion is that leaders of African states have succeeded in mobilizing a position of international weakness to achieve (primarily financial) benefits. In Bayart's words,

> the leading actors in sub-Saharan societies have tended to compensate for their difficulties in the autonomization of their power and in intensifying the exploitation of their dependants by deliberate recourse to strategies of extraversion, mobilizing resources derived from their (possibly unequal) relationship with the external environment.[53]

In this elite-centered perspective, self-regarding African leaders sit at the helm of states which are grafted onto society rather than rooted in it, something which forces them to look abroad for resources that can secure their rule.[54] This view has been criticized by Christopher Clapham for reducing politics in Africa to a static game of rent-seeking and for glossing over the vast differences between states and politics across the continent.[55] However, Clapham also praised the concept of extraversion for transcending an image of Africa's leaders as 'neocolonial puppets' and for capturing their skillful manipulation of foreign states and aid agencies. African elites, argues Ian Taylor, 'have generally proven themselves excellent arch-manipulators of the international system.'[56] For the purposes of this paper, I borrow from Bayart not a theory of the state or the idea of an essentially African form of politics, but the notion that 'subjection can constitute a form of action'. The colonial subtext, I argue, offered itself as an idiom in which this could be achieved.

Firstly, Sierra Leone's political leadership could use the subtext to invoke a sense of responsibility. This was well illustrated in a BBC news report in which the British reporter asked a number of blunt questions as to whether Britain was on a neocolonial adventure in Sierra Leone. Tony Blair refuted the notion that Sierra Leoneans would like to see the return of colonialism: 'They're not keen to have an old colonial master back... What they are prepared to do, though, is to acknowledge that in order to make the country what they want it to be, they are at a point in their history when they need help. And they are smart enough to realize that and to get that help'.[57] This answer differed sharply from that of Sierra Leone's Finance Minister Samura Kamara. When asked whether he did not think it was odd that Sierra Leoneans were so eager to have the old colonial master back, he smiled: 'I want them to play a much bigger role. They should take leadership. You can see in the Francophone countries, whether overtly or discretely, the French are very strong'. This contrasted starkly with Blair's confident assertion that he 'would be run out of the country pretty quickly' if he tried to return in the capacity of colonial master.[58] Unlike Blair, Kamara presented the former colonial power's interventionist role as similar to that exercised by the French; thus suggesting that the relationship between Britain and Sierra Leone was a normal exercise of Great Power responsibility.[59] 'Is this a form of neocolonialism?' the reporter wondered. 'I would not put it that way', Kamara replied. 'It's a kind of partnership. The global architecture for development has changed. You need a partnership. I know, we need them, but I'm sure somehow they will also need us. So it's different from the old boss and servant type of relationship'.[60]

By portraying Britain's interventionist role in the country as part of a global architecture for development, and by reframing 'dependence' as 'interdependence', Kamara eschewed the suggestion that they were being put under colonial administration again. Specifying just how Britain would need Sierra Leone in the future was not necessary; but the suggestion that Sierra Leone could one day come to Britain's rescue served a purpose. When the reporter used the word 'neocolonialism' to suggest that there was something suspect about his warm invitation to the colonial master to play a much stronger role, Kamara in fact seemed more eager to allay British discomfort with playing empire in Sierra Leone than to pay homage to his country's sovereignty.

Recruiting foreigners into the security sector

This seemingly backwards dynamic where the weaker party was urging on a reluctant patron to compromise its sovereignty was clearly illustrated by the negotiations about the extent of British involvement during the early stages of the British intervention. From the outset, President Kabbah clearly wished to see foreigners take leadership of the country's main security institutions: '[I]t is striking how welcoming the Sierra Leonean executive was of its former colonial masters, appointing Keith Biddle as police chief, and suggesting that David Richards should become the Chief of Defence Staff'.[61] In fact, there is evidence that Kabbah wanted a much deeper involvement in the SLP than he actually got. Keith Biddle remembered how he had to convince Kabbah that a less interventionist model was the way to go: 'I thought the original idea, which Kabbah wanted, which was that we virtually took it [the SLP] over— we didn't fancy it. Once we got on the ground and we realized what the dynamics were, it wasn't the thing to do. And we convinced everybody, including Kabbah, that it wasn't.'[62] In other words, Kabbah did not resist the reproduction of colonial relations of authority, he actively promoted them.

Such 'proxy governance' where foreigners 'are temporary stand-ins for local authorities who are unable or unwilling to perform the needed administrative tasks themselves' is well known from other international interventions in places such as Namibia, Bosnia, Kosovo and East Timor.[63] In line with the image of imperial imposition, however, proxy governance is assumed to be a 'mechanism that peacebuilders have used to promote liberal norms'.[64] This forecloses the possibility that host governments may draw their own benefits from initiating such arrangements. Indeed, our case bears this out. Firstly, it was reasonable for the Sierra Leonean executive to expect that senior British consultants appealing directly to their employer would be able to raise more funds than domestic candidates with little experience in fundraising and liaising with foreigners. This concern is likely to have reinforced Kabbah's personal opinion that there were few domestic candidates suitable for the position of Inspector General of the SLP.[65] However, a second and even more important reason for initiating such proxy governance stemmed from Sierra Leone's politics, and was exacerbated by the volatile situation at the time. In his 1999 Independence Day address, Kabbah lamented how the country's development had been hampered by 'four major military coups, two counter coups, at least five attempted coups, and four "palace coups"' in just three decades.[66] Outsourcing control of institutions with a history of staging coups, a history only too familiar to a president who had been ousted from power just months earlier, was therefore a way of shoring up the government's fragile hold on the country. If this was a powerful renouncement of sovereignty, it could therefore be interpreted—at least from the government's point of view—as a way of safeguarding it. By actively initiating proxy governance of the country's security institutions, Kabbah deftly helped secure British support in an extremely volatile context. Reminiscent of how individual colonial governments relied on imperial forces in times of emergency, this in effect expanded the coercive apparatus available to him.

The tug-of-war about the extent of direct involvement described above flies in the face of the common criticism that international state building stifled the sovereignty of the states which became subject to it.[67] At first glance, the governance structure that crystallized in Sierra Leone seems close to Stephen Krasner's proposal for 'shared sovereignty'; an institutional arrangement that involves precisely proxy governance: '[T]he engagement of external actors in some of the domestic authority structures of the target state for an indefinite period of time'.[68] In such arrangements, 'one core element of sovereignty—voluntary agreements—would be preserved, while another core element—the principle of autonomy—would be violated'.[69] However, Krasner's idea of 'sharing' contains very little scope for understanding how weaker parties could use the same institutional arrangements to further their own autonomy. Our case reveals that the Sierra Leonean government was not a passive recipient of British military and police aid, but exercised a political will extending far beyond cooperation and consent on the terms offered to it. In fact, its accommodating attitude included a veritable recruitment policy of British advisers-cum-commanders. Since this agency was aimed at increasing direct foreign influence in the country's security sector, it challenged internationally recognized notions of sovereignty and thereby placed the British government in an awkward position. In fact, the British delegation seemed much more anxious to comply with notions of sovereignty than its Sierra Leonean host. Curiously, the image of sovereignty as a shield protecting the weak from the interference of the strong seemed reversed; it was the British who had to invoke sovereignty in order to establish limits on what they could and could not do. Fearing a 'dependency culture', the British government therefore limited its initial plans for military assistance to three years.[70]

The above account suggests a difference with regards to how sovereignty structured reform in different domains. Against the Sierra Leonean government's request for a British Chief of Defence Staff, it was considered 'important in terms of presentation' that the British commander in charge of restructuring the armed forces was to be designated 'Military Adviser to the Government of Sierra Leone'.[71] Sovereignty was therefore perceived (by the British) to be more constraining in the military sphere than in the field of policing, where the appointment of Keith Biddle as IGP did not cause problems. This indicates that donors are more flexible in their dealings with state institutions outside the domain of 'high' international politics.

We can make sense of these negotiations about sovereignty by recalling the concept of extraversion. If strategies of extraversion work precisely by turning the government's survival into something which internationals have a shared stake in, it is clear that leaders may see the infringement of the principle of autonomy as an acceptable way of enhancing *de facto* autonomy. Wendt and Friedheim argued that international security assistance helped clients reap benefits by embracing the identity as 'weak' or 'subordinate':

> Weak states are not naturally given [but] created and sustained by providing an external base to certain actors that enables them to seize power and avoid difficult policies necessary to create domestic legitimacy. By enabling regimes to survive that otherwise might not, in other words, security assistance creates identities that have an 'investment in subordination'.[72]

Similarly, Wendt and Barnett theorized that 'dependency on security assistance in geopolitical structures of informal empire tends to create elites whose definitions of security are those of external patrons rather than the masses'.[73] However, like Krasner's focus on how strong states must rethink their approaches to essentially passive 'collapsed and failing states', this conception endows the leaders of those states with little real agency. Anticipating instead the local reactions that violations of domestic autonomy would provoke, Krasner gave an exceptionally blunt piece of advice to internationals: 'For policy purposes, it would be best to refer to shared sovereignty as "partnerships". This would more easily let policymakers engage in organized hypocrisy, that is, saying one thing and doing another'.[74] In Sierra Leone, exactly who engaged in organized hypocrisy is not so straightforward. As we have seen, 'partnership' was a disarming trope the Finance Minister could use when confronted with the word 'neocolonialism'. Moreover, 'saying one thing and doing another' was not only the domain of internationals worried about their reputation, but a key characteristic of extraversion.

Secondly, this activism illustrates a weakness in the donor conceptualization of 'local ownership'. Local ownership is held by practitioners and academics alike as a critical precondition for the sustainability of international state building, and refers to 'the extent to which domestic actors control both the design and implementation of political processes'.[75] However, as Simon Chesterman argues, the 'rhetoric of ownership [presupposes that] a political vacuum exists prior to the arrival of international staff'.[76] Donors therefore concede that local ownership in the early phase may be limited to securing 'buy-in' or endorsement of initiatives that international staff design and set in motion. Even such limited ownership is taken to be 'a critical component of sustainability', meaning that it will lead to a situation where the 'host nation takes on responsibility for [security] forces and reform programs'.[77] Kabbah's activism may be seen as an example of such 'buy-in' and participation early in the reform process. In this case, however, Kabbah's exercise of ownership was not directed at a rapid take-over, but at keeping the international presence for as long as possible. This form of local ownership fundamentally challenges the linear assumption that reforms will move from heavy international involvement in the early phase to increasing local responsibility in the later stages. What obstructs this sequence from playing out might not be the common problems identified by donors, such as the predominance of donor priorities and timelines over local involvement, but that 'locals' cognizant of the benefits of keeping internationals in charge work actively to keep it that way. This may explain why a 2004 evaluation of UK-led post-conflict reconstruction attributed the difficulties in fostering local ownership partly 'to a lack of energy, expertise, will, and resources on the part of the Sierra Leone government'.[78] To claim that 'local ownership is abundant in policy but absent in practice'[79] is therefore to neglect forms of ownership which does not fit the stylized image of the donor discourse.

Activating colonial knowledge

If what has been said so far creates an image of Sierra Leonean extraversion as indiscriminate groping for foreign involvement of any kind in their ailing security sector, it is inaccurate. Conflict attracted a multiplicity of foreign actors offering different forms of assistance, but not all of them were met with equal enthusiasm by their Sierra Leonean hosts. The multinational police advisers from the UN CIVPOL found themselves at a disadvantage not just because they struggled to coordinate and mediate between the widely different policing cultures composing the mission. They were also at a disadvantage because SLP officers recognized that the Commonwealth team represented a historical legacy that was the source of institutions and professional standards still very much alive in the country. Sierra Leonean leaders were highly aware and proud of the imperial imprint on the police. This historical backdrop is important in order to appreciate the political will to receive and comply with British help in the police sector, but also in order to understand why British reformers described SLP officers as having an 'intuitive' understanding of community policing and as being 'highly receptive' to change. It meant that, from the outset, there was a degree of mutual understanding about policing, and law and order generally. Asked about which models of policing he looked to for inspiration, an Assistant Inspector General (AIG) responded: 'We always look up to Britain, you know, we were British colonized'.[80] Another AIG indicated how this was important in implementing reforms: 'It was much easier, in fact, for Keith Biddle to be able to play and do policing in Sierra Leone, because what he was practicing here was similar [to the UK] in terms of the Policing Act, arrests, procedures, and practical policing. We were already aware of how policing worked in the colonial era'.[81]

In the case of President Kabbah, these shared understandings actually derived from direct personal experience. Kabbah served as an Assistant District Commissioner during the late colonial period, and in this capacity, he was in close contact with the police during late colonial reforms. According to Biddle, Kabbah remembered the period as an 'age of stability and calm' where the police had properly functioning vehicles and regularly provided him with intelligence. The significance of this memory was elaborated on by Biddle:

> Well Kabbah's history, he's an interesting guy, he is a well-educated guy and he was a District Commissioner [DC] in the Colonial Service... So when you say to him 'we need to integrate the security system', and you talked to him in a lot of modern terms, he, eh, asked us lots of questions. If we said 'what we want to do is set up a district and provincial [Security Committee]'—he'd say, 'I remember those from colonial times'... A lot of Kabbah's thinking was conditioned by the past, like everybody else. And he could relate to what went on in the late fifties when he was a DC. So yeah, we could capitalize on that.[82]

The ability to activate the president's colonial experience to rally support for reform was a factor which was of course unlikely to offer itself to international state builders very often. It was also an open question whether a different president with a different personality would have gotten along as well with the British reformers as did Kabbah. However, Kabbah's personal history was not unlike that of many local partners to state building elsewhere, and is worth recounting. Joining the UNDP a few years after independence, he spent most of his professional career as an international civil servant, assuming a number of senior administrative positions at the UNDP headquarters in New York in the late 1980s. That left Kabbah with little experience from Sierra Leone in the decades after independence; and it was precisely his absence that set him up as a conciliatory figure upon his return to a country embroiled in civil war in the early 1990s. With regards to policing, this meant that his frame of reference was more strongly coloured by the colonial experience than it would have been had he remained part of the country's politics after independence. To the British, Kabbah's long-time absence made him appear as a sensible man who understood what his country needed, from a neutral point of view.

In practical terms, his late arrival on the political scene, and his image as an uncharismatic technocrat, offered some valuable opportunities. Firstly, he did not have strong personal ties with anyone in the SLP senior leadership, especially as several of them had been selected as stalwarts of the opposition party. This meant that the British were free to reshuffle the senior management as they saw fit. But his disaffection from politics had a more basic implication— it allowed for the activation, or perhaps the manipulation, of a kind of knowledge with clear affinities to the reformers' expertise. When asked just what part of Kabbah's background Biddle could capitalize on, he singled out his 'knowledge on how he believed the colonial police was a very effective community-based police force'.[83] While Biddle let on that he deemed this 'knowledge' rather dubious, he clearly did not hesitate to allude to it in order to get Kabbah to back his initiatives. When 'talking to him in a lot of modern terms' did not work, framing things in a way familiar to colonial times proved a better strategy.

This shows that the colonial past could be mobilized by the British as well as the Sierra Leoneans, although at a different level. Appealing to Kabbah's memories of colonial practices was a way to create 'local ownership' of the reformers' favoured ideas about community policing and decentralization; ideas which could easily be squared with principles of colonial administration. In other words, while British respondents were noticeably less comfortable than Sierra Leonean respondents talking about the 'special relationship' between the two countries as an extension of colonialism, they found it useful to invoke this past in a professional capacity.

Mobilizing the subtext in the SLP

Having so far concentrated on how the colonial subtext was mobilized in the relationship between the executive and the leading British reformers, we need to consider more closely how the subtext was at work within the police organization itself. Even a cursory glance at the literature on police reform suggests that seeing eye to eye with political elites is not going to be sufficient to effect large-scale institutional change. According to Peake and Marenin, reformers convince a typically skeptical institution by finding 'champion[s] within the institution whose practice/policy platform one is trying to alter' and establish reform as part of the 'routine managerial practices of police administrators'. The administrators, in turn, need to be connected with '"translators" within the organization who make meaningful what is general advice, who translate the jargon of advisors into police lingo, and who have the capacity and the will to insist that reforms be executed and sustained'.[84]

However, in the SLP, the problem seemed to be the opposite of distrust. Instead, British reformers reported being revered as representatives of the colonial masters and met with submissive attitudes. This was something they found awkward to talk about. In the words of an adviser to Sierra Leone's Military Police: 'People will say to you, you were the colonial master so we have to listen to you. In Europe people would be mortified at someone saying something like that'.[85] This is not to say that British reformers eased into the role of 'colonial' officials without reservations. Biddle was in fact quick to distance himself from colonialism: 'I said to them, "I'm not your master". I don't believe in colonialism, it's something in the history of Britain—I'm not your colonial master, and I don't want to be."[86] Rather, it is to say that the narrative associating British rule with order and progress had a concrete implication; it allowed the British reformers a freedom of action which Sierra Leoneans could only wish for. Biddle candidly described how his image as the 'white Inspector General' was useful for getting things done:

> Well just basically everybody thought I was right. If I said, 'look this is the way to do it' people would say 'ah, he must be right, he's the white IG'.... And so I got away with things I don't think an indigenous IG would get away with. My successor, Acha, he said to me, 'I'm gonna have to do things differently now.' He said, 'you could say things and do things that I can't. Because I have to live here when I retire and you don't'. So to a degree, yeah he said it right; Acha has to spend a lot more time consulting, listening and trying to persuade people, whereas I'd do some of that, and then say 'right, well this is how it's going to be done, let's get it done'.... So yeah, did we capitalize on it?—well you'd be a fool not to. Didn't overdo it but, yeah, I'd work on it when I had to.[87]

Biddle's Sierra Leonean successor, who took office in 2003, stressed that his mentor had taught him to value 'humility' and to appreciate people 'individually rather than [for their] status', and seemed proud that they had 'similar approaches' to leadership. He confirmed, however, that the Briton had a confrontational style which meant that he 'at times would come at people very strongly'. Echoing the praise of Biddle that one heard from almost everyone in the SLP, he connected his effectiveness with an image of a man you did not want to get on the wrong side of: 'He had a lot of people…he made sure he pushed them out of the organization before he left. A lot of them'.[88]

This testimony suggests that the subtext was not just a mutually beneficial factor; a set of representations that could be mobilized by both parties to facilitate reforms in various ways. It was also the texture of an irrevocably unequal relationship, which had implications for how the reform played out. 'There was this mentality upon their arrival of a new colonial approach', recounted one senior SLP officer, arguing that they played a game of 'divide and rule' within his organization.[89] Another high-ranking civil servant observing the reform up close recalled that the most promising young officers were in fact those who voiced criticism against the British approach. These officers, he claimed, were brushed aside 'just like in colonial times-.[90] An officer with twenty-five years of experience who formerly headed the Special Branch, described the working relationship between Sierra Leoneans and the British in the following way:

> I'm being very personal in my answer here. There was this mentality upon their arrival of a new colonial approach. Blacks in general have always had a mentality of slaves, it's in the psyche. The history of the colonial era didn't help. They came again with their divide and rule policy. Some were sensitive to it, others were not. For the rank and file, they [the British] were seen as semi-gods who could not fail. Some of us realized they were humans, and it is human to err.[91]

The reference to 'slave mentality' was uncommon and broke starkly with the more familiar tropes which portrayed the return of the British as the advent of a new 'partnership' or simply as 'help'. The AIG recognized the importance of the colonial era, but rather than as a source of mutual understanding he viewed it as something which increased his colleagues' susceptibility to the 'divide and rule policy' that characterized a 'new colonial approach'. A key figure in the Office of National Security indicated that a similar dynamic was at work in the armed forces:

> The people who voiced opposition were looked on as the troublemakers, but they were not! I would look at them as the best. But the young British officers thought otherwise…[T]he sly officers ingratiated themselves with the white men to look good, and profited from it. On the other hand, a small number of people who protested and told the truth were marginalized. I'm sorry to say it; it's the same that happened in colonial times. Critics were brushed aside.[92]

While it is not possible to generalize about the British effort as a whole, these accounts suggest that criticism and truth-telling could be at odds with the concern for building momentum around certain models and policies, and achieving results quickly. This suggests that even in contexts where there is widespread mutual understanding and sympathy between external interveners and local hosts, there is little to prevent 'partnerships' almost indistinguishable from colonial relations of authority from stifling critics. While this is certainly an important feature of international interventions generally, it should not serve to cover up other and perhaps less politically correct aspects of the same relations. There is no reason to doubt that the enthusiasm, and even open admiration by many lower-ranking SLP who drew no direct personal benefit from the reform extended to the British reformers, was genuine.

Conclusion

This paper has explored how social representations of the colonial past influenced the (re)introduction of a British policing model and the British-Sierra Leonean reconstruction relationship in general. It challenged the tendency to use terms like 'imperialism' and 'colonialism' to make normative judgments, arguing instead that their significance may be productively analyzed in the interactions of local 'hosts' and their foreign 'partners' in concrete instances. From this vantage point, colonialism appeared as a complex subtext which offered a repertoire of actions to the supposedly weaker partner as well as to the stronger one. The Sierra Leonean government drew on popular feelings of filial affection between the two countries in order to pull their former colonizers into the ailing security sector, and to restore their police service. The British capitalized on the 'intuitive' understanding of policing that could be recovered from this history, and on the submissive attitudes they were met with to implement the policing model they championed. Thus, the suggestion that the absence of anti-colonial sentiments may be a sign that 'Sierra Leoneans don't have sufficient pride in themselves and their country'[93] obscures how the active mobilization of the colonial past could serve purposes quite different than a return to colonialism. Against the image of Western-led interventions suspending local sovereignty, policing became a field where sovereignty and local ownership were exercised to prolong and deepen the intervention.

The harnessing of historical relations of dependence for domestic political purposes was not unique to Africa. In a quite different context, Geir Lundestad has shown how Britain itself 'attempted to influence the Americans in the direction of taking greater, not lesser, the interest in their affairs' during the Cold War.[94] During the first decades of the Cold War, Western Europe recognized direct American influence as a way to reconstruct its war-torn economies and defence establishments. The US was therefore allowed privileged access to areas that had previously been jealously protected in the name of national sovereignty; it became an 'empire by invitation'.[95] In fact, the backdrop of war and the worry over the fate of democracy that characterized US-European relations in this period allow us to see that there were striking parallels between Europe's 'extraversion' towards the US and Sierra Leonean strategies for obtaining essentially the same kind of assistance from Britain.

Against this background, the representation of colonialism in Sierra Leone as a time of order and welfare, on the one hand, and the slightly embarrassed willingness of British reformers to play the role of 'masters', on the other, may not be so exceptional after all. Yet this subject has received little attention because it challenges the cherished donor goals of equal partnership and local ownership, and probably also because international state builders are reluctant to talk about it. This is unfortunate, because whatever the well-meaning intentions behind this neglect, it hides forms of agency that challenges dominant understandings of sovereignty and local ownership in international interventions.

4

POLICING DURING AND AFTER APARTHEID

A NEW PERSPECTIVE ON CONTINUITY AND CHANGE[1]

Jonny Steinberg

Scholars writing about policing in contemporary South Africa have been preoccupied by continuities between apartheid and democratic policing. This is certainly understandable. Together with the prison, the police was arguably the apartheid institution black South Africans reviled most. Changing the manner in which it engaged with civilians was among the most potent projects a democratically elected government might accomplish. The will to police differently was surely very powerful indeed.

In the early years of the democratic era, South Africa was awash with ideas brought in from abroad by a left-leaning criminological establishment, one that emphasized the artful business of preventing crime over the blunt business of fighting it. New and benign forms of policing were written into the constitution itself, into legislation, and into the South African government's overarching philosophy on crime policy, the National Crime Prevention Strategy, published in 1998. The police's military rank structure was abolished and the name 'Police Force' was replaced with 'Police Service'.

How interesting then to discover that these newly labelled bottles contained old wine. Under the aegis of such soft-sounding names as crime prevention and community policing, the old paramilitary model of exerting unilateral control over urban space quickly re-emerged: night-time invasions of township neighbourhoods by squads of heavily armed men backed by airborne support; the indiscriminate arrest of young men by the truckload; widespread police violence both against detainees and on the streets.[2] By 2010, barely a decade and a half into the democratic era, even the new labels and bottles were gone. Police ranks were remilitarized, signalling a naked return to an apartheid legacy.

This trajectory in policing has provided much food for thought and scholarship has indeed been feasting on the ironies.[3] Why has the most reviled of apartheid's institutions been so very slow to die? Why, indeed, has a democratically elected government gone out of its way to coax it back to life? These questions are intellectually satisfying. They push us to enquire into the limits of transition more generally. They press us to ask, for instance, whether South Africa's transition might best be understood as a mere surface movement in a deeper *longue durée*; whether the underlying structure of society does not require a certain measure of coercion to preserve itself, irrespective of whether political representation is democratic or determined by race.[4] They ask, too, whether apartheid-style policing is not in fact popular among the poor, which, in turn, opens up enquiry into the endurance of old mentalities. Perhaps most interestingly, these questions open a window onto how the democratic state is acquiring legitimacy and suggest that an authoritarian populist regime may well be in store.[5]

While these questions are undoubtedly important, a preoccupation with continuity risks blinding scholarship to what has actually changed. I argue in this article that what has changed most since the end of apartheid is the relationship between policing and political order. This has changed fundamentally and the consequences are very far-reaching indeed. During apartheid, and especially during its last fifteen years, the structure of the police force, its culture, its ethos, its career trajectories and its spirit, were animated by the task of containing an insurgency against the state. In the democratic era, the structure of the police force, its culture and its spirit, are increasingly shaped by the task of managing conflict in the ruling party. The difference is profound and the implications ripple right to the edges of the organization, fashioning even the manner in which street life is policed. My argument is that if we want to understand how South Africa is policed, we should be concerned, not just with continuities, but also with a rupture in the relationship between politics and state coercion.

High and low policing

To make sense of the trajectory of the last thirty or forty years of policing in South Africa, I draw upon Jean-Paul Brodeur's famous distinction between high and low policing.[6] By high policing Brodeur means policing that aims to protect the political order. He has in mind the work of agencies like MI5 and MI6, the CIA, the national security units of the FBI and, in apartheid South Africa, the Security Police and the National Intelligence Service. By low policing he means 'everyday policing as performed by uniformed agents and detectives'.[7] Put another way, low policing polices horizontal relationships between individuals and corporate entities while high policing protects the state from those who intend to destabilize it.

There are a number of lacunae, obscurities and ambiguities in the distinction between high and low policing. For instance, the idea of 'high policing' would seem to encompass both the defence of a constitutional order against those who intend to subvert it and the defence of a political incumbent against those who intend to challenge or unseat it. Also, it is not certain where high policing ends and low policing begins because the distinction between fighting crime and defending the political order is often famously unclear. Indeed, shoring up a political order by fighting crime is a well-known strategy of governance.[8]

We shall see later that both of these ambiguities lie at the very heart of South African policing and that the distinction between high and low is never clear or unproblematic. Brodeur's delineation nonetheless remains extremely helpful, not least because those tasked with the business of managing states do themselves invariably distinguish between high and low policing, even if not in Brodeur's language, and the fact that they do so shapes the nature of policing and police institutions a great deal.

The distinction between high and low policing has undoubtedly held central place in the minds of South African state managers, past and present. Under apartheid, high policing stood at the apex of the South African Police and veritably dwarfed low policing. The national police leadership was invariably recruited from the Security Branch, never from the Detective Service or the Uniformed Branch. The personnel in these latter two branches were in general not as well educated, were understood to have stunted career paths and played only a *pro forma* role in shaping the strategic direction of the organization. The Security Branch, which accounted for just 13 per cent of police personnel at its high point in 1987,[9] was the centre of the organization and its concerns shaped the entire organization's priorities.

This situation came to a rude end at the dawn of the democratic era. Quite simply, the new government did not trust the police organization with matters of state security and systematically suppressed its capacity to conduct high policing. During the first six years of democracy, high policing in the South African Police Service (SAPS) was entirely dormant. In its stead, low policing blossomed. Uniformed police leaders were appointed to manage the organization as a whole; discourse about uniformed policing dominated the ways in which policing in general was spoken about. This amounted to a sudden inversion, one that has barely been written about, its implications largely unexplored.[10] I argue that the implications were enormous, that during this transitional period, in which low policing dominated, the South African state entered into a new, unprecedented relationship with its citizenry, a relationship that has largely passed scholarship by.

In retrospect, this turned out to be a short transitional period; it lasted precisely six years. In 2000, the first black police commissioner in South African history was appointed. Crucially, he was both an outsider—he did not come through police ranks—and was an ANC veteran who had lived much of his adult life in exile. Through him, the ruling party began to establish control over the organization and as it did so, it coaxed the organization's high-policing functions back to life. The purposes for which it used high policing were radically different from those of its apartheid predecessor—the ruling party began to use organs of high policing primarily to police itself. And so, a circle closed. High policing found itself back at the apex of the organization, as it had been under apartheid. Yet the animating purposes of the organization had changed as had its relation to the political order. I will show that this was to impact upon policing in general. Finally, I will use this narrative history to reflect more abstractly on continuity and change and how to understand the ways in which they interact.

The South African Police in the age of counter-insurgency

If we are to understand the police organization South African democracy inherited, we are talking of the one that began to take shape in 1978, the year PW Botha became prime minister, for this moment marks a turning point in South African statecraft and in the history of state security in particular.

Prior to Botha's premiership, the high-policing organs within the South African Police (SAP) were at the very centre of strategic thinking on state security. It was a police detachment, rather than the army, that was sent to Wankie in Rhodesia in 1967, the scene of Umkhonto we Sizwe's first armed initiative since the banning of the ANC.[11] It was also the police that advocated for and designed South Africa's invasion of Angola in 1975, and that shaped South Africa's thinking in regard to the impending end to white rule in Rhodesia in the late 1970s.[12] In part, the police dominated state security because the National Party government did not trust its Defence Force until deep into its reign. Its British-trained, English-speaking officer class lingered into the 1970s, its commitment to the Afrikaner nationalist project dubious at best.

Botha's ascent signalled the SAP's decline. For one, Botha had spent the past several years as minister of defence and had finally built a trusted, Afrikaans-speaking, Nationalist-supporting officer corps. Moreover, he abhorred the SAP's manner of conducting high policing, which he regarded as amateurish and corrupt.[13] A sitting police leader was never again to play an influential role in the formulation of state security strategy under apartheid.

At the centre of Botha's security strategy was a previously moribund interdepartmental bureaucracy called the National Security Management System (NSMS) accountable to a high-level body called the State Security Council. All manner of government departments were represented in both organs, but the military was its heart. From now on, the formulation of security strategy would bypass parliament, the National Party caucus, and, indeed, the cabinet. Through the NSMS, swathes of government became directly accountable to military strategists.[14]

The military under Botha was heavily influenced by French counter-insurgency theory and tried to fashion a hearts-and-minds strategy tailored to South African conditions.[15] That need not detain us here. More important, for our purposes, is that within the NSMS establishment, the Security Police was assigned an important but decidedly subordinate position. It was to gather intelligence on and contain the ANC and its domestic allies, but under the direction of the NSMS. Its role in implementation was seen as decisive, its contribution to strategic thinking minimal.[16]

Thus, the SAP's relation both to itself and to other organs of government was shaped primarily by its role in high policing. A former senior-ranking security policeman recalls the 1980s thus:

All government institutions, agencies and units functioned as one entity with the same objective: to protect South Africa against communism in all its facets: armed resistance, protests actions, uprisings. We understood that we were a cog in this machine. We understood that we took our direction from outside police ranks.[17]

Another former security policeman I interviewed joined the police with a university degree in hand, and yet, eccentrically, chose to work in the Uniformed Branch. He was soon approached by the Security Branch as a potential recruit:

When I asked why they wanted me, they said: 'Listen, we have to sit in meetings with the military where we look pretty stupid. You have a higher degree and you speak eloquently. We want to train you to operate in those meetings.'[18]

Yet if the Security Police's involvement in high policing as a whole was that of a junior partner, the fact that it conducted high policing lent it absolute dominance inside the police. According to an informant who worked in the Security Police from 1982 until its demise:

The Security Branch was seen as the elite. If you really wanted to advance, you had to go there. And yet only the best went through—to get a nod from them meant that you were special... It was inconceivable that somebody could be appointed National Police Commissioner without going through the Security Branch. To rise through the ranks of the Detective Service, or, even worse, the Uniformed Branch, meant little—you weren't really going anywhere.[19]

As for the Detective Branch:

They were considered primitive by the Security Branch for they had no intelligence capacity at all. They would put their heads down and investigate one crime after another. They were considered to be robots rather than thinkers. But they were salt-of-the-earth people with an enormous professional ethos and they relished the chance to investigate a Security Branch member. They felt big pride when they were tasked to go after one of the Gods.[20]

As for the Uniformed Branch: its relationship with black civilians was considerably more complex than *pro forma* accounts of apartheid policing may suggest, but there is unfortunately not the space to explore this complexity here.[21] Suffice it to say that the 1980s was a very dark time for uniformed policing in South Africa. Within the SAP itself, the Uniformed Branch was considered the bottom feeder of the organization, its members the least educated, its work the least important. Its relationship with black urban civilians was at its bleakest. As the uprisings against apartheid gathered pace in the early and mid-1980s, uniformed police officers who lived in urban townships were forced to flee their homes. Whatever measure of 'ordinary policing' that had once been possible was extinguished.[22] Police now entered black urban spaces only in large numbers and in paramilitary fashion.

As the uprisings escalated, recruitment into the Uniformed Branch swelled. While the ratio of police to civilians had been stable for much of the twentieth century, it escalated suddenly and dramatically in the early 1980s, and especially in the late 1980s—between 1985 and 1990 the total number of SAP personnel jumped from 41,000 to 85,000.[23] Recruitment was hasty and panicked. A new and dramatically abbreviated training regimen saw the emergence of a much maligned sort of policeman known in popular parlance as a *kitskonstabel*—an 'instant constable', a euphemism for a thug hastily dressed up in a uniform. By the time the ANC was unbanned, it was common that the Uniformed Branch was poorly managed, technologically backward and adept at very little. Most important of all, it was considered something of a virus among the black urban population. In the early 1990s, uniformed officers who returned to the townships where they once lived were figures of shame.[24]

Democracy and the ascendance of low policing

The four-year period between the unbanning of the ANC in 1990 and the first democratic elections of 1994 was extremely awkward for the SAP. Its leaders knew that the organization would soon have to serve a new dispensation, but the nature of this dispensation was still under negotiation. They knew that the organization would soon have new political masters, but were not sure whether these masters would even tolerate their presence.

Among a host of other measures, the Security Branch was disbanded in 1991 and absorbed into the Detective Branch under a new name, the Crime Information Service, tasked with gathering intelligence on organized crime. As the new name suggests, police leaders anticipated that the organization could only survive the transition if it abandoned high policing *in toto* and transferred its intelligence-gathering knowledge to low policing.[25]

And yet, of course, the idea of policing organized crime complicates the distinction between high and low policing in two ways. First, practices historically associated with high policing—the penetration of organizations by covert means—are now transferred to low policing.[26] Second, organized crime is itself understood as a threat to state security, especially insofar as it involves the corruption of state officials and political representatives. Whether they realized it or not, what the police leaders of the early 1990s were in effect proposing was that the Security Branch of old be given licence to spy on the politicians and bureaucrats of the new order.

67

This proposition was obviously intolerable to the ANC. In retrospect, it can be said that the decision of the early 1990s to dissolve the Security Branch into the Detective Branch and thus to blur the distinction between the detection of crime and political policing polluted the entire Detective Branch in the eyes of the ANC and signalled its decline.

The ANC came to power at the end of April 1994. During its first few months in office, it eased the police's national leadership out of their posts and searched for new leaders inside the organization. By early 1995, the organization was under new management. Although many of the new figures were white, apartheid-era cops, they were unlike any leaders South African policing had seen before. Among the most influential new strategists were Uniformed Branch careerists, an unprecedented development.[27] Many had travelled to the developed world in the early 1990s where they had discovered a new language and now used it to engage their new political masters.[28] This language had little to say about high policing, or indeed, about crime detection. It spoke primarily of uniformed officers; it spoke of them as problem-solvers, as officers who developed ongoing relationships with civilian constituencies, as officers who entered into an open-ended dialogue with those being policed.

Uniformed policing, for so long the organization's bottom feeder, became an emblem of policing as a whole. The very language through which South Africa began to understand the transformation in the relationship between cops and civilians was almost exclusively a description of uniformed policing.[29] The status of the detective service quickly diminished and the work it did all but disappeared from the language in which the organization spoke about itself. At police-station level, the detective branch became accountable to the Station Commissioner, who was invariably a uniformed officer. The detective service was thus humbled and scorned; both its leaders and its rank-and-file understandably took the new course of events as an insult.[30]

A great deal thus changed in a short space of time. High policing, which had until recently commanded the organization as a whole, now disappeared from it completely.[31] The Detective Branch, whose members had despised the practitioners of high policing as an arrogant and unaccountable lot, were now diminished because of their association with high policing.

How did the blossoming of low policing, and of uniformed policing in particular, change the relationship between police and civilians? It is here that scholars have become too fixated with continuities at the expense of a larger picture that is considerably more nuanced and more interesting.

It is true that many continuities soon emerged. Township residents, especially younger ones, were not very welcoming of a police presence, despite the new uniforms and the new language, and police often resorted to doing their work in large numbers and aggressively, especially on weekend evenings, in part as a measure of self-defence.[32] It is also true that the organization was large and unwieldy, the skill base of the Uniformed Branch very poor; it was thus easiest, in Ted Leggett's inimitable phrase, to 'herd police into large formations' and aim them at civilians.[33] And it is also true that police leaders discovered, to their pleasant surprise, that many civilians, especially the residents of townships and shack settlements, took comfort in the spectacle of large paramilitary presence on the streets.[34]

And yet paramilitary policing only accounted for what uniformed officers did for a very small portion of their working hours. For much of the remainder of their time, they were doing something South African police officers had never done before—they were responding to calls made upon them by black civilians. If this observation is simple, it is deceptively so, for the implications are quite profound.

Egon Bittner has famously argued that legitimate policing is made possible by the demand for it. When people demand policing, they quite literally pick up the phone and call for it. What they are calling for are officers licensed to wield asymmetrical force to intervene in situations where things have spun out of control.[35] Such policing had barely existed in the history of black urban South Africa. Police had certainly entered black people's private spaces at will, but seldom because they had been called—in the main, they entered people's homes to enforce pass laws.

When democracy came, a dam wall burst; black civilians began calling police in high numbers and police responded. In the eight-year period that I periodically accompanied police on patrol, the uniformed officers I followed, whether in the ghettos of Cape Town or the shack settlements on the periphery of Johannesburg, spent the bulk of their time responding to calls from civilians. More than anything else, this what uniformed police now did.

Strong historical residues must of course have shaped these police-civilian encounters. The sort of authority police possessed when they entered private black homes under apartheid must have spilled over into post-apartheid encounters, with all the ambivalence that this implies. But a new relationship was nonetheless being forged. The idea that in a moment of trouble a protective state might be at the other end of the phone, that it would respond personally to your call during moments of strife, was novel in black South Africa, and must surely take an important place in any examination of the phenomenology of citizenship in the early days of South African democracy. It was in these exchanges between people in trouble and uniformed cops that at least some of the unwritten rules of a new relationship between citizens and state were worked out.

These questions are understudied. South Africa's murder rate began dropping precipitously in the mid 1990s. Why it did so remains something of a mystery. It is quite possible that the normalization of policing had a great deal to do with it. After all, most murders transpire when things get out of control. Until the mid 1990s, across swathes of urban South Africa, there was no authority to call upon at such times. From the mid 1990s on, there was.

In any event, I think that a satisfying account of uniformed policing in the early democratic years must speak of a mosaic, or a cacophony, or even of a confusion of clashing elements. Many things were going on at the same time. Under the aegis of a new language of risk, police were saturating township spaces in high numbers and behaving at times like an army of occupation. The violence they might mete out in such situations was extreme. Yet an officer who participated in one of those melees might, during the very same shift, have entered a private home because he was called to do so, and protected a child from a drunken man. He may have done so poorly or reluctantly or in a manner that caused great damage over time. That is not my point here.

I am suggesting that police were entering into multiple relationships with civilians guided by multiple logics. Which relationship was activated moved in sync with a range of rhythms—time of day, density of crowds, private or public space, the preponderance of one gender over another among the civilians the police encountered. Scholarship has yet to give an adequate account of these rhythms. One possible reason for this omission is a fixation with continuity. Such a fixation takes a thin and rather frail slice out of a rich and uneven relationship.

The return of high policing

In 2000, Police Commissioner George Fivaz's term of office ended. His replacement was Jackie Selebi, an ANC career veteran. At the time, Selebi was heralded as South Africa's first black police chief. But the colour of Selebi's skin was less important than two other attributes. The first was that he was not a policeman and was thus tasked with running an organization of which he had no knowledge and with understanding a profession that was not his own. Second, he was an ANC cadre who owed his appointment to South Africa's new president, Thabo Mbeki. To understand the significance of these attributes, one must have a sense of the ANC's circumstances at the time.

In politesse, the ANC is referred to as a broad church. In more straightforward language, it is an organization whose social base is immensely varied, the political perspectives it must contain and manage breathtakingly diverse. The ANC's strength at the inception of South African democracy was its capacity to capture as its own the meaning of what it meant to be black and to aspire. And yet black South Africa was massively plural: it contained eleven language groups, a diversity of life experience ranging from deeply rural to hyper-urban, a large and well-organized trade union movement, a host of aspiring business interests, and much else besides. All sorts of people cohabit in the ANC: managing the organization entails forging an unlikely consensus.[36]

Thabo Mbeki became president of the ANC and of South Africa in 1999. He came to power with a robust sense of what was needed economically, and his plans, which involved tight fiscal management, wage restraint and limited privatization, were greeted with hostility by a host of ANC constituencies. And so the question of how Mbeki would both manage the economy his way and hold together the organization was not an easy one.[37]

At the same time, a new class of black capitalists was growing through opportunities opened up by the ANC's control of state power.[38] The questions of ruling party politics, of corruption and of access to new wealth among the politically connected were thus fast becoming horribly entangled. At the very time that Mbeki came to office a highly controversial state arms acquisition programme was underway. Why the government had embarked on such massive expenditure and who might be benefitting from it were questions being asked with increasing urgency in public discourse.[39]

Given this combination—an organization whose consensus was fraying together with the rise of new forms of high-level corruption—criminal investigation acquired a new political salience. To put it bluntly, controlling the agencies that investigated corruption was fast becoming a crucial tool of political management inside the ANC. For the question of whom criminal justice agencies went after and whom they left alone became critical to determining who would control the ANC in the near future. The discretion of the leaders of investigative agencies became explosively political.

As we have seen, the police were pretty much disbarred from doing this sort of work from 1994 on. Until 2000, Mbeki restricted very carefully who might spy on members of the political establishment. The NIA was permitted to do so because it was tightly under his control. And, in 1999, Mbeki gave the green light to the establishment of a powerful investigative agency in the Justice Department under the authority of the National Director of Public

Prosecutions, but only after he had thoroughly reformed the prosecution service, ridding it of its federal structure, centralising authority in the National Director, and appointing a trusted client to this position.

With Selebi's arrival in the South African Police Service (SAPS), it became possible to entertain the prospect of turning the police's investigative machinery on ANC politics. This Selebi began doing with gusto from his first weeks in office. At the time, I was in regular contact with several senior police officers in various parts of the Detective Branch, including Crime Intelligence. I thus received an ongoing account of the new relationship Selebi was forming with the Detective Branch. Five months into Selebi's term of office, an informant told me this:

> You sit in your office and the phone rings and its Jackie's office summonsing you. You go to him and he informs you that you have been assigned to a team to investigate x. You raise your eyebrows because x is a household name, a heavy-hitter in public life. You ask Jackie what you're investigating him for and Jackie says: 'It doesn't matter. Just bring him down.' You find that the people working with you on the case are from other units. None of us is accountable to his commander. We are accountable to Jackie personally. The budget from our investigation is drawn from a covert slush fund. So it is all informal. There isn't even a record of what we are doing.[40]

While Selebi was assembling these informal, task-specific bodies, he also began dismantling a raft of formal organizations in the detective service. In a wide-ranging restructuring exercise announced in 2004, Selebi decided to disband the entire slew of specialized units in which much of the detective service investigated crime.[41] Members of these units would be dispersed to police stations across the country.

Selebi's stated motivations were mildly populist. He argued that the structure of the Detective Branch kept its most skilled personnel at a remove from those who needed them most—ordinary people. If poor and working people were to be properly policed, he argued, the most skilled police officers in the country should be working as close to the ground as possible, in police stations.

Various experts warned that the restructuring Selebi proposed would not so much redistribute skills as destroy them. Specialized units were the institutions through which the police organization retained and passed on specialist knowledge. They were receptacles for the recruitment and training of skilled personnel. Dispersing their officials across South Africa's 1,200-odd police stations would in effect dissolve the institutions in which the knowledge of investigative work was housed.[42]

In any event, the effects on the capacity of detectives to do their work was immediate. According to a former detective, now a scholar of policing:

> If you were in the Serious and Violent Crimes Unit, you arrived on the scene of a crime at 3am, and you had in your cell phone the numbers of everyone you needed to help you do your work—someone in the dog unit, another in forensics, another in the drug unit. All those people were gone now, dispersed to police stations. Detection is a collaborative exercise. After restructuring, there was nobody left to collaborate with.[43]

One can of course do no more than speculate about Selebi's reasoning. But it appears on the face of it that among his primary concerns was his capacity to see into the Detective Branch. All of these specialized units, each with its own corporate identity and each working in relative autonomy, represented so many pockets of opacity. And each was tasked with looking into serious matters that at some point may result in the monitoring or investigation of figures in politics and in business. Interestingly, one of the last of the specialized units to go was the one tasked with investigating corruption in police ranks. Its autonomy was starker than any other detective unit—it was not obliged to divulge whom it was investigating to the Police Commissioner. Shortly before it was disbanded, its commander resigned after Selebi demanded to see its open dockets.[44]

While this dismemberment of formal investigative institutions was underway, the proliferation of ad hoc, informal investigative activities described above gathered pace until they became something of a tradition. Increasingly, Selebi became personally involved in a host of on-going, complex investigations. Each was run by an informal team. Many team members were not even serving police officers—a number were former officers whom Selebi had registered as informers and was paying out of the police informer fund. To access this money, Selebi had to register each of his personal projects as a covert operation.[45]

By 2007, the ANC had become embroiled in a succession battle of epic proportions. Whether investigative agencies were acting impartially became the most important and controversial matter inside the ANC, for the question of who would lead the party and country turned on a number of corruption cases, most especially that of the main contender for the ANC presidency, Jacob Zuma.

Jackie Selebi was at the heart of the imbroglio. After the assassination of a famous, and famously dodgy, businessman, Brett Kebble, it emerged that among the many informers Selebi had recruited into his maze of covert operations was a mafia boss who now stood accused of murdering Kebble. It appeared, too, that the mafia boss had paid Selebi sums of money. South Africa's chief prosecutor attempted to bring Selebi to trial and promptly lost his job as a result.[46]

What are we to learn from this eventful seven-year period, 2000–2007? Most obviously, that political policing, having been abolished from the organization, had returned to its apex. But it had returned in such a different form and with such different consequences.

It is true that in the 1980s, discreet bodies within the Security Police were opaque, corrupt, and, indeed, thoroughly heinous, operating in a twilight world between organized crime and the state bureaucracy. These were the bodies, most famously the eerily named Civil Co-operation Bureau, charged with treacherous and illegal aspects of counter-insurgency like targeted assassinations.[47] But they were discreet and secretive and sealed off from the main body of the organization. For the rest, the Security Branch was a Weberian bureaucracy, albeit not a sterling exemplar of one. It was animated by a central purpose formulated by a high organ of state; it recruited and trained its personnel bureaucratically; it developed habituated, rule-governed procedures to gather information and to retain and transmit know-how.

The Detective Branch Selebi left behind was a very different beast. His impulse was to break down bureaucratic regularization and to disrupt the institutions through which an organization gathers and retains knowledge. In their stead, he formed numerous overlapping, ad hoc bodies centred around himself. It would be wrong to see this tendency to erode institutions as the result of the proclivities of one police leader. Something more systemic was afoot. In Brodeur's terms, the nature of high policing had changed. While it was once animated by an external threat, it was now a mechanism through which a very plural and rancorous ruling party managed itself. It was this environment that broke down institutions and replaced them with personalized networks. More specifically, it was two features of the environment: first, a broad-based liberation movement, housing a very diverse array of political complexions, but bound to stay together to keep an electoral majority; second, a new mode of wealth accumulation highly dependent on state access. It was the combination of these two factors, above all, that gave post-apartheid high policing its character.

Political policing and uniformed policing

Thus far, I have argued that post-apartheid political policing has shaped the Detective Branch in important ways. What of political policing and the

Uniformed Branch? This theme is best addressed by following a chain of events that began after Selebi's departure.

After Selebi's patron, Thabo Mbeki, lost the ANC presidency in December 2007, Selebi went on extended leave. He resigned from the police in 2009 and was convicted of corruption the following year. His successor, Bheki Cele, quickly became famous for his bellicose talk and then infamous for his decision to remilitarize police ranks, signalling, on the face of it, a naked return to an apartheid legacy.

As with Selebi, the best way to understand Cele's significance is to get a sense of what he did institutionally. During his time in office, Cele built a new institution *de novo* in the Uniformed Branch and its appearance on the landscape of South African policing proved extremely important. The institution was called the Tactical Response Teams and its members were trained to apprehend highly armed and militarily trained gangs of robbers. The rationale was that ordinary police officers were not trained to apprehend the armed gangs that committed cash-in-transit heists, for instance, or robbed banks, and that what was required was a group of personnel trained to approach culprits who could be assumed to resist arrest in groups using lethal force.

The Tactical Response Teams Cele built were large and pervasive enough to respond rapidly anywhere in the country. Nine provincial teams were formed in 2009, each with roughly a hundred members.[48] And then, in February 2011, when the teams were less than two years old, something odd and disturbing happened. During a process of bureaucratic restructuring, the Tactical Response Teams found themselves under the police division responsible for public order policing. Carrying live ammunition, and trained to confront militarily-trained suspects using lethal force, they were put in front of street protests and demonstrations. The results were very alarming indeed.

Beginning in mid-2004, violent street demonstrations became a feature of the South African landscape. Across the country, crowds would periodically gather, their grievances usually concerning housing shortfalls, or the delivery of utilities or local government corruption, and set fire to or damage government property. Initially, these violent protests were policed with a light hand. Between their inception in 2004 and 2009, four people were killed by police during demonstrations. There was something of an escalation of deaths in 2010: three people were killed by police in protests that year. And then, in February 2011, precisely the time that police trained to use maximum force became involved in policing protests, the number of civilian deaths at these protests rocketed: eleven dead between February and July that year.[49]

Following a particularly scandalous incident in a small town in the eastern Free State, where television footage captured an unarmed protester being shot dead at point blank range with a rubber bullet, the Tactical Response Teams were withdrawn from public protests. After a long hiatus, they would appear again at a platinum strike at Marikana on 16 August 2012, where, famously, thirty-four striking miners were shot dead by police.

Why was lethal force used in this way? The violent service delivery protests that began in 2004 are complex phenomena; the crowds that form are socially diverse and harbour a range of interests, motives and ideas.[50] For all their complexity, though, many of these protests are organized by card-carrying ANC members, sometimes by office bearers, and many of those in the crowds vote for the ANC. Among other things, these violent protests are arenas in which constituent parts of the ANC compete for power.[51] To have an organizational opponent's office burned down by an angry mob is, after all, an effective way of undermining his legitimacy.

In this light, the decision to deploy police trained to use maximum force begins to make some sense. Just as exercizing discretion about whom to investigate for corruption becomes a mode of managing the ruling party, so the question of which protests to quell with violence becomes a weapon mobilized in intra-party conflict. In a careful analysis of the policing of violent protest from 2004 to Marikana, David Bruce has suggested that decisions about how to police protests are made case by case. He suggests, too, that there is evidence in some cases that specific protest leaders are singled out for violent treatment.[52]

If, under the SAPS's first ANC-aligned police chief, the work of the Detective Branch was increasingly shaped by the task of managing the ruling party, it appears that, under the second ANC-aligned police chief, this new logic of high policing began to reach into the Uniformed Branch too. How far and how deep into the Uniformed Branch the politics of ruling-party management will reach is impossible to say in advance. But it is worth noting that we are only nineteen years into the new order, and that the new relationship between political order policing that began to take shape in the mid-1990s is still young, many of its manifestations and consequences still dormant.

Conclusion

Scholarship on policing and political transition in South Africa has expended a great deal of energy trying to understand why there have been so many unexpected continuities. This is understandable. But it is also important to examine what has changed. My argument here is that the character of both uniformed policing and detection altered rapidly and with much consequence after the end of apartheid. This is because the things the political order required from policing changed quickly and decisively.

Underlying this story is a set of observations about the broader question of change. That there will be many continuities between an old regime and a new one is surely unsurprising. After all, what does the new have at its disposal other than the instruments it has inherited from the old? But the question of which instruments from the old survive and how they are modified is the crucial one. At the risk of crafting a formulation that seems too simple, old instruments generally survive only when agents in the present find a use for them. Those that are not useful die of neglect or are actively destroyed. And so, in this instance, an analysis of what has been preserved and what has changed hinges, in the end, on the question of how a ruling party in the here and now governs itself.

The analytical principle at stake may sound simple, but it is not nonetheless crucial. To understand what survives from the past, one's analytical eye must focus on the present.

5

HISTORICISING VIGILANTE POLICING
IN PLATEAU STATE, NIGERIA

Jimam Lar

Over the decades, successive Nigerian governments have grappled with the
provision and maintenance of law and order, and guaranteeing the safety of
citizens. Amidst the state's inability to meet this primary duty and expectations attached to it, the citizenry has been constrained to turn elsewhere.
While state institutions remain the primary statutory bodies responsible for
policing and the maintenance of law and order, over the years a plethora of
groups have emerged and have made claims to providing policing services. In
approaching the study of policing in contemporary Africa, we are therefore
confronted with a policing landscape that is characterised by a plurality of
actors and practices. My focus in this chapter is on analysing the historical
emergence of such community policing groups in meeting policing needs in
Plateau State, Nigeria. The chapter traces and shows an otherwise little known
link between the plural policing landscape of colonial Nigeria and the evolution of a new plurality of policing, that began to emerge in the first decade
after independence and has continued to evolve in response to changing
political and social context.

I argue that the latest and current feature of this plurality is characterised by the activities of the Vigilante Group of Nigeria (VGN), a semi-official citizens' policing organisation registered in 1999 with Nigeria's Corporate Affairs Commission. The objective of the VGN as is clearly spelt out in the organisation's constitution is to support state agencies (particularly the Nigerian police) in combating crime and general maintenance of law and order in society. Therefore, plurality in this context refers to a policing landscape that actually bridges the state and non-state divide. Furthermore, I argue that an example such as the VGN questions the formulation of vigilante practice as something which solely confronts and contests the writ of the state. The chapter argues that in studying current policing practice in Africa we have to take into account the role of non-state actors, not always as a spontaneous communitarian response to a weak or absent state but rather as an extension of the state. Plural policing as historically evolved and currently practiced in this part of Nigeria is about statecraft from below. I argue that this should be embraced in the initial circumstance, not just as current policing practice but also as the future of policing. My understanding of vigilantism is informed by two key sources: firstly, I have relied on conceptual insights drawn from existing literature, with emphasis on sub-Saharan Africa; secondly, the paper is equally informed by data generated from research interviews and archival research carried out in Plateau State, Nigeria,[1] from November 2011 to January 2012, and from July 2012 to January 2013.

Conceptualising and contextualising vigilante policing

There is a growing body of literature that has examined the various types and diverse functions of vigilante groups and non-state policing structures in Nigeria. These existing studies are a reflection of Nigeria's pluralistic landscape, focusing on the activities of vigilante groups, local militias and local private guarding outfits. The research has particularly focused on the southern zones of Nigeria;[2] there has also been some research work on the religious functions of non-state actors in northern Nigeria,[3] and recent research on the role of non-state security actors, particularly ethnic militia groups, in mobilization and group violence in some of central Nigeria's conflict theatres.[4] Other studies also show how the phenomenon is unfolding amongst minority ethnic groups of the Niger Delta[5] and the Middle Belt area.[6] Therefore, it is difficult to address this phenomenon in Nigeria collectively, as with most Nigerian phenomena it is a product of a very pluralistic society, with varied histories.

The classical conceptualisation is that which understands vigilantism as a response to state policing failures: vigilante groups emerged and are still active because of the failure of the postcolony and this leaves gaps in the provision of services, security included. Vigilantism therefore feeds off unsatisfactory provision of law and order by the state.[7] I do recognise that some of the vigilante groups studied in different parts of Nigeria fit the conception of a quest for order, directly or indirectly linked to the inability of the state to police the totality of its territory. However, I argue that this response to policing failures does not necessarily amount to state weakness. Vigilante action could equally create a contrasting variation. Fourchard makes this point quite convincingly where he argues that instead of looking at vigilante groups as a supposed decline of the police force or weakness and failure of the state, we should consider them as an attempt to introduce forms of community policing,[8] clearly showing the top-bottom dynamic of non-state policing in Nigeria.[9]

The approach and understanding of vigilante groups in this chapter is drawn from the notion that understands vigilantism as everyday policing, as Buur and Jensen[10] argue that there are contexts where vigilantism can be understood as a form of community-based policing, in constant interaction with the state (police) and society. Consequently, vigilantism is constitutive of a policing landscape that is characterised by plurality of actors and of practices. Also important to the conceptualisation of vigilantism in this chapter is the attention that Fourchard gives to the historical process.[11] While an ethnographic understanding of vigilante practice is clearly useful, we gain more insight when we explore the historical trajectory. I therefore trace continuities and discontinuities in plural policing practice from its early colonial and postcolonial versions to the more recent, organized and structured form. Finally, Gratz's analytical notion of vertical encompassment[12] explains how vigilantes set out to gain legitimacy by demonstrating effectiveness over time. In this chapter, vertical encompassment illuminates our understanding of the evolution of vigilante practice from isolated local night patrols on a small scale to setting up roadblocks and performing policing duties in collaboration with state police. Across this historical trajectory vigilante groups migrate from punishments informed by the given cultural context to a hybrid of practices that includes mimicking statutory institutions (police and courts), showing movements and shifts of practice and punishment across historical periods, migrating from one legal code to another, and creating new legal codes over periods across different generations.

The origins of plural policing

In the literature that analyses the historical development of vigilante practice in Nigeria, key periods are identified: the civil war (1967–70) and its aftermath in the early 1970s; the years of the IMF-inspired Structural Adjustment Programme (1986 to the early 1990s); and the period since Nigeria's return from military to civil rule in 1999.[13] While I recognise the importance of these periods in the evolution and development of the trajectories of vigilantism in Plateau State, the insights generated from my research also show that the end of the civil war coincided with another important administrative reform that had a strong impact on the emergence of vigilante policing in Plateau State. This was the dismantling of the Native Authority Police, one of the earliest components of Nigeria's plural policing landscape.

However, before analysing these periods the chapter will first provide an outline of the political history of Plateau State and the roots of plural policing. Plateau Province, initially made up of Jos and Pankshin Divisions, was carved out of Bauchi and Muri Provinces in 1926. The chapter focuses on two main areas of the former province. While the urban city of Jos, situated on the Jos Plateau, is critical for my study of urban plural policing, the main data for the chapter was drawn from the former Shendam Division of the Plateau Province. The Shendam Division during the colonial period was the land area situated on the right bank of the Benue River, south of the central Nigerian Plateau. It is the low-lying continuation of the lower Benue plains,[14] formerly part of Wase District in Muri Province, and formerly known as Lowland Division. As an administrative unit of Nigeria's federal state structure, Benue-Plateau was created in 1967; sub-divided into Plateau State in 1976, with Nasarawa state then carved out of Plateau in 1996. Jos was the administrative headquarters of Plateau Province and has been a state capital since the Nigerian regions were divided into states in 1967.

Since September 2001, Jos and its environs have witnessed incessant episodes of sectarian violence. Jos, a city of about 1.6 million people, is located in the central Nigerian 'Middle Belt', a socially diverse zone of mostly minority ethnic groups. While the chapter is focused on a history of policing institutions and the agency of policing actors, in order to understand the relational analysis that follows in subsequent sections of this chapter it is important to grasp the historical relationship between the minority groups of Plateau State and the large Hausa-Fulani emirates of northern Nigeria.

To understand this, there is a need to briefly recapitulate the history of the relationship, and highlight some of the main factors that defined the representation of Hausa-Fulani in the consciousness of the peoples of the former Plateau Province. Two key points will suffice; the wars and historical experiences occasioned by the extension of the Sokoto Jihad to the non-Muslim communities; and long standing derogatory references to these areas as a backwater used for the purposes of slave raiding.

Prior to British colonization, institutionalised Hausa influence in the Middle Belt had been limited to a few emirates,[15] established following the Sokoto Jihad in the early nineteenth century, within the Middle Belt area; a system which Ochuno (2014) has termed scattered 'systems of emirate control that nominally oversaw some non-Muslim peoples while pragmatically ignoring others.' Memories of these experiences are still alive across the present Plateau State. British colonisation introduced an administrative policy that placed non-Muslims under the control of emirates for the purposes of indirect rule. This misreading of precolonial relations between the emirates (like Bauchi and Zaria) and the non-Muslim groups on the Plateau highlands and in the Jema'a area was continually resisted throughout the period of British colonisation. The culmination of this resistance was the rise in a collective Middle Belt consciousness.[16] This explains why even contemporary sectarian violence in Plateau State occasioned by identity politics is easily associated within the consciousness of the hitherto non-Muslim groups of a historic perceived risk from Hausa-Fulani hegemonic tendencies. Having provided the historical political context as a basis to understanding my arguments and analysis, the chapter now turns to the roots of plural policing.

The forebear of the Police in Northern Nigeria was the Royal Niger Constabulary (RNC), established in 1886. The RNC was the enforcement arm of the Royal Niger Company, principally founded to secure and advance British commercial—and imperial—interests in the territories of what became Northern Nigeria. The RNC played a vital role in forcefully suppressing the discontent of the 'natives', allowing George Goldie's Royal Niger Company to carry on with the task of advancing British colonial interests.[17] By the early twentieth century, as colonial conquest took shape in the Northern territories, parts of the RNC naturally evolved into a colonial government police force. However, by 1907 a colonial policy to re-organise the police was already in place. The official reasons given for this re-organisation was the lack of coherence in police oversight—referred to then as the 'dual control' of the police, which was exercised by the resident administrative officers on one hand, and the chiefs of constabulary on the other. The argument for reform relied on the understanding that the system led to a multiplication of duties, and misconception of authority.[18] There were, however, more reasons beyond the official narrative. Rotimi rightly argues that it was principally to win the support of the northern emirs, as it permitted them to use their indigenous palace guards (*dogari*) as police. Secondly, the policy was much in line with the emerging colonial administrative policy shift from 'rule through native chiefs to rule through native chiefs on native lines'.[19] Significantly, this turning point marked the official recognition of local palace guards as Native Authority Police, starting in Kano and expanding to other parts of the northern territories in 1908.[20]

The Native Authority Ordinance of 1916 and the Protectorate Ordinance of 1924 therefore further empowered emirs and chiefs to maintain law and order in their domains. Thus, they had the authority to recruit people as security agents. Scholarly analyses of the Native Authority (NA) system have emerged with varied opinions. Whitaker, in one of the earliest publications and perhaps a conservative take conforming to the modernisation thinking of the period argues that the NAs are to be seen as necessary participants in the process of transformation, a symbiosis of tradition and modernity.[21] In other words, political developments did not take a linear process from 'traditional' to 'modern'; rather it was a complex fusion of both elements, consequently creating a form of transformation, something new that emerges, which cannot be described as traditional, but can neither be said to be to be modern. Dudley takes a different approach: he argues that the NA system disrupted the transformation process, pointing out that the political authorities who at the time were not receptive and adaptable to change, found useful tools in the Native Authorities.[22] Dudley situates his analysis further on in the context of late colonial Nigeria and the early years of independence within the roles the Native Authorities played during party politics. Dudley's main contention was that because of the funds the NAs controlled at the time, they were able to intervene at the local level in support of the parties of the state, actively involved in political mobilisation, coercion and oppression of all opposition. Furthermore, a system that situates so much power and control in an individual (an emir or a chief), placing high stakes on loyalty above all other thinking, is anything but transformative.[23] Perhaps the most enlightening take on the Native Authorities is the viewpoint of Yahaya, in his study aptly titled *The Native Authority System in Northern Nigeria, 1950–1970* the Native Authority is regarded as a political organism with corporate self-interest and as an institution for the making and application of law at the local level.[24] Yahaya rightly argues that,

> ...to speak of N.A. interest implies that it is not simply an institution of local government, but an organizational manifestation of a social force in society. As a politi-

cal institution, it will (sic) be expected to maintain law and order, to balance interests amongst the social forces, and to supervise the allocation of resources in the society. It is in the sense that the governments expected the N.As to function; however, they have been seen to act inconsistently. The discrepancy between the stipulated roles and the actual performance of the N.A. may not be fully understood until it is conceived as an organization of social force.[25]

The NA as a social force is therefore an institutional interest group, which is composed of various social groups; at the local base, we find the traditional ruling class, which includes the emir or chief, the district heads, the village heads, titled officials and employees of the Native Authority.[26] Here also included is the enforcement arm, the police.

Convinced of this new system of policing amongst the Northern Nigerian emirates, the colonial administrators began to consider implementing it in the more decentralised, acephalous southern provinces of the then Protectorate of Northern Nigeria. This was against the advice of local administrative officers, principally because there was largely no existing culture of *dogarai* amongst these groups.[27] Eventually the NA police in these areas had a substantial percentage of non-indigenes, largely from the northern Hausa groups. By the late 1930s to the early 1940s, NA police were operating across the length and breadth of the Northern region. As Rotimi notes, in the Hausa emirates they had metamorphosed from being the personal staff of the chiefly authorities in pre-colonial times, with no fixed remuneration, to stipendiary officials of the Native Administration.[28]

In the aforementioned southern provinces inhabited by the acephalous groups or decentralised societies, however, a dynamic emerged; it created problems on two fronts. Firstly, the local colonial administrative officers who were daily relating to these people recognised the challenges, because of the introduction of the centralised emirate-like system amongst groups that were previously loosely organised socio-politically along clan structures, with chief-like priest figures at the clan level providing juridical and spiritual guidance. In the Annual Report of 1932,[29] the Resident Officer of Plateau Province noted the difficulty to establish the principle of indirect rule amongst communities that previously had no paramount chiefly institution, though in the Plateau Province there were three exceptions[30] where centralised structures existed. The transition to a powerful paramount chief-like figure encountered resistance in some areas and the balance of stability and instability was to say the least precarious. To make this clear it should be understood that the polities or ethnic groups of the Plateau, prior to British rule did not constitute single political units. So while, the Berom, Ngas, Goemai, Mwaghavul, Eggon and Tarok, for example, were in their own right ethnic polities with particular common languages, each group was constituted by several separate independent political units.[31] 'Thus, among the Berom there were the separate independent polities of Du, Zawan, Fan, Gyel, Forum, Vwang, Kuru, etc. Among the Mwaghavul there were the independent polities of Pianya (Panyam), Kerang, Pushit, Bwonpe, Mpang, Mangun, Kombun, etc. Among the Ngas there were the Dawaki, Kabwir, Tuwan, Per, Ampang, Garram, Wokkos, et cetera.'[32] Among the Tarok, there were the Bwarat, Sa'a, Che, Lagan, Jat, Laka, Gyang, Pe, Lohmak, Gbak, Singha, etc. Each of these small polities of a particular ethnic group had their own priest chief, or system of socio-political organisation. Therefore, when paramountcy is mentioned, it refers to the British ambition to have a single overall chief for the Angas, Mwaghavul and Tarok, for example. This is what the policy of indirect rule set out to achieve amongst the ethic polities of the Plateau.

It was within this context that a Native Authority Police was established, so in the eyes of the people in these societies the chosen individuals who were made paramount chiefs were provided with a tool to oppress and intimidate. The idea that the Native Authority Police Force (NAPF) was populated by a 'stranger' population—of Hausa *Dogarai*[33] brought in from other Northern Provinces—worsened the situation of day-to-day policing.

The perception of the Native Authority and the NAPF amongst the non-Muslim communities can be understood along the lines of what Mahmood Mamdani has referred to as 'decentralised despotism',[34] a regime of institutional differentiation characterised by a bifurcated system with two forms of power used to govern 'colonial subjects'. Urban power was dependent on the language of civil society and civil rights—the rights of the colonisers. Rural power on the other hand was characterised by community and culture, ethnic groups reconstituted as Native Authorities administered by customary law. While rights governed citizens, subjects were governed through a range of different arrangements. Under the system, most of the colonial population were subjects because the status they had was derived from a putative customary law which colonialism used to compel Africans into the commodity chain of imperial capitalism. Citizenship was reserved for colonial officers and the few who were in their service. Africans were subjects of the colonial state but also subject to its discipline via so-called custom and tradition.

As it relates to the security roles, the structure of what was then the colonial police force has critically shaped the relationship between the state and society then and continued to do so in post-colonial Nigeria. The goal was to overcome the legitimacy crisis and to achieve the extractive, accumulation and taxation objectives of the colonial state. As the foregoing narrative has demonstrated, the colonial state, its legitimacy crisis and its preoccupation with 'law and order' threw up a specific state structure, state personnel and institutions to achieve these objectives.[35]

Ibeanu and Momoh rightly argue that while there is variance in the understanding of insecurity from the colonial to the post-colonial context, and the forces that constituted such threats to security equally vary, in both cases 'security has had an unchanging and fixated meaning. Security is about the state; it is both the prerogative and obligation of the state and its controllers to protect themselves, and it is in this context that the Nigerian police emerged.'[36] In sum, the post-colonial Nigerian Police Force (NPF) and the NAPF were not attuned to be in the service of ordinary citizens, neither were they obligated to operate under certain democratic norms and principles; peoples of the colony were subjects who were not practically entitled to be protected by the state. It should be noted that conceptualisations of security are not necessarily state-centric; personal security and the security nexus around the family and community as observed by Baker[37] are valid and should not be discounted. The bottom-line here however, is the fact that in post-colonial Nigeria the people logically developed a culture of not expecting the state to protect them.

From NAPF to Yanbanga

During the colonial administration, the NAPF Yandoka[38] system amongst the ethnic groups of central Nigeria had already come under some fierce criticism. In a memo to the residents of the provinces in August 1937, the chief commissioner of police was clearly concerned about the recruitment, training and efficiency of the Yandoka. While he advocated for better training and improvement, he was resigned to the fact that Yandoka in certain 'backward' (rural) parts would be relegated to the position of village watchmen (guards).[39] The Divisional Officer in charge of the Shendam Division (later renamed Lowland Division) of Plateau Province was even more damning. In an assessment of Yandoka in 1944, he lamented that the Yandoka had failed to efficiently discharge their functions, as the force was filled with illiterate and semi-literate personnel who were little more than messengers.[40] Nevertheless, despite the criticisms, the Yandoka continued, largely because there was no alternative.

There were several attempts to reform the Yandoka institutions and provide better training for the men. In the late 1920s, the colonial administration of the Northern Provinces desired to arm the Native Authority Police. The idea emerged from the office of the lieutenant governor of the then Northern Provinces with input from his residents and strong support from the inspector general of police, Northern Provinces. The lieutenant governor had in fact already recommended the importation of the first batch of the weapons for the use of the Kano, Sokoto and Ilorin NAPFs. The belief was that arming such Native Authority police might be useful in cases of emergency and for affecting the arrest of dangerous criminals.[41] In a letter to the secretary of state in charge of the colonies, the officer administering the government (OAG)[42] at the time, having expressed his support for the policy then went on to discourage it in the same letter. It is worth quoting him at length. He wrote:

> The policy of Government, however, with regards to the maintenance of armed forces by Native Rulers is set out on page 304 of Political Memoranda (1918 edition), and on page 325 it is expressly stated that Native Administration police may not carry firearms. If the Native Administration police are armed, it may easily happen, as the system develops, that within a measurable period of time there would be a large body of armed men, directly under the control of native chiefs, the potential danger of this (sic.) cannot be overlooked...[43]

This shows how seriously the Northern Nigerian government in Kaduna had regarded the NAPF as a policing arm. It was however obvious that once the bigger picture of the British global colonial experience was considered, the last thing the British wanted to do was to arm a policing force that was constituted by several ex-servicemen from World War I, some of whom still harboured grudges against the demobilisation process. While the British trusted these men to fight as comrades in arms during the war, they could not be trusted within a landscape that was still presenting strands of resistance to colonial rule. The recruitments in 1926 represented the engaging of ex-servicemen from World War I, and the recruitments in 1946 were drawn from World War II veterans. The colonial principle of recruiting ex-servicemen as local police, and as staff of the Native Administration in the Plateau province began after World War I and continued after World War II, whilst these men were being recruited to engage in police work, their major source of socialisation and experience had been in the art of soldiering.

Recounting his time in Nigeria, Mr. Robin Mitchell,[44] a former colonial police officer who served in Jos, Sokoto and Minna Provinces of Northern Nigeria, made the point that the effectiveness and efficiency of the NA Police varied across the region. It depended on the chief or emir overseeing the police, and the general situation in each Native Authority. Some were easy to police and nothing much was heard from them, but there was constant turmoil in others, largely because of the activities of the NA police and the high-handedness of some chiefs and emirs. Ultimately, the Native Authority police were not given arms, but apart from their primary role of policing the designated Native Authority area, they remained a very important and significant enforcement arm of the traditional rulers. The emirs and particularly the chiefs could not enforce their authority and rulership over their populations without this critical enforcement arm.

Having served its purpose during the colonial era, the NAPF survived the first decade of an independent post-colonial Nigeria; however, amidst the local government administration reforms of 1976, the government abolished the NAPF and qualified officers were subsumed into the Nigeria Police Force (NPF). The reforms had varied impacts across the country. In areas where there had been a long history of centralised chiefly political institutions, the re-organisation of the role of traditional rulers in the day-to-day running of government, while stripping them of all their statutory powers, did not necessarily affect their authority and social legitimacy. Traditional rulers in such areas continued to enjoy the loyalty and support of their communities. A contrast was found among the minority ethnic groups of central Nigeria; particularly groups that prior to colonial conquest had a socio-political system that was regarded as acephalous—or non-centralised. The local government reforms reduced such chiefs to mere ceremonial heads of their communities, as the role of chiefs as a sort of executive head of the community or ethnic group had not had sufficient time to develop and to be recognised by the people.

In place of the chiefs came local government administrators: the new system created a third tier of governance, the Local Government Area and its council. The traditional rulers were still around and were not going to go away; this left them in an ambiguous situation. On the one hand, they were stripped of their statutory authority and no longer ran local administration. On the other hand, within the context of emerging ethno-nationalism, they had emerged as an important rallying point of ethnic identity, and it was in nobody's interest to revert to the pre-colonial era when these societies were organised and administered according to the clan delineations. Subsequently, the chiefs began to seek out creative means to maintain a hold on their communities. They introduced the practice of bestowing traditional titles on prominent elites from the community or outside; they developed customary legal codes to respond to the need of maintaining control of land and land use; and they championed the introduction or continuation of traditional festivals and celebrations. Furthermore, traditional rulers helped establish vigilante groups, to help maintain law and order within their domains. The vigilantes are referred to as neighbourhood watch groups or vanguard groups, and colloquially by the Hausa term *yanbanga*.[45]

There is clear evidence to show that traditional rulers under the Native Authority system were using the Yandoka as their personal force, reducing them to Dogarai.[46] For instance, the village heads, the district heads and chiefs all partook at various points in the mapping, assessment, collection, and delivery of tax to the relevant colonial authority.[47] There are several accounts of corrupt and fraudulent practices by the chiefs, where the chiefs exploited the people by collecting illegal tax in the name of the colonial state and then embezzling it. Mangvwat narrates how:

> The chiefs... and their relatives enjoyed the period of tax assessment and collection, which usually took place from October to December, because it afforded them the opportunity to amass plenty of livestock and grain, which the peasants (people) had to auction in order to obtain cash for the payment of taxes. This was in addition to the outright confiscation of properties by some chiefs, purportedly for entertaining tax officials on tour even when no taxes were due. Indeed...some of these chiefs forced some of their subjects to pay taxes twice a year by refusing to issue receipts to the latter when they had duly paid their taxes in the first instance.[48]

The people also became wary of the chiefs and began to devise strategies to outwit them. An elderly man, Ali Dakshang in Dadur town of the Langtang North local government area, now in his late eighties, narrated a case of how he outmanoeuvred the local chief in the 1950s.[49] In one account the local chief was wont to demand livestock to entertain visiting colonial officers, in such cases whoever is called upon to provide is expected to oblige. However, the people became suspicious when it was realised that some livestock collected were later to end up in the chief's herds. The most fattened of animals that were made ready for the market were sent out to relatives in more remote villages out of the sight of the chief.[50] The atrocities perpetrated against the people of the Plateau province by the chiefs during tax collection formed an important dimension of colonial exploitation and terror, but it also engineered fervent resistance, sometimes leading to open riots, there were cases in which some of these chiefs were murdered.[51] The colonial accounts and oral records from this period show how the Dogarai and the Yandoka, as the enforcement arm of the chiefs were involved in cases of arbitrary arrest on the order of the chiefs, there also cases of indefinite custody of persons designated as accused over long periods without trial.[52] What the state reform took away with the disbandment of the NAPF was replaced with vigilante groups—*yanbanga*. In our area of research, recruitment for the first generation of this practice came from civil war veterans. In Langtang North, Langtang South and Shendam local government areas (LGAs) of Plateau State, the idea to establish a community-based neighbourhood watch group emerged from the palaces of traditional rulers. In a council meeting in 1971, the then Ponzhi Tarok (the Tarok paramount chief) called the attention of his council to the rise of crime, robbery and general lawlessness in his domain. He lamented that the unfortunate developments had a correlation with the dismantling of the NAPF without adequately replacing it with an alternative institution.[53] Traditional rulers were concerned about their loss of an enforcement arm. In 1975, the Nigerian government implemented the comprehensive local government reform, which was to re-organise the role of traditional rulers. The traditional rulers were stripped of all their administrative powers, hence if they were to muster any sort of relevance and influence they had to be creative. The establishment of the *yanbanga* in the mid-1970s is therefore best understood as an attempt to regain some semblance of authority by the traditional rulers.

Post-civil war vigilantes

Having made the decision to establish neighbourhood watch groups, the traditional rulers found a very reliable and ready-made group to champion the idea and become the major driving force for the return of a plural policing landscape: war veterans, who were demobilised after the Nigerian civil war and were mostly frustrated by the ordeal of having their army careers cut short, were keen to lead the way in recruiting and training selected young men to serve their communities as *yanbanga*.[54] I encountered several men, now in their 60s, who had served as *yanbanga* in the 1970s and met a few of the civil war veterans in Langtang North Local Government Area who were a critical part of the establishment of *yanbanga* in the area.[55]

The *yanbanga* of the 1970s were content to maintain a particular kind of socio-traditional order that was informed by customary legal codes; largely answerable to traditional rulers, their actions and functions in the communities derived from cultural norms, values and traditional codes of law and order. However, it should be noted that because at the time Christianity had also

gained root amongst these communities, it was equally influential in informing what vigilantes regarded as a contravention of law and order. This created
a scenario in which on issues where Christianity and tradition agreed, there
was a convergence of codes of law and order. However, it was not all smooth
sailing as points of disagreement emerged in situations where the dual codes
were in conflict. One such scenario was the denigration of traditional ancestral cult practices of Christians amongst the Tarok: here the church found
itself on opposite sides with the traditional religious adherents, and several
adherents of traditional religion were equally members of the vigilante group.
This was the case in communities of the Plateau Province where there had
been an established practice of ancestral cults providing a specific variant of
pre-colonial policing services. In spite of the major headway of Christianity in
the Plateau lowlands, ancestral cults have retained considerable prominence
and importance, in some communities up till the present; the scenario
observed is best described as a landscape of religious duplicity, a sort of a
biformity of practice. This does not refer to adherents of different religions
living together, but rather a considerable number of people who are active/
passive adherents of different religions. The culture of masquerading and
ancestral cult worship indeed has different functions and cultural roles in a
general sense amongst the peoples of the former Plateau Province particularly
the Tarok of the Plateau lowlands, variously religious, political and aesthetic.[56]
Vigilante membership included both Christians and traditional religion
adherents; often there were tensions amongst such groups.[57]

Another important feature of these groups at the time was the fact that they
were organised at the community level. Their roles were largely limited to
preventing and responding to robbery and petty crime in the community. The
punishments they meted out to suspected culprits who were found to have
contravened societal norms and values and broken traditional codes varied
depending on the crime committed. Two kinds of crime are instructive here.
First was the most common crime of theft, one of the classical reasons for
establishing vigilantes. The object of theft ranged from small-scale domestic
livestock such as sheep and goats, to cattle and stored grains. Where a suspect
was found to have committed such a crime, the routine of punishment would
involve public flogging usually at the chief's palace or the town square, followed by a procession with the suspect dancing at the front amidst songs of
mockery and jest, a practice Pratten[58] observed amongst the Annang of south-
east Nigeria, referred to as the dance of shame. The *yanbanga* of the 1970s
tended to merge societal legal codes with traditional religious practice.

Secondly, capital punishment as a possible punishment for contravening serious codes of the ancestral cult such as leaking secrets of the cult was practiced. This was a case of vigilante policing informed by different codes of law and different values. Therefore, within a given territory, there were different legal regimes at work, to some extent a plurality of practice and punishment. Judgements and subsequent punishment were restorative but also largely punitive. Therefore, an individual found guilty of an offence such as theft was fined a goat but could also be publicly flogged, and also subjected to the dance of shame around the village or the market square.[59]

Structural adjustment and the quest for order

Another important epoch in the evolution of vigilante policing in Nigeria and particularly Plateau State is linked to the implementation of the Structural Adjustment Programme (SAP) from 1986 and the impact it had on state policing.[60] In the period from 1970–78, the Nigerian military government enjoyed a period of high export earnings from petroleum revenue, the so-called oil boom which ushered in a rise in public spending. The Nigerian military government embarked on a massive spending spree, hosting and organizing international cultural festivals, for example the Festival for African Arts and Culture (FESTAC) in 1977, and local sports competitions, giving huge bonuses to workers, and an array of public works—education, health care, public infrastructure—all without proper investment in the productive capacity of the economy. Unfortunately, the 'oil boom' was soon to become 'oil doom.' After the international drop of oil prices the revenues of the Nigerian government dwindled; the reason for this was obvious: Nigeria was running a single-commodity economy and agriculture, which was formerly the mainstay of the economy, had gone into decline. Olukoshi notes that manufacturing and unemployment had also gone into massive decline and from 1980–83; over one million workers were retrenched.[61] Despite huge public protests, the military government followed the prescriptions of the World Bank and the International Monetary Fund to implement large-scale austerity. This austerity cut across all sectors of Nigerian society. There was a period of massive state withdrawal from public services. The provision of public security and the maintenance of law and order—a statutory responsibility of the police, which at the time was already not in good shape—went from bad to worse. The government, in response to growing crime and lawlessness, turned to the citizens for a solution. There are several accounts of individuals who remember this period and narrate how it unfolded. In an interview with Maiangwa[62] Chenvong Vongbut,[63] the current vigilante group leader of Langtang North LGA, he recalls the process of establishing the vigilante groups in the mid-1980s as follows:

> The then Ponzhi Tarok [traditional ruler, chief] was called upon to Abuja [this is circa 1988]...they were told that there is [sic.] a shortfall in manpower. We used to have 'yan sandan NA'[64] but now they have been discarded...and we only have the police who are grossly insufficient.... There is a need to select some people who would fill in the gap.... When they arrest any criminal, they should take such suspect to the nearest police station...for further investigation, so that we can restore order in the land.... When the Ponzhi Tarok returned, people were selected, and I was among those selected.... We were given appointment letters; the DPM[65] of the local government signs the appointment letter.... We continued working [and] at the end of the month, they give us allowances.

Police numbers were insufficient at this time due to the lack of resources from the government to employ new police officers but also for the training and retraining of those already in service. The allowances paid were monthly stipends paid to the vigilante groups. This was a case of vigilante policing established by the state to respond to a shortfall in policing numbers, as a result of the state cutting down on critical social services. The mantra from the state police, borrowing from international trends at the time, was all about community policing as a panacea for high crime rates. In public advertorials, citizens were encouraged to 'help the police serve them better'. This was the beginning of police/vigilante co-operation in Plateau State. The vigilante groups at that time began to believe they were operating as an extension of the state. The roles and functions of vigilante groups expanded: they provided information—intelligence—and arrested suspects and handed them over to the police.[66] They also worked in conjunction with market authorities across Plateau State to maintain law and order in local markets.

They however continued some of the practices and punishments from their predecessors of the 1970s. The dance of shame continued in some cases as a precursor, before suspects were handed over to the police.[67] The practice of tying armed robbery[68] suspects to trees particularly when they were caught or arrested at night was widely practiced. Corporal punishment was equally continued. Again as with the vigilantes of the 1970s, within a given territory there were two key jurisdictions at play: a plurality of practice and punishment characterised by vigilantes working in cooperation with state institutions and observing statutory practices on the one hand, and on the other hand still drawing from their own codes of punishment.

Post-1999—the Vigilante Group of Nigeria (VGN)

In the seventeen local government areas of Plateau State, there are vigilante groups operating with clear hierarchical structures, drawn from and recognised by the communities they serve. The divisional police officers (chief police officers) in charge of these local government areas are aware of the existence of these vigilante groups. The extent to which the police are aware of the activities and operations of these groups varies across the state. In some local government areas there is close monitoring and supervision; in others the situation is much more relaxed. These groups are local branches of a national organisation, the Vigilante Group of Nigeria (VGN). With its headquarters in the city of Kaduna (former capital of the Northern region at independence in 1960 and current capital of Kaduna State), the VGN is the officially recognised umbrella body of vigilante groups. According to the group's national leader Alhaji Ali Sokoto, the group has members and branches in all the thirty-six states of the federation.[69] Though the VGN was formally registered only in 1999, the origins and history of vigilante groups in Nigeria and Plateau State dates back much further as we have seen.

The characteristics of vigilante policing create a phenomenon that is not sustainable. Largely unpaid,[70] there is a tendency for the vanguard to become the vandal. Consequently, vigilante groups largely have short life spans, as, when their activities get out of hand, the state through its agencies is quick to put them in check. However, over time they re-emerge. The post 1999-vigilante groups in Plateau State and other parts of northern Nigeria demonstrate how vertical encompassment[71] evolves. Vigilantism has increased in prestige; consequently social legitimacy and popular acceptance at present is very high. The process of recruitment gives us indications: forms are filled, the local chief has to vet all potential recruits, followed by an interview process by the local police. For the successful few, uniforms are procured, identity cards are issued and rudimentary paramilitary training given. As part of a national association, vigilante members in the current typology are keen to be identified as extensions of state institutions. They actively participate in policing duties such as arrest, detention and interrogation of suspected criminals. In most cases, they hand over the suspects to the police.

There are broadly two categories of vigilante engagement with the police: those who are embedded in the police stations subordinate to the police and those who work independently but in close cooperation with the police. In current practice, what is observed is the adoption and use of two legal codes: a statutory code based on vigilante groups' understanding of state policing, and vigilante codes that have been drawn from historical practice. The motivations for joining the vigilante are also twofold. First, as already mentioned, being a vigilante brings prestige and authority. The idea of going on patrol and having the power to arrest and to punish is a huge motivation for many of the young men who get involved.

The second motivation relates to the political economy of being a vigilante. Simply put it creates a means of a livelihood. At first glance though this is not clear; when the researcher first poses the question of what motivates individuals to volunteer, earning money and favours are not admitted as a motivation; rather altruistic factors are mentioned. However, after spending several weeks on night patrol with the groups it becomes clear that vigilantism is not an altruistic pastime. To patrol the town at night means not only policing the town's residents: it is also policing night travellers who are either arriving in the town or passing through to a neighbouring or a distant destination. Usually from 11:30pm or 12:00, midnight roadblocks are set up with logs of wood and wood planks with a line of nails dangerously sprouting out. From afar, an approaching vehicle sees the bright light burning off a thread soaked in kerosene. At first commuters would assume that police officers man the checkpoints; only when one arrives at the roadblock does one realise that one is dealing with a local town vigilante group. Sometimes the routine takes just a few minutes: asking about identification, where the travellers are coming from, and their destination. If the vigilantes are satisfied, they allow the vehicle to proceed; if they are not, they request the commuters to disembark and they commence a check. I have witnessed episodes where drivers arrived at our checkpoint with their fists clenched motioning to hand over money, but on some occasions they were berated and accused of trying to hide something. Parts of the research area still remain unstable and insecure and have witnessed cyclical violence; in such regions lorry drivers are suspected of trying to hide arms. On other occasions, the vigilantes may take the money and allow the vehicle to pass. Usually in the morning, all the men assemble at the local chief's house for some kind of a debriefing session, after which they disperse to reconvene in the evening.

Since 2001, there have been recurring episodes of violent conflict in Plateau State. While there is much controversy and contestation over the 'ownership' of the state capital Jos and other communities, discourses on where the blame lies for the several episodes of violence is also a major topic of debate.[72] What is however clear is that vigilante groups have been very active in perpetuating collective violence. Vigilante groups adapted to the new insecurity and were important local actors in the crisis. Polarised along religious and ethnic lines, their significance metamorphosed from vigilance against crime within the community to constituting the most serious threats posed by armed militias.[73] As Higazi has argued, the intersection of vigilantes and militias was situational; where there was less violence vigilantes were more prominent, but elsewhere their functions merged. Vigilante groups hitherto responsible for providing security within their immediate communities emerged and were mobilised as 'ethnic' and 'religious' militias. This role of 'defending the community' in time of violence thus bestowed a particular kind of legitimacy on vigilante members, that legitimacy which comes from the ability to protect the community during times of violence being perhaps the most important—more important than cultural and historical notions of masculinity.[74] It is important to however make the point that vigilante groups were not homogenous and they were constituted by young men from different religious and ethnic backgrounds. Therefore, during periods of violence where mobilisation was around ethnic and religious identity, the *yanbanga* were themselves polarised along ethnic and religious lines during the crisis in areas affected by violence. These divides have remained in some areas.

There are, however, towns I visited during my fieldwork where vigilante practice has emerged as one of the forums that is actually bringing feuding communities together again. A prime example is Yelwa, formerly a major commercial centre of the Plateau lowlands. Yelwa town was in ruins following several episodes of violence from 2003–4; in fact it was the unfortunate massacre of Muslim residents of Yelwa in May 2004 that necessitated the Nigerian government to declare a state of emergency in Plateau State. In a group interview with the Vigilante Group of Nigeria members of Yelwa in November 2012, I could see a semblance of cooperation amongst the Christian and Muslim residents of the town, the local leader of the vigilante group Alhaji Dahiru Garba[75] a retired police officer pointed out that:

...after the crisis here, still there was lack of trust amongst the Christians and Muslims, so you see the stakeholders in the community suggested that there should be a joint vigilante group, as it was before the crisis. Every Sunday evening we meet here [at the vigilante local office where we were having the interview] for brief lectures, about two hundred of our members. We know the law and we usually do parade just as the police do, so religious leaders and the peace committee saw how we were successful in our work, they immediately identify with what we are doing saying they will support us, and we are currently living and working together with no problem.

Conclusion

In this chapter, I show how vigilantism in Plateau State, Nigeria, is traced back to the demise of the former NAPF, although through different periods they represent evolving categories of Nigeria's plural policing landscape. The earlier phases of this plurality transpired in the wake of the Nigerian government's policy in the mid-1970s to reform local government, and the subsequent attempt by traditional rulers to re-assert some semblance of influence and authority. In addition, the chapter argues that contemporary vigilantism is a product of a socio-political historical process. In our understanding of this process, we are able to show continuities and discontinuities concerning the role of actors, as there are always members carried over from a preceding era of vigilantism; equally, there are new members with new practices. The chapter explores important epochs within the historical trajectory on a macro level, showing how these epochs affected the social landscape at the micro level, establishing links we otherwise may not have noticed. Furthermore, the chapter shows how vigilante groups operate based on different legal codes, some statutory, others influenced by the historical experience of practice carried on from one generation of vigilantes to another. It is also clear that while vigilante practice may emerge and be sustained on the grounds of quest(s) for order, in our case the dominant theme of vigilantism is not contestation with state authorities; rather it is actively emerging as a means by which the state hopes to extend its reach. In other words, vigilantism is not necessarily strictly a function of state weakness. My analysis of the origins, organisation, structure and functions of vigilante groups suggest that there are contexts where they are part of the state, or at least in their action they constitute an extension of the state rather than belonging entirely to the realm of the non-state.

The demarcation of state and non-state in some contexts is blurred, but vigilantism as a social phenomenon is relational to the state, and the state in this conceptualisation could be the state actual, the state potential, the state symbolic or the state as an idea. As Abrams argues, the most important question to consider in our study of the state is how 'the idea of the existence of the state has been constituted, communicated and imposed.'[76] The study of vigilante groups requires that we consider the state in context, with content generated from its discourses and practice. In this respect, the paper is a departure from contentions and arguments where vigilante groups reject the politico-legal authority of the Nigerian state.[77] The paper rather suggests that vigilante groups actually end up supporting the state and its agencies. I am in agreement with arguments that have cautioned us from always concluding that the increasing prominence of non-state security actors is an automatic feature of state decline in power and authority.[78] Vigilante groups analysed in this paper mimic the state and attempt to be an extension of the state. It is important to note that, while vigilante practice and other forms of plural policing do in some ways demonstrate the inability of the Nigerian state to govern the totality of its territory, vigilante practice also speaks to the practice of statecraft from below, and through their interactions with state institutions vigilante groups actually extend the state's legitimacy.

We can also consider what broader implications these arguments have for the wider concerns and comprehension of this chapter. I would suggest that they provide a new perspective into our understanding of vigilantism, and on a more general note plural policing in Nigeria. Earlier studies on the Bakassi Boys, the Oodu'a People's Congress (OPC) and the Hisbah (Sharia Police) had, at their core, examples of vigilantism that were driven and situated within the social formation of identity. Another popular theme was the conception that understood vigilantism in the logic of contesting the authority of the state.

However, at the same time as the Bakassi Boys, the OPC and the Hisbah were emerging on to the scene, the VGN was being registered; consequently the structures, organisation and practices of vigilantism were being further transformed with the active approval and involvement of the state. What has emerged from my study reveals that the vigilante group I have studied (the VGN) does not comply with the dynamics of ethnic and religious category as the basis or the logic of its mobilisation. While it may be pointed out that the formation, and its current leadership in most of northern Nigeria is converged around a Hausa group dynamic, its membership is diverse and does represent the larger heterogeneity of society.

Finally, I would suggest that the arguments offer us insights into the understanding of the state and its everyday operations. In sum, vigilante practices both expose state weakness and at the same time represent statecraft from below. The two are not mutually exclusive. Vigilantism seeks to fill in for the weaknesses and through 'negotiated' arrangements that may be incorporated by the state to supplement and complement state police. What then emerges is a relationship best described as what Mbembe calls 'conviviality'. Here the relationship is characterised by 'dynamics of domesticity and familiarity inscribing the dominant and the dominated within the same episteme'.[79] Vigilante practice is influenced by different legal codes; therefore this creates a plural landscape of actors, jurisdictions and practices.

PART II

WHO ARE THE POLICE IN AFRICA?

6

WHO ARE THE POLICE IN AFRICA?

Thomas Bierschenk

This chapter addresses the question: who are the police in Africa? As stated in the introduction to this book, this question represents a call for a globally comparative historical sociology of the police as an organization and profession. The question is raised here—implicitly at least—as to whether generic commonalities exist between police organizations and police officers throughout the world, which are also shared by the police in Africa. The question is also asked as to whether the category 'police officers in Africa' is sufficiently independent as an object of study, and this, in turn, points to another question lurking in the background as to whether 'Africa' is itself a meaningful sociological category of study.

However, international comparative police research is underdeveloped at present and appears to be almost entirely absent in relation to Africa.[1] Thus, it is only possible to provide some pointers as to the direction in which the answers to these questions could be sought. Therefore, at best, this question encourages us to carry out comparative research that has not yet been done.[2]

In a comparison of police forces in the global North and South, the question ultimately arises as to whether it is possible to observe variations that make African police forces fundamentally different as organizations to their counterparts in the North. In this text, I argue that, like all state organizations, we should understand police forces as heterogeneous bundles of discourses and practices that do not form a coherent whole governed by a single logic. This kind of view is similar to Gluckman's position in his famous debate with Bohannan regarding the possibility of intercultural comparison in the area of the law.[3] This debate is of interest to my argument insofar as it revolves around the concept of culture. For Bohannan, cultures represent coherent units with clearly delineated boundaries ('systems'), which are organized around central concepts.[4] Seen from such a culturally relativistic view, these systems are, therefore, both unique and incomparable. Gluckman, in contrast, sees cultures not as systems but as 'hotchpotches' of practices and their justifications, which are only loosely connected with each other. According to Gluckman, it is entirely possible to compare these individual elements of a culture with each other. In comparative international police research, we face a similar problem and I propose to resolve it by adopting an approach similar to Gluckman's. In accordance with this kind of 'non-essentialist' approach, it would appear particularly interesting to me not to compare police organizations *in toto* with each other, but to compare instead the individual elements (discourses, practices) of police organizations and police work.

Based on this premise, I work on the hypothesis that ethnographic police research—as developed from the 1960s and 1970s for many countries in the global North and as also carried out in Africa in recent times—that focuses on practices will reveal more commonalities than differences between the police 'here' and 'there'. The contributions to this book testify, not least, to this. And yet, it is far from easy to define what should be identified as a 'commonality' and what as a 'difference' as this depends on the selected degree of abstraction. From an ethnographic perspective, the specific features of African police organizations appear to be only gradual differences. Hence, what is involved here are nuances and modulations, which do not lend the police organizations in Africa an 'essence' of their own but, perhaps, a particular hue.

This text is divided into three major sections. In the first I ask the question 'how to compare' and propose three possible comparative dimensions in response. Based on some examples, in the second section, I explain the elements of police organizations that can be compared. To conclude, I attempt to outline how 'macro differences' which emerge very clearly from the comparative analysis can be explained, or, to put it another way, whether and how differences that may be observed in the individual elements cumulate to form qualitative differences. As with all ethnographic studies, the challenge here is to explain differences without essentializing them and without altering the object of study, that is without 'othering'. In this context, I also consider the role of culture, history and organization as possible explanations for local-specific forms of police. To conclude, I appeal for reciprocal comparisons as an approach to global police research.[5]

Three comparative dimensions

The hypothesis of a fundamental isomorphism between police organizations throughout the world may only appear surprising at an initial glance. It becomes less remarkable when we realize that the police is a classical travelling organizational model or 'transversal object'.

Travelling models and reciprocal comparison

Following Behrends, Park and Rottenburg, I understand 'travelling' organizational models as technical or organizational plans (of action) or blueprints.[6] The level of refinement and sophistication of such 'plans' can differ considerably; in the course of their 'travels' around the world, they are repeatedly copied, altered and transferred to other processes or fields. Travelling models can have different dimensions and concern both the form of state police organizations and individual elements of them. African police organizations as we know them today were introduced during the colonial period in Africa; in terms of their general manifestation and many of their individual elements, they are shaped by the organizational styles of the former colonial metropole to the present day. This emerges very clearly, for example, in the distinction between the police and *gendarmerie*, which is found mainly in the former French colonies but not in the former British ones.[7] Many aspects of these 'journeys' remain largely unresearched, however: we do not know how these models travel, which zones of contact exist and how it is possible, for example, that the outward appearance of the Ugandan police force bears an astonishing similarity to that of its Bavarian counterpart.[8]

Incidentally, the fact that today's police organizations are shaped by the styles of the former metropoles does not mean that such models always travel from the global North to the South. On the contrary, recent historical police research in relation to Great Britain drew attention to the fact that ideas, practices and personnel circulated in all directions between the different colonies and Great Britain.[9] Indeed, some authors argue that modern ideas about policing developed in the colonies and were introduced to England from there (and then re-exported again).[10]

It could be argued that historical moments involving particularly close connections exist and that the current phase of 'neoliberalism' constitutes just such a moment. The police have become an object of global social engineering.[11] Over the past twenty years, intensive efforts have been made to reform the police sector in many countries, partly in a context of comprehensive 'security sector reform'. This reform was triggered, on the one hand, by the 'African Spring' of the period around 1990, but it was also motivated and financed in many respects by foreign donors. The latest period of intensive—if frequently also contradictory—reform, has also created the context for the increasing research interest in the police in Africa.

African police as 'bureaucrats in uniform'

Apart from isomorphisms with the police in the former colonial metropoles, I would also argue, second, that police forces in Africa often share the specific features of their functioning with other African state bureaucracies. The police is part of the state apparatus—it consists, so to speak, of 'bureaucrats in uniform'.[12] This consideration points to another comparative perspective that would merit more systematic attention in the future. Empirical ethnographically oriented research on state bureaucracies and public services in Africa (which inspired the ethnographic police research in Africa, on which this book reports, in part at least) emerged in recent years under the heading of the 'state at work'.[13] One of the main benefits of the research studies carried out under this heading lies in the considerable rectification of the previous fixation by (mostly political science) research on the African state on the issues of 'corruption' and 'neopatrimonialism'. Detailed scrutiny of the findings of this research points to commonalities which appear to be shared by many public bureaucracies in Africa (the police, legal system, education system, public health sector). I will examine some of these commonalities, which, in turn, constitute relative differences to the global North, below.[14]

History: path-dependency and sedimentation

Thirdly, it is also possible to compare the 'police today' with 'police before'—a perspective that is already contained in the aforementioned concept of travelling models. The form currently assumed by police organizations everywhere is the outcome of path dependency and entangled history. The influence of the colonial metropoles that provided the models has already been mentioned. In the form they assume today, however, African police forces are also the product of their own individual history.

The concept of sedimentation appears particularly useful to me when analysing organizational development. In most cases, organizational innovations do not simply replace existing arrangements but accumulate like layers of sediment. The consideration of the individual elements of bureaucracies—the personnel, codified rules, practical norms, legitimizing discourses—reveals accumulated 'temporal layers' within them, which refer to very different historical periods.

The shaping of today's police organizations by their colonial heritage and the cumulative experience of the population with these police forces are particularly important in this context. Like many European police forces, until well into the twentieth century, these colonial police organizations scarcely reflected the modern political principles of separation of powers and equality before the law.[15] On the contrary, they were repressive, racist and primarily guided by the principle of maintaining power. With the exception of the systematic racism, all of the elements found in this colonial police organization found their way into the post-independence period.[16] This observation is important for the deconstruction of the myth that can still be encountered in relation to the great distance between African populations and the institution of the police and the state in general: as demonstrated by the high demand for police services, the population does not fundamentally question the institution of the police. The criticism is directed instead at the inadequate functioning of the institution.[17]

The simultaneity of the non-simultaneous, which is contained in the idea of sedimentation, is, of course, a characteristic of all bureaucratic organizations. However, it appears to be particularly prevalent in African police forces and in the state apparatuses in general: elements of the repressive colonial state can be found operating in parallel to the very latest trends in neoliberal administrative reforms like 'participative police work'.

In view of the frequent restructuring of the security sector, however, what exactly is meant by 'police before' is often far from obvious. For example, in the French colony of Dahomey, today's Republic of Benin, different police organizations (urban police in the strict sense, which were limited to the major cities in the south of the country; prison guards; district guards/*gardes de cercles*; the 'indigenous' gendarmerie, etc.) were established at different points in time, and underwent numerous name changes and temporary amalgamations. The staff of these various repressive organizations mostly originated from the occupying forces. In 1923, a national police force was established from these different elements, while the gendarmerie remained part of the military. During the Marxist-Leninist regime (1974–90) the police and gendarmerie were (partly) united on an organizational basis—a process that involved considerable (re-)militarization—and in 1990 a police force was established that was clearly separate from the gendarmerie.[18] In the Democratic Republic of the Congo, various police forces have been repeatedly restructured since independence and private and state, military and civil security organizations have been amalgamated. The current Congolese police force includes former soldiers and rebels.[19]

Is 'Africa' a relevant unit of study?

All of the comparative statements made here must remain largely hypothetical, as the available research is still very patchy; in Africanist research, it is important to avoid the unfortunately widespread tendency of applying limited knowledge from one corner of the continent to all of its countries. Even if the perspective is limited to sub-Saharan Africa, the spectrum ranges from South Africa, a country with a developed capitalist economy whose average GNP exceeds that of some European countries, to Niger and Mali, two of the poorest countries in the world, from countries whose territory exceeds half of that of the European Union (Democratic Republic of the Congo) and whose population (Nigeria, 180 million) is equivalent to over one third of that of the European Union, to mini-states, whose territory (Cape Verde Islands, 4,000 km²) is exceeded by the overwhelming majority of German federal states, and whose populations (Cape Verde Islands, 520,00 inhabitants) are smaller than those of a number of German cities. These extreme internal variations render the idea of starting with 'Africa' as a unit of research a fundamentally dubious one. This raises the question, however, as to which categories would be appropriate for such a global comparison—a question that must remain open here.

Elements of comparison

I will now present a series of aspects and elements of police work in Africa, which could be the subject of a future comparative analysis—needless to say, the list is not definitive.

Police idea and police practices

Analogous to the distinction made in the recent empirical research on the state, I propose to differentiate between a 'police idea' and 'police practices'.[20] On the one hand, we have a global image of the police as an established and clearly defined organization with transparent rules, which represents the organizational core of the general function of policing. This perspective, which is also internalized by the actors themselves, probably explains why the idea of 'police' has a relatively high recognition value everywhere. However, this globally circulating idea of police, which shapes both public perception and the official self-image of police organizations themselves, only loosely coincides with actual police practices everywhere. The image of a coherent and clearly defined organizational form of 'police' as part of the state apparatus correlates with varying professional practices involved in 'doing police'.[21] It in no way excludes the co-production of 'policing' in the interaction between state and private actors. In addition, practices which reinforce the idea of state can be differentiated from those that tend to undermine this image.[22] As is the case in the state apparatus overall, just as historical practices can contribute to reinforcing or undermining this idea of police, there is tension in all police forces between the homogenizing idea of police and heterogeneous practices.

Police, bureaucracy and state

Police, bureaucracy and state everywhere interact closely with each other. However, from a sociological perspective, this relationship is underdetermined.

The police is related to the state in two ways. Following Weber, in terms of the institutional character of the state and its domination function, the police is the internally directed bearer of the state monopoly on violence.[23] Accordingly, it also covers the state's monopoly of regulation (or monopoly of legislation) in relation to the constitutive people and state territory. This function emerges clearly in the commonplace reference to the police as the 'guardians of the law'. In terms of the organizational form of the state, the police is one of many state sub-bureaucracies.

From a sociological perspective, both descriptions—the police as bearers of the monopoly of violence, and as a bureaucratic organization—only cover some of the societal functions and professional practices of the police. Only some of the observable practices carried out by the police can be described as law enforcement. Laws and the eventual recourse to the monopoly of violence are merely one of several resources available to the police in their professional activity. This can be referred to as the selective application of the law. On the other hand, the functions of the police also extend beyond law enforcement: maintaining social peace is identified in the literature as a key function of everyday police work.[24]

Likewise, the labelling of the police as a bureaucratic organization only reflects reality in part. As is the case for all state organizations, the everyday functioning of the police and everyday police work are shaped instead by a tension between formal norms and informal practices.[25] The everyday practices of police officers everywhere are based on different moral orders (or registers), of which the bureaucratic order, which refers to the state, is merely one. Like all bureaucrats, police officers must deal with the fundamental bureaucratic paradox whereby it is their role as bureaucrats that brings them into contact with the problems of the lifeworld while a purely bureaucratic logic is not sufficient for the management of these problems. However, it could be argued that for the police the state is not merely one regulatory idea among others, but something that ultimately formats police practices. All other forms of policing arise, so to speak, 'in the shadow of the Leviathan'.[26] For, if the work of the police often does not exist simply in the enforcement of laws, thematizing the possibility of their enforcement constitutes the crucial power resource for the enforcement of interaction orders.[27]

Statehood—which like other abstract categories (capitalism, Islam etc.) is not accessible through direct ethnographic observation—is, therefore, a quality of police practices that emerges from them. It could be argued, following Beek, that one important difference between the global North and Africa lies in the fact that the bureaucratic order is more 'taken for granted' in the North than in the South.[28] Here, it clashes more intensely and explicitly with other moral orders; here, the project of state domination is more precarious and fragile. As a result, it requires more conscious decision-making and greater practical and emotional investment on the part of the police and its staff.

Police and policing, the public and private spheres

The specific nature of African police work cannot be simply sought, however, in a particular aspect that may appear typical at an initial glance—i.e. the limited range of state police organizations in many African countries. Since the 1960s, ethnographic police research—albeit focusing on the global North—has repeatedly drawn attention to the fact that a state-organized police force in the modern sense is merely a specific expression of the social function of policing.[29] This applies to all societies, and not only those of the global South. Private forms of police work long preceded the state attempts at monopolizing this function. In addition, private forms of police work go hand in hand with state police work to the present day; without the support of private police work, effective state police work would be impossible. The state police organizations that have emerged in Europe since the nineteenth century never constituted the sole policing instance, even after this point in time. The majority of social conflicts throughout the world are not resolved through police intervention even in cases in which responsibility lies with the latter according to the legislation. Instead, different forms of private policing prevail. These range from informants and contacts ('friends of the police'),[30] without whom the work of criminal investigation departments would have no prospect of success, to phenomena referred to generally under the heading of vigilantism and to private security firms. To these are added other phenomena like the private sponsoring of the police by business people, something that may be particularly common in Africa.[31] As is the case with corrupt practices, the boundaries of the public and private are permanently called into question by these phenomena. These boundaries are also exceeded when police officers are forced to avail systematically of their own private resources—for example mobile telephones and motorcycles—in the exercise of their official functions.[32]

The regulation of social conflicts by the state police in their official role tends to constitute an exception, however. It could even be argued that state policing is only effective if the police do not have to manage the majority of the conflicts, for which they are responsible in principle. It has been demonstrated for Africa that many interface bureaucracies are surrounded by fields of action, in which private actors adopt important supplementary or auxiliary functions in individual areas. Hence, formal public organizations like the police 'dissolve' at their edges, so to speak. Without these private actors, the public function of the state bureaucracy in question could not be fulfilled. In the context of education, this phenomenon has been described as the 'shadow education system'.[33]

Limited human and material resources

Given the limited material resources and steering capacity of many African states, the belief in the civilizing mission of the police collides perhaps to a particular extent with the realities of police work there. A banal reason for this—and one that is often ignored by ethnographic studies—is the frequently low police density. Whereas in Germany, for example, there is one police officer for just over 300 inhabitants, the corresponding ratio in Mali is one for almost 1,700 people.[34] Moreover, the Malian population is considerably younger; thus the proportion of young men—a priority clientele of the police everywhere—is considerably larger. The country is also three-and-a-half times bigger than Germany and considerably less accessible by road, and the Malian state has less than 1 per cent of the per capita sum spent by the German state on its population available to spend on its own citizens.[35] Furthermore, in a certain way, the rapid social change underway in Mali, in particular the high rates of urbanization, is reminiscent of the context in which the modern form of the police emerged in Europe in the nineteenth century.

Accordingly, in countries like Benin, Ghana and Mali, the presence of police forces is limited to the cities with rural areas being largely 'police-free'. It could be argued that due to the current reductions in public budgets in Germany, it is also possible to observe a certain withdrawal of the police from the territory. However, the relative inadequacy of staffing levels in the Benin police force is exacerbated by the insufficient material and technical resources available to it. For example, there is no guarantee that a police station in a medium-sized African city, which is responsible for 100,000 people distributed over a radius of 100 kilometres, will have a single functioning vehicle.[36] The radio equipment may not work either so that the police officers are reliant on private mobile telephones to communicate with their superiors. Office equipment and materials are also lacking, as are the modern resources of criminal technology. This, in turn, generates additional work, as the police must rely almost exclusively on eyewitnesses when fact-finding, a process that is far more time-consuming for investigators than the collection of circumstantial evidence.

The heterogeneity and opacity of African police organizations

To these resourcing problems are added the marked peculiarities of the internal organizations, which make the police forces in Africa highly heterogeneous structures—'archipelagos of elements'.[37] It must also be stressed here that this is not intended as an absolute difference to police forces in the global North. Bureaucracies everywhere are 'loosely coupled systems',[38] which present considerable grey areas between formal norms and informal practices and whose 'self-generated complexity' renders them opaque environments,[39] even for their participants.

However, the ethnographic police research of recent years has shown that this circumstance arises in an exponentiated form in African countries. African police organizations are characterized by a high degree of internal norm pluralism—the product of frequent policy changes, missing and, also, contradictory reforms triggered by very different donors, opportunistic individual decisions and an endless series of micro reforms at local level.[40] Despite the comprehensive production of official norms (in the form of ordinances and provisions), large parts of the system are not covered by these norms. There are unexplained contradictions between many texts, particularly because they are frequently formulated on an ad hoc basis with a view to resolving individual problems. Other texts are ignored by the administration, even wilfully. The actors—even those whose main occupations are affected by them—are not familiar with many of the relevant texts or lack access to them. In addition, important decisions by the administration are not actually produced in written form.

This organizational opacity involves, in part, a consciously generated lack of transparency, which is used as an instrument of power—by the upper echelons of the police vis-à-vis subordinates and by the police vis-à-vis the population.

A basic principle of the functioning of public bureaucracies in Africa appears to lie in the fact that, in the main, the interface agents are abandoned to deal with their problems themselves. Under such circumstances, professional behaviour—particularly if it is based on an idea of the public good and responsibility towards subordinates—can require conscious deviation from bureaucratic norms, above all when these norms are clearly obsolete and impossible to implement. Informal practices can, therefore, contribute to the improvement of the sporadic efficiency of state action. At the same time, however, ad hoc measures, which may be entirely reasonable in individual cases, reduce the overall efficiency of the administration, which fragments into personalized networks and semi-autonomous cells. In most cases, this is tacitly accepted by the superiors and leads to a high level of organized hypocrisy, which, in turn, reduces the predictability of processes for all participants. It is difficult to sanction divergent practices in this context. As they explain it themselves, all of the participants are forced to drive in this mist without a compass and must operate 'by line of sight'.[41]

This circumstance can be demonstrated in many sectors; I will present it here briefly based on the example of human resource management, recruitment and promotion policies, and the corresponding career strategies in Benin.[42] The conditions for access to the police professions and the qualification profiles change frequently, sometimes on an annual basis. The corresponding entrance examinations and those leading to promotion are held irregularly, if at all. In addition, the regulatory requirements governing promotions changed frequently from the 1960s and frequently alternated between the cancellation of existing regulations and their re-formulation. This led to the repeated reclassification of the personnel—a measure that was accompanied by an abundance of transitional provisions. These were not always recorded in writing and certain requirements in terms of educational qualifications were eliminated for them or other compensatory measures introduced.

These changing recruitment criteria and modalities are difficult for the candidates to understand and follow. The constant to-ing and fro-ing with regard to recruitment requirements, the implementation of entrance tests, and the duration and content of the basic training has resulted in the existence of police officers of the same rank who were subject to very different access requirements and whose career trajectories differ considerably. Their basic training can differ considerably in duration, depending on the availability of trainers, and be more or less military in nature; moreover, the content of the non-military part can differ completely. Thus, despite being equal in rank, these police officers can have very different levels of knowledge and experience. Cases are often found, in which officials hold posts, for which they are not actually qualified—a phenomenon that is familiar from other sectors of the public service in Africa, for example hospitals where nurses do the work of doctors (and are even addressed as *docteur*) and cleaners do that of nurses.[43] Significant inconsistencies in status are not uncommon, for example a simple police officer may have a school-leaving certificate or university degree while his superior has only an intermediate school certificate, and a police trainer trained by Europeans may have a lower rank than the police officers he trains.[44] Moreover, it is entirely possible for two officially registered police officers with the same seniority, training and pay grade to be paid completely different salaries.[45]

Police officers and gendarmes try to counter the opacity of the bureaucratic organization by adopting ingenious career strategies. The tension between official and practical norms in human resource management, on the one hand, and the multiple strategies adopted by the officials to overcome it, on the other, not only produces a high level of diversity in the categories of police officers and internal bureaucratic segments, which is surprising for such a bureaucratically rigid organization. It is also a source of widespread frustration among police officers and bureaucratic cynicism. Administrative processes that are supposed to unfold automatically require considerable personal investments in terms of time, money, social capital and political influence on the part of those involved. This is known as 'lobbying' in Ghana and referred to as *suivre le dossier* in Francophone Africa. A considerable proportion of the officials' energy is used in working against their organizations. It means that careers can only be planned to a limited extent and career progression depends to a largely unpredictable extent on not only qualifications but, ultimately also, chance.

In addition, finally, the environment and state organizations of relevance for police work, for example the legal structures and parliaments which are responsible for creating the legal conditions for police work rarely fulfil this task; they function in accordance with similar principles, which, in a negative feedback loop, renders the conditions of the police work more difficult in turn.

Organizational and professional self-image

Modern bureaucracies are not just technical constructs but must also be understood as moral orders ('orders of life' as defined by Max Weber), and the bureaucrat must be understood as a moral person. 'Bureaucracy...presupposes an ethical formation on the part of the bureaucrat, a bureaucratic vocation, as opposed to a more or less blind obedience to rules and orders'.[46] A corresponding ethical understanding of bureaucratic office is, therefore, the necessary complement to the discretion of the bureaucrat and, specifically, the condition for the limiting of bureaucratic tendencies in the negative sense.

With respect to widely disseminated culturalistic stereotypes, it must be stressed that this ideal image of the bureaucrat (police officer, teacher, judge) is also very common in Africa. It is taught in the police training institutes and police schools, its formulations—for example the 'ten commandments of the good policeman' in Benin—can be read in many state offices. The extent to which this image of the correct and responsible official is part of the external representation of many state authorities is very striking, in fact. This official model, which formulates high professional ideals, has been appropriated by many police officers, at least discursively. As is the case on other continents, its function lies less in controlling behaviour than in the legitimization of the organization to the outside world and the generation of an *esprit de corps*. Similar to that of judges, the official self-image of police officers is one of *automatons* who apply the law mechanically. As was established for other officials in Africa, the description of their functions by police officers themselves is heavily influenced by the highly idealized topoi of the educator and 'guardian of the nation'. As a self-image, it has quasi-religious traits.[47]

115

Despite the knowledge of the unattainability of the bureaucratic ideal, the belief in it sustains the everyday practices of the police. Moreover, the African public assumes that in the (alas unattained and unattainable) ideal case, police officers will take direction from the idea of state. A large part of the public criticism of the police, which is also expressed in Africa, is not rooted in a kind of cultural alienation from this institution but in the awareness of how far removed its everyday practices are from this ideal.

However, the police constantly exceed the imperatives of this model in their everyday work, as they must permanently weigh up the options between different action options and contradictory norms. The police legitimize this contradiction with the need to adapt to the realities of everyday African life, which are, in accordance with this view, characterized by the deficits of their own organization, on the one hand, and by the 'backwardness' of an 'uncivilized' population on the other (and this, in turn, legitimizes their self-designation as educators). Using a military metaphor, Beninese police officers (and other public servants) constantly refer to the fact that 'c'est le terrain qui commande'—like a good soldier, you have to adapt your practices to the terrain in which you move. This kind of everyday theory of the resistance of the local population almost expresses something akin to the dominant life attitude of Beninese police (and other public servants), with which they manage the wide-ranging normative dilemmas they face in their everyday professional lives.[48] These highly idealized attributions also provide a striking contrast with the motivations behind the choice of this profession, which tend to focus more on accessing a secure income or—*on n'a pas trouvé mieux ailleurs*[49]—the lack of realistic alternatives.

Precarious interaction formats

These under-resourced and overworked police officers encounter 'strong' societies, which, somewhat similarly to the situation in the USA, learned to keep the state at bay over the course of long historical processes. In their interactions with people, police officers in Africa know even less than their European colleagues about the people they are dealing with and how they will react (and whether their own superiors will ultimately support them in the event of a conflict). As they perceive it, they operate in hostile environments. This is reinforced, in turn, by the fact that, due to the lack of resources, police officers tend to limit their presence to the police stations and to 'missions', in which they can present in large numbers, for example at traffic checks.

As is the case everywhere, the encounter with the citizen in Africa, for example during traffic checks or police patrols, is also a process of negotiation, in which reference to the legal situation is only one of the possibilities availed of and, indeed, only as a last resort.[50] Like all police officers, the African police 'under-apply' the law (a fact that does not exclude them from over-applying it in the case of certain population groups). They base their behaviour on the people with whom they are interacting and the situation involved. The perceived status and behaviour of the interaction partner is of crucial importance here and is assessed using the key criterion of 'respect' (towards the police). This is also known from police studies carried out in the global North.[51]

However, in these encounters, African citizens often have a degree of agency that is far greater than that found in the global North and which ranges from the use of violence, evasion or flight to the opportunistic use of social relations and the media, witchcraft and political resistance. The police must take these different action options into account situatively in their own actions. As a result, encounters become highly unstable events with very unpredictable outcomes in most cases—not least because, as mentioned above, the legal situation is characterized by considerable grey areas and does not, therefore, represent a certain basis for police action.

A communication idiom frequently availed of is that of sociability, which, in turn, forms the context for the presentation of gifts. In these precarious interaction formats, the 'dash', e.g. the handing over of gifts of various sizes, becomes the modal form, so to speak, in which these interactions proceed. Corruption, which is embedded in a language of friendship, is the form of interaction, on which both sides can agree (even if this agreement is often grudging).

How can differences be explained?

This list of elements for comparison of how African/non-African policies work could, of course, be extended. This is not possible for reasons of space and, in any case, the aim here has been to kindle interest in such comparisons.

The question arises, however, as to how we should understand difference—which undoubtedly exists and to a considerable extent. African public bureaucracies are clearly not particularly successful at the production of public goods such as education, justice and social order.

Macro differences as the cumulative result of micro differences

If we do not want to explain these differences in terms of a somehow fundamental other 'essence' of African states, we must understand them in detail as the accumulated outcome of many small differences. The difference between African and other, let us say, European police forces does not, therefore, lie in the fact that they work on the basis of completely different criteria. They function largely on the basis of the same criteria, however these are differently characterized and their 'mixing ratio' is different. The impression that major differences ultimately exist between them, e.g. in terms of efficiency, is not the expression of a different 'essence' but the result of many small differences which ultimately generate a different quality.

As in a chemical process, macro-difference emerges, therefore, from the interaction of many small different factors and mechanisms. These, in turn, are only loosely linked and cannot be depicted by a single principle, for example neopatrimonialism or corruption. Moreover, it is precisely this loose link that brings stability to the difference; the alteration of a single factor does not as a rule change the entire outcome. In other words, attributes of policehood that may appear to be 'typically African'—for example widespread corruption— are overdetermined: they are not conditioned by a single factor but by a series of factors.

In these 'loosely-coupled systems',[52] individual elements are overdetermined: they are not explained in a linear fashion by a single factor. This can be illustrated by the example of police violence. The use of violence by the police is a compensation strategy adopted in the absence of other truth technologies (for example, fingerprints). However, it is also sustained by similar social practices in other areas of society like family and school. Corruption is a result of low salaries and is driven by local forms of politeness and other cultural 'accelerators'.[53]

Culture, organization and (colonial) history as explanations of police practices

A central question that arises in the context of intercultural comparisons of police work concerns whether the observed functional mechanisms and professional practices can be explained by cultural characteristics, history or organization. As has probably become clear, my preferences tend to lie with '(colonial) history' and organization. It is certainly true that the vast majority of basically justiciable conflicts in Africa never reach the police, not to mention find their way to the courts. They are resolved in myriad ways by very different (state and non-state) regulatory instances on the ground. This is not an 'African' phenomenon *per se* but a universal fact. What appears to characterize the cases observed in Africa is the relatively minor role that state instances still play in conflict resolution.

Nevertheless, it seems dubious to me that primarily 'cultural' explanations should be sought for this. On the contrary, the African populations have a series of very practical reasons for not taking their conflicts to the police. In my view, what is significant here is less the lack of demand than the inadequacy of the supply: the modern police simply function badly in the eyes of the population, based on its own claims and based on international comparison. It is quantitatively overstretched by the demands of society, remains influenced by its colonial genesis and lacks any serious attempt—including on the part of the many donors—to find a form, in which the orientation based on universal legal principles can be brought into harmony with the realities of a poor developing country. In this regard, it actually does resemble the public service in (West) Africa as a whole.

Global police research: for reciprocal comparisons of transversal objects

Police organizations are 'transversal objects' *par excellence* and are particularly suited to 'reciprocal comparison'. Following the historian Espagne, I understand transversal objects as relatively bounded empirical phenomena which are a result of transfer processes that took place in the past in the context of European imperialism and colonization.[54]

However, such a perspective alters the problem of 'otherness' which is also constitutive for anthropology. In the classical phase of ethnographically based anthropology, researchers, all of them western ethnographers, were faced with empirical phenomena which were unknown to them *a priori*, and of which they had to make sense. Today, in the presence of transversal objects, the boundaries between the known and the unknown are drawn differently, and ethnographers are no longer exclusively Westerners. In fact, they belong to a globalized body of experts who are confronted with a set of institutions and organizations that are spread throughout the world, and who are (or should be) in constant dialogue with other experts from other disciplines and professions. While the temptation in some academic circles in the political or administrative sciences is to view these institutions in the South from the confines of a (ethnocentric) Northern conceptual framework and from a universalistic perspective (similar to the way in which, for example, many comparative political studies rely on quantitative data), in contrast, the temptation for many anthropologists working in Southern countries, is to exoticize or essentialize these objects from a particularistic perspective.

What is needed, instead, is the development of a 'symmetrical' social science that consigns the both epistemic and methodological 'great divide' between 'Them' and 'Us', South and North, Africa and Europe to history, and at the same time allows for the relativity of particular 'Northern' perspectives.[55] In this context 'reciprocal comparison' means comparing 'transversal objects' with each other without a concrete temporal-spatial manifestation of this object forming the comparative yardstick for other manifestations. This book represents an important step in this direction.

7

SOMEWHERE BETWEEN GREEN AND BLUE

A SPECIAL POLICE UNIT IN THE DEMOCRATIC REPUBLIC OF THE CONGO

Laura Thurmann

'Just keep away from uniformed people, then you'll be fine.' It was on one of my first days in the Capital of the Democratic Republic of the Congo when a member of a private security organisation (who paradoxically was wearing a uniform) gave me that piece of advice. By 'uniformed people', he was referring to a small group of military and police staff who had become involved in an argument on the other side of the road. All of them were wearing uniforms and berets and were armed with AK-47s. At first glance, the only difference in their appearance was the colour of their apparel: The military staff wore khaki and green uniforms while the police officers wore dark blue suits.

'Keeping away from uniformed people', obviously was not a solution for me as I was about to plan my research into police in Kinshasa, but this situation first sparked my interest in police/military connections in the Democratic Republic of the Congo. In western countries, there seems to be a clear distinction between the military that is responsible for external security and the police whose duty it is to maintain law and order in the interior of the state.[1] Even police organisations such as gendarmeries that are assigned to the Ministry of Defence are clearly separated from the army by conducting civil police work to protect domestic security. Meanwhile, in many African countries it seems to be difficult to distinguish between police and military tasks.[2] Recent studies of civil servants and state organisations conducting policing in Africa deal mostly with issues of corruption, everyday functioning of organisations, institutions or modes of work and the interplay between a multitude of different actors to maintain law and order. Olivier de Sardan describes the vicious circle of impunity and corruption.[3] Justaert outlines the role of the Security Sector Reform (SSR) in the DR Congo and analyses the relationship between the police reform and local governance.[4] Police/military connections, however, are rarely studied in the scholarly literature on policing.[5] Beek and Göpfert point out that in many African countries, '[M]ilitary and other paramilitary organisations are also charged with tasks of law enforcement and the maintenance of public order' and can therefore be perceived as policing institutions as well.[6] Admittedly, they discuss neither the military nor paramilitary aspects of civilian police services nor the way in which it affects their day-to-day work. Literature about the Congolese police may illustrate the common history of the police and military, the paramilitary character of the police in general or the problem of demilitarization within the framework of the Security Sector Reform. Yet there is still a lack of empirically based literature analysing the role of police/military connections in today's police units in the DR Congo.

This paper is based mainly on informal, semi-structured and narrative interviews with members, trainers and sponsors of a special police unit in Kinshasa, as well as observations in the unit's base. For the duration of my research, I worked as an intern in one of the organisations that financed the police force. The role as a member of an international organisation facilitated the field access but also restricted my research in some ways. As I had to abide by their strict security guidelines, it was not possible for me to conduct any observations of the unit's work outside their base. I was able to observe the way the special police officers interrogate suspects and witnesses as well as record keeping processes and their daily interactions with civilians or other police officers. All I learned about their intervention, search and arresting derives from the stories the police officers and their co-workers told me about their work. Hence, a lot of my data is based on the self-image and the perception of the work in a special unit as portrayed by the police officers. To obtain a more profound insight into the unit, I also consulted internal documents and reports elaborated by international organisations that supported the unit since its foundation in 2008 and development until today.

After gaining independence in 1960, there was a persistent 'overlap connection' between the police and the military in the DR Congo.[7] Many police units are still influenced by a military self-perception of the police in general. Before analysing these military images of the Congolese police unit, it is important to define what I mean by military. There are two levels to this term. First, there are the qualities and rules that determine military organisations either by law or by the organisation itself. Kraska and Kappler describe military as 'a set of beliefs and values that stress the use of force and domination as appropriate'.[8] This 'force and domination' is normally directed at an external enemy of the state, except for situations of civil war.[9] The 'set of beliefs and values' are those qualities that are directly associated with the term military in many countries around the world. It is not just the German Armed Forces, who advertise their profession by emphasizing values like camaraderie, steadfastness, discipline, bravery and staying power.[10] The South African Army portrays its forces as ethical, honest and disciplined and calls for honour and patriotism, while the Russian military underlines duty, honour and service in the interests of the homeland as the key values of the forces.[11] These virtues demanded of soldiers are mostly produced by military organisations to advertise their professions and to create a standard identity among the ranks. Being brave and honourable might be a motivation to join the army which often does not conform with the second level of the term that defines associations which civilians relate to the term 'military'. By defining an organisation or a type of behaviour as military, civilians tend to refer to forms of harshness, inhumanity or even brutality. Especially in post conflict countries like the DR Congo, people often associate soldiers with war, fear and violence. Assuming that the special unit in Kinshasa is seen as military might be a problem in regards to Martin's assumption that police work is only possible if there is mutual trust between the police and the civilian population.[12] Police work, as Bayley defines it, can simultaneously refer 'first, to what police are assigned to do; second, to situations they become involved in handling; and third, to actions taken in dealing with situations'.[13] When writing about police work here, I refer mainly to how police officers conduct tasks that they 'are assigned to do' e.g. 'patrolling, investigating, directing traffic, counselling and administering' and that are defined by the organisation.[14] By using the term civil police work, I mean those parts of police work in which the police are in immediate contact with the civilian population and thus rely on their cooperation and trust in the police institution.

In this paper, I examine the police/military connection in a special police unit among whom I conducted three months of anthropological fieldwork in 2012. It was founded, financed and trained with the support of two international development aid organisations[15] within the framework of the Security Sector Reform. After a short survey of the history of the Congolese police and military I outline the creation, organisation and self-image of the unit. I analyse the connection to military structures and functioning with regard to the influence of European trainers and the framework of the Security Sector Reform. I will show how a special unit creates a balance between a military self-perception and civil police work and how they place themselves among the forces in green and blue and the civilian population.

Historical background and foundation of the unit

Following Hills, I assume that in most African states, the police have a paramilitary character due to their 'historical legacy and environment'.[16] Therefore, it is essential to provide a brief overview of the history of the Congolese state security landscape before going into detail about my work with the special unit. During the Belgian colonial rule, policing was carried out by the Force Publique that served as military and police at the same time, as well as the Gendarmerie, all consisting of white Belgians and some local police forces that worked as inferior units.[17] After independence in 1960, Belgian forces withdrew from the country. As Belgians occupied the majority of the senior positions in the police and the government, the Congo was left in a highly unstable political condition.[18] With 'fragmented' police structures and 'without adequate leadership', it was practically impossible for the remaining forces to fulfil peacekeeping duties and maintain law and order in the new state.[19] Many police officers acted as private forces for local politicians or joined the army to earn more money and secure favourable positions while the first UN forces who arrived in the DR Congo after independence took over the majority of the policing in addition to their military tasks.[20] President Mobutu founded the first integrated police force in 1966. The Police Nationale Congolaise (PNC) was created as a concept uniting local police forces and tasking them with providing 'public safety and salubriousness, and carry out surveillance'.[21] In fact, as a police officer told me, the PNC was 'not at all apolitical' at this time and seemed to be 'nothing more than Mobutu's private security company'.

In 1972, police in the Congo, then called Republic of Zaire, were seen as increasingly inefficient because of their constant rivalry with the remaining gendarmerie forces. Subsequently, the two forces were dissolved and reunited to form a new Gendarmerie Nationale that was replaced by the better trained and equipped Garde Civile in 1984.[22] During the conflicts that became known as 'war of liberation', the Alliance des Forces Démocratiques (AFDL) created a new police force under the rule of the first president Kabila. This force was an ensemble of personnel made up of former members of the Gendarmerie and the Garde Civile, as well as some military staff.[23]

The PNC as it exists today was founded and first included in the transitional constitution of the state in 2002 that 'defined the separation of powers independence of courts and basic civil liberties'.[24] In five articles, the police are defined as an institution that cares for 'public security, the security of persons and goods, the maintenance and restoration of public order as well as the special protection of the high authorities'. Furthermore, the Congolese police need to be 'apolitical' and 'objective' in all work situations and only operate at the service of the Congolese Nation.[25]

With the establishment of these articles that stipulate their tasks and roles, the police as an institution was enshrined in law for the first time. Still, these changes could not be directly implemented in practice. State institutions and the police in particular were still described as 'weak and corrupt'.[26] Since the first elections in 2006, many organisations have worked in conjunction with the Congolese state to create democratic institutions. It took another three years to launch the police reform, which is still in force today. The Comité de Suivi de la Réforme de Police (CSRP), consisting of the concerned Congolese ministerial authorities and different international partners, have drawn up a plan which aims to create a police service that is close to the public and civilians, fully apolitical and demilitarised within the next fifteen years. They demanded the demilitarization of the police and a strict separation of military and police forces.[27] In the framework of this reform, many special units arose in the DR Congo.[28] Various national and international state organisations and non-governmental organisations tried to fashion a better image of the police and establish a working cooperation between the police and the civilian population. As Martin outlines, trust in the police by the civilian population is essential for their everyday functioning.[29] Loader points out that an increased police presence leads to a higher sense of security in many Western countries.[30] Meanwhile, in the DR Congo, both military and police personnel are more likely to be perceived as a threat by the local population as '[m]uch of the violence against civilians in the protracted conflict in the DR Congo is perpetrated by state security agents.'[31] While Dahrendorf describes the frequent cases of sexualized and gender based violence as 'largely perpetrated by members of the armed forces' in Kivus, the US Bureau of Democracy reports on the engagement 'in illegal taxation and extortion of civilians' of the police and military throughout the country.[32] Being close to the public while conducting police work thus seems to be a challenge for the newly formed units. Apart from the low wages of 20 to 60 US dollars per month and the lack of equipment, the Congolese police force find themselves in a vicious circle of ill repute among the local population and civil police work malfunctions.

The unit in Kinshasa where I conducted fieldwork is a special force that fights organized and gang crime in the capital and environs. In 2008, the PNC started a pre-selection conducted by the local commissariats in Kinshasa. About eighty police officers were chosen to take part in a three-month training workshop and a protracted selection procedure. Instructors of the PNC and an international organisation tested the candidates' personal, intellectual, psychological, physical and professional skills. Finally, the instructors chose about forty police officers to form the new special unit. One year later, ten more officers in the Police Judiciaire[33] were added to improve the unit's investigative qualities. So far, the police officers have received further training and education in special investigation and intervention techniques, securing evidence and crime scenes, protecting victims as well as driving cars and motorbikes, record taking and first aid. Thanks to this multifaceted training, they are able to fulfil all tasks of civil police officers' work as well as those of special intervention units akin to those in Western countries without the help of other commissariats or special intervention groups. The trainers are both national and international police instructors working in development projects in the framework of the SSR. However, most of the trainings are conducted by police officers from different European countries. During training and workshops, they work actively with the Congolese police officers to teach them European police models. Although they all have different backgrounds from various European policing institutions, the instructors present themselves as homogenous European police which in reality do not exist in this way. They impart an idealized idea of European police as a non-corruptible, apolitical, objective state security institution.

The special unit is clearly male dominated although initially women should have comprised 20 per cent. In reality, they comprise a mere 7 per cent 'because of a lack of physical productivity', as one of the instructors told me.

A look at the structure of the police force shows clearly that it is based on a military model. The unit consists of six groups, four of which are in charge of investigation while another is responsible for search and the remaining for intervention. These groups report to a six-person leading management team know by the French military term *État major*.

A military police unit?

When I chose the special unit as my main field of research and started collecting theoretical data about the foundation and the trainings, I discovered a promotion video that shows some parts of the basic trainings. This fifteen-minute film portrays the police officers being taught some special police skills by European trainers. The viewer also sees a very disciplined unit lining up, marching briskly, saluting and singing some kind of anthem written for their unit. 'We are real police officers...' the officers sing while standing in rank and file which in my opinion, supports almost all traits associated with military personnel—but not police. That first impression was intensified when I first went to the unit's base accompanied by three representatives of their international partners.

When we arrived at the unit's base, the police officers were ordered to line up in the courtyard of the police station while their commanding officer, Colonel Mbala, informed us about the creation and development of the unit. After his short speech, he asked me to explain briefly the aims of my research and work with the unit. When I finished, the commandant stepped forward and asked the members of the unit: 'Who is this woman?'. 'Madame Laura' the unit chorused. 'And what is her profession?'—'Anthropologist'. 'What will she ask you?'—'Questions!', 'And what will you do?'—'Answer!'. This little question-and-answer game went on for quite some time before the commandant advised the police officers to go to the assembly room to prepare for their first conversation with me. They marched into the building in lines of two and in step.[34]

Military terminology and the construction of symbolic power

When discussing military/police connections in the DR Congo, a striking aspect is the terminology that defines the status of the police officers. When I first met the commanding officer of the unit, he was introduced to me by some members of the unit as '*le Colonel*'. In the process of demilitarization, many former soldiers or gendarmes lost their military ranks. By joining the police, they were given 'civilian' police titles, but the attempt to rename higher positioned officers only worked on paper. In formal documents or letters, the commander of the unit bore the title 'Commissaire supérieur', but in practice all of the subordinate police officers and even the European instructors called him by his former military title 'Colonel'. In fact even the European trainers did not use Colonel Mbalas' civilian police title. This phenomenon exists, as a member of a European organisation told me, not only in this special unit. Throughout the DR Congo, police officers—especially those in leading positions—tend to use military titles to define their status. It is striking to find this phenomenon in a special unit such as the one I worked with even though it is highly influenced by European civil police models. One of the officers of the Police Judiciaire explained this phenomenon a few weeks later:

> You see, these policemen are former military. They see it as a debasement to be called Commissaire if they are used to being called Capitaine, Mayor, Colonel... *'Commissaire'* could also be a civilian. That title doesn't show that you are a courageous, powerful man who wants to fight for the country.

By using the military title, the commanding officer of the unit creates symbolic power, defined by Bourdieu as a form of power that is not legitimised by law and exists only as long as it is accepted by the subordinate group.[35] The greater part of his authority is legitimised by the loyalty and respect of his subordinate police officers who call him by his military title and salute him accordingly. In fact, they demanded that everybody else acknowledge the commander's authority. Every time I went to the base to talk to the police officers, they first sent me to the Colonel to get his permission to conduct more interviews or to spend time with the officers. Even after having spent more than two months with them and although the commanding officer told me repeatedly that I was free to come and go at my discretion, they still insisted that I get his permission before talking to me.

Not only the commander's authority is, to a large extent, based on symbolic power. According to Loader, this form of power is indispensable for the performance of civil police work in general.[36] This phenomenon is known and directly used in the special police officer's work as one of the members of the unit described it:

> We work both, in uniforms and in civilian clothes. Both at the same time I mean. When we have an operation, it works like this: some of us, those who don't wear their uniform, are looking for the perpetrators. That is good because they can talk to the local population. You can't go to a woman and ask her what happened if you are wearing a uniform and a rifle.... But when we found some [criminals], the others

intervene in uniforms...we need the uniforms to show our authority and earn the people's respect.

The importance of uniforms as instruments of power was mentioned in almost all of the interviews I conducted at the unit's base. As I was working as an intern for the international organisation that sponsor the unit, I expected my presence would be perceived as a way of securing new material or financial support. The fact was that of all the things they were short of, like a steady flow of electricity and running water, stationary, resting places for nightshifts etc., the lack of new uniforms mattered most to the police officers. Nearly all of my interview partners told me that the uniforms, which had been made for the special unit and which they received from their European partners four years ago, were all worn out and not useful anymore. The new ones they got from the PNC were the 'normal police uniforms and not made for special units', as one member of the unit told me. 'When we look like normal policemen the people will be afraid. With special uniforms they will see that we are the special unit and they will be more cooperative. We don't have the respect we need with normal police uniforms.'

The special police officers assume that a special uniform might lead to a better reputation. As they wear civilian clothes or standard police uniforms, they are not perceived as a special police force. They experience the same notoriety as other police officers in the DR Congo. A member of the unit stressed that the ignorance concerning the unit is a problem that 'cannot be solved in one day. The people who know [the force] come from far outside the base as they know that they can trust us. But as most people don't know that we're different, they won't come here to see how we treat their cases.'

A US police expert working in the DR Congo stressed that in Western countries the motivation to conduct police work might to a large extent be based on the use of high-tech equipment, weapons and uniforms. Although the special unit was well equipped by the European police project in 2008, most of its material is battered now and does not give the unit a feeling of pride or power. With their disciplined, strict behaviour the unit offsets the lack of symbolic power based on their equipment. They picture their work as 'a fight for the country' and see themselves as war heroes thus giving the unit an identity in which they find personal motivation and a feeling of pride.

Concept of self and the enemy

The feeling of pride became even more striking when I asked one of the police officers what motivates him to do the everyday work. He answered: 'I am very proud of being in this special unit. Sometimes it's hard, really hard. It's like there's war every day but I like to fight. ... I want to serve the country, that's why I'm here.' Another member even stressed the military organisation of his unit by pointing out that he is motivated by the discipline and the military framework as well as the strict hierarchies of the force. 'That's why we do such a good work.' Many members of the special unit opined that the police acted as a defender of the country and this was stressed in most interviews I conducted. The constitution stipulates that the police 'serves the Congolese nation', the SSR is also supposed to focus 'on local needs policing rather than act entirely as an agent of the state'.[37] With statements like 'I want to fight for my country' or 'It's also the love for our country that motivates us to work here' the police officers show strong sense of patriotism. They declare their 'enemies' the perpetrators they are arresting for not being part of the state. On the one hand, the concept of an enemy strengthens the sense of community among the unit. 'When we fight against the gangs in the suburbs we act like a football team. We all play together to root out the criminals,' a policeman explained. On the other hand, it seems contradictory to term these people 'enemies of the state' as they are part of a movement that has sprung directly out of society. The gangs the police officers declare their enemies are mostly part of the *phenomène Kuluna*'. The term 'Kuluna' derives from the Portuguese *Coluna* for column. It describes groups of young men armed with stones, machetes or other hand weapons that attack and rob civilians in the suburbs of Kinshasa.[38] A policeman told me that many of the members of the Kuluna are underage, often former street children or homeless youngsters who were abandoned by their families. 'Most of them grew up somewhere on the streets in the suburbs. They just never left the streets of Kinshasa.' So most of the unit's 'enemies' can be described as part of the Kinoise population. Additionally, many of these groups are even accompanied by members of the police and military. With the help of uniformed people armed with rifles, gangs have increased their power as they commonly consist of youths armed only with stones, bottles or machetes. Thus in some cases civil servants might even take part in these groups and are then declared enemies of the state. By declaring villains in the conflict inner and external enemies, the special police officers locate their tasks between police and military work—somewhere between green and blue.

By taking an external view of these observations, one could easily think that there is no difference between the special unit and military staff performing police work. Taking a look at the self-perception of the police officers, I soon found out that to a large extent they still set themselves apart from soldiers and other police units. A member of the unit told me that the unit was much more disciplined, better trained and worked under a strong sense of rigour, almost like the army. The difference was that he would never go to war; he does not want to have blood on his hands even if he feels a bit like a soldier: 'I don't want to shoot people. The police don't shoot people.' One of his colleagues added that they are not allowed to use their guns. 'We have these AK-47s but we don't use them to shoot. Other policemen do, soldiers do, we don't.' They know that they can be judged for firing their guns or being violent other than in a case of self-defence or to protect a victim. During an interview one of the officers added:

> We had a long and hard training, we were taught by European police specialists and we worked hard to be what we are now. We are proud to be a special unit like that.... We are the best of the best, I would say, because we learned everything. We know about the law, we know that you cannot keep a suspect in custody for more than forty-eight hours and we know we can't shoot.

The distinction from military staff became even more obvious in an interview with one of the higher-ranking officers. 'I had a military education. ...I would have liked to become a soldier but I was too intelligent, too intellectual to go to the army. My father didn't want that so he told me to join the police instead.' On the one hand, the members of the unit are motivated and inspired by military structures and attributes. On the other hand, they feel different and are often better trained and educated than military personnel.

Perception of the instructors

When talking about the military self-image of a unit that is highly influenced by their instructors and financial supporters of international organisations, it also seemed important to examine the perception of the Europeans that have been working with the unit. Many of the European partners appreciated the police officers' great motivation and how they conducted their everyday work. Two European experts on policing even approved of the commanding officer's severity and the harsh discipline. They explained:

> The unit is really polyvalent; they can do all kinds of tasks. ...They are trained in so many different fields, that they can do almost everything without the help of other units. ...A lot of the unit's effectiveness is due to the strong leadership qualities of the commander. I can't say that this unit would be the same without the severity of the Colonel.... They are disciplined but also close to the people. ...All this makes the unit a real democratic police force.

It is striking that the Europeans value a commanding structure that equates to the 'Quasi-Military Command Model' that is 'intended to foster strict and unquestioned discipline for rapid mobilization in emergency and crisis situations'.[39] These kinds of leadership models and military influence are quite common in special police forces, according to a member of an international organisation: 'This unit is a special police force that fights against violent gangs and organised crime in Kinshasa. Of course they cannot be as close to the people as some kind of neighbourhood police.'

He compared the unit with US SWAT teams, which operate in high-risk situations and are often organised in a military manner. The Congolese unit is trained and specialized in rapid mobilization and operates in high-risk situations. Still, the member of the European partners forgets that to a large extent the unit's daily work is based on talking to civilians or patrolling the suburbs of Kinshasa in plain clothes which cannot be equated with the tasks of a SWAT commando that only intervenes in emergency and crisis situations.

The special unit's 'polyvalence' as the two police experts put it, was stressed in nearly all of the interviews I conducted with the police officers' European partners. Asked what made them polyvalent, a member of the unit told me about the training in multiple fields but also about 'going to war' against the gangs and at the same time using their minds and empathy to connect with the local population. In my opinion, the polyvalence that the international co-workers stressed and praised might even be based on the connection between the identification with military attributes and civil police work.

Conclusion

Structures and behaviour that we see as military should not be equated with military work. In the same way police officers whose self-perception and motivation is influenced by military terminology do not necessarily see themselves (or should be seen) as soldiers. As I outlined, the Congolese special unit acts, on the one hand, in a military manner. On the other hand, it works along with the population and performs civil police work as defined by the law. What does demilitarization of the police mean? Is it important for the Security Sector Reform to remove military aspects of the police if they are to fulfil civil police work? Police as defined by the western world as a guarantor for internal security in general are, according to a French police expert working in the DR Congo, 'a western concept that cannot be applied to the Congo'. According to Jörgel, the SSR might even be a 'Eurocentric idea' and in many countries you can even find civil police forces like the gendarmerie or the carabineri that are assigned to the Ministry of Defence and act as a part of the military, yet remain close to the public.[40] Hills sees the insertion of gendarmerie-like police organisations as a possible way of enforcing the law in post conflict societies, since these units 'are equipped with armoured vehicles and mounted weapons and can fight as light infantry but are also trained to maintain public order, conduct investigations make arrest and direct traffic'.[41]

The special police unit in Kinshasa has both a military and local police character. They intervene in uniforms and in plain clothes to create a balance between civilian police work and authority through symbolic power expressed through their uniforms, weapons and strictly disciplined behaviour. The police reform in the Congo aims to create a police force that is strictly separated from the military just like the European police model. But as Hills outlines, '[t]here is no universal understanding of the purpose of the police as an institution'.[42] Both European models of police work and Congolese military history influence the police unit in Kinshasa. The idea of a completely demilitarised civilian police force in the Congo might, like the idea of the SSR, really be a 'Eurocentric idea'.[43] When I asked a member of the unit whether he would prefer a civil or military way of being a police officer he answered: 'Well, neither. I just like being a policeman'.

8

MOONLIGHTING

CROSSING THE PUBLIC-PRIVATE POLICING DIVIDE IN DURBAN, SOUTH AFRICA

Tessa Diphoorn

In December 2008, I was on night shift with Brian, an Indian armed response officer in his late thirties, who works for a large armed response company in Durban, South Africa. We were parked on a rather busy street across from a grocery store. At one point I observed a white male standing outside the grocery store who was talking on the phone and swearing loudly at the person on the other end of the line. I commented about his loud behaviour to Brian and he casually told me he's a police officer who does this 'on the side'. He is a detective, but also guards the store for the owner who is a good friend of his. Brian explained that many police officers, from all ranks, are engaged in security-related work to earn extra money. He told me it's what they call 'moonlighting'.

This night shift with Brian is part of my research project on armed response officers in Durban, South Africa. Based on twenty months of ethnographic fieldwork between 2007–10, I explore the occupational culture of the armed response sector and analyse their policing practices and interactions with others, such as clients and state police officers. Armed response officers make up a part of South Africa's private security industry, which is valued at approximately 2 per cent of the country's total GDP and is the largest worldwide.[1] In 2011, there were 8828 registered private security providers, entailing a growth of 60.77 per cent since 2001.[2]

Armed response officers are labelled as private policing agents that operate in private spaces and are not accountable or available to all citizens. This is in contrast to state policing, which is executed in public spaces and (ideally) serves all citizens. Yet in the policing literature there is growing recognition that the public-private dichotomy does not reflect contemporary policing practices. Public policing is increasingly privatised, 'commodified',[3] and incorporating a 'business-like ethos',[4] while private policing is increasingly punitive and executed in public spaces.[5] Studies have also identified numerous policing bodies that contain both public and private characteristics, such as 'hybrid' policing bodies,[6] which are 'neither the public police, private security or some form of voluntary initiative'.[7]

My research contributes to this discussion and I argue that armed response officers are engaged in 'twilight policing', which refers to policing practices that occur in a twilight zone between state and non-state policing: they are public and private policing entanglements.[8] They are simultaneously performing state and non-state practices and thereby engaged in what Lund calls 'unstately stateliness'.[9] I also argue that state police officers shape twilight policing and I will show this by focusing on moonlighting, which refers to police officers that are engaged in undocumented security-related activities outside their work.[10] This can range from a police officer who works as a bouncer or owns a private security company. This does therefore not refer to 'privately paid public policing'[11] or 'user-pays policing'[12] that operate with the consent of the larger state police apparatus. Rather, moonlighting here concerns security-related work that does not appear in official records or occur through official channels.[13] In this chapter, I will analyse moonlighting from a historical perspective to show how it is connected to the relationship between the South African state and the private security industry. In doing so, I will also show how state police officers contribute to twilight policing, that is, engage in practices that blur the distinction between state and non-state policing.

The private supplement to the state

According to my informants, moonlighting did not exist in South Africa before the 1970s when police officers primarily earned their extra income in other sectors, such as construction work. During the 1980s, the private security industry experienced an exponential growth due to its alliance with the apartheid state and moonlighting flourished.

Before the 1970s, private security primarily operated on industrial sites, such as the mining industry.[14] During the 1970s, state forces were increasingly called upon to deal with political unrest. After an upsurge of strategic attacks conducted by the African National Congress (ANC), such as the hit on a fuel plant outside Johannesburg,[15] additional manpower was needed that would not deplete state resources. This was primarily supplied from the 'crime prevention sector'.[16] Through various changes in legislation, tasks that had previously been under command of the state police were outsourced to the private sector.[17]

The main legislation was the National Key Points Act (NKPA) 102 of 1980. The NKPA implied that the security provision (predominantly guarding) of particular strategic sites deemed crucial for national security would be taken over by the management/owners of these sites.[18] For private security firms, NKP sites were lucrative and 'propelled the security firms into elite status'.[19] Although companies were motivated by profit, they did not frame themselves in market-based terms, but primarily identified with the discourse of state sovereignty.[20] In this process, private security firms (and the individuals employed by these firms) formed alliances with the state.[21] The industry was the 'major "hidden" supplement to the state police'.[22] Yet although the responsibility of security provision was transferred to private individuals, authority and control remained in the hands of the state.[23]

The Security Officers Act (SOA) of 1987 and the accompanying Security Officers Board (SOB) strengthened this collaborative relationship.[24] The SOA was the start of a formal state regulation system to monitor and control the (predominantly black) workforce of the industry. It entailed compulsory registration with the board and laid down the rules with regards to disqualification and withdrawal of registration. Before the SOA, an informal screening system existed in which company owners used their contacts with the South African Police (SAP): the SAP first checked a potential employee, and if 'cleared', he became viable for employment in the industry. Yet this informal system was not fool-proof and the industry and the state realised that tighter regulation was needed, as the owner of a guarding company working in the industry at that time stated:

You see, during the 80s, when the ANC went crazy with planting bombs all over the place, and on strategic places too, things changed, the industry exploded. There was once a bomb explosion on Smith Street outside the White House, you know that building where they used to renew the *dom passes*[25]... well... yes, I happened to be in the area. ... I drove to the site and quickly noticed that the *watchman*[26] that usually worked on that site was missing. Now everyone, including the police, assumed he was dead, but I knew better. He was ANC, a spy. You see, in that time, the ANC was smart, they knew that watchmen were posted at important sites, strategic for the South African government, and they infiltrated this sector. Four out of the twenty-seven bombs that went off in Durban, planted by the ANC, were on my sites, I worked those sites...and in all of them, the guard was involved, they were ANC...they used many ways to enter the industry to attack the South African government. For example, they would go to jail, pay bail for some criminal and then force him to work as a guard, as a spy for the ANC. ...This is how it all got started, the SOB, we needed a way to screen the guys coming in. We needed to know that these guys were okay, and not going to bomb the sites where we had our money coming in. So we worked with the SAP and the Ministry and got this up and running together, it was good for both of us.[27]

The SOA thus emerged through collaborative efforts between the industry and the state: it had 'the very purpose of developing a relationship between the state and private security companies'.[28]

'The old boys' network'

The alliances between the industry and the apartheid state—on both national and local levels of policing—created and maintained the 'old boys' network'.[29] This refers to a string of social networks among white men operating within the industry and the apartheid armed forces. Singh (2008) describes it as a 'club' where 'membership was exclusive and largely restricted at the administrative levels to those with police, intelligence and military backgrounds'.[30]

Similar to the state armed forces, the private security sector was a white man's world. At the outset, the industry comprised of white expatriates from Kenya, Zimbabwe, and Zambia who immigrated to South Africa.[31] As time passed, the industry recruited soldiers from the South African Defence Force (SADF) and officers from the SAP, a process referred to as 'poaching'. Companies also purposely profiled themselves as former state police officers,[32] thereby 'borrowing, as it were, the symbolic power of the police as a means to enrol customers and boost sales'.[33]

Many police officers and SADF soldiers left the force to establish their own companies. Several entered the armed response sector and operated as 'one-man shows'.[34] This refers to individuals that policed the streets with a walkie-talkie from their vehicle and with their own firearm for a handful of clients.[35] An example of a former 'one-man show' from my research was a police reservist who set up his own company in the early 1990s. His company started as a free service and as word spread among his social networks (particularly from his time as a reservist), community members increasingly requested his assistance. The company slowly established a community base and then converted citizens into clients and expanded into alarm installation.

'Poaching' and 'one-man shows' show how state officials left the force to work in the private security industry. Yet there were also many police officers that decided to benefit from both worlds through moonlighting. Many police officers decided to stay with the state police and engage in security-related work during their off-hours as an extra source of income, as a former police officer highlights:

> We were asked to do this, because of our expertise. But also because of the image, the symbolicness, you know? When collecting a debt, a man in a police uniform was more effective; people assumed you would arrest them. We basically used our role as law enforcement officers to persuade people to do things, to enforce our authority in other areas. And people paid us nicely for it. It was good income for us. It was perfect for many of us who didn't wanna leave the police, but needed the extra money. I wanted to do both, and I could, so I did.[36]

Many policemen worked as bouncers, bodyguards and armed escorts, or were engaged in private banking, debt collection and the eviction of squatters. Bouncing was the most common entry point. In the 1980s, most doormen were policemen that earned between R 80–100 per night. Although the bouncer was dressed in civilian clothing, people knew he was a policeman.

By the end of the 1980s and into the early 90s, the state police and the industry worked together and resembled each other. Brogden and Shearing demonstrate how private security companies used comparable equipment to the SAP and SADF and operated correspondingly, particularly through the use of force.[37] Private security firms provided logistical, technical and personnel support[38] and the SAP often relied on the extensive surveillance activities of the private sector.[39] As former colleagues with existing working relationships, cooperation between the public and private forces was rather natural. Although working for a different agency, they shared the same objective, namely to safeguard white privilege. These alliances and social networks provided an environment for moonlighting to flourish and current forms of moonlighting are based on the social connections developed during this period. Many former policeman described it as something that 'everybody did', although it was not openly discussed: 'Back then, all policemen did it, it was a normal part of the job, it's what you did on your off days, but nobody talked about it, explicitly...it remained hush, hush'.[40]

'A conflict of interest'

When Nelson Mandela won the elections in 1994 and apartheid rule came to an end, moonlighting was rife through the alliances between the industry and former regime. This increased during the transition period when many police officers and military personnel who were not amalgamated into the new armed forces (either by force or choice) entered the private security industry, both domestically and abroad.[41] This further consolidated the 'old boys' network'.

The post-apartheid state initially viewed the private security sector with suspicion as it was seen as a part of the old order. The state feared these companies would transform into private militias and overthrow the ANC government.[42] Moonlighting was also frowned upon and this exacerbated when it received a lot of negative publicity in the mid-1990s. With the explosion of taxi violence in the early 1990s,[43] news surfaced that many policemen were directly involved, as many policemen owned taxis or had invested in them.[44] This was particularly problematic with cases in which police used their firearms off duty. The Ministry of Safety and Security intervened by changing the 'standings orders' of the Police Act. This amendment stipulates that police officers are allowed to engage in other income-generating activities, but that they must apply for permission from their station commander. Additionally, certain sectors, such as the private security industry, are forbidden.[45]

The South African state also wanted to increase control and regulation over the industry, as the SOA was seen to protect 'the economic interests of a white-dominated and controlled industry'.[46] In 2001, the Private Security Industry Regulation Act No. 56 of 2001, monitored by the Private Security Industry Regulatory Authority (PSIRA SOA transformed into), replaced the SOA and implemented various new amendments.[47] Certain forms of security that were previously excluded, such as in-house security, locksmiths, and private investigators, were now regulated by the state.[48] The composition of the Council was also addressed: while the SOA Council contained six officials from the industry, PSIRA's council lacks industry representation.[49] Furthermore, the new legislation also prohibits police officers from working in the private security industry. If police officers are registered as security providers, the first step is to deregister them. If they continue to operate, they are charged for operating an unregistered company.

Therefore Police Act and PSIRA legislation prohibit moonlighting. This is primarily because moonlighting is seen to create a conflict of interest. Policemen can easily use their authority to acquire clients: attending a crime scene as a police officer one day, he/she can return the next day as a sales rep to acquire the client.

> Take the case of a bouncer. Where is his loyalty? Let's say the club he works for, is raided for whatever reason, such as possession of drugs or under-age drinking, or whatever.... Will the police officer work as a policeman and assist the raid or will he lay allegiance to the owner and assist him?[50]

The question raised in the quote is of even more significance when these police officers use SAPS resources, such as vehicles and firearms. Moonlighting was therefore not openly discussed during my fieldwork.[51] During a joint interview with two owners of security companies, they said: 'It's not safe to talk about it, they'll have you arrested'.[52] Whether or not this is true, it emphasizes the clandestine element of moonlighting.

Yet moonlighting still occurs. Many informants claim that the punishment in the police is not severe and discouraging. If a police officer is engaged in security-related activities he/she did not request permission for, he/she is departmentally charged for 'misconduct' or 'failure to disclose other employment'.[53] The punishment is usually a fine and dismissal is very rare; this only occurs if it is linked to a serious crime. A police reservist provided an example of a police officer from a specialized unit who had his own private investigations company. When this became known, he was charged departmentally and instructed to stop with a final written warning.[54] PSIRA prosecutions are also not experienced as threatening, because they are referred to the SAPS and the majority of these cases are never dealt with. As a PSIRA inspector said to me: 'eventually it is up to the police to police their police—we police the industry, must we now also include the police?'[55]

However, I argue that moonlighting still occurs due to encouragement by both the industry and state police officers. It is regularly described as 'a part of the policing game' and a way of assisting each other. As one company owner said: 'I ask a lot of policemen to do work for me. I need the expertise, they need the money, it's a great deal. So why not?'[56]

Partnership policing

This attitude is fostered by the 'partnership policing' strategy envisioned by the South African state. As an inherent part of the liberalization of crime management, the SAPS embarked on a 'more managerialist approach'.[57] The name changed from the South African Police (SAP) to the South African Police Service (SAPS) and particular activities, such as the guarding of government buildings (such as police stations) and vehicle tracking, were outsourced to the industry.

The state also outlined a new policing strategy in the 1996 National Crime Prevention Strategy (NCPS) and the 1998 White Paper on Safety and Security. In addition to the focus on community policing forums (CPFs), the NCPS also envisioned a 'multi-agency approach'[58] whereby the government would work alongside other actors, such as the private security industry, to combat crime. A new paradigm of police emerged that 'was not merely about transforming the police; it was also about transforming society *through* the police'.[59] The 'partnership policing' strategy outlined the structure for security networks between the state police and other policing bodies. Yet it also implied that any form of partnering was 'only to be established on the SAPS' terms, i.e. strongly controlled and directed by police managers at police station level'.[60] Private security firms would function as 'force-multipliers' and the 'eyes and ears' to assist the state police.

Public-private partnering was therefore envisioned along the lines of the 'junior-partner' model, a model that has been identified as the common structure for public-private policing partnering worldwide.[61] This entails a strict hierarchical structure, in which the public police is the 'senior' partner and private policing bodies are the 'junior' partners 'whose role is to give the public police whatever assistance they can to help them do the job of "real policing"'.[62]

Yet despite the strategy, there is still 'no formal national co-operation agreement in existence between the SAPS and the private security industry'.[63] The result is that partnering primarily occurs through operations established by local municipalities and police stations.[64] The most common form of official cooperation occurs through Ground Operational Co-Oordinating Committee (GOCOC) meetings.[65] These weekly meetings are organized by local police stations, at which outside members, such as representatives of private security companies, ward councillors and chairpersons of community organizations, are invited to discuss crime and share 'security data'.[66]

Contemporary moonlighting

A lack of a national formal partnership entails that interactions between police officers and employees from the industry are predominantly informal, ad hoc, and are primarily based on social connections. Moonlighting exemplifies this.

Contemporary moonlighting includes police officers engaged in body guarding, business visits, bouncing, debt collection and vehicle tracking. Body guarding pays around R 250–R1000 per day and bouncing pays between R 300–R 600 (approx. 20–40 USD) per shift. One police reservist claimed that police officers approximately earn up to R 5000 per month through moonlighting.[67] Guarding is also common, in which police officers wear company uniforms and are paid approximately R 500 for a few hours work.[68] Escorting clients and resource transfer was also mentioned; one informant stated that armed escorting a truck to Johannesburg and back to Durban could provide approximately R3000.[69]

Private investigation is also common and is referred to as a system of 'lick, stamp and mail'. This entails that private investigators do the work and then 'lick, stamp, and mail' it to the police.[70] In turn, police officers also provide private investigators with assistance. In fact, many informants claim most private investigative work is based on active cooperation between private and public bodies, either as a paid service or through reciprocal exchanges. Vehicle tracking is stated to be the most lucrative type of moonlighting.[71] While accompanying an armed response company in May 2010, we chased a hijacked car with a tracking company. When we brought the arrested suspects to the station, I talked intensively with the two trackers. They initially stated that they were former policemen, but then admitted that they are still policemen that work as trackers on their off-days. They refused to tell me how much they earned, but stated 'it was the best way for us to make money'.

The type of moonlighting that carries the most implications concerns police officers who own private security companies. Several ex-police officers provided lists of policemen who owned companies and I knew several individuals on this list. In fact, two of them were informants I spoke to regularly, yet denied any engagement in moonlighting. One of them once stated to me: 'I am very proud to say that I have never been engaged in any form of moonlighting...I have always been able to keep the two completely separate'.[72] Yet other informants used this same police officer as an example of moonlighting, 'He's been doing it for years, everyone knows it—you can see him, driving around in his police vehicle, checking up on his guards'.[73]

Owning guarding companies is the most common; 'All policemen have a few guards, it's almost like their uniform'.[74] Police officers generally employ between ten to twenty guards, so that it is not too obvious. Maintaining guards is easy, as they can be inspected during their shifts. Due to PSIRA legislation, the companies are not enlisted as theirs, but are registered in someone else's name, such as a relative, a police informant, or friend.[75] This is referred to as 'fronting', which is claimed to facilitate illegal behaviour and activity.[76] A police officer once mentioned: 'You're not allowed to own a company or do the physical work, but you can manage it'.[77] The only way to uncover this is to analyse the flow of money through financial audits. Although PSIRA has the legislation to implement such audits, this is rarely done.[78]

Decreasing or changing?

In their study on security intelligence networks in Ontario, Canada, Lippert and O'Connor argue that interpersonal connections based on the migration of personnel from the public police to the industry have demised and thereby no longer affects the sharing of crime intelligence between the two policing bodies.[79] In my research, moonlighting was also claimed to be less prominent for two reasons. The first is the rise of corruption. One police officer explained that extra income is currently generated through 'spot-fines', that is demanding a fine (accepting a bribe) on the spot: 'Why work as a doorman for R 500 if you can make a docket go missing for R10,000?'[80] Other informants highlighted that 'sponsors' have replaced moonlighting. This refers to policemen demanding 'sponsors' from private security employees, such as a portion of a guarding salary, in exchange for 'police assistance'.[81] One police officer phrased it as a form of 'police-man influence':

> For example, the owner of a hotel or bar wants to know where the road blocks will be on a certain night, so I'll offer to give him that information every week, as long as he'll have the bouncing and guarding done by a company that I suggest...if he says no, I can play a very dirty game and he knows it.... So they almost always do it....[82]

This police officer further narrated how the company he 'suggests' will provide him with financial benefits. The claim is therefore that police officers no longer earn extra income by directly conducting security-related work, but using their authority as police officers to arrange financial deals with the private security industry.

For many informants, the difference between moonlighting and corruption was racially tinted, where 'white policemen do security work, black policemen do spot-work'.[83] Due to state policies of affirmative action, white policemen have fewer promotion prospects and are more dependent on extra income generated from moonlighting. Their jobs are more at risk and they perceive moonlighting to be less risky than corruption.[84] Others claim that white policemen are more involved in moonlighting due to their social networks in the 'old boys' network'.

This ties into the second given reason for a decrease in moonlighting, namely the demise of the 'old boys' network' that consisted of white men. With decreasing numbers of white police officers in the force, the old boys' network is less pervasive and influential. The result is that there are fewer interactions between policemen and private security officers, particularly owners, thereby decreasing moonlighting opportunities.

> A lot of white cops have left.... I'm not gonna be received with open arms by a black policeman who wants to help me out. If the police still had a lot of whites, or if more companies had black employees, or representatives, then the relationship with the SAPS would be much, much better. And the benefits too.[85]

Policemen currently entering the industry do so in lucrative sectors, such as investigations or vehicle tracking, or enter companies at management level. Police officers do not leave the force to become armed response officers, as had been the case during the 1980s. One could thus assume that the old boys' network does not affect interactions between armed response officers and police officers, as they were never colleagues.

However, I argue that although the old boys' network may be less influential and only evident at the level of management, it continues to influence on-the-ground interactions between armed response officers and police officers. For example, many informants referred to a former police officer who is currently the owner of a large company, who is stated to have

> bought out the whole station, all those guys are working for him, protecting his clients and his interests. They're not policemen anymore, although they wear the uniform. They do police and private security work at the same time. That station is filled with corruption, political games, all money. Money from the industry is leading them, not passion.[86]

Additionally, companies managed by former police officers who have social ties to the state police are preferred by police officers. In my research, I repeatedly observed how particular police officers gave preferential treatment to armed response officers working for a company managed/owned by a former police officer. This preferential treatment did not only concern sharing crime intelligence and conducting patrols, but also condoning the excessive use of violence by armed response officers. This was particularly the case for community-based companies, in which the owners would utilise their social connections with the local police station to 'resolve' the matter.

Furthermore, it also occurred in a contrasting way, which I describe as an 'old boys' feud'. This entails that armed response officers are (unlawfully) penalised due to rivalling relationships between company owners/managers and police officers. There was one particularly hostile case in my research and it involved the owner of a community-based company, who was a former police officer, and a high-ranking police officer at the local police station. The antagonistic relationship originates from the 1980s when they were both police officers. To complicate matters further, the police officer in question also owns a guarding company (a clear form of moonlighting) that competes with the company. Due to his status as a high-ranking officer, he regularly, and sometimes illegally, exercises his authority. The result is that the armed response officers from the community-based company were regularly mistreated, particularly in comparison to security officers from other companies. The 'old boys' feud' that exists at management level therefore influences the daily practices of armed response officers, particularly their interactions with police officers.

Conclusion

Moonlighting therefore shows how personal networks and social contacts between individuals of different policing bodies influence the nature of policing. It is an explicit example of a policing practice that contains both public and private elements. Moonlighting blurs the boundaries between public and private policing bodies: it is a direct form of 'boundary-crossing'.[87] This makes it increasingly difficult to distinguish between public and private officials, as a police reservist explains:

> It's difficult to separate with all this intermixing between the force; guys from SAPS are connected to the private security, and private security guys are doing police work, it's all mixed up. It doesn't have to be a problem—we are all here to fight crime. But it becomes a problem when there's a conflict of interest, when someone steps on someone else's shoes...uses their position on one side to influence the other. It's a problem when the law no longer matters.[88]

Twilight policing therefore refers to armed response police officers who are increasingly policing public spaces and resembling the state police, but it also includes state policing practices executed in the private sphere. Moonlighting emphasizes how state and non-state policing practices influence each other.

Furthermore, I also argue that this highlights the importance of ethnographic fieldwork that can uncover the importance of social ties. In the South African context, we can only understand moonlighting by analysing the relationship between the South African state and the private security industry, particularly historically. The alliance between the industry and the state fostered an environment for moonlighting, and the contemporary lack of a national framework showing clearly how daily interactions should occur is fuelling this further.

9

RISK AND MOTIVATION IN POLICE WORK IN NIGERIA

Olly Owen

In Gida State Police Command's Administrative Office, next to the Commissioner's private office, a printed A4 poster is tacked to the wall above Inspector Kenny's desk. It reads:

IF YOU WANT TO KNOW WHO YOUR FRIENDS ARE, WAIT UNTIL YOU FUCK UP AND SEE WHO IS STILL STANDING BY YOUR SIDE. Signed DSP A——— O———.

This chapter deals with the role of risk and motivation in the lives of ordinary officers of the Nigeria Police Force.[1] It shows how officers perceive risk—especially career risk—as emanating both from everyday contingencies of the job, and from the disciplinary hierarchies of the force, and consequently how it informs officers' motivation. At the same time, the risk-mitigation strategies they employ, centring on evasion and dissembling, aggregate and pattern into discernible effects at the level of the whole institution. In previous research I outlined ways in which Nigerian police, beset by severe material limitations, resolve cases primarily by relying on craft skills learned and deployed in prac-

149

tice.[2] This chapter expands the frame by looking at the systemic imperatives into which such practices aggregate; repeated iterations pattern into informal principles which structure the actions of officers and the policed public as much as do law or formal bureaucratic requirements.

For police officers, a case must simultaneously fulfil three separate but interdependent requirements; first, it must satisfy the complainant and deal with the matter at issue; secondly it must allow the officer to maximise agency and personal advantage; and thirdly it must avoid putting the officer at undue risk. The chapter attempts to resolve the interplay of officers' craft and instrumentality, within a context of primarily 'upwards-facing' accountability (to superior officers) and an ever-present potential for risk which is often uppermost in officers' minds. This interacts with management practices, themselves sometimes shaped by very instrumental and personal motives, and sometimes designed precisely to forestall, minimise, and remedy the 'known unknowns' of risk in the work of policing. The nature of police work, preoccupation with personal risk, and these evolved management practices, all combine to produce effects of the state institution prominently visible in the public sphere.

I begin by examining what police officers understand by risk and its consequences in the police world—either as physically damaging to the person, or to their fortune and career, whether directly or vicariously. I illustrate the overriding preoccupation with career risk, the constant possibility of advancing and retarding personal prospects, especially by use of informal management practices such as punishment postings. The second part characterises police management as based on a duality—a combination of bureaucratic rule which centres on discipline, with informalised action which has material social and economic consequences—a combination which patterns officers' behaviour, attitudes and expectations. Management practices which encompass institutional imperatives, personal advantage, and risk mitigation structure both senior officers' decisions and subordinates' responses in mutually constitutive relationships mirrored elsewhere in the postcolonial world. Thirdly, I illustrate the relationship between such management practices and the motivations for police officers to carry out their work in particular ways and to particular ends. At the 'sharp end' of both events and institutional disciplinary logics, subaltern police officers invest in diverse strategies of risk-mitigation. The chapter therefore examines the limits to disciplinary modes of managing subordinate officers, and the unintended tendency to produce simulation, dissembling and inertia. It concludes by noting implications for our understanding of the wider organisation of the state, and for the meanings it generates in everyday life.

Risk in police work

A constant preoccupation with risk is not limited to the police. Everyday life in Nigeria is fraught with nebulous, unpredictable and only hazily-known risks: travel is a risk; places and situations of unfamiliarity are risk; and most of all, other people are a source of risk. This clearly articulates with a general milieu of low trust in society and 'radical insecurity' notable in vernacular culture. But risk also manifests in ways specific to police officers. The nature of police work, but also institutional modes of responding to and managing problems, generate unique risk factors. The most obvious is direct physical harm to the officer. Policing is a dangerous profession, no less so in Nigeria, with high levels of armed crime, dilapidated infrastructure, and frequent political and communal unrest. Deaths in the line of duty, by violence or accident, are common. Many more die prematurely from infections and preventable diseases, medical negligence and road accidents in a country where the average life expectancy is 51.[3] Photocopied posters with a photograph and caption 'In Memory' or 'Gone too soon', sometimes accompanied by the widow's bank details, are common sights outside police stations.[4] While I was writing my thesis, one officer with whom I worked closely was shot dead in an ambush. My fieldwork coincided with the beginning of the Boko Haram insurgency; this hit home one day when in my company, an inspector from Borno State received a call telling her that a family friend serving there had been followed home and assassinated.[5] Police officers know the criminal geography of Nigeria—which places are notoriously 'hot'—and although some seek postings to hotspots such as the commercial centres of the south east to really learn policing, to 'acquire relevance' and to make money, others actively avoid them. A long-serving rank-and-file officer tells a group of us:

> Even though I have two years to retirement, if they post me to Anambra I will tender my resignation [that is to give up rights to pension]—that they mean to turn my wife into a widow.[6]

Life is also hard for those who survive close encounters. In March 2010 I am with the commandant of the Mobile Police[7] Squadron based in barracks behind 'B' Division, a neat military figure in olive-green combat fatigues with clipped hair and moustache. He calls me:

'Come and see this man' (he shouts) 'Sergeant!' and asks 'How does a policeman walk in your place? Is it like this?' He makes the sergeant show his disabling limp. 'See a man the police has spoiled.'

The commandant expounds on the injustices, and even selects two men for me to interview in his office. One, a veteran of 18 years' service, survived a collision between a police truck and a bus. Because Gida State's hospital was on strike, the sergeant had to seek treatment at hospitals in neighbouring states. Eventually, he travelled to his family home 330 km/200 miles away to see a traditional bonesetter. During the three years he was off work he received his salary, but no contribution towards medical fees, which he estimated at N240,000, or US$1,478.[8] The police institution does not simply neglect officers injured in the line of duty; there are insurance schemes designed to pay out on loss of life or injury. In practice, however, claims and payments can be delayed or diverted by the private-sector insurer or the administrative hierarchy, so that claims are often not received on time or in full, if at all. In such circumstances, it is easy to see how officers who do not possess the reassurance of a fatalistic outlook or a naturally confrontational personality may wish to place their personal safety before their duties.[9]

Even outside their workplace and working lives, personnel often feel no safer than other members of the public. They may even feel less safe, as dealing with crime and misfortune on a daily basis they remain constantly aware of their vulnerability. Police status itself does not confer any guarantee of safety outside the confines of duty hours, especially as in order to limit the potential misuse or loss of police arms, officers are not permitted to take weapons home; so police officers are just as vulnerable as anyone else, especially if they live outside the barracks, which can house only a small fraction of officers. Moreover, officers are often selected as targets of violence if caught in, for instance, an armed robbery on public transport. Therefore many go to lengths to hide their occupation whilst off-duty. Some don't carry their police ID card when they travel; if found with it 'armed robber will kill you straight'. In the 35°C heat of dry season, some constables came to work wearing overcoats in a flimsy attempt to hide their uniform. And an officer who came into the Community Policing office to read the copy of police in-house newspaper *The Dawn* refused to take it with him when offered, as he did not want to be easily identified as a policeman. Physical risk and hardship then is an ever-present factor. But it is not perhaps as constant an influence on behaviour as is the preoccupation with the nebulous issue of career risk.

Early in my fieldwork, 'B' division's DPO,[10] Chief Superintendent Okechukwu fell foul of the powers that be over his handling of a fight between farmers and nomadic Fulani herders. Okechukwu was ordered to relocate to semi-rural Ogidi Division, an economic backwater some thirty miles away, notorious for youth and political unrest, and with only around thirty officers.[11] Some months after, I travelled with a couple of officers to visit my former DPO's new post. Close to our destination, we encountered five or six youths under the age of 20 blocking a badly potholed section of the road. Carrying picks and shovels, they were ostensibly collecting contributions for repairing the road, but the lack of actual repair and the iron sheet they held across the remaining portion made it very clear that this was polite extortion. I was travelling with an out-of-uniform assistant superintendent and a corporal, so was prepared for their aggressive status-assertion, and was profoundly surprised when the senior officer gave a N100 (US$0.65) note to the youths. Registering my surprise, the corporal (driving) explained 'it is just because of God'[12] whilst the senior officer bashfully added that if we hadn't given them something, we could have been delayed. My second surprise was to discover on clearing the roadblock that we were less than 200 yards from the police station.

At first I was keen to ask the DPO how the youths could operate an illegal roadblock so close to the station, but the answer soon became abundantly clear. Welcoming us, CSP Okechukwu showed me his brand new station, and then the smoke-blackened ruin of its predecessor next door, set alight by angry youths during the 2007 election, when it had housed the local headquarters of the Independent National Electoral Commission (INEC). As he described his division, a picture emerged of a hotbed of unemployment and political thuggery, where numerous aspirants enlisted youths in their continual struggle for limited state offices and goods. Further, of the officers available only around half were of sufficient length of service and rank to carry weapons. The tricky balancing act of policing the area became apparent: with such limited resources and such a politically vulnerable position, which managerial officer (especially one whose fingers had been recently burned) would risk provoking unrest? Far better to leave the youths to the relatively victimless crime of petty extortion from passing traffic, which at least provided an opportunity for them to support themselves, while incurring relatively little risk to the police or the DPO's wellbeing or career, leaving him in peace to hope or lobby for eventual transfer.[13] As we left, I turned to the assistant superintendent (ASP) with me and remarked how close the youths' roadblock had been to the police station. 'I was praying you wouldn't mention that', she said, 'it would have been in very bad taste'.

The story reveals two things: the first, public order as a balancing act, the finely negotiated limits to the supposedly authoritarian police, I have explored elsewhere.[14] The second is the salience of career risk in the policeman's world-view. In such a particularist social context, where private social capital often trumps or at least contests with the formal-legal citizenship order, the officer faces huge risk embedded in who precisely they are dealing with and what can happen if they get it wrong. Mishandling a matter involving a sensitive social group or a high-status person, for instance, can bring unexpected and swift career reversal.[15] Unpredictable events such as these can ruin an unlucky officer's career at a stroke, an act of God or carelessness with lasting consequences and limited prospects for redemption.[16]

Caprices of misfortune such as the above are things which can happen to anyone as a result of a lack of skill or luck, and as such are digested by others as admonitory and educational tales. The misfortune officers really resent, however, is vicarious risk—that finger of blame and suspicion which can fall upon one person entirely as a result of the actions of another. This normally occurs because something has happened for which a scapegoat must be quickly found in order to satisfy the demand for accountability from above or outside.[17] Due to the hierarchical and unidirectional nature of information flows in the police institution, where only orders flow downwards and only compliance flows upwards, it takes an officer of rare audacity and backbone to resist calls to identify a scapegoat; more commonly the buck is simply passed down the chain. As vicarious risk implicates things which happen indirectly under an officer's responsibility, the scope for it, and preoccupation with it, grows with seniority; the job of the managerial officer with hundreds of constables, corporals and inspectors under their command, but very much not directly under their supervision, is replete with the daily possibility of incurring this kind of vicarious blame, and bereft of ways to hedge against the unforeseen. Therefore, a senior officer must learn to live with the possibility of unheralded episodes with profound consequences.[18]

Dutsin Bature's neighbouring 'A' Division, including a national transport junction and a busy adjacent market, was replete with opportunities for vicarious risk to derail the DPO's career, especially the frequent convoys of senior government officials passing through to Abuja. One day such a convoy encountered a problem by the junction's motor park.[19] In the process, one of its out-of-state mobile police escorts shot and killed a bystander before moving on, leaving the local police to deal with the consequences. Responding to the outpouring of public anger, Gida State's Commissioner of Police (CP) detained 'A' Division's DPO at the State Headquarters. Another senior officer drew my attention to this as an example of how blame is allotted instead of addressing the actual problem—a situation made possible because no matter who was responsible, 'to the public, it's all "police"'. The CP's tendency to make quick resort to scapegoating was particularly resented by some officers in the command, who felt keenly the humiliations endured by their fellows, such as 'A' Division's respected veteran DPO, who was embroiled a second time just a few weeks before his retirement. This time a serious road accident had occurred on the Abuja route. By a quirk of communication, the Inspector-General[20] had heard about it shortly afterwards and called the CP, who was not yet aware of it, and thus felt he was made to look incompetent. For this embarrassment the DPO nearly lost his post, and was only rehabilitated after eminent community members 'begged' the CP to let him stay until his imminent retirement.

Significantly, this event was relayed to me by a constable in 'B' Division, underlining that these vicarious falls from grace were, like everything else, common knowledge and subjects of gossip throughout the State Command; thus all the more painfully resented by their subjects.[21] Neither is this exclusively a concern for managerial officers. Shortly before my arrival in Dutsin Bature, a constable was arguing with a mob of local youths in a crowded market in the old town area, who then attempted to take his weapon off him. He fired at them, killing one person. This was the second fatal police shooting in a short time; in order to calm public tempers the commissioner of police decided to make an example of the officer. After disciplinary proceedings he was dismissed, prosecuted by a criminal court and imprisoned. Although this was met with public approval, serving officers relayed the incident to me as an example of unfair and undeserved vicarious risk. They felt that the severe punishment for what they considered self-defence was brought about on account of the earlier unrelated case, and the public backlash and political heat that the relatively lenient disciplinary treatment of the earlier shooter had incurred. While the Nigerian public may feel they are policed by a force which is only minimally accountable to them, it is interesting that the police conversely feel they are extremely vulnerable to misdirected and populist ad-hoc accountability, making the police often wary of the public, even if (like CSP Okechukwu) few police officers would ever openly admit it.

The snakes and ladders of police fortunes

Contrary to the popular imagining that police officers enjoy complete impunity for misdemeanours against the public, there are in fact often consequences. But rather than being formal and public, often they are quiet internal punishments such as unfavourable postings and transfers, comprehensible most clearly in the internal registers of the police system of values, merit and advancement. Malcolm Young underlines that in the British police, fear of the 'wheels coming off'—uncontrollable and controversial consequences which may bring the police institution, and thus the officer's seniors, into disrepute—is often the prime preoccupation in strategically negotiating everyday challenges.[22] Thus responses to crime and public order incidents are informed by an influential consciousness of how it will look from 'above'. The equivalent preoccupation in Nigeria is sometimes referred to as 'embarrassment'—a choice of terminology which reflects acute sensitivity to social status and hierarchy, within a wider society where public performance of rank and respect are heavily accented. Management responses to controversies are tailored to the minimisation of embarrassment and curtailment of controversy. A typical strategy is to immediately transfer and replace a DPO or other senior officer who has presided over an episode in which deteriorating relations with the public have embarrassed the force; a fresh face is a key part of the effort to rebuild relations, as with CSP Okechukwu after the 'Fulani case' above. This also has practical utility in separating the officer in question from the environment where they might continue to do damage, at the same time punishing them by exile. Thus the forlorn constable I meet at a remote post in Gada Biu village was sent there after Inspector Daniel at Dogonyaro sub-station discovered he had tipped-off a suspect that the police are looking for. Such administrative punishment-by-posting has the advantage of being fast, flexible and if needs be, reversible; and as such, sidesteps the constraints of formal procedure. It also bypasses the difficulty of finding concrete evidence for a misdemeanour which everyone knows has been committed but has been skilfully covered-up. Equally, it references a non-formal register of values—since all postings of the same rank are in theory equal, a bad posting is only a punishment informally, in its substitution of income opportunities, comfort, and the ability to mix with people of status, with discomfort, penury and boredom.

In fact, even when there is no specific case against an officer, the transfers are a failsafe standard operating procedure. In June 2010 I hear that a friend in the bomb squad, who recently transferred to an oil-rich Niger Delta state, had already been transferred again, to another Delta state, apparently because of an explosion which happened at the Government House shortly after his arrival. I ask a former colleague in Dutsin Bature's bomb squad why he was transferred to what after all was not a punishment posting. The Inspector answers:

No, they even want to issue query to him.[23] But it's not a punishment posting, they just do like that. Like if anything happen at Government House [here] now, they will transfer them. It's in case of insider.[24]

Such episodic ups and downs add an element of unpredictability to a police career which officers struggle to mitigate. Sometimes it may be possible to cushion the effects with the help of allies external—such as the elders who came to 'beg' for the DPO—or internal: Inspector Kenny complained to me about the officer who has not 'remembered' him since he helped shield him from a disciplinary investigation ordered from Abuja. But often events are entirely out of the officer's control. The police officer lives in fear of the episode that can 'spoil your file'.[25] It may help to think of the wider career of a Nigerian police officer (especially a senior officer) as the board game Snakes and Ladders—slow and routine progress along the board is interrupted by capricious throws of the dice, which may either rapidly boost an officer's advance beyond their expectations, or bust them back down behind their peers and hopes. But as career risk is a combined product of incident and management, understanding it necessitates further examination of management practices themselves.

Management and motivation

'Police job is a good job, but we ourselves make it to be a sufferhead job.'[26]

Police management, beyond the mastery of bureaucratic procedures, is also centrally concerned with the management of risk. Sometimes this is embedded in standardised practice. For instance, in order to minimise the risk of accidental or hot-headed shootings of members of the public, it is a standard rule not to issue firearms to officers with less than three years' service; after which they are expected to have developed the experience and judgement to be better-trusted.[27] Mostly, however, the management of risk in the police is responsive and reactive, as in the incidents related above.

The preoccupation with risk also produces a tendency to reserve decision-making at the highest practicable level—as a police friend tells me when I am lamenting an acquaintance's inability to get satisfactory service from the counter staff at his local station, often 'you have to go up to go down'. In April 2010, I am with a chief superintendent in charge of a large Lagos division with over 300 personnel. His phone buzzes with an SMS, which he reads and then calls for the S.O.,[28] telling him:

'Someone sent a text saying "one Sergeant Richard from this division just swindled my friend of 4k, I don't believe I have to make this a matter for the CP"—it came from the Area Commander—do we have any Sergeant Richard?' The S.O replies 'No sir.'

Therefore, they conclude, it must be someone from the autonomous SARS unit which shares the building.[29] This sort of thing, the CSP says, is always happening. He means the confusion, but I note instead the prevalence of having to deal with personal complaints from offended 'big' people. This prompts us to recognise the heavy, if necessarily intermittent, reliance on personal direct management; intervention and supervision by senior officers as and when a matter becomes of consequence. If the job of a DPO still is, at times, akin to the supervisory regimental soldiering described by colonial-era officers, at others it demands the most direct intervention, as personal accountability will be demanded by the police hierarchy, and upon it rests the fate of the senior officer's career. In fact the tendency is self-reinforcing, as equally risk-averse subordinates learn to take their cue only from the direct orders of the senior, rather than proceeding automatically, as we shall explore below. This reinforces both internal and external expectations of 'Oga-ism'— the personalisation of authority in the boss and their personal disposition, rather than in rules or procedures.[30] Thus, eventually, a situation is reached where supposedly routine functions such as recruitment and promotion regularisations are in fact only carried out through periodic and specifically ordered 'exercises'.[31]

A hierarchical and restrictive institution, where instructions flow downward and accountability upward, reproduces particular kinds of managerial mind sets. Prime among them is an accent on discipline. That 'police is a discipline institution' is axiomatic, and the disciplinary code is the usual means to redress the plentiful unintentional or intentional shortcomings of junior officers. CSP Okechukwu (at least before his fall from grace) was known as a hard man, a strict disciplinarian, who plentifully administered administrative punishments such as putting officers inside the cell or behind the counter when caught absenting themselves from duty on private business. Sometimes, an inspector tells me, as many as half of those in the cells may be officers on disciplinary punishment. All senior officers have their quirks—some are sticklers for cleanliness in the station, others for correct uniform, or timeliness.[32] But discipline is more complex than the simple coupling of misdemeanour-and-punishment. In Uttar Pradesh, India, Jauregui identifies discipline as a trope which not only controls junior officers' behaviour, but subjects them to particular possibilities of exploitation while severely limiting their options for redress. Constables feel 'humiliated and exploited...under the guise of maintaining discipline.... Many of them do not see their being disciplined as part of a process of learning the "right ways" to be part of a greater whole; instead they understand that they are considered inferior as subjects'.[33] The 'dictatorship' of senior officers encompasses 'refusal of leave, loss of allowances, or the enforced toleration of barely tolerable living conditions'.[34] Discipline, while ensuring standards, also provides for seniors to more fully possess the labour of subordinates, silence their attempts at contestation, and ensure that their will (whether contiguous with the official intentions of the institution or not) is carried out.

This disciplinary subjectivity equally applies in Nigeria, where it is more onerous on some police than others.[35] MOPOL, says Dutsin Bature's squadron commander, are luckier than many because of the autonomy of their dual command structure;[36] but ordinary divisional police are in effect totally subject to the CP's authority, so dare not complain. The highly personalised powers of public office in the postcolony are central to the manifestations of discipline: not simply a continuation of colonial hierarchies and autocracies but a reworking and intensification of their most unequal aspects. The MOPOL commander contrasted his own police 'upbringing' under a British-trained officer, to the norms of Nigerian hierarchical relationships:

> In the UK, we were taught that they relate—this is my colleague, this is my colleague (gesturing to officers sitting on nearby bench) but here is more master-servant, or do I say master-animal? If you, a constable, are here [gestures to spot right next to him, to indicate an inappropriate proximity of subordinate to superior] you will die and go to hell.[37]

Such relationships combine in particular ways with the abuses which become possible within them. Extracting value from juniors become easier when strictures of discipline limit their ability to appeal, so if a senior officer diverts transport allowances, for instance, there is little the constable can say. And because the policing job must be done, within the framework of orders backed by discipline which leave no room for argument, lack of resources is not a reason to neglect duties.[38] Thus officers use their own phones, motorbikes, petrol to do their jobs, a factor which becomes a salient part of their subaltern consciousness. As the MOPOL commander continued:

> We use junior officer more or less as a tool; or an animal. When he goes to road [mimes an officer raising his rifle barrel, and shouting stop, park well!] he will be thinking first of that 300 naira he took out from pocket to reach that place.[39]

*Management and the arts of resistance: Discipline and dissembling
at the roadside*

The managerial styles and performance of senior officers are watched closely
from below, and understood in particular ways. A mobile corporal guarding
the CP's house later tells me, for example, his approving opinion of the commandant I have been speaking to:

He will tell you go to so-so place, if you see someone with gun, fire him,
collect the gun; if you see someone with cutlass, fire him, collect the cutlass,
don't worry, I am behind you.[40]

In this context the subordinate approves that his boss is, in the MOPOL
terminology, an 'operations man', a leader of integrity who doesn't leave his
men unprotected in order to preserve himself from risk and controversy. The
leadership which wins approval from subordinates is about their feeling protected and empowered to carry out their orders. More often, however, the
narrative is one in which the senior officer oppresses, and the subordinate
evades as best they can. Jauregui illustrates the implications in a passage worth
quoting at length due to its strong relevance to the Nigerian situation:

Constables will often adapt, and sometimes even advance, by engaging in unofficial
modes of responding to their plight—what some might call resistance, what others
might call survival, and what still others might call corruption, cronyism, or indisci-
pline. Constables wield their own 'weapons of the weak' (cf., Scott 1985) including,
but not limited to: foot-dragging; falsifying evidence or other data; taking voluntary
leave (unnecessarily); taking bribes for seniors and under-reporting the actual loot to
pocket some extra themselves, or 'doing *jugaad*' and taking the help of a powerful
politician or local *neta* (leader) or 'system operator' of some other sort, who is sympathetic to them for personal or political reasons... Of course, if such practices have any
effect at all, they only render temporary 'solutions' or satisfactions, not any sort of
structural change or improvement. And beyond mere inertia, such practices have
detrimental effects on a security infrastructure that is already sagging under the
weight of corruption, politicization, and brutalization.[41]

An equivalent important example in the Nigerian context is the problem
of supervising 'road work'—checkpoints, ostensibly deployed for crime control, which quickly become opportunities for officers to extort money from
traffic. One of the most lucrative ways for officers to make additional income,
they are also one of the most commonly-cited negative public experiences
with the police. The widespread belief is that checkpoint extortion is part of a
revenue-farming practice of 'returns' in which a portion of the money is remit-
ted to seniors. This would provide one explanation why the practice has

proved so hard to stamp out in its most lucrative heartlands, the highways between eastern Nigeria's commercial centres. Shortly after assuming office in January 2012, Inspector General M.D. Abubakar announced the removal of all police roadblocks, a measure intended to restore public confidence. Although this was widely effective, shortly afterwards media and web forums on policing began listing complaints from areas where checkpoint extortion was continuing.[42] It seems that far from being evenly implemented everywhere according to the principles of a rational centralised bureaucracy, the directive had somewhere lost power. A closer look illustrates the power of the aggregated 'powerless', suggesting a more nuanced picture than assuming duplicity and disingenuousness by the police institution.

Contrary to popular myth, the NPF does on occasion catch and punish perpetrators of checkpoint extortion. Early in fieldwork, I am told that the Inspector-General's Monitoring Unit caught the last DPO of Dutsin Bature's 'E' Division collecting money on the road. I am also told that they must have been tipped off, as they went straight to where the money was kept in the bush. As a result of this, two constables were dismissed and the ASP queried and retired a year early.[43] Yet such crackdowns often take less predictable turns. First, the hierarchical nature of policing itself introduces room for slippage. In March 2011 an officer recently transferred from the east shared his insights on 'road work'. He pointed out that investigative missions sent from headquarters are only as good as their leadership. Often, the senior officer assigned will make themselves comfortable in a hotel and order an inspector to perform the actual task; thus already the decision whether or not to enforce, or to simply use the opportunity to extort the extortionists is instantly devolved: if the inspector is an avaricious type, says the constable, he may demand perhaps N40,000 (US$244) to drop the issue. After all, enforcing such orders is not free from risk. The same officer related how covert 'sting' operations, in which 'plainclothes' monitoring unit personnel were deployed to catch officers extorting at night-time roadblocks, ran into their own problems; faced with the prospect of loss of career and livelihood, he said, guilty officers sometimes chose to open fire on the officers sent to catch them, claiming afterwards, with some plausibility, that they had mistaken the 'plainclothes' men for armed robbers trying to ambush them in the night.

If the investigated take full advantage of the creative possibilities of reworking the disciplinary hierarchy's logic, it may not even come to confrontation. The same interlocutor explained that the best way to 'get away with' road work is to go and stand some distance from the point at which you have been

161

ordered to deploy. That way, when the commanding officer receives a complaint that the unit has been extorting money, you can point out that this was not where you were ordered to stand, so could not possibly have been you. This breathtakingly elegant and insolent solution is a simple and sophisticated response perfectly pitched at the institutional logic itself. It is cast entirely within the framing of obedience to authority. As the subordinate's defence is based on an appeal to the evident fact that he could not imagine wilfully disobeying an order, the senior officer cannot possibly argue with the premise of the defence without tacitly but consciously admitting that his orders are being routinely disobeyed. It is a dare, a gambit. Either the complaint is correct, and the senior officer is shown to have no effective authority over his men; or the officer's authority is real and effective, which dictates that the complaint must be wrong. The subordinate's level and calculated response invites his superior to call his own authority into question. His logic is straight from Morgenstern's *Impossible Fact*.[44] And whatever the superior opts for, the disjuncture between what was supposed to happen, and what has apparently happened according to the complainant, adds that element of doubt which undermines the certainty needed for effective disciplinary intervention. Nigeria's particular contribution to the arsenal of weapons of the weak, then, is dissembling; the artful recasting of the language of the state into its practical negation. The patient work of subaltern termites powerfully undermines the timbers of the disciplinary house; police, like criminals, and in fact everyone else, are fluent in the broad array of evasive and dissembling techniques. 'Nigerians,' Inspector Daniel reflects in wonderment, 'are too clever. In fact, they are three clever.'

The additional result is that this dissembling and evasion revalidates the accent on personal direct management, as in its absence the mechanistic obedience of the subordinate cannot be assumed. The only certainty a senior officer can really have is that which comes from personal knowledge of what a subordinate is likely to do in a given situation. This is why a young Assistant Superintendent tells me why he wants to 'mobilise':[45]

> Why mobile? I've done everything—DCO, CID, transport—if I become CP how will I know if commander mobile is telling me lies?

Note also the corollary; personal direct management also works in reverse—the subordinate must also engage in personal intervention vis-à-vis the superior and the wider system. For instance, all officers receive yearly salary increments. But to make sure that the amount is actually implemented on your payroll, rather than diverted by financial administrative staff, it is strongly advisable to visit the Mechanised Salary Scheme office in state headquarters around the correct date, to check personally that the procedure is being followed. Such interactions add a huge and distracting burden on officers' working and off-duty time.

Management, morale and performance

'The main problem with police is motivation' claims the Mobile commander, noting that this impacts how officers face the public. 'Even it's better for mobile', he admits, because a MOPOL constable might—for instance—spend a month on rotation guarding a private company with salary supplement. But in large part their morale also rests on managerial culture, as he explains:

> Because of starting as PSO (Principal Staff Officer) to one Oga who trained with whites I treat my junior as colleague... (they come to you saying) 'my child has been admitted (to hospital), I need 3k, I didn't get annual leave since 2 years, make I visit my grandmother'. If you take care of this, your men will be happy. By the time you say 'go well' and talk civilly to people, don't hit them, go well and take care, they will leave feeling good. But if all you know how to say is [acts] 'What is this? I will dismiss you!' (the constable will be thinking) 'What is this to talk of dismiss?' And this is the attitude they take to the public—transferred anger.[46]

Transferred aggression, and the transferred humiliation of the subaltern of the state, then, is a central driver of police officers' aggressive performance and exorcism of their status anxiety on the public. The experience of subjugation in work (and the Mobile School's notoriously rugged training, which the MOPOL commander notably does not indict), can produce a mind-set (again, in the commandant's words) 'that people don't respect you if you don't brutalise them'. Sometimes, this reaches crisis proportions and boils over. The commandant tells me the story of the sergeant who stops a car, and asks to look in the boot. The passenger, in an argumentative mood, asks why he should comply, since he didn't do anything wrong. The sergeant sprays the car with bullets, removes his uniform and clothes, and goes home.[47]

Between the rock of institutional disciplinary order, and the hard place of being frequently ordered to act in ways which are designed to benefit senior officers' personal, rather than professional, interests, subordinates quickly learn the difference between 'do as I say' and 'do as I do'. Nigeria's public sphere characteristically joins paternalist enjoinders to good behaviour and responsible citizenship (TV ads from the National Orientation Agency to shun tribalism, or showing Independent Corrupt Practices Commission staff teaching schoolchildren songs about the evils of corruption) with the most blatant and shameless manipulations and misuses of public finances and procedures. The energy put into producing this dissonance and hypocrisy is striking. The result is that Nigerians are naturalised to a high degree of fluency and sophistication in mastering the twin contradictory registers of what is espoused, and what is done. Bierschenk observes that West African bureaucrats in general feel betrayed by the state and locked in a relationship of mutual pretence with their employer and its ideals.[48] The MOPOL commander illustrates:

> If the C.O. gets two million, (sits, and mimes putting it under his seat) and says 'here, take small'—why will they not collect money?

This dissonance, of course, makes the enforcement of discipline even more problematic. In the intimate sphere of the police institution, everything the senior does is visible to the subordinate. If the subordinate is painfully aware of the financial good fortune which may accrue to superiors and the very small crumbs which may trickle down to him, what, apart from discipline, is to deter them from working on their own initiative? So paradoxically, while the imperative for personal direct management restrains subordinate police officers' formal room for agency and initiative, keeping them on a short lead, another powerful motive exists for them to deploy their own initiative plentifully in informal, instrumental and subversive ways.[49] Since only discipline and punishment, and not often rewards, flow downwards, and since credit for good work by subordinates is often taken by superiors, there are few institutional incentives to perform maximally. As Station Officer's clerk Godwin says,

> There is no reward for doing good work in police. If they can dismiss Nuhu Ribadu, who get more prosecution than any other person in fighting crime, then there is no appreciation of good work. If you do good now, do it for yourself, and it's just you that knows.[50]

Maier notes the recurring disjuncture in Nigeria of situations such as that of two public servants sharing the same office, one may be diligent, timely and hardworking, and the other avaricious, absentee and negligent.[51] We should observe that the mitigating factors in motivation often come from outside the institutional structure; personal morality, whether framed by strong personal spirituality or other imperatives, plays an unsung part. Even personal convictions have their limits however. Politics in particular presents a risk few can afford to ignore. The same officer tells me what he feels is the ultimate discouragement:

> If it is threat to the nation, we will engage it strongly. But when it is something political it makes you to just stay back.[52]

Mitigating risk

The mitigation of risks and dangers inherent in police work concern both the institution and the individual. On an institutional level, commanding officers may evolve tactics and working practices designed to make interventions more effective while minimising the risk to police officers.[53] Thus at the volatile hotspot of Ojudu Junction, where Akpai youth militias repeatedly clashed with each other and with police, MOPOL units tried patrolling accompanied by community elders, in order to combine a display of strength with appeal to mediation and moderation. They also reversed the usual policy of not sending officers recruited from the area to do public order interventions,[54] instead deliberately posting Akpai-speaking officers to see if militants would be as ready to fight 'their own people'. Such tactics serve a dual purpose—restoring public order, while also trying to minimise risk to the police.

More personal responses to risk vary. Some rely on spiritual help: in addition to Christian and Islamic prayer, some officers resort to older repertoires of power and protection. This was not often openly discussed, because many consider forms of traditional spiritual protection the disreputable preserve of dark forces, often associated with crime and impropriety. Mostly, however, police officers invest most of their efforts in personal risk mitigation strategies.[55] I observe three major strands: the absolute minimising of action which could trigger adverse outcomes; forming and maintaining of potentially advantageous relationships; and the simulation of obedience combined with a minimalist and instrumentally self-serving approach to compliance.

Firstly, avoidance: police officers may moderate their behaviour to minimise risk in the course of their work, to the extent that they are reluctant to perform core law and order functions without direction from above. Their actions become primarily concerned with self-preservation, especially when dangerous unknowns such as prominent persons, political forces and angry mobs are involved. The mobile commander tells me of a shooting at a high-profile political rally in nearby Kwararafa town. Opposition party activists were decamping to the ruling PDP, and some mobile men posted close by had gone there because they wanted to meet the local government chairman 'because of their welfare'.[56] While they were there, at the fringes of the event a group of political thugs abducted another youth political activist, bundled him into a car and driving only a small distance away, shot and killed him.

Ordinarily, my men would have just let go, finish,[57] but because they weren't meant to be there they lacked the confidence to deal with it, because of the risk of 'who told you to' and who were the guys? Ordinarily you shouldn't require someone to tell you to do your job.

Here we can vividly see how officers may develop an extreme aversion to doing anything which may trigger an unmanageable outcome without specific orders—they are after all unlikely to be disciplined for just doing nothing, which is not itself an offence.

Secondly, many serving police officers devote a lot of time and interest to investing in networks of personal relationships and loyalties which may provide useful leverage when needed. In this, they are partnered by a public which often engages police via particularistic relationships with officers. One day in Lagos I accompany a non-police friend to visit a constable at his work; they have become close, says my friend, since the constable stood up for him when he had a traffic accident with a tanker driver.[58] My friend explains that he likes to visit the constable occasionally, and help him with a little money, 'so that he and I will grow together'. Such dyadic relationships may be formed in the course of police work, or they may utilise pre-existing social capital. In many cases officers may attempt to use the same vertical connections which enabled them to navigate recruitment and posting throughout the course of a career.[59] In this way, shadow networks of allegiance and patronage thread through the formal institutional mappings of power relations.[60] The extent to which cultivating dyadic relationships can pay off was vividly underlined in 2010 when President Goodluck Jonathan appointed Hafiz Ringim, previously commissioner in Bayelsa State when Jonathan was governor, as inspector-general over the heads of a cohort of more senior officers.

More broadly, the social insurance of mutually advantageous relationships can form strategic bridges to whole constituencies, including powerful stakeholders such as the media. The State Command's Police Public Relations Officer (PPRO) role is image-maker not just of the police but of the commissioner personally, and must try to ensure media representations of both are 'on-message'; some other officers replicate the same effort informally, cultivating their personal networks of media contacts. Dutsin Bature's area commander frequently drank with selected journalists, nurturing a relationship with his bar bill which safeguarded his public image in return for the privileged access this gave the journalists.

Thirdly, superiors and their orders can be avoided but entire systems cannot; instead much of the time dissembling and simulation is the order of the day. Police officers rarely resist, but more often fudge or incompletely implement, orders they do not like. The similarity with modes of resistant subalterity elsewhere should not surprise us.[61] But the trope of 'resistance' is not exact enough to capture the mode in which this dissimulation is produced, and neither does the figure of the subaltern adequately capture the sense of play with which it is deployed. Mbembe more accurately recognises that in post-colonial Africa, political domination is often met not by resistance but by subordinates' connivance, imitation and 'conviviality'.[62] The Nigerian vernacular expression which fits best is 'lack of seriousness'; implying a lack not only of gravity but of personal commitment to the task in hand. This is manifest in multiple ways: when the diligent Godwin is away, his assistant detailed to log out and issue weapons from the magazine simply piles the AK-47s in a heap on the floor and goes to sleep on a bench, leaving the evening shift to help themselves; Corporal Friday Kassam sheepishly explains that he accidentally shot a gaping hole in the thin plywood wall between the SO's office and the bomb squad because he had left a cartridge in the breech of his shotgun 'in case I enter bush, see rabbit'.

Watching the evening shift parade before beat duty at 6pm, ostentatiously yelling their commands, cracking to attention, throwing their arms around, overdoing the marching steps, smirking and generally enacting a very conscious *Keystone Cops* parody of embodied police discipline, I was reminded of Mbembe's concept of 'simulacre' or pretending.

> The postcolony is, par excellence, a hollow pretence, a regime of unreality (*regime du simulacre*). By making it possible to play and have fun outside the limits set by officialdom, the very fact that the regime is a sham allows ordinary people to simulate adherence to the innumerable official rituals that life in the postcolony requires.[63]

Furthermore, says Mbembe, in postcolonial regimes where the relationship between rulers and ruled is based on simulacre:

> Strictly speaking, this process does not increase either the depth of subordination or the level of resistance; it simply produces a situation of disempowerment (impouvoir) for both ruled and rulers...although it may demystify the commandement, even erode its supposed legitimacy, it does not do violence to the commandement's material base. At best it creates potholes of indiscipline on which the commandement may stub its toe.[64]

I wandered back inside pondering the validity of applying this to the policing context, where the 'ruled' in question, subordinate officers, are also a constituent part of the state. Later I attempted to explain my badly-recalled understanding of Mbembe to the Assistant Superintendent with whom I shared an office. She looked puzzled for a moment, and then said 'Ah! You mean like when the CP calls and you answer [mimes picking up phone, and lying] "Yes sir, we are on our way there now in large numbers." Is that it?' Mbembe's concept was readily recognised by its own practitioners, who constantly play at obedience while also maximising their room to evade its strictures.

Conclusion

This chapter makes some preliminary conclusions of significance to wider questions of policing, and of the nature of the Nigerian state. One final example draws these together. On 14 June 2010, the replacement DPO of 'B' Division is in a bad mood. My notes recall:

> He's in the cell on the warpath because the suspect from the cement factory has tipped the Charge Room Officer (CRO) money to be allowed to sit outside, and now some of the CID suspects are there too, or locked in the SO's office as there isn't room in the cell. The DPO tells the CRO that as far as he's concerned, they *are* all in the cell, and it's on his own head: 'If anyone escapes you are dead. In fact, let me put it in writing. Because you are just out there playing around.' Then later, he is starting again, 'post guard outside that cell—cell guard—I don't want to hear of any woman going inside that cell.'

This exchange showcases the dual product of a situation fraught both with risk and with an inability to conclusively enforce authority. A meeting of issues of discipline, management, obedience and vicarious risk, it embeds some interesting dynamics. Firstly, note that the CRO has departed from his duty to engage in allowing privileged comforts to an influential prisoner, an activity possibly lucrative in the short term, and potentially helpful in the longer-term creation of future dyadic relationships. He clearly sees the advantage (itself an investment in a sphere which may mitigate the risks, discomforts and uncertainties of a police career) as easily equal to the risk of disciplinary action to which he is exposing himself. And he does this under a rubric of tempering bureaucratic indifference with humanity, which has a widely-held legitimacy. Secondly, although the DPO's ire has been raised by the perfectly proper managerial concern of poor cell security and possible escape, in his response the formal disciplinary option has been disregarded. It is striking that for reasons best known to himself the DPO does not enforce the formal rule; instead, his threat is just to mitigate his own risk by 'putting it in writing' thereby leaving the CRO exposed at the mercy of the institution's disciplinary mechanism. This he later backs up with his own direct personal managerial intervention (posting a cell guard) which entirely bypasses the CRO formally detailed to that responsibility. The DPO in question may not have been a particularly good divisional manager—he certainly made it clear that he did not enjoy the job—but his behaviour is instructive in revealing some of the choices and constraints around risk and the deployment of managerial power.

What does this prevalence of risk, of disciplinary modes of dealing with it, and of subaltern modes of evading it, mean more broadly? A pattern emerges. Extreme risk-aversion on the part of officers whose primary concern is second-guessing risk, looking after personal direct interests in order to cushion institutional misfortune, aggregates into a systemic tendency for the institution to do the same, resulting in a minimal and reactive, rather than active and interventionist, form of policing. And what does this imply for the organisation of the state? If what holds true for the police applies to the state in general we could characterise state institutions, and therefore the state itself, as cautious and restrained in their writ and actions over wider society, a reactive, semi-detached and somewhat *laissez-faire* governmental machinery quite different to the intensity and transformational intent of authoritarian or developmental states.

Such a system encourages consolidation of personal position at the expense of energetically implementing the state's formal rationale. The institution thus becomes inward-turned. Public interest becomes self-interest, security becomes self-preservation, and short-termism supplants institutional aims. Belying its Hobbesian pretensions, the state in practice, subject first of all to the internal concerns of its institutions and their risk-averse, career-conserving servants, is cautious, tentative and uneven. The state itself is both authoritarian and remarkably powerless. As far as the wider effects of such a state on the society it creates, and of the meanings created by the experience of such a state, both on its servants and subjects, we can do no better than to return to Mbembe:

> Pretence (le simulacre) becomes the dominant modality of transactions between the state and society, or between rulers and those who are supposed to obey. This is what makes postcolonial relations relations of conviviality and covering over, but also of powerlessness par excellence—from the point of view either of the masters of power or of those whom they crush.[65]

10

FIGHTING FOR RESPECT

VIOLENCE, MASCULINITY AND LEGITIMACY IN THE SOUTH AFRICAN POLICE SERVICE

Andrew Faull

On 26 February 2013, Mido Macia, a 26-year-old Mozambican taxi driver, was handcuffed to the back of a South African Police Service (SAPS) van and dragged hundreds of meters through the streets to the Daveyton police station outside Johannesburg. Two hours later he was found dead in his holding cell. An autopsy would reveal that he died of hypoxia, a lack of oxygen to the brain, after suffering extensive internal bleeding.[1] Prosecutors interpreted this, and blood spatters on Macia's holding cell walls, as evidence of a beating at the hands of police at the station.[2]

Much of the incident was captured on the cell phones of bystanders at the crowded taxi rank at which it began. Footage showed police officials attempting to restrain Macia in order to effect an arrest, apparently because his taxi was illegally parked. Macia resisted and police handcuffed him to the inside of the van, presumably in the hope that he would surrender and climb inside. He didn't, and as he hung awkwardly from it, with only his wrists cuffed to the inside, the driver of the police van pulled away.

At the bail hearing for the nine SAPS officials charged with Macia's murder, one of the accused, Warrant Officer Ncema, told the court that Macia had insulted him as a useless policeman when he had tried to arrest him.[3] Importantly, this alleged insult and the resisting of arrest, unfolded in front of dozens of bystanders.

Right from the start then, one particular account of what happened that day appeared very likely: a member of the public challenged the authority of SAPS officials; he disrespected them. He was not rich or middle-class; he was not a South African. His challenge was made in a crowded public space, in daylight. The SAPS officials involved felt humiliated. Once they had secured him in the privacy of the police station, they punished him for publicly embarrassing them. They beat him and he died.

Violence is deeply ingrained in South Africa's history, its society and its constructs of masculinity. James Gilligan suggests that violence is a human response to feelings of shame, often linked to inadequacies relating to masculinity and feelings of place in society.[4] In South Africa, becoming a police official means being given a chance to escape generational poverty and climb the social and economic ladder. But is it enough?

This chapter presents data gathered through participatory observation that suggests that violence is seen by some SAPS officials as a means of gaining the respect of its public. As such, the chapter considers the manner in which attitudes and understanding of the use of violence in South Africa shape the practices of some officials in the SAPS and how these are informally imbedded in the 'doing' of police work in South Africa.

From mid-August 2012 to mid-April 2013, I spent over 800 hours with detectives, patrol officials and station staff at four SAPS stations. Two of these were in the Cape Town metropolitan area and two in a rural part of the Eastern Cape. The research was ethnographic and involved shadowing station staff as they went about their daily routines. My objective was to try to understand who police officials thought they were and how this shaped police practice.

A rich literature on mostly Anglo-American police culture stretches back to the mid-twentieth century. This has explored and described how police organisational culture shapes police practice, as well as the performances, drawing on Goffman, which police officials enact during their duties.[5] Data was usually gathered through ethnographic research and suggested that, as summarised by Reiner, the characteristic of police occupational environments were: a sense of mission, cynicism and pessimism, conservative outlooks, machismo, racism, pragmatism, suspicion, isolation from the public and solidarity among colleagues.[6] It was, and for many still is, believed that these traits emerge(d) out of the unique environment in which police work within the democratic state, attempting to 'maintain order' while constrained by legal policy and law.[7]

Additionally, police have the right to use state sanctioned force in their work and operate with great breadth of discretion. Much like Michael Lipsky's other 'street-level bureaucrats'—those government workers with whom the public most often interact—police officials came to be understood as employing techniques that deliver a form of service often incongruent with that outlined in policy but forged within a set of limits imposed on police by the structure of their work.[8]

In the 1990s researchers led by Janet Chan began to question the automatic acceptance of these police organisational traits.[9] Yet in 2009 Bethan Loftus showed that at least in the United Kingdom, many remain valid.[10] In my own work as a police reservist (volunteer), as well as in my ten years of research experience with South African police, I have noted many similarities between the literature of these countries and my experiences of the SAPS. Further supporting evidence is found in a range of ethnographies conducted in the SAPS since the late 1990s.[11]

Informing much of the early literature on police culture was Goffman's work on symbolic interactionism.[12] Researchers used his notions of the 'front' and 'back stage' to explore the manner in which police managed their performance depending on the situation or member of the public whom they faced. They were described as bureaucratic entities needing to ensure their own political survival in a political space in which the justification for their existence remained ambiguous. This is because police have little impact on the root generators of crime, yet for many in South Africa and elsewhere, it is police who are seen as the primary custodians of safety and order. As a result police engage in ritual performances and myth making to suppress doubt over the legitimacy of the 'police prevent crime' narrative on which they rest, and promote images of assailants who only they can stop.[13] In South Africa these ritual practices include politicians speaking of 'war on crime', suggesting police must 'kill the bastards' in order to 'push back the frontiers of evil'.[14] These messages emanate out of and feed back into South African society's general acceptance of violence as a solution to violence and other challenges.

While much can be said of the informal, policy-skewed rituals that police officials in South Africa regularly perform, this chapter is most interested in the informal use of force. As such it builds on von Holdt's suggestion that contemporary state bureaucracy in South Africa in part aims to ensure black class formation while seeking to save face where mistakes, incompetence or criminality are present.[15] It also highlights the danger of a class-building project in an occupational environment that encourages the use of force.

The first station at which I worked, Nyanga, serves a number of Cape Town's older and most violent townships. I began work at Nyanga in mid-August 2012, shortly before the 16 August killing of thirty-four striking mineworkers by police at Marikana in the north west province of South Africa. In the months following the incident, I regularly raised the topic of Marikana with the police I shadowed at the four stations. Although some expressed sadness at the killing of the workers, almost without exception they tried to convince me that the police officials who had pulled their triggers that day had done so legitimately, lawfully, and correctly; that they had done nothing wrong.

These responses were not surprising. Solidarity and peer protection are long established characteristics of police organisations.[16] But I believe there is another reason SAPS officials so quickly defended the slaughter of thirty-four men at the hands of their colleagues: they abhorred the idea of being disrespected. It was clear within my first weeks at the station that the majority of officials working there did not believe the communities they served respected them, and did not believe South Africans in general respected them.

Station mythology abounded with stories of police attending complaints and returning to their vehicles to find the tyres slashed or wheels stolen. I was told foot patrol was not possible in the area because the community would stone patrollers.[17] Many police refused to walk the fifty meters to a shop next to the station for fear of being attacked for their firearms, while others told me that when they were off duty they would not admit to strangers that they were police officials because this would put them in danger. They saw these (potential) violent attacks as signs of disrespect.

How did this mythology about respect and the lack thereof manifest in the daily work of police officials? While many of them talked of the need to treat the public with respect in order to earn their trust, this sentiment was seldom extended to groups thought to be regular offenders. These tended to be young men, usually African or coloured and poor, who comprise large segments of South Africa's population. With these groups, it became clear that many officials believed respect was earned through force.

The following example is illustrative. One night I was on patrol with two crime prevention members, both young male constables.[18] It was shortly after

1am and the streets of the township were empty. Members of the Tactical Response Team (TRT) drove past us in the street. While not belonging to any station, they were deployed in the area as a 'force multiplier' to perform 'crime prevention' duties. I asked the constables what they thought of the TRT, referring to a popular investigative journalism television programme, which had recently portrayed them as abusive.[19] The driver responded, 'They are good but we don't have a backbone in the police. They don't appreciate what the TRT are doing and so they are demotivated.'[20] The 'we' he was referring to was the SAPS at large, and the 'they', the TRT. He went on, 'Since they have been deployed here there has been a big decrease in crime. People respect them.' I asked why he thought people respected them and he said, 'Because they beat people.... If they have suspects they torture them and the person gives up everything. It's good.' I asked whether he knew what kind of techniques they used and he said, 'They use that one with a bag over the head of the old days.'[21]

Of course this is only hearsay. The constable might never have seen such acts taking place, nor was he able to provide me evidence of a post-TRT crime decline. And yet even if it was without basis, it is important that the constable presented the story in this manner, suggesting that torture and violence reduce crime. Shearing and Ericson remind us that in the police organisational context, stories are rich with symbolic power and lay a foundation of strategies and knowledge, which guides police action.[22] Holdaway adds that the selection of some themes, like torture, over others, lends them credence. It gives them power in informing organisational identity and culture.[23] The chosen theme in this case is that violence earns respect. For Marks, by foregrounding certain themes in police stories and hiding others, particular actions are legitimised within organisational discourse.[24] These in turn help police to view particular actions as common sense.[25] For Loftus and Waddington, police stories or 'talk' are in fact a form of police practice, bringing life to the occupational culture.[26]

Having noted this literature, consider another story that emerged at the Nyanga station. During the Monday morning detective branch meeting, an officer announced that 'we almost lost detective X yesterday'. The story that followed went something like this:

> Police were called to the area following information that a man was in possession of an illegal firearm. After apprehending the man a shootout broke out and the suspect was hit eleven times. Detective X was passing by on the way back from his own crime scene. Caught in the line of fire, a bullet from the shootout passed through the back window of his unmarked state vehicle, missing his head by a

couple of centimetres, and exiting through the windscreen. When the standby officer from the detective branch arrived on the scene to support his traumatised colleague, the police who had fired the shots were found picking up their bullet casings, covering their tracks.

A few days later, following a reconstruction of the crime scene by senior detectives in the branch, a new version of the story emerged, shared with me during a private conversation. It went something like this:

Plainclothes police were called to the area following information that a man was in possession of an illegal firearm. They took the man into the street and started beating him. The man tried to flee the beating and the plainclothes police opened fire, hitting him eleven times. Detective X was passing by on the way back from his own scene. Hearing the gunshots and seeing the commotion in his rear view mirror, he stopped his unmarked state vehicle. The police involved in the shooting saw what they thought was an interfering passer-by stopping to watch them. Wanting to send a message to him that he should stay out of their business, that they didn't want witnesses to their crime, they fired a shot directly at the driver's seat. The bullet passed through the back window, missing the driver's headrest by a couple of centimetres, and exiting through the windscreen. The bullet was intended for Detective X. When the standby officer from the detective branch arrived on the scene to support his traumatised colleague, the police who had fired the shots were found picking up bullet casings, covering their tracks.

Although the shooting is not in doubt, some details of these narratives remain conjecture. Yet they are important. That this latter narrative emerged within the detective branch of a SAPS station is particularly telling. It indicates that the narrative is plausible to those within the SAPS. It suggests that some police officials expect such behaviour from their colleagues, that it makes sense to them in their experience of the organisation. They accept that SAPS officials might go as far as using lethal force against strangers if they deem those strangers to be interfering and disrespectful of their occupational choices, even if those choices involve murder.

My second research station was Cape Town Central. It was located in the heart of the city, serving busy commercial and residential spaces. Many of those who populated the space of the city precinct had more social and economic capital than the police working there. And yet it was at this station that I realised what might be a golden rule for those not wanting to unleash the violence of the state in South Africa: don't challenge a police official.

I came to this conclusion based on two observations:

1. Police at the station used the charge of 'riotous behaviour' to arrest anyone whom they wanted to punish or teach a lesson to, including those who disrespected them;

2. Persons who continued to challenge police once they had reached the confines of the police cell holding area had a good chance of being physically slapped into silence, despite the holding area's CCTV camera recording the abuse for station and provincial management.

Contempt for a disrespecting public is not unique to the SAPS. Loftus writes of English police putting civilians through an 'attitude test', stopping people for casual questioning with little intention to arrest. Civilians pass the test by 'being polite, apologising or admitting guilt, essentially by feigning respect for the police'.[27][28] The act serves as a reminder of police authority.

At the Nyanga and Peddie SAPS stations, a version of the 'attitude test' played itself out in a frenzy of stop and searches.[29] Young men, in their teens or early twenties, were routinely stopped and patted down as police searched for weapons and drugs. The young men invariably consented by throwing their hands in the air or leaning against the police car. Knives and other implements thought to be weapons were routinely collected but the men were never taken into custody. It seemed that this exchange was so routine that each knew his or her part and none were in danger of failing the test.

But it was in the holding cells at Cape Town Central, the space in which detainees are 'processed' before being allocated a cell, that I witnessed a more violent version of the test. People were slapped and punched, sworn at, laughed at and ignored, often only because they dared to ask a man in uniform why they had been brought into police custody.[30] In addition to the CCTV camera recording the scenes of the room, these abuses took place in front of other police, none of whom ever intervened in the business of their violent colleagues. Indeed, removed from the public gaze, it might be said that this violence was for the most part a performance by (male) police for (male) police, an intra-group enactment of how violence earns respect. The performance of, and silence around violence in this private space served to remind police of their occupation's unique allowance for the use of force. And while this informal and violent approach to problem solving went against all SAPS policy, the silence around it made it organisationally acceptable. It is this silence, what the literature calls the 'code of silence' and which is a characteristic of so many police agencies, that allows abuse of force and other violations to become routine in the SAPS. Considered within von Holdt's framework of South African bureaucracy, this silence can be seen as a form of 'face saving'.[31] Police officials from the lowest to the most senior ranks know that abuse of force scandals severely taint the image of the SAPS and so are unlikely to report colleagues' abuses, whether they approve of them or not.

On a number of occasions police officials told me that otherwise non-compliant civilians would suddenly obey their instructions after a slap to the side of the head. The information was shared with me as though it were a confidential trick of the trade, the magic slap that brings respect. In less violent jurisdictions police command such respect by issuing a fine. But in South Africa, where SAPS officials see fines as belonging to the lesser realm of traffic and metro police, it seems the *klap*, or the threat of one, is still considered the currency of the day.

I also spent time at Bell SAPS in the Eastern Cape, a small station responsible for policing a number of rural villages. There the use of violence took on different forms. Most importantly it was not always physical. The station precinct and the tasks carried out were very different to those of the city stations. Due to the size of the precinct and the number of villages within it, urban-like patrol was not a feasible option and police-public interaction was far less common (the police presented themselves as conducting 'patrols' but these tended to involve passing through a selection of villages once every other day). It was also apparent that police working in the area felt, far more than their rural counterparts, that the communities in which they worked respected them. There might be a number of reasons for this, including the fact that within the rural precinct police work was one of the only 'professional' occupations other than teaching available to residents. It may also relate to the comparably light criminal case burden which the rural police faced (twenty cases per month rather than 3000 at the two city stations). And yet these police still, in part, saw themselves as disciplinarians. When a mother accused her son of stealing money from her bedside drawer, police were called to 'teach him a lesson'. After putting him in the back of the van they sprayed him with pepper spray and hit his feet with a wooden stick. They wanted him to tell them where the money was. Similarly, but with a different form of violence, on two occasions community members reported teenage girls who had slept at their boyfriend's homes without parental consent. To punish them the station commander shouted at them and made them sweep and mop the station floor. This they did with tears in their eyes. They had been successfully disciplined by the state, at least for the moment.

Why violence earns respect

There are a number of interrelated interpretations of why many police believe the use of force earns them respect.

Peter Manning notes that in addition to enforcing the occupational culture's view of the law, police officials in any jurisdiction in part enforce their personal conception of order on those they police.[32] Many of these conceptions are formed outside of the police organisation, drawn from personal upbringing, primary socialisation at home, at school and in society more broadly. Drawing on a range of research, Anthony Collins suggests that many forms of violence have been normalised in South African society. He believes that in many contexts it is 'socially accepted...commonly understood as benign, necessary, justifiable'.[33]

The Centre for the Study of Violence and Reconciliation's (CSVR) study on the nature of violent crime in South Africa also identified 'perceptions and values related to violence and crime' as one of the factors behind the high levels of violence in the country. Their summary states that:

> [The widespread tolerance of violence] reflects widely held norms and beliefs which see violence as a necessary and justified means of resolving conflict or other difficulties...[including] the perception by young men that they need to be able to use violence to protect themselves and to obtain the respect of others.[34]

In this context, while the acceptance of violence is widespread in South Africa, it is most accepted by young men. Seedat et al. have convincingly suggested a strong link between constructions of masculinity in South Africa and the fact that young men suffer grossly disproportionate levels of violence and victimisation in the country.[35] This, Kopano Ratale suggests, is in part a result of the young men's inability to live up to popular expectation that men should earn good money, be virile, show leadership and be physically and mentally tough.[36] Ratele and Letsela have suggested that 12 per cent of premature male deaths in South Africa are the result of what they call 'masculine beliefs' characterised by sexual dominance and risk taking, and that such traits are amplified in male-heavy environments.[37] Police stations have historically been populated by men and saturated by cultures of machismo.[38] Although the SAPS has made great strides in gender representivity so that in 2016, 35 per cent of its workforce was made up of women, a disproportionate number of police working on the streets are still men. This may in part be because women are considered a risk to themselves and their partners when working on the streets, while men are expected to bravely face danger and risk. Such attitudes would again be a product of a gendered beliefs.

The fact that many of the SAPS officials I met, both men and women, had grown up in and/or continued to live in areas saturated by violence was clear. For example, a Nyanga captain started a parade briefing by telling his colleagues that he had passed his friend lying dead in the street on his way to work, shot on his way back from a party the previous evening. Similarly, a Cape Town constable told me her teenage son had been taunted and attacked by neighbours until one day he stabbed one of them and they died. When I met the constable her son was on trial for murder.

In these contexts, SAPS officials, particularly men, should be viewed as members of communities and families where violence, particularly violence by men, against men, has been normalised as a tool for solving problems and earning respect. It is therefore unsurprising that many members of the SAPS embrace the view that violence teaches lessons and solves problems, or that it builds respect.

The pervasiveness of such views and the manner in which they reach beyond the police occupational world came to the fore on a number of occasions during my fieldwork: I will briefly describe two such instances below:

In the first, Detective A arrived at work one morning with a swollen lip. When I asked him what had happened he told me a story about his having intervened to break up a fight outside his house between a friend of his and a stranger. During the scuffle he had been punched in the face. When I asked whether he had opened an assault case against his attacker he laughed and said, 'No, five other neighbours joined in and we put that guy in hospital.' Despite being a representative of the criminal justice system, Detective A had chosen immediate and violent retribution in response to being punched.

The same was true of Detective B who came to work one morning wearing sunglasses over a black eye. When asked what happened he told me he had been drinking with family when one of them had grabbed one of the children by the hair and pulled. Detective B had told his guest not to do this and the guest had punched him in the eye. When I asked whether he had opened a case against the man Detective B smiled and said, 'No, I'm going to wait until he's forgotten about it all and then I'm going to get him.' The inference was that the revenge would be violent.

Both these examples, I believe, further illustrate the manner in which violence is a common part of many police officials' lives, both on and off duty. Recognising this helps explain why the illegal use of force is seen by some police officials as legitimate. It also sheds light on why in some instances police may be correct in thinking the public want them to be violently forceful with certain people. Examples of this public demand were evident at the rural police station. There police appeared most at ease with the belief that communities supported them in punishing residents. None of the three examples mentioned earlier—the two teens sleeping at their boyfriends' homes or the son accused of stealing his mother's money—were intended to be dealt with by police in a formal manner. No dockets were to be opened, no names recorded in any books. Instead, it seemed residents called the police to scare and punish the teenagers in a manner that would 'teach them a lesson'. The mother of the boy wanted him to return her money while the residents who reported the girls wanted them to realise their behaviour was socially and culturally unacceptable. In these examples it was as if the police were being called to perform a sort of punitive parenting.

Similar dynamics played themselves out within the police stations. On a number of occasions during my research in Cape Town, managers would compare their subordinates to children, suggesting they were ill-disciplined. They threatened them with organisational sanctions in the belief that this would 'correct' them. At other times police officials told me they were doing the work of parents while on patrol, teaching errant school children what was right and wrong by taking them into custody and lecturing them, but also slapping and kicking them at times. None of this was officially recorded. Some officials told me that they beat their own children because it was how they had been taught discipline when they were children themselves. Yet many social observers accept that South Africa's colonial and apartheid history, particularly its entrenchment of migrant labour, tore many nuclear families apart. In its wake it left children raised without parents, nurture or nutrition, often replaced by violence and neglect.[39]

The individual, familial and community normalisation of violence in South Africa is at times bolstered by public figures in leadership positions, who believe that a threat of violence delivered by the state will reduce crime and build respect. This view is supported by a litany of aggressive rhetoric from politicians over the past decade.[40] In March 2013 the country's president, Jacob Zuma, stated against all other evidence that South Africa is not a violent country.[41] His comments were delivered in defence of the country in the weeks following para-Olympian Oscar Pistorius's shooting dead his girlfriend, Riva Steenkamp, in February 2013, and the litany of negative international media coverage that followed. And yet in 2006 Zuma was reported as saying that as a young man he would 'knock out' a gay man if one had stood in front of him (inferring the man's presence would be taboo and violence would be corrective).[42] Furthermore, it was reported in 2011 that Zuma had appointed Bheki Cele as national police commissioner to build a 'mature, visible police force that brought back its fear factor...[and portrayed an image to the public] that says the police must be feared and respected.'[43]

Other leaders have romanticised violence. In March 2013 it was reported that the provincial minister for education in the Eastern Cape province, Mandla Makupula, told a gathering of school learners that they didn't have any rights. Referring to a learner who had taken his father to court because he didn't want to go to initiation school, he told learners, 'I wish he could have been my child, I would have hit him on the head with a knobkerrie and he would have gone to that initiation school crying.'[44] The department defended his comments, saying '[he] recognised that this was an engagement with young people with a limited attention span, it was important that his remarks were interspersed with a high level of humour and reference to day-to-day experiences.'[45] This defence is equally emblematic of the problem, unintentionally confirming that violence is a daily experience in the lives of youths, but presenting it as acceptable humour.

In a country where the threat of violence is literally and rhetorically used to teach respect, and where violent crime threatens the populace's respect for government,[46] it makes sense that some power structures, particularly those deployed within the SAPS, would tolerate, even encourage, the use of violence and force to 'beat' a respect for the state into the population.

Hornberger offers one compelling explanation for the prevalence of the use of violence by SAPS officials. Exploring attempts to introduce human rights policing into the SAPS, and having observed the normalisation of violence in daily policing, she suggests SAPS officials resort to violence because they lack the personal reference point required to position themselves in the middle class, human rights-oriented front stage of policing.[47] She writes that instead

> most police officers [invest] in the backstage [which allows] them to get respect from colleagues... The image of potency allowed by the backstage has helped police officers to remain motivated and avoid feelings of humiliation and inadequacy... [which arise] where formal education standards are missing, where promotions have come to a halt, where challenges to masculine identity are seen as threatening, where the difference between middle-class values and police officers' bias towards lower and working-class values becomes insurmountable.[48]

During my 2012/13 fieldwork but also in conversations and interviews with police since 2004, there have been individuals who have bought into a discourse of mutual respect, believing that if they treat people with respect, they will be respected. Indeed, focus groups and social attitude surveys both suggest this is what South Africans want from police,[49] the approach known as procedural justice or procedural fairness. But my recent experience suggests that the organisational script in which violence earns respect, remains stronger than that of human rights and mutual respect, and is growing. Too many police believe it is their role to punish.

Masculinity, the 'good old days' and 'peanuts'

Most police work in South Africa focuses on male bodies. This is particularly true of the police gaze (surveillance), stop and search, and violence. In such contexts, a playing out of archetypal roles emerges: hero and villain, cop and crook, but almost always 'man' and 'man'. Antony Whitehead suggests that in contexts where a man's sense of being a man comes into conflict with another man as a man, '[v]iolence by [either man] may be regarded as functional in maintaining an idealised and internalised sense of manhood in the face of external realities that point to his inability to do so'.[50]

I am not suggesting that every male SAPS official is inherently violent, nor that those who are violent necessarily represent a 'hegemonic masculinity' against which all other male SAPS officials measure themselves—although it might.[51] As Morrell et al. point out, violence in South Africa is commonly enacted by many men, but this does not automatically make it an element of a national hegemonic masculinity.[52] Rather, it is the realm in which violence is practised—in this case the police organisational context—that can establish violence as a legitimate part of hegemonic masculinity, while outside of the organisational realm the violence might remain viewed as illegitimate. Is this what was reflected by my subjects' defence of the Marikana shootings?

Another explanation for the acceptance of violence is the mythology that exists around apartheid policing. This includes the idea that because police could previously shoot liberally, crime levels were low and police were respected. This belief results in statements like this from a warrant officer interviewed in 2009:

> Crime is out of control. If they manage to change Section 49 [so that police can shoot more easily], we will be back where we were before. The reason we are where we are is that the criminals have no respect for us. They have far too much leeway; they have far too many rights in this country. Our hands are literally tied behind our backs. I'm not saying we should go out and shoot and kill everyone running around, but they need to give us back our respect. When they give us back our respect, the crime rate will come down.[53]

It is easy to idealise the past. Despite most officials acknowledging the abuses of the apartheid police, both black and white, police still imagine that organisation as one that was characterised by meritocracy, justice and respect.

And while the past is continually re-idealised, many SAPS officials have only negative things to say about the present, both about the government of the day, and about the managers who steer the organisation. Many disrespect and distrust the people they share offices with, locking drawers and doors each time they leave their offices, even if only for a minute. One might say that some police officials are dangerously close to losing respect for themselves.

Consider, for example, that none of the officials I asked wanted their children to become police officials when they were older. Instead they stressed the importance of education and study as keys to 'better' occupations. Jonny Steinberg found the same emphasis on education among police in Johannesburg.[54] In that, and in subsequent work, he has suggested that some South Africans, in some contexts, do not consent to being policed by the SAPS, do not recognise their authority.[55] In effect they disrespect them.

As mentioned earlier, when off duty, some police in my study would not tell strangers that they were police officials. They framed this as if the revelation would put them in danger. Many avoided using public transport while wearing their police uniforms, instead carrying these in bags and changing before and after work. Might there be an element of shame to their concealed occupation? Consider the view of a senior officer interviewed in 2009:

> It's becoming embarrassing for me when I am at a private place, for instance at church, and they ask me, 'What do you do?' and I say, 'I am a police officer.' You can immediately see for yourself—these people, if you don't know them well, they will immediately withdraw a bit and think you are corrupt, or illiterate, or a poor performer. It's sad that that's the association with the police.[56]

Many of those who joined the police since the turn of the century did so because the illusion of a meritocratic society, in which they could be whoever they wanted to be, had failed to materialise. Joining the SAPS provided the best job security and income they could find. In 2009 I interviewed a young constable who told me 'I can't provide for my family.... The sad part of it all is that I live in a shack. It is hard for me.... I stay in the police because the family has got to eat.' At the time I suspected he was looking for sympathy and bending the truth. I knew how much money SAPS constables earned and I knew it was far more than most South Africans. And yet, I was very familiar with both the organisational and public discourse that said 'We can only expect so much from police because they are paid so little.' It is one of the few subjects relating to policing on which the public and average police official seem to agree. In 2007, as part of a review of research and action on police corruption in South Africa in which this discourse looms large, I compared the salaries of teachers, nurses, fire fighters and police officers to test the assertion. My research showed that police consistently earned more money than these allied professions,[57] and yet there was no comparable public discourse of sympathy for the others, with the possible exception of teachers. Since then SAPS salaries have continued to increase at a rate above that of inflation. Despite this, police officers are not afraid to complain about the 'peanuts' they are paid. It was something many of those I shadowed were unhappy about, a mark against them for which they were not responsible.

What was frustrating about the 'peanuts' narrative was that when compared to South Africa as a whole, police earned very good money. This does not automatically mean that they do not deserve better remuneration or conditions of employment, but does mean that compared to the average household, police are well off. Their incomes are particularly good if one considers that recruits are only required to have a matric (high school) certificate.

One attempt to define the 'middle-class', though perhaps a more accurate term would be 'middle-income' in South Africa, points to an 'actual [household] median' of R3,036 (£171.70) per month and an 'actual middle' as R1,520–R4,560 (£85.90–£258) per month based on 2008 data.[58]

By comparison in 2006 SAPS constables started work on a salary of R5,916 (£334.60) per month,[59] with additional housing, clothing, medical and thirteenth cheque benefits and annual pay progressions. By June 2010 this figure stood at R8,461 (£476) per month with the same benefits[60] and by 2013, I was told in the field, it was approximately R12,000 (£678.70). In contrast to these salaries but in line with Visagie's analysis, the 2011 national census suggested that the average annual income for a female-headed household was R67,330 (£3803.30) while for male-headed households it was R128,329 (£7249). Combined, the average household earned R103,204 (£5837.12) per year.[61] However, considering the race-skewed distribution of wealth in South Africa, this data is misleading. In 2013, 50 per cent of SAPS employees were classified as 'Male, African' and 29.4 per cent as 'Female, African'.[62] The national census shows that amongst these groups, average income was significantly lower at R60,000 (£3393.54) per year.[63] Similarly, 10.6 per cent of the SAPS workforce was classified 'coloured'.[64] The census shows that in 2011 coloured-female headed households earned an average of R51,440 (£2905.70) and coloured male headed households R112,172 (£7249). At a basic level then, 90 per cent of the SAPS workforce, on average, earns significantly more than the equivalent national medians.

The starting salary of a constable is twice the average income of an African male-headed household in the country. And yet as Visagie points out, 'the middle group in South Africa, comprising 4.2 million households, is quite poor,' and 'The relatively affluent middle class still includes, in its lower ranges, households with a very moderate level of income, i.e. R5600 total income per household per month.'[65] While lower ranking SAPS officials might not fall within this 'very moderate' pay range, it might be accurate, to consider theirs a 'moderate' income.

As obvious as the mediocrity of these salaries might be it was only during my recent fieldwork that I came to fully appreciate just how far these salaries are stretched. As I travelled with SAPS officials as they collected or returned colleagues to their homes before and after shifts, I became more aware of the relative poverty in which many SAPS employees still live. While salaries might be good when compared to national averages, they are hardly sufficient where an official is a sole breadwinner responsible for the support of unemployed parents, siblings, and children, often split between two provinces. This is particularly true if a constable aspires to enjoy the more luxurious fruits of the country's grossly unequal democracy in which material gain is desired, celebrated and respected more than almost anything else.

Bringing it back to violence

So how does this all link back to police violence? David Bruce has suggested that many South Africans suffer low self-esteem and insecurity about their status among peers, and that this feeds the country's high levels of inter-personal violence, particularly violence perpetrated by men.[66] Citing research that correlates low self-esteem and an inflated concept of self-worth as drivers of aggression, he suggests that the most disadvantaged citizens would not necessarily be the most violent. Police officials are certainly not the country's most disadvantaged.

Similarly, James Gilligan has posited that any form of violence is motivated by a feeling of shame and a desire to replace it with pride.[67] He notes that violence is almost always enacted by those who have been socially shamed by the structure of the societies in which they live. In other words, where for example unemployed persons or a particular ethnicity or sex is socially marginalised and looked down upon within a stratified society, the recipients of that downward gaze are most likely to resort to violence to regain their self-esteem. He notes that this is particularly true amongst men in social systems that prescribe very different gender roles to men and women, and in unequal societies. In such societies, as in South Africa, men are celebrated for being brave, aggressive, virile providers. When these men find themselves in social circumstances that are looked down upon by society, such as when they are unemployed, and if they have not been taught alternative coping mechanisms, they are likely to resort to violence as a means to reclaim a sense of masculinity.

Anthony Giddens makes an astute observation on feelings of shame as they relate to personal identity. He writes that shame is the manifestation of anxiety as it relates to the narrative one seeks to sustain to maintain a cohesive sense of self. As such, shame bears directly on self-identity.[68] He contrasts shame with guilt, suggesting that the former should be understood in relation to the integrity of the self while guilt is only derived of feelings of wrong doing. Taking this into account, while SAPS officers might know their abuse of force might be 'wrong', possibilities of manifest guilt may pose less of a threat than the threat of manifest shame, which could be brought about in the absence of violence as a tool to teach respect.

Giddens goes on to cite Lewis and suggest that 'bypassed shame' is born of unconscious anxieties of self and to feelings of ontological insecurity, consisting of repressed fears that the narrative of self-identity cannot withstand the pressures on its coherence or social acceptability. In short, he argues, pride comes from a self-narrative that can be sustained, while shame manifests where that narrative of self begins to crumble under societal interrogation. The latter includes lack of coherence in ideals, the inability to find ideals worthy of pursuit, as well as instances in which goals are too demanding to be attained.[69] One might imagine all of these to regularly manifest in the lives of particularly young South Africans who find themselves working in the SAPS, having never before imagined themselves part of the organisation but having turned to it due to a lack of alternatives.

It seems quite plausible that some members of the SAPS experience a form of emasculation as they move from their home to their work lives. If true, this is likely most pronounced among black African officials, many of whom are drawn from the margins of the working class and are most likely to be the sole breadwinners responsible for the upkeep of extended social networks. Black African males currently represent over 50 per cent of all SAPS personnel.

Of course constructions of masculinity in South Africa are not neatly delineated by race. Reflecting on, and generalising, the violence of a white police official, Kerry-Gaye Schiff suggests that:

> the need to conform to strong cultural standards of masculinity within the context of the police can lead to a severely restricted coping repertoire that is unable to conceive of solutions to problems other than within a narrow range of behaviours that are mostly rooted in violence.[70]

These male officials, who as South African men tend to be raised and live in environments that expect men to provide for their families[71] (often extended families: grandparents, nieces/nephews included), find they are unable to. They have failed in the most intimate of spheres, because they cannot provide for themselves or their family the life that society imagines they should. Moreover, they feel disrespected in the most public of spheres, because they wear the blue of the SAPS. This compounded emasculation echoes that experienced by black African men in the colonial and apartheid-era labour systems. Emasculated by slave-like power structures and removal from family life, many asserted their masculinity in part through violence,[72] a means by which to reclaim some self-esteem.[73] It seems quite likely that some men within the SAPS seek their respect through violence at work because of the manner in which South Africa's gross inequality, past and present, leads to unmet expectations and emasculation.

This is not to say that many police officers are not proud of their position and of the organisation, or that it is only feelings of emasculation and shame that motivate the delivery of violence by police. South Africa is a country in which violence is normalised by the state and family, from the home to the school and to the state's response to crime. What I am suggesting in this chapter is that within the SAPS there are many men whose middle-class aspirations have failed to materialise as envisaged. For those without alternative coping mechanisms, and with its historical culture of force and secrecy, the SAPS workplace provides a stage for the acting out of a script which reminds its actors that there is little in the world that is more manly than beating another man into submission.

While these trends were most apparent in the city, they were not absent in the rural setting. There, police believed villagers respected them based in part on their ability to scare, punish and harm with public consent. As such they made themselves available as public servants whose capacity to use force to address social or familial fractures could be requested without official record.

Police in democratic societies are given the right to use reasonable force in the delivery of their duties in order to contribute to the development of safe environments. Yet it is for this very reason that police can become a threat to security.[74] If the extra-legal use of force or violence becomes normalised within a police agency's organisational culture, if it becomes a tool for the lazy with which to problem solve efficiently rather than by following official prescripts which might require more time and effort, then the SAPS is in danger of reclaiming its apartheid-era image as being the state's violent fist.

Conclusion

I spent the week of 26 February with detectives at Cape Town Central police station. When, on the morning of the 27th, I asked three of them if they had heard the news about Macia's death, they expressed disgust at the actions of their colleagues. Two of them literally dropped their heads in shame, preferring not to make eye contact as they wondered out loud how police officials could do such things. But just the previous day these same detectives had tried to convince me that it was normal to assault young men if they were found walking the streets of Cape Town's townships at night, asking rhetorically 'Why are they there, if not to commit crime?'

So while there are limits to what many police consider a necessity for violence in their work—dragging a man behind a police van, resulting in his death, perhaps representing that limit—many embrace an underlying logic that says the state allows police the use of force because force and violence prevent crime. This logic suggests that if police are forceful enough, civilians will, out of fear, respect the state and South Africa will be at peace. But as Gilligan points out, all the evidence suggests that the greatest product of punishment and violence is more violence. Once societies stop causing violence (through police, prisons, social stratification), violence will disappear from society by itself.[75]

Of course there are many SAPS officials who abhor violence of any form. But they tend to turn a blind eye to the violence of their colleagues. And so the message too often communicated by police is that it's okay to use violence to solve problems. Their violence serves to remind South Africans that the agents of the state can be as threatening to their safety as any 'criminal', and begs the question: does a police organisation and its members, in embracing such violence, deserve the respect of the population? Probably not, but considering the context in which many live and work, might police officials be forgiven for thinking they do?

When, at his bail hearing for Mido Macia's murder, Warrant Officer Ncema told the court Macia had insulted him, it is likely he was looking for sympathy from his audience. When presidents threaten violence against gay men and MEC's threaten violence against learners, one might spare some sympathy for a police official, humiliated in public, possibly humiliated daily, for thinking that violence is the logical tool with which to teach lessons and earn respect. Unfortunately for Ncema and his co-accused who maintained their innocence throughout the trial, the court did not agree. In November 2015 the eight former SAPS officials were sentenced to fifteen years in prison for the murder of Mido Macia.

PART III

HOW ARE THE POLICE DOING
THEIR WORK?

11

POLICING BOUNDARIES

THE CULTURAL WORK OF AFRICAN POLICING

David Pratten

The contributions in this section focus on the state police forces of Mozambique, South Africa, Ghana and Niger. They take us behind the scenes in the training, recruitment and routines of African police officers and into the complex social and political interactions between police and public. It is here, in the interstices of public and private, official and popular, that the real work of policing happens. Who will protect, prosecute and punish, and which case or complaint will fall inside or outside the domain of legal remedy? These are issues that are learned in the craft of police work and are subject to everyday contingencies, improvisation and discretion. These chapters investigate the boundaries between the prescribed and the practiced. From the perspective of the practice of everyday policing we are introduced to the importance of these boundaries; two are especially striking—the institutional boundaries between policing authorities, and the normative boundaries between official and popular legal orders. Given the potential slippage of these institutional orders and cultural norms, we find that the practices of boundary-making are of primary importance in our understanding of the 'cultural work' of policing in Africa.[1]

A striking feature of boundary-making and negotiation in African policing is institutional—a result of the challenge to the state's monopoly on policing. Globally policing has 'entered a new era, an era characterized by a transformation in the governance of security'.[2] This new paradigm of privatized and decentralized policing complicates our common understanding of the state's provision of security, its monopoly of force, as the essential function of government. Analysts of policing and security around the world now speak of complex patterns of 'overlapping agencies,'[3] of 'plural networked policing,'[4] and no longer accept the conceptual priority of the state in these new security networks.

It is striking that in Niger and Mozambique, with such different legacies of colonial governance, for instance, that the policing landscape is shaped by the cooperation and collision of police and chiefs, gendarmerie and chefferie. The 'fractured sovereignties' of policing in these cases offer important examples of the ways in which governments are not just devolving power in decentralization and post-conflict reconstruction exercises, but promoting and 'accepting new bases of legitimate government.[5] Collaboration between chiefs and police, and between the customary and civil spheres are based on working out the boundaries between the two. What is the chief's business, and what matters should be brought before the police are highly contingent questions. The contested boundaries between these realms link these contemporary portraits into a long historical trajectory of intersections of the criminal and customary codes that ties contemporary criminology to the historical ethnographic record.[6] The sedimentation of norms, laws and institutions from different historical eras and traditions has produced considerable scope for negotiation and bargaining between them. And as Olivier de Sardan has argued this superimposition of various types of law, and the way that successive forms of political power have been interleaved in the political domain shape the ways in which this complex legal landscape is policed.[7]

The formal and practical norms of policing are in constant flux and are neatly captured in the process by which cases are brought to the police. In Niger for instance, a matrix of institutional incentives and moral imperatives produces procedural pathways that determine how and by whom cases are heard. These practices are shaped by fear of falling into the 'legal funnel' and the predatory hands of the state apparatus, evaluations of the relative power and effectiveness of police and chiefs, and are critically determined by the ways in which policing 'bends' according the origins, identities and ethnicities of protagonists. In Niger, as elsewhere across the continent therefore the boundary between a police case and one that can be dealt with or withdrawn into the familiar, customary realm is vigilantly policed. Whether a case crosses these boundaries from civil to customary is decided in part by the protagonists and in part by the police who evaluate its material, moral and legal credentials.

The definition of cases and domains is also a key aspect of the cultural work of policing in the Mozambican case where the constitution of policing is based on formal collaboration between police and traditional chiefs. The boundaries between criminal police cases (importantly defined according to the drawing of blood), and so-called 'social' cases (including adultery, divorce, debt and land) retained for chiefs are redefined and rehearsed, but remain prone to collapsing. Where localized registers of crime, justice and punishment are inflected in contemporary practice, in dealing with witchcraft for instance, so these boundaries are re-imagined not in terms of state practice but within the familiar domains of healers.[8] As a consequence, it is important to discern how those who step into the void of disorder and de-centeredness and establish routine by knowledge and practice do so by grasping the importance of how cultural patterns are articulated to systems of political domination.[9]

One key set of boundaries refracted in this light therefore is the intersection of moral orders regarding right and wrong, and the legal codes according to which infractions are prosecuted and punished. This opens up distinctions between state and non-state, official and unofficial, state-sanctioned and 'popular' notions of justice that in turn become implicated in one another. While 'popular' justice is often structured in terms of 'legitimate' targets and appropriate punishments, these imperatives produce notions of justice and law with different kinds of imaginaries from those available in the official sites and representations of justice and law. This is never simply a matter of 'folk' notions of law and justice versus state-sanctioned ideas of justice. Although they are locked in unequal relations, they are enmeshed in one another.[10]

As Mary Douglas said, 'any structure of ideas is vulnerable at its margins'.[11] The 'cultural work' invested in policing boundaries is starkly defined and repeated so routinely because in practice these boundaries are precarious and are shot through with ambiguity and complexity. What is legal, legitimate and right needs to be rehearsed, to be practiced, to be performed in the face of this precarity. In highlighting this point these chapters also draw our attention to the formal and informal rituals and routines that define secure spaces and policing subjectivities. In this post-colonial context of 'metaphysical disorder'[12] and 'radical uncertainty',[13] it is important to recognize the cultural work that seek to conjure up 'safe, imagined communities'.

Routine performance is central to the processes by which the boundaries of moral communities are constructed, and how legal subjectivities are inscribed in and on the bodies of law-keepers and law-breakers. In the context of policing in Ghana, drills are key to instilling this shared imagination of police service. Contributing to a subjectivity fostered in the legitimacy of stateness and self-discipline, these parades act as 'bureaucratic ceremonies' in which officers perform an idealized vision of their organization and themselves. Elsewhere these boundaries are shaped by routine and ritual in other ways. Food consumption amongst police patrols in secluded locations around the Johannesburg metropolis, for instance, constructs a sphere of 'positive conviviality' from an environment of 'negative sociality' beyond it. Just as nocturnal vigilante patrols mark out an idealized map of their village community,[14] so these police patrols produce not only physical but cognitive boundaries separating good from evil, legal from illegal, order from disorder.

The way in which the aesthetics of difference are marked onto on the bodies of police and criminals and across human and animal symbolic divides is significant in this light. In the Ghanaian police academy therefore instructors tell recruits that 'you are an animal, you are not a human being, you are coming from the forest, you are now going to be trained to become a human being.' This initiation into the social world for police contrasts with those performative practices which emphasise the transgressive animality of criminals. At official policing ceremonies in Mozambique, for instance, prisoners are paraded in front of a public who are reminded of the non-human characteristics that criminals possess. These prisoners are like crocodiles and leopards, the public is told; the criminal is represented in witch-like guise, a spectral form which attacks at night transformed as an 'evil' animal. As these contributions demonstrate, it is important to account for the historical tenacity with which embodied semiotics of difference mark police from criminals. These practices differentiate insider from outsider and enable us to interrogate the moral imperatives and aesthetic evaluations that people in different contexts make of their actions on the bodies of others.

The focus in this context is on the construction of categories in which the classifications of purity and impurity and good and evil, are constituted cosmologically within a moral order of the world.[15] These boundaries are also marked in other ways. The significance of food in marking inclusive and exclusive social relations amongst South African police patrols captures this ambiguity precisely. Food offers a powerful symbolic repertoire through which the ambiguities of power and social relations are addressed; '... although eating was a sign of wealth, physical health, and patronage—it could also be the avenue for bodily waste and death'.[16] For Johannesburg's cops food sharing and consumption is a fine and precarious line. What keeps a police officer out of trouble (cool drinks, sheltered spots, convivial networks), can also put him in trouble (awkward obligations deriving from accepting hospitality). The complications brought on by the intimacies of social praxis warn Johannesburg's police officers to maintain their boundaries since when they eat with the public then they may be compromised and have to work for them.

Across these ethnographies of contemporary policing in Africa we see that policing needs to be related to its own cultural logics and political imperatives, not as ideal types but as practice. No easy logic inflects national or global trends to local practices of policing, and no simple model of state-society relations captures the ambiguous nature of contemporary policing in Africa. The fracturing observed in these dynamics of political authority over policing opens up the scope for alternative, non-state, logics to insert and implicate themselves into policing practice. That the institutional and normative foundations of policing in Africa are plural and complex, however, is not to say that the boundaries between police and alternative policing authorities, or between legal and popular codes of justice are simply blurred. Against this context of plural policing authorities the very categories of 'crime' are mutually constituted across official and unofficial divides, and the 'cultural work' of defining the boundaries of what counts as a crime and who counts as a law-breaker and law-keeper, is intensive.

12

THE BELLY OF THE POLICE

Julia Hornberger

Beyond the metaphor: Taking eating and drinking seriously

There are probably only a few motorists in South Africa, who have not had the experience of being stopped by a police officer and instead of being given a fine for a real or imagined traffic violation are being asked to buy him (or her) a cool drink.

As the cartoon suggests, it is such a common thing that the 'cool drink talk' amounts to something like the twelfth official language of South Africa.[1] Despite this ubiquity, but probably because it is 'merely' a consumable (or a small amount of money indexed/bracketed as immediate equivalent for a cool drink)[2] that is at stake in changing hands here, this would mostly be captured under the heading of 'petty corruption'. To call it petty corruption is to mark the distinction between a less consequential form of corruption and the seriousness of, for example, white-collar corruption; or what in South Africa has come to be called tender deals. These deals involve huge sums of (state) money and are seen as having the power to cause a real effect—both short and long term. They produce a real advantage for some, mainly ascendency into a

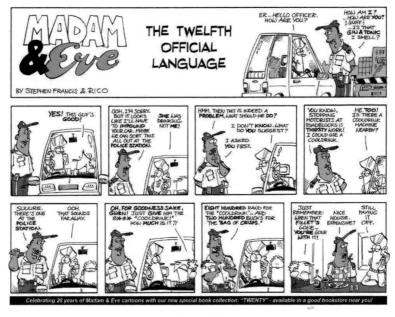

Figure 12.1

newly-rich class and continued political influence, and real disadvantage for others, such as the disruption of essential services and access to justice. In contrast, to call corruption 'petty' expresses annoyance but not outrage, redundancy rather than crisis.

Likewise, when we speak about 'the politics of the belly', the analytical term shaped by Jean-François Bayart,[3] the figures of the belly and of eating are merely used as metaphors to describe the intertwining of political and social life that has captured the state in Africa. It metaphorically captures the social behaviour—the wheeling and dealing—of big men and political entrepreneurs, but it does not take the role of food and eating, and the role of body in corruption, seriously as such. In fact, Bayart hardly even bothers in his famous book to go to the popular and ethnographic roots of the expression. Yet it is a vernacular expression which is tightly connected to the role of eating as a way of building personal power through sustenance, but also very closely connected to witchcraft and the possibility of actually being poisoned. All this has been left out as he elevates the vernacular expression to conceptually describe the destruction of public goods and their appropriation for private gain.

In this chapter, I take issue with this way of underplaying the role of food, and eating and drinking, in relation to corruption and state-craft in general, and to policing in particular. I argue instead that the actual exchange of food is one of the most consequential forms of corruption—at least in quality. It keeps a hold on the parties involved and it has the power to create mutual obligations that far outstrip the power of abstract generalized money exchange. In fact, so this paper argues, food and drink fundamentally structure police work, and how police officers relate to one another and the community in their everyday work. In turn, food and drink, taken literally, provide a powerful lens through which to understand policing.

Classical anthropological studies have shown the powerful social and cultural dimensions of food. They have mainly highlighted the ritual and sacrificial dimension, in which food taboos, such as not being allowed to eat one's totem,[4] or who is given which part of a hunted animal,[5] bring a certain social order and social hierarchy into being; while sharing a sacrificial meal connects and transforms people on a transcendental plane.[6] In a structuralist understanding, food affords the elements for an overarching logic of mental categories. For example, in Levi-Strauss's accounts of 'The Raw and the Cooked',[7] or 'The Culinary Triangle',[8] the raw is what is still in the hands of nature, while the cooked is that which has been socialised through human alteration. Various objects can then be arranged in relation to one another on a continuum between these two ends. Mary Douglas similarly explains Levitican food rules by showing that what is taboo is that which defies certain basic categories.[9] That which is out of place becomes dangerous and is seen as polluted. Here food is woven into, and holds together, mental and social structures.

More recent studies of food, drink and the stomach have brought about something of a revival of a focus on eating and digesting in social science. Anthropologists in particular have brought new perspectives to highlight the material and the ethical side in relation to the social and political nature of food. These newer studies add to older functionalist, structuralist and semiotic approaches to food an understanding that includes the very substance and character of the food and drink being taken in without falling into a purely nutritionist understanding. Such approaches argue that, while the meaning of food is cultural and contextual, and produces all kinds of social formations, there remains an interesting necessary connection to the actual practice of how and what is consumed.[10] Manning describes how a toast cannot be a felicitous toast without a real drink in hand; and how the actual drinking of coffee provides the material infrastructure on which a certain sociality can thrive: without the excuse of a real coffee, the famous coffee house talk would be rudderless and awkward.[11] In a similar way, remaking the boundary not so much of the semiotic and the material, but the social and the biological, there are studies of food in relationship to biochemical bodily processes. Landecker describes a recent shift from the understanding of food as energy or fuel to food as environment.[12] Food as environment highlights how we imagine a person and their personality not just being shaped by social and political context but also by the interaction of the molecular self (i.e. DNA) with the molecular nature of food. This is noteworthy as it signifies a process that takes place in-between the social and biological, and disassembles the boundaries between the organism and the environment 'causing definite ontological upset about outside and inside, about "the social" becoming the biological' through bodily 'regulating transaction zone[s] with the ability to transforming passing objects'.[13] Metabolism in a way then is a relational process—that which emerges as it mediates between the domains of the social and the biological aspects of nutrition. In Hylton White's work, the social is made through food that in turn has been exposed to a particular environment.[14] In the countryside of South Africa's KwaZulu-Natal province, animals such as chickens are inscribed with ethnic identity, being 'white' when industrially produced, or being 'Zulu' when raised as part of a rural homestead. More important however is that this ethnic indexing of food, which also points to different forms of the circulation of money and labour, means that the shared eating of these animals allows for very different ways of forging of social relationships and for connecting ethically with others: one reflective of impoverished rural proletarianisation, the other of culturalist kinship arrangements. Such ethically differentiated forms of being in the world, and of connections with others enabled through food, is also what occupies Annemarie Mol.[15] She suggests a new understanding of an embodied ethic on the basis of our relationship to food. Instead of being caught up in a dietary understanding of our body either leaning toward discipline and thrift, or indulgence and pleasure, she suggests a position of appreciation which involves both 'cultural appraisal and physical taste'. 'Appreciation', so she posits,

> is a fascinating term. Rather than excluding the body from ethics by being suspicious of it, making excuses for it, or hoping to liberate it from moralism, it suggest the possibility of an ethics that involves the body. In an ethics that involves the body, being attentive to the 'the good' is not imposed on the body by a mind that is rational, but cultivated as a personal capability that is as physical as it is mental.[16]

These studies make for an exciting range of perspectives on and through food. While not necessarily in accord with each other, they produce an awareness that food creates many kinds of social formations, and that it does so by also bringing together what are often considered discrete domains. Food entangles people in particular material realities, exposes the body to its environment and context in unexpected ways, and offers ways for thinking what it means to be—both bodily and ethically—in the world.

What these studies often avoid, though, is extending these same insights to questions of the law and the state, alongside other political abstractions. There are studies that describe global or national inequalities through circuits of trade and the production of (global) food commodities such as sugar and bananas. Yet while they foreground the political economy that produces these circuits they do not discuss how the state itself is being shaped by the intake of food. What I want to do here then is to bring together the question of food and the kind of embodied relationalities—even embodied ethics—that it produces, on the one hand, with questions of policing and the state that are otherwise mainly discussed in terms of heightened instrumentality and functionality, on the other. There have been many attempts to describe the permeation of the state by society. To talk about food and the state however is an attempt to go beyond the kind of already abstracted and congealed social formations—ethnicity or class—that might capture or shape the state in their interest. Instead it takes the state straight to what is according to Simmel one of the most shared human social commonalities:

> Of all the things that humans have in common, this is what they have most in common: that they have to eat and drink.... By virtue of the fact, however that this primitive physiology is an absolute human commonality, it becomes the content of shared action; the social formation of the meal emerges; the exclusive selfishness of eating is being tied to a frequency of being together and of being accustomed to being unified in such a way as it is rarely achieved through higher and more spiritual instigations.[17]

Empirically, this paper is based on many years of ethnographic work with the South African police, mainly in Johannesburg. In fact, the issue of food and eating, and the following case of the meaning of the cool drink, goes back to the very first days of my fieldwork with the police, in 2001. Interestingly it is only now, some fifteen years later, that I have come to write about it. It seems I first had to prove myself by writing about obviously serious issues regarding policing, such as questions of violence and justice, and universals such as human rights, before I could delve into the cultural nitty-gritty and anthropological particularity and 'otherness' of the police.

And to be honest, it is again an awkward moment to do so. I can feel the tension between an attempt to write about a police officer's metabolism and the political mobilisation and outcry over the lethal brutality of the police and its increasingly oppressive role in some of the most conflictual encounters of this society, such as at Marikana. Marikana is where on 12 August 2012 anti-crime police units of the South African Police Service (SAPS) were called in to end a so-called wildcat strike by platinum miners. The miners refused to disperse and the police ended up killing thirty-four people. One of the critical issues was the involvement of Cyril Ramaphosa, a prominent ANC politician but also a board member and shareholder of the Lonmin conglomerate that owns and runs the Marikana platinum mine. He had apparently used his political influence to portray the miners as criminals and to compel government to dispatch the police to push ahead with a forced rather than a negotiated solution.[18] The result was that once again in South Africa the police were seen as the brutal arm of the state and of capital, made to choose the wrong side of the people. Little, it seemed, had changed not just since apartheid but, going even further back, since the early days of the South African Union, when in 1922 the South African police (together with the military) was sent in to quell a white miners' strike and hundreds of workers were killed.[19] Regarding Marikana, some commentators might dare speak about the bad public order training of the police and the impossible job they are given in dealing with protests.[20] But as John Soske has declared, 'counterfeit mourning', 'every last goddamn liberal evocation of untrained police who thought they were in danger', and 'every lazy media "revelation" about the situation's many and imponderable nuances only serves to obfuscate what happened' and to 'deflect from demands for real justice and accountability'.[21]

Reciprocally, though, this means that our knowledge of what the police is becomes more myth than understanding, more hyperstylisation, projection and inference than insight into the peculiar social phenomenon the police is, and the way it makes, reflects and refracts the society in which it operates. It is therefore that I persist with this rather whimsical and seemingly light-hearted topic, to get us to understand policing from a less obvious angle. It is through the idea of food that I think I can throw some light on how police are entangled in and made to do things which then often allow us to see them as mere instruments. Meanwhile what is often at play is a complicated division of agency across a set of entangled and embodied social relations, above and below the institutional level. Corruption, meanwhile is always considered a hot and relevant topic, but even here we should maybe start to see how it works its way back and forth through our bodies and our cultural cosmologies, and how metabolism, in the literal and not just the metaphorical sense, is part of its dynamics.

Hot and cold policing

So let me take you back to these first days of my fieldwork with the South African police. This was in 2001. I was working with police in an area of Johannesburg called Sophiatown and had been lucky to find a police officer, Inspector Musi, who was willing to take me with him on patrol through the area and beyond. He was a talkative, highly reflective man. He could endlessly 'sociologize' about the people he was working with, both his colleagues and the various rich and poor people living in the diverse neighbourhoods across which the Sophiatown policing area stretched. When doing this he radiated a particular calm and composure. But this was a fragile state. As he explained to me, it could easily change into a heated encounter, both with colleagues but even more so with people of the area. These encounters could escalate from situations under control to situations out of control. From one moment to the next, things could turn against him in unforeseen ways, he explained to me: a colleague blackmailing him, a senior reprimanding and shaming him, a person opening an unfounded case against him, him losing his temper and being provoked to use violence. These were all situations that could potentially destroy his carefully laid out plans to get ahead, to be promoted, to earn more money, to live a better life. The way he described it, it was as if they were always just around the corner, these moments which could ruin him and change his whole life-course.

It was therefore also that he got very stressed on a hot summer day. We were just embarking on that day's crime prevention patrol, when he realised that he had forgotten to take some essential equipment along with him when he had rushed out of his room at the police barracks in the morning. He knew it was not right to leave the policing area, but he mumbled some excuse about why he needed to drive back to his quarters, where he fetched a little portable ice-cooler that fit perfectly between the two front seats of the police van, two plastic cups, and a litre bottle of cool drink. We then stopped, by now back in the policing area of Sophiatown, at a bar in the neighbourhood of Westdene, where the owner welcomed Musi with a convivial handshake. The familial gesture clearly indicated their acquaintance. The bar owner happily helped Musi out with filling his cooler with ice on Musi's request. Back in the car

Musi prepared two cups with coke and ice and said to me, already much more relaxed, 'now we can get started, now I am safe'.

This speaks to a well-known South African cosmology of hot and cold social transactions, where, as Jean and John Comaroff note, 'thirst' and the 'polluting effect of heat' imply 'simultaneous physical and social disruption', signalling 'interference in the orderly actions and transactions that maintained viable being in the world'.[22] In the policing area of Sophiatown, and in the life of a policeman, such interferences could easily occur where a 'viable being in the world' was not only historically questioned in terms of the past atrocities of the police under apartheid, but also as police often found themselves pulled between people's strong desire for the power of the state combined with a practice of entitlement towards the means of the state.[23] Added to this was the absence of an experience of policing as a public, non-partisan and legitimate institution. A policeman could one moment be called into a private household to intervene and resolve a conflict and be cursed and condemned in the next by the mother of the household for arresting her son, who caused all the trouble.[24] It is in order to walk this thin line between being compelled and condemned, that the cooling medium of the ice-cold cool drink becomes pivotal, 'quenching the thirst' and cooling 'the heat engendered by a threatening world'.[25]

Eating together

Food also structures the everyday pathways of police in terms of conviviality. Eating together is a powerful way of connecting people to each other,[26] and this is as much about what is eaten as it is about where it is eaten. Whenever I was working with the police, great consideration would go towards what they would eat for lunch and where they would obtain it. Few of them brought food from home. I suppose it was a welcome reason to interrupt their patrol or investigations to drive to a familiar food place, where they knew what was on the menu. And there was no shortage of lived racial, ethnic and class clichés about who preferred which food, anchored strongly in experiences of sustenance and wellbeing and translated into perceptions about identity and belonging. As Fischler states,

> ...eating the same food is equated with producing the same flesh and blood, thus making commensals more alike and bringing them closer to each other. The perception that 'you are what you eat' seems universal. It holds that, when absorbing food, a subject absorbs at the same time salient features of the food. If eating food makes

one become more like that food, then those sharing the same food become more like each other.[27]

Fast food chains would provide common ground, but were generally considered too expensive to be frequented on a daily basis. Generally however, preferences for either *vetkoek*, *pap* or *biryani* determined who would end up working in a team with whom. As much as seniors might have wanted to impose a more cross-racial approach, they knew they did not have much choice but to give in in to those preferences, if they wanted their officers to be happy. The wrong food and the wrong commensals would have made for much discontent, more even than unpaid overtime.

What was interesting was that police officers, especially when they were in uniform and driving in a marked car, or had bought food in an area where they were well known, preferred to drive to a quiet spot, be it the parking lot of the art gallery in downtown Johannesburg, the Highlands ridge in Yeoville, or some other park in the suburbs, or the dead-end of an alley, to eat their food in peace. As they explained to me, repeating the sense of being constantly exposed to a socially threatening world, it was better to be out of people's view, as they would otherwise immediately make nasty remarks about cops being lazy and useless. This sense of embattlement even more so strengthened the sense of the boundaries of positive conviviality within and negative sociality without. The intimacy which eating together produces,[28] in addition to revealing the ultimate humanity of the police, was clearly at odds with the kind of ambiguous expectation people had of them: to be state officials ready at any time to be at people's service and disposal, and yet somehow also embodying the awesome powers of the state—sometimes evil, sometimes favourable, but a power beyond the human need of nourishment. In return, police did not want to be contaminated by the people whose areas they were policing, and for which they were often full of contempt and social disregard. Exposing their food to people's eyes or even only faintly invoking the idea of having to share food with their policing subjects, brought about a sense of repulsion, which was rather to be avoided.

Both these aspects then—the power of eating together and turning people into intimate equals and friends, and the necessity to stay cool—point immediately in their combination towards another dimension in which food comes to structure policing. It is the dimension that makes for the tragedy of the belly: namely, that both these aspects are linked to the impossibility, in the end, for police officers to stay cool, and their nearly inevitable entanglement in hot relations with people that compromise their identity and discreetness. This is especially the case as police are expected to engage in so-called community policing and to build intimate connections and relationships of trust and care with the people of the neighbourhoods they police. Just remember the convivial handshake between the owner of the bar and Inspector Musi. Inspector Musi later told me that the owner likes him to come to his venue and always offers him something, a drink or some food. 'He likes it when a police car is standing outside.' This practice refers to what I have elsewhere called 'my police—your police', or the informal privatisation of policing.[29] It is a practice whereby people do not imagine policing as a public affair to which they have free access. Instead, it is only through building up special bonds with particular police officers that one can get a share of the kind of protection that the police has to offer. Here then, the police do not ask for a bribe but are offered something, often something to eat, by someone from the neighbourhood as they are passing through a venue, in order to attract police like flies. This potentially detracts from the charge of trying to corrupt them, as offering food is always ambiguous enough that it might still be considered to be just an innocent courtesy or simple nicety. I have seen manifold manifestations of this practice, and they were definitely performed in a kind and courteous way, but they were never just a nicety. They always had some real—policing—effect. It could be a petrol station, for instance, that allows its Nescafe machine to run for free at night when policemen of the area are out on a special crime prevention operation. I have seen this petrol-station swamped in blue, visited by seven marked police vans and twenty uniformed officers at once, who came together there at 3am to warm up by taking multiple rounds of sugary coffee before returning to their cars and veering off into an endless night. The calculation here is that a petrol station that has the reputation of being a police hang-out would make an unattractive target for a robbery.

Mostly however this happens on a one-to-one level, such as with the police officer who had become a real fan of green tea and would always get a freshly brewed cup of the invigorating liquid from a Chinese restaurant in Cyraldene, personally served by the owner or his pretty daughter. Also here, a police car could regularly be seen standing outside the establishment, providing some measure of personal protection.

Food trappings

These exchanges happen seemingly in a casual way and often seem hardly like an exchange at all, more like a contingent coming together of circumstances that can easily be disentangled again. Yet it only appears so casual since what we see is not the actual forging of the bond or the redeeming of the pledge, but simply a reconfirming, at best a deepening, of an already drawn-out relationship. And anyway, the more delayed the return of the gift, the stronger the relationship.[30] How very binding and at the same time entrapping these relations are became clear when I was working with one Inspector Chetty, this time in downtown Johannesburg. Inspector Chetty was trying to win the trust of some Bangladeshi migrant traders. One of the traders had found the courage to come to the Johannesburg Central Police Station to complain that fake or corrupt police officers were extorting money from him and fellow Bangladeshi traders. Men in police uniform would stand in front of their street vending tables and would chase potential customers away until all the traders had paid up a certain sum of 'protection' money. And Inspector Chetty, a highly motivated police officer, trying to make human rights work, had hoped to convince them to all lay charges. Yet in order to overcome the foreign traders' strong mistrust of police he had to be more than just correct. He had to be extra nice to them, and to prove his commitment he had handed out his personal mobile number as a kind of guarantee. The traders however instead of collectively laying a charge and being cajoled by this to follow a path through the formal legal system, insisted on keeping things on a personal level with the inspector. With his phone number now at their disposal, they hoped to call him out when the corrupt policemen returned, or at least to be able to threaten them back with their special connection to 'their own' police. In order to further rewrite the relationship in this direction, they treated the personal mobile number of the officer as a gift which they reciprocated by inviting him to a restaurant owned by one of them, where under the pretext of meeting more traders and to offer him some tea on this hot day, they in fact dished up a whole meal for him. Inspector Chetty protested vehemently, but having sat down at one of the tables already he hardly could refuse the roti and curry they served him. While not quite the Durban curry the Indian South African inspector might have been used to, there was also an assertion of sameness by the traders here, by not just offering any food but food that they assumed he would find familiar. They then also all stood around him while he was eating and expectantly awaited his judgement. Foregrounding what was eaten and how it tasted, this gave depth and authenticity to the very act of reciprocity, and defused some of the instrumentality to the transaction. Yet, in the following weeks, no official charges were ever opened, and Inspector Chetty received various calls from the traders to remind him of them, and that they might need his help in the future. He was torn as to whether he should attend to these calls. His chances for a formal case faded away, but he also felt bad just cutting them off. He did so in the end and after much agonising, by switching his phone off to stop the calls, but at a price of great frustration and bitterness, that his work was going nowhere and he had now even lost the appreciation of the traders who were in a seriously exploited and weak position.

While this case speaks of either subverting an officer's work into some form of informality, or alternatively merely frustrating that work, the following story shows that the sharing of food can actually be highly compromising and lead towards a path of illegality. It also shows that this is not just an issue of an informal grey zone of people living at the margins of society where lines between private and public naturally blur, but one which also takes place at the very heart of the establishment, where those lines are much more clearly drawn, yet maybe even more so undermined.

We have now arrived in the year 2012. By this time I was working with the Commercial Crime Unit of the South African Police Service. The conversation about the role of food started because I had brought some strawberry muffins along with me. Inspector Mokoena was jokingly wondering if they were really allowed to eat those muffins, implying that I was maybe trying to bribe them. Inspector Sithole, the head of the unit, worried that I might be offended, quite seriously responded that I was their friend. 'No worries, guys, she won't ask anything in return.' But even though he was defusing the suspicion of bribery, the situation had obviously triggered some further thoughts about the connection between food and corruption in his mind. He went on, making clear that now a long story was to come:

I remember, some long time back, there was this Mister M, and we were coming to his house and as we arrive, we see this table laid out, and all this food on the table. M was in trouble at the time. He was one of these ANC guys who got rich with mining. So we come to his house and there is all this food on the table, and it is clear he is going to invite us to eat with him. When we saw this, we knew, the moment we eat with him, we now have to help him. There were cases against him. But you know how it goes. These guys are clever. The moment somebody opens up a case against them, they open up a counter charge. And then they want you to help them with their counter charge. So we quickly made up an excuse, that we had received this call, and that we had to go. He was not impressed. He really wanted us there and eat with him. It was clear from all the food. But we said to ourselves, we can't do this. Tomorrow we have to arrest this guy. It won't work if we eat with him. If you eat with them, then you have to work for them. That is how it goes. So we rather left quickly and avoided getting drawn in.

And so we do come back after all to the issues that were at stake in Marikana: to policing and mining and politics, and to new riches and their compromising entanglements. However I am coming at this from a very different angle. I have often heard people ask about the disgraced former Police Commissioner Jackie Selebi, how it could be that it was for a pair of shoes and some expensive suits that he could be corrupted. But what should become clear from what I have been talking about is that it is not a quantifiable monetary sum that determines the hold that exchanges have on people and the obligations they produce. It is much more the quality of the bribe that is at stake here, and the potential it holds to structure conviviality and sociality. Ethics here, instead of being resolved through the stomach,[31] actually becomes complicated, if not foreclosed. Money remains a rather thin device, in the way it can create abstraction and generalise exchange. In food in contrast, a variety of elements come together. On the one hand, the 'right' food is the basis for sustenance and wellbeing. At the same time, what is considered the 'right' food or drink is very much determined by the environment in which the police have to manoeuvre, and yet food creates both boundaries and deep embodied solidarities. As we have seen, to keep all these aspects in balance and to keep relationships 'cool' is sometimes exactly what gets policemen and women into trouble. The cool drink Inspector Musi employed to manage the precariousness of his situation is exactly what got him in trouble, even if only in a small way. Getting the ice for free from the bar owner, and the bar owner happily helping him so that Musi would 'protect' his place, produced an intractable intimacy which could not simply be resolved. And yet, exactly without a certain closeness, without a certain level of involvement and exposure to the heat, the police cannot do his or her work. Yet it is at the brink of this exposure that police are quickly pushed, drawn in and seduced by relationships, which then tend to overheat. This we saw in the case of Chetty, and even more so in the investigation of the political mining magnate. Police then find themselves constantly being suspended between protecting their discretion over the powers they have been given, on the one hand, and the constant threat that they will themselves be consumed, on the other hand, by the actions, judgments and projects of the people they are policing.

Bittersweet ending

Managing the uncomfortable embodiment of policing and the impossibility of the line police have to walk between being members of the state and of society

211

simultaneously, often leads to their being burnt up in the always looming defeat and the eruption of violence meted out by themselves or by others against them. Alternatively, withdrawing and avoiding the challenge leaves them frustrated and drowning in bitterness about the futility of their work. What we then see is that such burning and bitterness are being purged through sweetness. Again the cool drink story already holds the key to this aspect. While the so-called cool drink might be momentarily cooling and thirst quenching, the sugar induced through these drinks quickly asks for constant repetition and upping of the level of consumption.[32] It produces an addiction and dependence, which makes them even more susceptible to offerings by society and reduces their ability to withdraw from socially capturing relationships.

The other drink loaded with sugar—of the fermented kind—is alcohol: a common staple of many of the police officers I have worked with over the years. Alcohol, even more so however, creates the illusion of momentary relief from the stress which straddling the constant exposure entails. Yet it produces in itself aggression and overheating, and therefore even more so requires a constant repetition. It is this final sugary aspect, which we see taking shape in the failure of fitness and growing bellies and police officers' love of afterhours bars and raucous *braais*. And while the frequenting of bars leads to further entanglement in the city, and the braais and the eating together of meat enforces police fraternity, the issue of metabolism works itself yet even deeper into what emerges as a particular police culture. In a way then, the dyad of hot and cold relationships, and the impossibility of resolving these, produces and gets superimposed by a secondary dyad of bitterness and sweetness. This then becomes the actual reality of policing and the structuring principle for the culture of policing that leads us to understand policing less as a question of law enforcement than as a practice of difference, which finds expression in the 'tragedy of the belly'.

13

INSIDE THE POLICE STATIONS IN MAPUTO CITY

BETWEEN LEGALITY AND LEGITIMACY

Helene Maria Kyed

Maputo police these days are notorious for extreme levels of corruption. Street level extortion of cash in exchange for a night outside the police station cell is common. In fact most foreigners have experienced that even the lightest breach of traffic rules or the failure to carry original ID papers can cost dearly. This is backed by (often drunk) officers with AK-47s and threats of being locked up. There is a sense of anarchy and impunity among street-level cops. This is paralleled by high level corruption cases right into the offices of the former minister of the interior, and by extra juridical killings by police, especially since the mid-2000s. Yet there is also another side to policing in Maputo, one that is more benevolent and adjusted to citizens' demands. It is not necessarily more in line with the rule of law and human rights principles of the post-war transition, but it is more locally legitimate. This is the kind of policing one finds inside the police stations, in the *sala de permanancia* where the resolution of social cases and minor crimes takes place. In these spaces the state police act as court-like forums, deliberating cases and facilitating resolutions, with the majority of cases never ending in court. This is despite the fact that the district-level judicial court is in sight, situated just 150 meters from the police station across the *praza*. Instead of being forwarded there, the police settle the cases through reconciliatory and compensational justice practices akin to those applied among 'community justice' institutions. These practices are often combined with short-term detention in the cells as a form of tangible, immediate punishment. This takes place on a daily basis, and is the norm of how the police work at the stations, not only in the poor suburbs, but also in the very heart of the inner city.

Such everyday policing practices are, however, rendered invisible to foreign reformers and national policy makers, because: first, they are outside the mandate of state police and therefore not included into any official records or statistics forwarded up into the system; and second, they are not brutal enough or so excessively illegal that they make it into the reports on human rights violations and corruption (as for instance the visible extortions on the street, the very poor prison conditions and the extrajudicial killings). This is highly critical, I argue, not only because it prevents an in-depth understanding of 'how the police works'. Blindness to the informal, benevolent practices within police stations also misses out on the most common interaction between police and people. Importantly, it is in these interactions that police authority is negotiated and (re)constituted.

While police officers do at times receive *agradicimentos* (thank you gifts) when they help recuperate money or goods, their handling of minor crimes and social cases outside the law is also a legitimacy issue. They respond to citizen demands for immediate justice so as to gain popular acceptance. A 'good' police officer is someone with whom citizens can negotiate settlements 'on the spot'. Thus despite popular views of the police as brutal, corrupt and inadequate, which correspond with official definitions of illegal police behaviour, many citizens actually prefer a police officer who does not strictly follow the law.

The informalisation of state policing is, I suggest, informed by the distrust that people—not least the urban poor—have in the legal system and the judicial process, which is seen as slow, expensive, and inconsistent in punishing wrongdoers. Thus they turn to the law in so far as it allows them to call on the police to facilitate a resolution, but hardly ever are they interested in persisting with the law—that is, to have formal legal process opened. This is because the law itself does not give a sense of justice, as Hornberger and the Comaroffs also suggest for South Africa.[1] Significant here is to understand the informal practices of the police as part of the legally pluralistic contexts within which police officers work and live. Plurality consists of an intertwinement of divergent conceptions of justice and of multiple actors who have a stake in the authority to make order. Thus state police not only have to enforce a law that they themselves at times find at odds with popular (and often their own personal) conceptions of justice. They also both compete with and depend on networks of partly state and partly non-state order-making actors, including community courts, community police, human rights NGOs, private security companies, neighbourhood leaders, and, in the more peripheral urban zones, traditional chiefs. This is a plural landscape that is far from uniform across the city, with great variety in who *de facto* performs policing functions and handles disputes and crimes from *bairro* (neighbourhood) to *bairro*.² In such a landscape the police have the advantage of being formal law enforcers, backed by the state's *de jure* monopoly on violence, yet this power is only really effective and popularly legitimate when mediated by other forms of justice and applied as immediate punishment.

In this paper, I first address the everyday work of the police inside the police station, analysing how they resolve the cases that they receive on quite typical days. Next I reflect briefly on the reason behind the police's strong engagement in informal case handling, arguing that this was informed by the wider plural institutional context where police officers have to compete with community and private actors to an increasing degree.³ The paper is primarily based on my own fieldwork at Police Station Nine in 2010 and among community police in the surrounding area in 2009–10. Station Nine is situated in District Two, a high density and very heterogeneous suburban area, which lies on the frontier that separates the richer inner city from the poorer residential areas. It is also on this frontier that there are large informal markets, drug trading and many unemployed youth, all aspects used to explain why the crime rates are so high there. My case study is supplemented by the insights of Sara Araújo (Station Seven) and Christina Dela Widenmann (Station One and Two) who conducted fieldwork in the inner city in 2009 and 2004 respectively.⁴

Station Nine—everyday case handling

The mornings were the busiest at Station Nine. Long rows of people sat in the waiting room on the benches or the floor. They waited to either report a case directly to the police or to have their case heard after parties had been notified by the police or forwarded to them by one of the 'community' structures. Some were also there to collect goods or money in compensation for cases of theft, fraud or debt that previously had been settled 'informally' at the station. Case by case they were called into the *Sala de Permanencia*, where two officers, on twenty-four hour shifts, attended to them. When busy at the station, cases were also heard, in parallel, outside in the hallway, half standing, and half sitting. The officers were very efficient. They did not stop hearings until the waiting room was empty, which easily meant three to four hours of case handling, before they could break for tea. When an official process was opened case handling took the longest time, because all details had to be recorded on the typewriter. This was referred to as *abrir processo* (open a process). When stated, everyone knew that this meant a formal legal procedure, involving the judicial court, across the street. Yet this was the exception rather than the rule.

During my fieldwork on average one out of seven cases was recorded as a formal process, and not all of these ended with an actual court hearing. They were settled 'informally' by the police officers on duty. This was possible because many cases could be defined as 'social'. The label 'social' allowed police and complainants to find solutions outside of the judicial court, which was by far the preferred option. This involved some form of agreed upon compensation for loss of goods, damage, debt or physical injury, which also marked, materially, a reconciliation of the parties in question, who quite commonly were related in one way or another.

In this context 'social' did not just refer to family and neighbour disputes, however, which officially should be dealt with by one of the state recognised community court forums. Social also included thefts, debt, fraud, consumer/ service conflicts,[5] and domestic violence, which were by far the most common cases received at Station Nine in 2010. These kinds of cases could during the resolution process be shifted between the categories of criminal offence and social dispute, depending on the justice desires of the complainant and the police officers' responses. Being categorised as a crime allowed the officers to draw in the law in the form of a threat to *abrir processo* and put suspects in the cell. Yet this labelling was in the first instance used as a way to persuade the accused to admit guilt and to accept certain resolutions that were in fact informal or non-judicial, such as to compensate the victim. This reflected how officers intermittently referenced state law and powers as resources, rather than as the defining features of what was primarily a mediating and educational role in bringing the parties to agree. Indeed, when the officers heard a case they would first attempt to reach a consensual decision between the disputing parties, or between the perpetrator of a crime and the victim, similar to what has been observed in the community court forums.[6] Only if this failed was a process opened. This was commonly the decision of the police officer, as it was only on very rare occasions that the complainant asked immediately for a legal process. In fact it was more common for complainants to press for the opposite, such as in a case where a mechanic had failed to repair a car and taken it for a drive where the officer concluded: 'you used the fuel of his car, and did not do the job. This is fraud. It means prison'. Hereafter the complainant, in a nervous voice shouted, 'No, no, I do not want to have a process, I just want him to fix my car'.[7]

The resolution process was characterised by being informal, flexible and adaptable to the case. The officers were in general very patient with the parties, not least if they were elderly and women. They gave them time to explain and defend their case. Officers could also spend a long time patiently explaining to complainants the formal legal procedures of a case when the perpetrator is unknown and how they should deal with matters. Although the official language is Portuguese, in these situations people were allowed to express themselves in Shangana, and if not both, then at least one of the officers could speak this local dialect. During hearings the officers acted as third party. They allowed space for the parties to sort out their problem, giving their opinion on right and wrong, and intervening only at intervals to help them talk out their issue. As money discussions are part of most case resolutions, a key role of the officers was often to help the parties to calculate the amounts and agree on a payment date, which was made binding after signing a declaration under police observance. The officers' role as 'facilitator' and 'mediator', however, co-existed with reference to law and legal procedures, and with the officers intervening to stop the heated discussions by asking for discipline and order in the room.

Resolving cases informally, 'calling upon' state law and violence

After hearing each of the parties the officers typically began by stating 'once the case is here with us, it is a crime that should be treated as a crime. We shall open a process'. However, here after they immediately allowed for negotiations by asking the complainant: 'What is it that you want?', or 'Why is it that you have come here?' If the accused admitted guilt such as to a debt or theft the police's main role was to help facilitate the repayment and provide a stamped paper for writing the declaration. Repayment was overseen by the police, and its enforcement was backed by the threat of opening a formal process, if payment was not done on the set date. The following case is instructive of how officers facilitated compensational justice:

CASE 1: The complainant brought a case of assault and disappearance of a cell phone to the station. The officer passed a notification to the accused to appear for a hearing the next day at ten o'clock. The complainant passed on the notification to the accused although usually this is supposed to be done by the local *circulo*.[8] Yet it was a Sunday, so no local leader was found there. At the hearing the next day complainant first explains that they were a group of six men drinking together on Saturday night. He went to greet a woman, but then her boyfriend, the accused, hit him twice and also grabbed his pocket. Later he discovered that he had lost one of three cell phones from his pocket. The accused denied having beaten the complainant but agreed that he put his hands in his pocket. The officer continues the hearing in the following way:

Officer: Now, what is it that you want [asking the complainant]?

Complainant: I want him to pay the cell phone that I lost and that he tells me what it is he thinks that I did. What problem is it that he thinks we have with each other? Because after I left the *barraca* [open bar] a friend of mine came in there and got the same treatment.

Accused: There is no problem.

Officer: Concretely what is it that you exactly want? What do you want us to write? Are you friends?

Complainant: No we are not friends, we were just drinking together

Officer: Then it is just a matter of opening a process

Complainant: I just want payment for the cell phone

Accused: About the cell phone I don't know, but I will take the responsibility, but I can only pay at the end of next month, because this month I already had my salary and I used the money.

Complainant: When will I know the date?

Officer: Make a declaration now, marking the date and the hour that you shall meet here [at the station] to pay for the cell phone.

For a while they discuss the value of the phone, based on knowledge of the make and of how old it is. The officer allows them to discuss but then after about five minutes he intervenes and asks: 'So what is going on? Have you agreed now?' They have and then the officer helps them to write a declaration. Each of the parties signs it, and it is taken by the complainant. The officer explains that it cannot remain with the police (that is, because this is not an officially registered case), but should be presented to the police on the day of the payment. The officer then warns the accused that if he does not pay on that date a criminal process will be opened against him. He also tells, in a moralising and disciplinary voice, both of the parties off for drinking and causing such problems as this case. He then tells them to go.[9]

This case also brings to light how officers tried to find aspects of 'familiarity' as an element of defining the case as 'social'—that is, when the officer asks the complainant whether he is friends with the accused. Being friends, family or neighbours made it easier to argue for an informal resolution process. Although in this case the two parties were not 'friends', they had been 'drinking together'. What tickers the final decision to have it resolved outside court is however the justice desire of the complainant. This is less complicated when the accused admit guilt and agree to pay. Conversely, when the accused fails to admit guilt during the hearing or to pay on the agreed date it is rather uncomplicated for the police to move the case (back) into the category of crime.

It is exactly the police's capacity to switch between social and criminal 'registers' that make them particularly valuable in facilitating non-judicial resolutions. The way in which the cells, as a form of state violence, were used, is particularly instructive of this capacity.

While mostly in the form of a threat the cell was frequently used as the violent element in informal resolutions. This could be when the accused, prior to the time set for a hearing, was arrested and brought in to the station from the neighbourhoods by community or sector police. Then they would spend some hours or even the night in the cell until the hearing took place. The cell was also used as a mechanism to pressure the accused to pay his debt or compensation. This happened when the amount was very high or when the officer (often based on the opinion of the complainant) believed there would be a risk of the accused running away from his agreement. In one case the accused was kept in the cell an extra day before a formal process was opened, thus giving him a last chance to repay his debt of 12,000 meticais (US$400) with the help of family members.

Importantly, whether pledged guilty or not, the cell was never simply seen as detention (which in any case would be exaggerated in such minor cases as theft of cell phone or smaller debts) but also as a kind of 'immediate justice' in the sense of a 'tangible punishment'.[10] It also happened that the accused was put in the cell for a while, because compensation was not seen as 'sufficient punishment' by police and victims, yet without this being 'too big of a deal' to open a process. For instance in one case, the police arrested a person accused of stealing a cell phone. He spent a few hours in the cell before the hearing, where he reluctantly ended up admitting guilt. First he tried to say that it was his sister's cell phone that the officer had found on him. Angry that he had lied the officer said: 'Ok we give back the phone. But first this one is going to jail'. As if well aware that this was an immediate form of punishment that would not lead to a court process, the accused smiled to the victim, stating 'I will go to prison, get my punishment and then I will greet you in a couple of days'.

This was confirmed to us by the officer later when he said the victim should come back to collect the phone after a couple of days when 'the thief has learned that he has done wrong [that is, by spending time in the cell]'.[11]

Thus the cell does not signify a formal procedure. The detentions were just as much used for disciplinary or educational measures as an element of informal resolutions. It is a quick and resolute form of punishment that is outside the complicated judicial processes. As one officer stated when I asked what would likely happen to two young men accused of physical aggression:

> He [the victim] will take us there [to locate the suspects] and they will be intimidated to go to the station. And if they do not convince us they will spend some nights here in the cells of the station for them to learn. Yet of course this will all depend on the offended agreeing.[12]

So again the emphasis is on agreement between the parties, yet with the police facilitating such by using the instruments they have available. Detainees also 'learnt their lesson' by doing chores for the police, such as cleaning the private car of the Station Commander or sweeping the floors of the *sala de permanencia*, under strict supervision by an armed police officer.[13]

When the accused did not admit guilt the 'calling upon' state law and violence to make sure that resolutions are enforced and agreements are made was even more apparent. In these cases the officers played a more interventionist role, asking investigative questions and at times postponing the hearings to a later time if witnesses were needed to elaborate the case. In some cases, suspects are held in the cell even in the case of smaller thefts, as a mechanism to see if this will get them 'to talk'. Another strategy that the officers used was to begin to record the names and addresses of the victim and the accused. This gave the impression that a process was being opened. Promises of pardoning the accused if things were returned also worked. The following case is a good illustration of how these aspects are played out:

> CASE 2: Two men are present at the hearing. One claims that his wallet with important work-related documents has been stolen on the street, after being pushed. A cell phone has also disappeared. The other is accused and was caught by the victim himself who brought him to the police. At the crime scene he was seen with another guy. During the hearing the victim claims that the person he has caught is the thief, but the accused denies, indicating that it was the other guy present. The officer then intervenes.
>
> Officer: So Sir would you like to open a process against this man?
>
> Victim: Of course.
>
> Officer: What is your name [asking the victim]?

The victim answers, and the officer then asks for address, name of father, birthday, workplace, which he writes down on a blank piece of paper—not on the typewriter as in a formal process. The victim works for G4S—the big multinational private security company, and he is thirty-six years old.

Officer: What is your phone number [asking victim]?

Victim: The phone is the one that the youngsters robbed from me also, and the number is only on the phone, I do not remember it. I was also supposed to call my job to say I cannot come now, but also the number for the job is only on the phone.

The officer then asks all the details about the cell phone—its make and the price. He writes it down and then he turns to the accused.

Officer: Sir, it is better that you begin to speak because if you do not speak it is going to be very difficult for me to help you. It is better that you begin to say where the things of this man are for your own good.

Accused: I already said to him that I did not steal from him. The youngster who took his things ran away and I never saw him in my life.

Officer: Sir, you are making us lose a lot of time with simple things and we all have a lot of things to do here. Please help us find out where your friend is.

Victim: I could even forget all this and withdraw the case if you give me my documents, because I have a little bit of time to hand them in, and if they expire I will lose my job.

Officer: This man says that he is ready to even forget the time that you are robbing from him if you give him his documents.

Accused: Ok I will speak with him [the other person present at the crime scene] and we will give everything to him [the victim]. But you have to understand that I had nothing to do with the assault, I only know him [the other person present] from there [the crime scene].

Officer: You were lying for what reason? You have made us lose a lot of time for nothing and this man almost lost his job because of you. Do you think this is nice? Carlos [other police] take this one [the accused] and bring him back with the documents and his friend so that we can give them some *chambocos* [strokes with a baton].

The police officer, Carlos leaves with the accused.

Victim: Will they only be beaten?

Officer: No, I just said this so he would not be suspicious. They will stay here at least two nights to learn that they should not do what they did.

Along with the cell and threats of force, bureaucratic elements, such as stamps, notifications and declarations, as seen, also constituted a strong component of informal resolutions.

Managing the registers and the paper work

The use of state bureaucratic artefacts and the power of the written word gave weight to the enforcement of informal resolutions. To this end it was important to know how to navigate the registers and the paperwork. This is significant because as one officer told a woman whose case of a stolen wallet, to her great dismay, ended in court although the perpetrator had already paid back some of the money missing from the returned wallet: 'Once the official process is opened, it is with the courts and then we cannot go back [that is, to make the accused pay his instalments].' Thus the officers typically first wrote down the names and the issue at stake on blank pieces of paper (as seen in Case 2 above) and not in the register and on the typewriter. Declarations and notifications were also on blank pieces of paper, yet with the police stamp, giving them an aura of officialdom. When it came to detentions, officers also had to keep the books in the right order. Detainees with a formal process were registered with the secretariat and once in this register it was not easy to negotiate as such data would be forwarded up the system. This is probably what happened by mistake in the case of the woman who lost her wallet.[14] Those without a process were only in the book of detainees, and in this case, all the officer had to do was to write that he was released without evidence (whereas in practice the case may have been resolved informally with the parties, or the detainee may simply have been released, perhaps based on bribes from family or friends).[15] The result is that the vast majority of cases heard by police never enter into any crime statistics or police records, thus making invisible a very substantial part of the police's work. Whereas this evasion of official registration allows police to handle issues based on popular justice demands, it also means that the most benevolent and service-minded aspects of police work is not accounted for further up in the system.

The point is that the station constituted a space not for law enforcement, but for negotiations and for talking out disagreements. This was facilitated by the manoeuvring of classifications and registrations to allow for informality.[16] Here I have focused more on minor thefts, but it should be noted that similar procedures applied to the many cases of physical aggression, domestic violence, debt, service disputes, neighbourhood disputes and family quarrels over property, that I observed. Three further aspects need attention, namely the presence of citizen-educational talks by police, not least in social dispute cases, police compassion, and the strong role of citizen participation in case resolution.

Citizen education, compassion and participation

In particular in family disputes, open fights and fraud the police officers commonly told off, in a deep disciplinary voice, the parties, also as they are then 'set free' or left to sort out their issues at home. In doing so the officers referred to norms and customs in the home and from their rural backgrounds, not to law and legal procedures. As such the officers took very seriously their citizens-educative function, yet without invoking state officialdom. This was often combined with long moralising talks, and the use of metaphors, to emphasise the wrong that had been done, and also to show that the officer was familiar with a given problem. For instance in one case of a mechanic who failed to repair a car, the officer brought up his own experience with an unreliable mechanic. In another case about the loss of building materials, the officer told off the accused builder for being too old to steal from a young woman the age of his daughter, calling him 'irresponsible'.

While the officers in this way placed themselves in a position of higher moral standing, they also familiarised themselves with the parties, at times to the extent that they chit-chatted with them. Fewer officers kept their distance, and tolerated very little loud discussion. The majority allowed for intermissions of chaos as long as order was resumed when they asked for it. Here there were also age differences. Young boys were treated as inferior and told off in harsher tones than elderly ladies and men, who were spoken to with respect and empathy if they were victims. The latter was particularly evident in what were indeed very petty cases, often involving women who clearly were poor or in a very weak position. For instance in a debt case a single mother came crying to the police station for help. She owed 300 meticais (US$10) to another woman. As she could not repay, the woman had taken her phone as a pawn. The phone belonged to her uncle and now she was in trouble. The officer took very good care of the woman and promised to help her by notifying both the woman and the uncle. In another case the officer defended a Zimbabwean woman who had sold two bags of onions to two local women who had failed to pay the whole amount, missing fifty meticais (US$1.50). He spent a very long time listening to the case and gave the ladies a real telling off for mistreating foreigners, who come here to work hard. He made sure that the two women paid their debt.

The familiarisation and compassion of police officer with complainants and their 'petty' issues (at least from a formal legal perspective), certainly points to a different face of the police in Maputo, otherwise notorious for corruption, indifference to poor citizens' security needs, and brute force. Such cases as the two just mentioned also point to the fact that the benevolent practices of the police are not just about getting a supplement to their income. They were well aware that the Zimbabwean woman would not share her fifty meticais with them, for instance. Compassion and understanding of the complainant's life situation can mean setting aside the law, as we have already seen. That this could go as far as including illegal businesses is evident in Case 3.

CASE 3: It is one of these busy days where cases are handled in parallel in the hallway, where I join the older officer, Fernando to follow his work. A young man who has an illegal lending business in one of the neighbourhoods comes up to Fernando with an old man whom he has brought with him to the station. The old man has failed to repay his loan after the due day was long over time.

Fernando Police: Why have you come here?

Moneylender: I want you to help me make him pay his debt to me. It is 5000 meticais.

At this point another police officer points out to Fernando that such business is illegal, but he just laughs and lets Fernando go on with it.

Fernando police: It's not a problem. They have such businesses everywhere in the *bairros*...they are so important for the local economy, because people can loan money cheap. The bank won't give the poor people any loans really. So let's come to an agreement [again now speaking to the moneylender and the old man].

Moneylender: He has to pay by next week.

Old man: That is ok, I will get the money.

Fernando police: Now you go home and make sure to pay the money. You must do this in peace. Don't try to do anything illegal...to take the law into your own hands. Then instead you come back here if he does not pay.

After they had left, Fernando told me and his colleagues in his defence that such cases can end up in severe forms of criminal offence such as physical aggression (as Fernando also indicated to the two parties). Because of this the police should help resolve debts, even when this regards illegal moneylending businesses. He also explained that traditionally and still now in the rural areas, the chiefs help resolve such cases to avoid crimes.

Case 3 is a good example of how the local embeddedness of police officers takes precedence over 'the rule of law' in many situations. Commonly this was justified as a crime prevention measure, thus referring the informal resolutions 'back' to law and order issues. However, it is also clear that the police did this not just for the 'law', but also (and perhaps even more so) out of familiarity and compassion for the life situations that people found themselves in.

The familiarisation of police with complainants, and the negotiated exchanges between them, was also mirrored in the level of citizen participation in police work. This also reflects a capacity problem. There was an acceptance that citizens did a great deal of the 'ground investigative' work in resolving their own (usually minor) crimes. Victims of theft and assault were given the responsibility to identify the accused themselves. The police expected people to make use of the available local structures to identify and bring forward the accused. As such, the police station officers were seldom in the field themselves, unless on regular patrols or when criminal investigation police were involved in more severe crimes. It was also uncommon for police to arrest individuals out in the neighbourhoods after being called by victims. Either they did not have transport or fuel to do so, or they found that cases were 'too petty'. Thus victims very often apprehended the accused themselves, perhaps with the help of neighbours or family members if they could not convince them to come to the station. Where community police were strong, people could use them to arrest and bring forward the accused to the station, yet in these instances, the case would usually have involved the community police from the outset (as I return to below).

Notifications were also commonly handed over to the accused by the victims themselves. Also in cases of larger thefts of for instance car parts, electronics or expensive phones the police station officers usually asked the victims to search for the stolen goods themselves at the black market. In one case a mechanic was asked to go to a black market named Estrela to identify his goods and only return to the police for assistance to apprehend the dealer. When the mechanic found the goods, he waited for two days until a police car was available and they were able to recuperate a few of the goods that had not yet been sold. There were also cases where the police were used as a third party to verify whether a suspect was guilty, as the police were seen to put more pressure on a person to plead guilty. In such situations the case was never opened as a criminal process but remained a kind of 'police consultation'. This happened when a mechanic was taken to the police station by the owner of the garage where he worked on suspicion of stealing a diesel injection pump. After consultation at the police station the suspect was released as the garage owner wanted to investigate the case a bit further, that is, on his own, without the police, before asking the police to put the mechanic in the cell. During the hearing of this case the police officer allowed the garage owner to decide the fate of the suspect, asking him directly, at the end of the hearing: 'So sir [garage owner] do you want that we arrest this man or not?', and when he replied 'no' the officer responded 'OK that is fine, and true, sometimes arresting is not the right thing to do' (fieldnotes transcript, 21.05.2010). The mechanic thereafter sorted out the issue with the suspect himself, and was not seen again at the station. What this underlines is how the police are used as one resource, among others, to settle disagreements outside the law. In 'exchange', the police rely on citizens to help them get their job done. Citizens help in locating criminals and stolen goods, before matters are brought under police control.

This begs the question, why do the police go to all this trouble of handling cases 'outside of the law', without registering and accounting for it?

Informality is not always corruption

According to Dela Widenmann, the presence of weak courts and the large discretionary powers of the police in Mozambique have meant that more and more cases are resolved directly by the police at the station, who at the same time see this as an opportunity to supplement their low incomes.[17] There is no doubt that in some of the cases referenced above there could be money involved for the police. For instance in the case of the stolen wallet, which mistakenly ended in court, the victim gave 200 meticais (approx. 3 USD) as an *agradicimento* (thank you gift) after the wallet was recuperated. This underlined the woman's frustration with the case ending in court, as she had indeed followed the 'informal resolution procedures'. However, gift giving was far from a guarantee in cases resolved outside of court. In fact, it was more common in larger thefts and huge debts that did involve the formal legal process. As such, informality is not always corruption, and official processes may be even more prone to monetary exchanges and to ideas about corrupt officials. A good example of this is when perpetrators are set free due to lack of evidence for the courts to proceed with the case. This commonly gives way to popular accusations that the perpetrators have paid the police and the judge to avoid punishment.

When discussing issues of corruption and informality, it is significant to note that gift giving and monetary exchanges are entirely legitimate as long as it is an element of the 'culture of negotiation'. Thus when a case has been settled between the parties and the resolution has been agreed upon the payment to the victim and to the third party negotiator is accepted, if not outright expected. However, when money or gifts are used to avoid a settlement or a punishment then it is regarded as amoral and corrupt. As Dela Widenmann writes, corruption is not solely because of 'greedy' police officers, but also because of citizens as 'corrupters', offering bribes to avoid arrest, to be released from detention or to avoid paying a traffic fine, for instance. According to police officers, bribes are most frequent as a means to interrupt the case flow in the judicial system. Thus police are paid for noncompliance with official procedures.[18] At Station Nine this was also the case, but the significant point to highlight is that noncompliance with official procedures did not always follow a bribe. Instead, monetary exchanges happened after the informal agreement had been set and were not compulsory. This suggests, I argue, that informal settlements by police were not solely motivated by opportunities for police officers to supplement their low salaries. It was also driven by issues of police legitimacy, associated with citizens' mistrust in the formal system and its inability to secure the kinds of justice that people demanded.

The police officers understand perfectly well that when a person ends up with a formal legal process there is no guarantee that the victims will be compensated for their loss of material items or in the case of assaults for their hospital bills. People are not privately insured and therefore have no other choice but to cover losses by consulting the perpetrator or his/her kin. Police officers are themselves residents of the area and are not well-off people with private insurance. Understanding local economic needs is crucial, and the police gain legitimacy from it. The example of the illegal moneylender is instructive in this regard.

Yet there is also another aspect to police understandings of popular justice demands. This has to do with the change in official police rules and culture in accordance with post-war human rights legislation and training. In a rather radical tone, the Station Nine Commander, explained to me how complicated it had become to act according to the law, and that this had reduced the police's capacity to deal with the really bad criminals. After this she stated:

> The population knows better how to punish the criminals, so that they will not do it [the crime] again. Here at the police station we have to follow the law...it is very complicated today. We can just listen and register and then we have to involve PIC, the attorney and the court. It is much easier out there [in the neighbourhoods]. They can do more and punish as they like...they burn them [criminals] if necessary. You know we should reintroduce capital punishment here in Mozambique, so that we can see an end to all this crime.[19]

At the same time she strongly supported compensational justice, albeit while 'on tape' denying that it also took place within her own walls: 'We only send cases to PIC [criminal investigation police] or back to the population'. A core issue for the station commander was that the police could no longer officially respond to popular demands for immediate justice and tangible punishments. Doing so informally, as did the officers in the *sala de permanen-*

cia thus constituted a way for the police to continue these practices. Yet now this was only possible in petty crimes and social disputes, which would not reach the attention of the media and international organisations, or put police at risk against armed and dangerous criminals.

The officers were very skilled in reconciliatory forms of case resolution, yet also constantly complained that they had too many of such petty cases, instead of focusing on the big crimes and letting the community structures take care of the rest. Even so the officers I knew were very patient, allowing for discussions to take place and engaging in even very cumbersome calculations of debt and repayments. For instance, in one case a woman owed another woman 550 meticais (US$18) for a sack of beans, and the officer spent over an hour discussing the instalments with the parties. Although such informal resolutions seldom give the officers any money or for that matter any recognition by superiors, they are an important part of doing the police job in a way that gives the officers some measure of popular legitimacy and relevance in light of the bad reputations they generally have. This cannot, however, be seen in isolation from the competition they meet in the increasingly plural security landscape.

Competition from community and privatised policing—the significance of violence

Informal case handling by the police cannot be seen in isolation from the increased prevalence of alternative policing and dispute resolution bodies, some of which are partly state-recognised and some of which are entirely privatised. The criminalisation of tangible punishments by police, notably direct actions associated with the use of force and cells has opened a 'market' for more privatised forms of violent order-making, outside of the police station. This is also what the Station Commander in the quote above hinted at when she said that today the population are better at punishing the criminals.

As I have discussed extensively elsewhere, violence is, if not outrightly 'outsourced' to community policing groups, comprising of young civilian men, or to private security guards, then at least taken up by such groups and by congregations of disgruntled citizens in instances of mob-justice.[20] The common explanation for mob-justice is that the police do not have the capacity and willingness to provide protection of citizens from criminals in poor neighbourhoods. Yet if you ask the police officers, it is because the law now restricts them from meting out immediate tangible punishments, as they have to protect the rights of the suspects.

Popular demands for tangible punishments, and police ideas about the necessity of force to reduce crime, have not changed, but the law has. This is supported by my observation that sector police officers at neighbourhood level 'outsource' the physical beatings of suspects to community police members, inside the walls of the sector police office.[21] Thus the officer is in charge of the case handling, yet when it comes to the physical interventions, the community police take over until the suspects 'talk' or the victim is satisfied with the punishment. Conversely, the community police, in cases of severe crimes, would commonly beat the criminals with the baton before they were sent to the police for the initiation of a formal process. The explanation was: 'We do this to make sure, for the victim, that at least the thug has been given a punishment. You know because when they end at the station there is not really any guarantee'.[22] This quote captures well how *de facto* there is a sense that the state police have lost their capacity to punish the most serious criminals in the neighbourhoods to private and community actors. The latter can mete out tangible punishments under the veil of 'the population' where the real perpetrators of order-making violence are difficult to pinpoint in a legal process. If a police officer does the same, he risks being reported for human rights violations or other official procedural corrections. Moreover, although the police do constantly try to bring community and private policing actors under their umbrella, so that their efforts ultimately boost state police authority, this constantly fails. Instead there is a co-existence of collaboration with competition for clients and authority out in the neighbourhoods.[23] This has had the odd effect that the state police handle an ever increasing amount of social disputes and petty cases, which were otherwise intended exactly for their community-based counterparts. Yet because these operate outside of regulation, and official recognition, they are rather the ones who tend to punish the 'real' criminals.

This situation by no means implies that the police act within the law, as we have seen, or that they do not still use violence. Yet in the everyday case handling inside the police stations, at the lower level of the force, there is a clear tendency for police work to be pre-occupied by those petty cases that are just significant enough to give them some level of popular legitimacy. This challenges the common notion that the space for negotiation and informal settlements are higher the further away one is from the police station in the neighbourhoods among community or private actors. In practice, the *sala de permanencia* allowed for just as much negotiation 'out there' with the population. A core, and significant difference was that 'formal process' and the option of detention was much more likely at the police station. If the purpose was to see the perpetrator physically punished, chances were better with the private and community actors.

Conclusion

In 2006 Lalá and Francisco concluded of UNDP's failure to 'democratise the police' in post-war Mozambique that: 'The public perceive the PRM [Police of the Republic of Mozambique] to be inefficient and corrupt. It is widely seen as unable to cope with an increase in the rate and violence of crime, especially in and around the capital of Maputo'.[24] There is no doubt that this view to some extent still holds true. Yet to focus only on the negative sides of the police and simply see these as a failure of 'the rule of law' and 'human rights' to gain a footing, as most observers do, misses the point. In fact, in the eyes of most of the Maputo citizens and police that I spoke with, the presence, rather than the lack of human rights and rule of law, are the cause of police incapacity to deal adequately with criminals. Setting aside the law produces justice. Law and state power are resources in enforcing informal resolutions 'outside' the law, not defining features determining the outcomes.

Drawing on Walter Benjamin, Julia Hornberger describes popular policing interventions as characterised by 'forms of tangible punishment and a remaking of order not mediated through a distant law, but through the use of police power as immediate threat and law-making power'.[25] This is very much in line with what I have observed at Station Nine. A core difference is that, even if violence is a constitutive element of informal, popular policing—as a threat and a 'back-up'—it is not the main form of resolution as in the South African township interventions that Hornberger looks at. Rather it is the 'softer' justice principles of compensation and reconciliation, mediated by notions of familiarity or by efforts to bring out familiarity and closeness, which constitute the main components of everyday case handling. Conversely, if citizens want to really make sure that perpetrators are physically punished, there is greater chance of success with the community police, who today constitute a strong local, informal sovereign in the Maputo neighbourhoods. Constrained by human rights and rule of law principles, the police's popular legitimacy is more likely (re)constituted through their capacity for informal resolutions that are responsive to the justice desires of complainants than for their ability to exercise their sovereign power and represent the law. This is the other, invisible and yet very significant side of the Maputo police, who are otherwise notorious for their corruption and illegal extortions. Without taking seriously and bringing into the considerations of 'invisible' side of Maputo policing, there will be little prospect of creating a 'genuine' police service.

14

MONEY, MORALS AND LAW

THE LEGITIMACY OF POLICE TRAFFIC CHECKS
IN GHANA

Jan Beek

When discussing police traffic checks in West Africa, civilians and scholars alike contrast the handover of money with law enforcement. But police officers all over the world do not enforce the law automatically. Indeed Waddington argues that the main characteristic of the police is the 'under enforcement of the law' by exercising discretion.[1] Ghanaian police officers have a particular way of under enforcing the law. Instead of focussing on practices often subsumed as corruption, handing over money can be understood as part of an interplay between various police practices, and its meaning emerges from this situational interplay.

At 7am, four police officers with the traffic police (MTTU) stood along the main road to Akansa in uniform. Constable Moses was positioned in one lane, Constable Doris in the other. Both held old newspapers in their hands. The inspector and the lance corporal sat on a small bench at the roadside. I tried to position myself next to Moses. When a car, lorry, or *trotro* (van for public transport) approached, Constable Moses raised his hand signalling them to stop. Then, he walked to the car. He checked the Driver and Vehicle Licensing Authority (DVLA) sticker and the insurance one. He scrutinised the roadworthiness of the vehicle. Finally he asked for the driver's license. He placed the license on his newspaper and checked it solemnly. Sometimes he asked the driver to leave the vehicle with a short '*bra*' (Twi: come), and led him to the other side of the vehicle to talk to him. The driver then gave a 1 cedi note (approx. 0.20 USD) to the police officer, hidden in the license or in his hand. I rarely saw this as my view was obstructed either by the newspaper or the car. The police officer then stored the money in his newspaper. Some drivers seemed friendly and amused while others were obedient and fearful. The passengers, huddled together in the *trotros*, often muttered derogatory comments that Constable Moses ignored. One *trotro* had loose tyres, and Moses lectured the driver about road safety and made him tighten the bolts. However, most vehicles were in a blatant state of disrepair. *Trotros* were over-crowded, and passengers rode on the back of unloaded trucks. Yet Moses allowed all vehicles to drive on in the end. For *trotros* and other commercial vehicles, the whole process was regularly shortened to a brief handover of the driver's license.

Not all vehicles had to stop. When prompted to stop, some drivers flashed their lights, honked, or just stuck their fingers out the open window or onto the windscreen signalling that they had already been checked at another police checkpoint. Then Moses allowed them to drive on. Ordinarily, he did not bother checking expensive government-marked cars or those belonging to NGOs. There were two exceptions to this routine. On one occasion, he stopped an Audi, but the driver only had photocopies of his license. Moses told him that photocopies were invalid. But the passenger, an older man, started shouting: 'Are you suspecting us? He has a driver's license. You can look at us and see that we are no criminals.' Moses seemed reluctant to pursue this. Ultimately, he told them to drive on. Another person was driving an old Volvo even though his license had expired. A long discussion ensued. In the end, the police officers prepared a form for him, thereby initiating a court case. The driver took the notice and left without a word. Until that point, all other drivers had convinced the police officers to let them go.[2]

Contemporary police researchers have a non-normative approach and understand discretion as a necessary interpretation of the written law in the face of complex everyday encounters.[3] While the notion of interpretation is helpful, some practices of the interaction at traffic checks only remotely refer to the law.

Bittner argued earlier in the text police officers use the law as a resource, but that their discretionary decisions are based primarily on moral considerations.[4] In his work on Taiwanese police, Martin develops the idea that police officers' decisions are based not only on law, but also on other moral orders. Expanding this concept, the various practices that police officers employ—ranging from checking cars, lecturing drivers, to taking money—evoke different moral orders.[5] Weber writes that interactions are orientated towards the order that actors perceive as legitimate in the context.[6] But he adds that in many interactions various contradictory, valid orders coexist (*Nebeneinandergelten*). Anthropologists researching legal pluralism similarly argue that actors switch between various legal orders according to context.[7]

Police officers use distinct choreographies, tools, and vocabularies that can be classified in different registers. Each register evokes one of the moral orders. The concept register is used here to distinguish these various practices and the underlying legitimating moral orders. Police officers evoke the law by acting seriously, by appearing unapproachable, by using their forms, and by talking about offences. The law register guides their actions and sets a moral order that legitimates them. Police officers use the registers of violence, law, social order, sociability, and market. They select and deselect these in the course of the interaction, often in parallel.[8] Register is meant not in a technical sense but as a metaphor for the organ stops of a pipe organ that can be selectively turned on and off to set a timbre—a technique called registration.

However, civilians and police officers do not necessarily categorise particular police practices in the same register; what police officers see as acts of sociability may be seen by civilians as market orientated practices; certain moral orders complement and infuse each other, but others create inconsistencies or contradictions.[9] While registration allows police officers to act flexibly and tap multiple sources of legitimacy, they are deeply insecure about both the meaning and hierarchy of these opaque moral orders. Ghanaian civilians are anything but victims of police intervention at traffic checks. Moses' uncertain reaction when confronted by a driver suggests that civilians could use various countermoves leading to outcomes unintended by the police officers. Civilians resist police officers by using violence, evasion, connections, the media, witchcraft, or politics. The ambiguity of the evoked moral orders allows civilians (and some police officers) to read the traffic check differently, pointing out fundamental contradictions between some of these moral orders. Civilians criticised the meaning of the interaction and voiced their demands on how the relations between the registers should be structured. Legitimacy at traffic checks is fragile and situational. However, police officers and civilians attempt to uphold a distinct hierarchy of registers. The state, or rather stateness, can be understood not as any essential characteristic of the police, but as a quality that results from a distinct interplay of registers in everyday interactions.

The interplay of registers at traffic checks

Ghanaian police officers rarely use violence, and it is especially unlikely during traffic checks. However, they threaten to use violence by their performance, by ostentatiously displaying the tools of their trade. During traffic checks, police officers often have an AK-47 assault rifle slung across their backs or have knives attached to their belts. Police work is characterised by the police officers' 'potential to use legitimate force'.[10] The violence register evokes a moral order of authority, the common-sense notion that police officers are sanctioned to use violence when civilians are not. By controlling a situation, police officers successfully perform 'the monopoly on legitimate violence for the realisation of orders'.[11] Most of their speech acts such as the harsh language of commands and threats are contextualised by this potential to use violence and are therefore inherently coercive.[12] Ghanaian police officers display their potential to use violence more overtly than police officers in other countries. But this indicates their insecurity rather than their dominance in the interaction. With the implied threat, police officers partially select the violence register at the beginning of the interaction sequence. The register remains selected parallel to their other approaches. Potential violence underlies all other practices. In Waddington's words, this potential 'imbues everything that the police do'.[13]

Police officers use the law by meticulously checking the car and its paperwork. The traffic laws in Ghana comprise thirteen distinct legal documents (the Road Traffic Ordinance from 1952, eight legal instruments, and four acts of parliament), which altogether list over 300 road traffic offences. Police officers could look at any random vehicle and then list a dozen offences, as hardly any vehicle complies with all traffic laws. Constable Arday explained: 'Every car has an offence on it. You just have to search for it.'[14] Police officers are not allowed to issue on the spot fines and are legally required to send the case to court. The local court will then issue a fixed fine, between 300 and 600 cedis (approx. 145 € and 290 €).[15] A MTTU police officer explained: 'The power of a police officer is his pen.' He thereby meant that he could always use his forms to end all discussions with drivers. The law register evokes a moral order distinct from the others, as it derives mainly from written texts. Both police officers and civilians therefore perceive this moral order as fixed and uncompromising. Police officers repeatedly quote the traffic offence and mention the court. Like violence, the law register remains partially selected; as Luhmann writes, the law remains citable in the background, ready to be used as a resource, if required.[16] The police officer's decision to enforce the law derives not just from the written text but takes other considerations into account.

If police officers in West Africa always enforced the law, they would paralyze the transport of goods and people.[17] Additionally, they would overburden the courts.[18] Enforcing the law is a last resort, not only in Ghana but also for police officers everywhere.[19] Still, the law remains highly relevant during the whole interaction. If the police officers do not discover any offence, they will let the car pass eventually. Thereby, the law codetermines all police officers' practices. Like violence, the law imbues everything police officers do.

But police officers refer not only to written law as legitimation for their actions. Instead, they lectured civilians constantly, ordered them to do maintenance on their vehicles—as in the narrated traffic check—or shouted at drivers that they were endangering themselves and others by not adhering to traffic laws. Paperman writes that such 'moral lessons' are hugely important for police officers because such lecturing allows them to legitimize their actions. Ghanaian police officers call this part of their job 'education'.[20] 'They [civilians] are like children, especially the ones from the villages', Constable Moses explained. The education metaphor refers to rules of conduct that everybody should adhere to and represents police officers as arbiters of this order. By lecturing, police officers select the social order register, pointing to the morals that in their view underpin the written laws. Both moral orders are infused with each other. Yet by emphasising social order and not explicitly referring to written law, they can adapt to situational exigencies and local moral discourses.

In contrast to law, social order is uncodified and ambiguous. The social order register allows for the inclusion of new morals and varying local social orders.[21] In their own words, police officers 'adjust' to the local conditions or perform 'policing in context'. In rural areas, they ignore overloading and passengers riding on trucks. Thus, not only do they act according to the economic situation, but also because urban areas are perceived to be more 'enlightened'. Furthermore, they applied the law if the driver defied them. Police officers' discretionary decisions are not based on the type or severity of the traffic offence, but on the way civilians reacted to the police officers' self-representation as arbiters of social order.

While police officers selected the mentioned registers, they were prepared to deselect them—to change the tone of the interaction. Lance Corporal Christian explained the interplay of the various approaches: 'Every car has an offence. We just want to do the right thing. They make up their mind and give you the money. I wouldn't call it a bribe. It is just a dash [British English: gift]. It's not perfect.' He refers to both the law ('offence') and social order ('right thing') registers, and in his depiction the civilian then offers a gift. After explaining the situation, police officers at traffic checks regularly asked drivers: 'What do you say?' Police officers thereby prompted them to decide how to resolve the situation. Police officers rarely asked for anything. Occasionally they said they were hungry or thirsty or asked civilians to 'find something for us' (in Twi: *Fabibi bra*). In their own words, they called these practices to *chop* money (in Twi: *di sika*; in British English: eat money) or 'to collect'.[22] All these expressions belong to the idiom of everyday sociability, in contrast to the vocabulary used as part of the law and social order registers. The sociability register enables police officers to 'consider' civilians, as they put it. It allows all involved parties to seek a 'compromise' in the face of legal regulations and social expectations. This may entail the exchange of personal gifts. But by selecting the sociability register, police officers became entangled in mutual considerations. Taxi and *trotro* drivers occasionally lamented that their business had been bad that day, and police officers then let them pass. If private vehicles owned by affluent Ghanaians broke any traffic laws, those civilians were expected to pay a higher amount, between 20 and 40 cedis (approx. 10 € and 20 €). While in Akansa, 1 cedi was the common amount of a *dash* for a commercial vehicle, the amount in Accra was often 2 cedis, reflecting the regional economic situation. The sociability register is structured by local concepts of what people consider appropriate and reasonable.[23]

As Lance Corporal Christian explained, resolving the situation like this is not 'perfect'. Police officers feel that the law and social order registers should always be upheld. Civilians often describe the handover of money as a *dash* or 'gift' rather than a bribe or corruption.[24] Concerning police officers in India, Jauregui writes that both sides do not inevitably see such dealings as corruption; instead they sometimes see it as necessary and effective improvisation.[25] Actors routinely hold and orientate their practices towards contradictory beliefs and make allowances for several moral orders. This leads to inconsistencies, but not necessarily to the invalidation of law or social order. Similarly, religious requirements are circumvented without necessarily subverting them.[26] When talking about the handover of money, police officers often muttered, 'We are all human beings', meaning that both parties to the interaction face financial difficulties and have to make ends meet. Civilians are keen to avoid the time and costs of a court case. Therefore, they want to circumvent the rules and criticise police officers that refuse to accommodate them.

The sociability register is similar to local forms of gifting and other specific social norms.[27] There are pre-colonial, colonial and postcolonial histories of such practices.[28] But it would be misleading to suggest that these practices derive from any West African culture. Instead, these practices are closely adapted to Ghanaian corruption laws. According to these laws, the prosecution must prove that the exchange 'smacks of a contract'.[29] By performing the exchange according to mutual sociability, police officers try to protect themselves from legal repercussions. Furthermore, Ghanaian law differentiates between two offences: corruption is a misdemeanour for both the official and the civilian; extortion is a second-degree felony for the official only; the latter is assumed if the official openly demands money.[30] If police officers do not openly demand money, the handover of money becomes a tacit agreement—it becomes corruption, not extortion. By making a complaint, a civilian would then also endanger himself, because both parties are guilty in corruption cases. Not all Ghanaian police officers know the relevant sections of the Criminal Offences Act, but they teach each other the main principles. Chief-Inspector Richard explained: 'Police officers who demand money do not know how to do it right. An educated detective like me, who knows how to talk, will just tell you go and come, and then the civilian knows he has to pay.' Practices of the sociability register are clearly adapted to legal regulations and cannot sufficiently be described as informal or cultural. Laws limit these practices insofar as they prevent those practices from becoming explicit business transactions. Even the way money is handed over is co-determined—or imbued by—law.

Yet often civilians do not perceive such practices as guided by sociability. They say these practices are orientated towards the market register. Ghanaians employ the same terms (*dash*, 'favour') and similar postures at market places. Clark describes Ghanaian food traders' bargaining practices and writes that emotional appeals to hunger and lifelong friendship are used to receive a *dash* as an added gift to the bargain.[31] Police officers at traffic checks do not bargain openly. But if the sum offered by the civilian is not to their liking, they simply ignore drivers to indicate their displeasure and continue checking other cars. Every time the civilian approaches the officer, the civilian raises the sum offered. Therefore, civilians may perceive these practices as strategic moves in a ploy guided by the market register. The practices of the sociability register and the market register are not clearly differentiated. This ambiguity allows both sides to categorise this phase of the traffic check as they please.

Still, the market register is a moral order. It has an instrumental dimension, but it is also about trust and reasonableness. Police officers accept that there are rules and limits for payments. If drivers signalled that they have already paid at another traffic check, police officers let their cars pass. Drivers thus only have to pay once per day.[32] As police officers were familiar with the routes of commercial vehicles, they could gauge whether the driver had already paid. But this practice is based on some degree of mutual trust. The commercial drivers trust the police officers to honour the tacit agreement. In turn, police officers trust the drivers not to feign a previous check. Additionally, the amounts drivers have to pay again show that payments are imbedded in legal provisions. The amount drivers have to pay depends on the seriousness of the offence. 'The higher the offence the more you pay,' explained Detective Lance Corporal Kpodo. The fines issued by the court sets the upper limit of the demanded amounts. The circuit court judge in Akansa explained in an interview that he always chooses the lowest possible fine in a bid to lower the amount that police officers could earn at traffic checks. Ultimately, negotiations could fail—as happened during the last check in the narrated episode— and police officers then reselected the law register.

Countering police registers

Police officers are not necessarily the dominant actors in the interaction sequence. Ghanaian civilians can employ several practices to counter police officers. In the course of traffic checks, civilians also set the tone. This causes uncertainty for police officers. Martin argues that Taiwanese police officers are constantly adapting their intervention to avoid such counterstrategies.[33] Similar to violence and law, counterstrategies are primarily potential practices. But this potential shapes all interactions because police officers have to anticipate responses. Civilians select one of several responses, not unlike the selection of approaches by police officers. Which response civilians select depends both on situational conditions and on the resources at their disposal, like their capacity to use violence, their connections, and others. Bierschenk understands violence, time, money, social relations, supernatural powers and status as currencies that clients use complementarily to influence the official process.[34] At Ghanaian traffic checks, civilians' responses can be categorised as violence, evasion, connections, media, *juju* and politics.[35]

Ghanaian police officers always have to expect civilians to use violence. This is similar to the potential use of the violence register by police officers. During fieldwork in Akansa, police officers stopped a driver at the barrier. But, as Lance Corporal Christian told me, 'The civilians didn't allow the policemen to search them'. Instead, the driver broke through the barrier.[36] The police officers chased the car to the next filling station. But there some bystanders defended the driver. The police officers fired some warning shots into the air and then retreated. Such confrontations were a monthly occurrence in police stations all across Ghana.[37] Civilians could 'not allow' police actions because of the insecurities police officers face when using violence. AK-47 assault rifles are not suitable for overpowering resistance. In addition, Ghanaian police officers were not sufficiently trained to use assault rifles or other forms of violence. Police officers are unsure how violent acts will be assessed in legal or popular discourse, and they are afraid of civilians physically overpowering them.[38] Detective Constable Doris commented sarcastically: 'Police officers only carry their weapons for fun. If you don't want to get a problem, you don't shoot.' Police officers rarely pursue civilians who challenge them and avoid any further conflict. Civilians in Ghana have therefore learnt that using violence against police officers is an effective response.[39]

Police officers everywhere have to deal with bystanders and their possible reactions to police interventions. While Ghanaian police officers often explain their actions loudly—selecting the social order register—bystanders do not necessarily accept their justifications. To avoid bystanders, police officers position themselves outside towns, avoid interventions in areas with a high likelihood of confrontations, and conduct their interventions as swift hit-and-run actions. 'You have to get out, arrest the *moto*, and drive back', explained Moses. Confrontations can escalate. Crowds of angry civilians killed three police officers on duty between 1990 and 2000.[40] Any overt challenge to police officers, especially by bystanders, subverts the legitimacy of police intervention. Successful police work is about avoiding overt coercion.[41]

Usually drivers used evasion to counter police traffic checks. Due to their monetary interests, police officers are interested in keeping cases at their level. They do not want to pass it on to the courts or to the appropriate police department. Therefore, civilians often waited for hours on end until police officers just gave up and let them pass. A civilian stated, 'They just waste your time'. While such an approach thwarts the police officer's expectation of a money handover, it entails an outward acceptance of the police's legitimacy. One civilian explained: 'You don't argue. You say: [putting his hand over his head to mime a beseeching gesture] "Oh, master, I'm sorry. What did I do wrong?" If you show them respect, you can work something out.' Publicly acknowledging the supremacy of the police officers' moral orders and spending time was often enough to circumvent handing over money.[42]

Civilians can openly defy police interventions, if they have connections to politicians, high-ranking police officers, or other officials.[43] Civilians at traffic checks regularly take out their mobile phones, call a number, and give the phone to the police officers. The person on the phone will claim to be a senior police officer or politician and order the police officer to let the civilian pass. The anonymous calls from people claiming to be a 'big man' are often enough to deter police officers, even if they cannot confirm the caller's identity. If the policemen do not comply with the demand of a real senior officer, he or she can hinder their promotion or punish them otherwise. Police officers have no access to official guidelines, which allow their superiors to punish even regular actions. Due to the unclear chain of command, any senior officer, regardless of his competence or location, can issue such commands. Because of the influence of politicians on senior officers, politicians can also order police officers to let drivers pass.[44]

Civilians use such connections all the time. This causes constant insecurity for police officers doing their everyday work on the street. The police have a saying that reflects the immunity of certain civilians: 'You cannot eat the meat of every vulture.' The potential of such counteractions has a profound, unsettling effect on the way police officers perform traffic checks. In most situations, Ghanaian police officers do not lecture confidently and do not read the law aloud. Instead, they are nervous and even argue among themselves. Police officers everywhere have to deal with complaints by civilians.[45] But Ghanaian police officers cannot rely on written regulations and police solidarity to the same degree as police officers in the global North. They lack the organisational framework that enables other police officers to control the interaction as dominant actors. While democratisation since the 1990s has improved the civilians' ability to counter police officers, no accessible and applicable legal framework for police work has counterbalanced this loss of authority.

When civilians use their connections, they openly subvert the police officers' social order register. Civilians also challenge the law register, daring police officers to cite the relevant traffic law. Police officers evoke a social order that is based on equality before the law and impartiality. Yet on the roads, they over enforce the law towards commercial drivers. Police officers react to the use of connections by largely avoiding private cars and focusing on commercial vehicles. They thereby reproduce social inequalities. Police officers thus inadvertently reinforce competing moral orders—the notion that some people are largely immune to the law. Some police officers questioned this and complained that 'justice is only for the rich' (Constable Gabriel).[46] Early police researchers understood the reproduction of social inequality as resulting from the police officers' power to label behaviour and practices.[47] However in Ghana the over-enforcement of the law towards specific groups emerges from the limits of police discretion and autonomy.

Even when civilians are unable to counter the police officers' requests during traffic checks, they can still shame and threaten police officers afterwards. In the wake of democratisation in the 1990s, many local radio stations have emerged. Radio listeners can call anonymously to complain about the police, often naming police officers. Police officers listen to these broadcasts anxiously, and are afraid that their names will be announced.[48] Such gossip reflects moral orders, reinforcing specific norms that are described as violated, and function as a social sanction.[49] Furthermore, such complaints can lead to internal punishments. Senior Officer Ndago stated: 'They [politicians or journalists] come to me, and when they want to annoy me they speak of "lack of supervision".' Then the allegation travelled down the chain of command until a junior rank received some form of disciplinary punishment.[50] Furthermore, civilians supposedly use religious practices to punish police officers that have extorted money. Police officers interpreted several deadly accidents of colleagues as *juju* attacks by civilians who had been abused by these colleagues. Police officers fear such retributions, and thus avoid antagonising civilians.

Up to this point, the described counterstrategies of civilians were mostly situational. In a sense, such situational responses to traffic checks are political. Yet civilians also attempt to impede traffic checks altogether, by more explicit attempts to change the landscape of traffic checks in Ghana. Chatterjee calls acts 'popular politics' that limit the possible practices by officials.[51] Public education in Ghana has subtly changed the public perception of police practices. The 'new generation', as police officers called them, more readily complained about perceived unfair treatment. Public outrage over traffic checks and barriers has prompted politicians to use their connections to senior police officers to limit the number of barriers and MTTU traffic checks. Since 2000, the number of barriers and traffic checks has gradually declined.[52] Three months before the 2008 election, the government managed to suspend nearly all traffic checks as a 'service' to the electorate. According to a regional commander, there was no new official policy, just a phone call from one of the ministers to abolish all barriers. Immediately after the 2008 election, police officers re-established traffic checks. Police officers in the narrated traffic check held the issue of the newspaper with the election results in their hands.[53] But political attempts to curtail traffic checks continued after the election. In 2009, the inspector general of police (IGP) circulated new guidelines. Accordingly, each *moto* check has to be authorised weekly by the deputy regional commander; the attached police officers have to wear nametags; taking any kind of gift is forbidden. These new guidelines were only partially implemented because the communication system between District and Regional Headquarters did not allow weekly authorisations, and because the administration had never issued any nametags. However, the police management attempted to limit the overt handover of money at traffic checks through these regulations. As senior officers in headquarters only profit indirectly from the money collected on the roads, they are not keen on protecting this practice. However, senior officers are reluctant to abolish barriers outright because they impede smuggling of illegal arms and narcotics. Additionally, senior officers are not sure that such orders would be obeyed. In January 2010, the IGP sent police officers from the Professional Intelligence and Professional Standards Bureau (PIBS) to arrest four MTTU police officers doing a traffic check. On the grounds that 196 cedis (approx. 100 €) had been found in their hands, they were indicted for extortion.[54] This was the first time since the 1990s that police headquarters had arrested MTTU officers so publicly.[55] Olivier de Sardan writes that the condemnation of corruption seldom leads to sanctioning or legal repercussions.[56] However, this has changed slightly concerning traffic checks in Ghana. While these arrests were one-off events, the anticipation of such and other responses has begun to fundamentally change police officers' practices at traffic checks.

Perceptions of the interplay among registers

The previous description of the interplay of registers at traffic checks followed mainly the police officers' perceptions.[57] Ghanaian police officers often lamented that 'Civilians don't understand', or that 'Their understanding is far'. Yet when listening to civilians, it became clear that they elaborately assessed everyday police practices. They simply did not share the police officers' understanding of what rationalities underlie police work. Research on the perception of police practices focuses on its legitimacy. Tyler and others define legitimacy in contrast to compliance based on the threat of violence or the promise of material benefits; they understand legitimacy as deriving from the general perception of state organisations and their adherence to law based procedures, i.e. procedural justice.[58] Using this general definition is difficult in an ethnographic approach. A mixture of convention, material interests, fears, and moral considerations motivates everyday compliance. Additionally, the law is not the only source of legitimacy. Applying the law without regard for other moral considerations is not necessarily deemed legitimate in Ghana. Overall, civilians did not ascribe legitimacy generally, but perceived it as highly situational and context based. Ghanaians detested traffic checks at barriers when asked about the police. But when asked about armed robberies, they praised barriers as an appropriate method of limiting the movements of armed robbers. According to Weber, it is only a possibility or chance that civilians perceive and treat officials' practices as legitimate.[59] Police researchers write that the legitimacy of the police everywhere is inherently fragile and has to be perpetually established in everyday encounters.[60] For an ethnographic approach, it is useful to develop how actors draw on various sources of legitimacy in their everyday practices, to ask what type of moral orders they evoke, and to study how such attempts are perceived and contested.[61]

Civilians describe traffic checks contrapuntally to police officers' perceptions, highlighting the handover of money. In Ghana, traffic checks have become an allegory for corruption. In a schoolbook, corruption was explained as follows, '[P]olicemen collect money without checking papers'.[62] Ghanaian movies likewise portray police officers as money-grabbing illiterates. Civilians everywhere use stereotypes to conceptualise police officers,[63] and in Ghana negative stereotypes are prevalent. Research on the Ghanaian police often reproduces this focus on corruption.[64] The fragile legitimacy of traffic checks is evident. But beyond the general condemnation of corruption, civilians' criticism of everyday traffic checks gives insight into their perceptions of what moral orders should guide police interactions.

Civilians did not criticise the use of the law. Instead, they complain that police officers routinely ignore it. In the shortened interactions with commercial drivers, police officers do not evoke the law in any meaningful way. By dispensing with the checking process and rarely sending cases to court, police officers lose the legitimacy the law provides. The actions of officials become 'counterfeit rituals', if they only use soft forms of enforcement.[65] Yet whether civilians perceive a traffic check as official police work, as legitimate based on law, depends largely on how police officers managed to relate the law register to other registers.

Despite the condemnation of police corruption in public discourse, civilians show sympathy with police officers and their economic needs when narrating specific interactions with them: 'They are also human beings, they have wives and children', a civilian declared after narrating a traffic check. Some civilians shared the police officers' perceptions of the handover of money as a sociable act in the face of the law. 'I scratch your back and you mine', a *trotro* driver commented. Boubacar, a local businessman, saw police officers' attempts to obtain additional income as understandable: 'It is necessary to survive. A policeman cannot live like a poor farmer. He has to dress well, needs a car, electronic equipment...to work for patriotism does not fill your belly. If you are poor when you retire, people will laugh about you.' According to Boubacar, taking money does not necessarily mean that a police officer is 'greedy'. In private conversations, Ghanaians distinguished very subtly between the various ways police officers obtain money. Few argued against tips to police officers after the official interaction had been concluded.

But Boubacar lamented repeatedly that, 'They [police officers] like money too much'. Likewise, other civilians did not condemn the handover of money inadvertently. Yet they said there was 'too much corruption' in the police. Even when perceiving the handover of money as a sociable act, civilians had different ideas what amount is reasonable and appropriate.[66] However, because the sociability and market registers are not clearly differentiated, this criticism can become more fundamental. 'Police are only after money', was a complaint often uttered by civilians.[67] By stating that the market register is the sole deciding one, displacing all other rationalities, this criticism reveals that the attempt to obtain money may subvert the legitimacy provided by the law and social order registers. The suspicion that monetary interests are involved undermines any other explanations for the police officers' decisions.[68] For civilians the police ceased to be an organisation that has the quality of stateness in these situations. They then describe the police differently. 'They do not patrol. They are doing their business', a neighbour complained. A circuit court judge commented that the police station looks 'like a market'. Most civilians do not complain that monetary interests and market rationality were part of the interplay of police registers. Yet in their perception, the market register displaces all others and thereby annuls the legitimacy provided by these.

In these moments of criticism, the registers and the evoked moral orders become clearly demarcated, revealing the emic notions underpinning them. Thus the contradictions between some of the evoked moral orders become apparent. These inconsistencies are not only problematic for the outward legitimacy, but also for the self-legitimacy of the police officers.[69] Violating the belief in the law publicly is inconsistent with their self-perception that relies on them being legitimated by laws and regulations. While civilians usually focus on the inconsistencies between the market and law registers, they also criticise the threat of violence, because it is directed against them rather than criminals. By pointing out that police officers always select the violence register in parallel, civilians draw attention to the unequal power structures in the interactions. Luhmann writes about the paradox of using negative sanctions; these have to be hinted at but become ineffective when apparent.[70] By emphasising the coercive elements, civilians subvert police legitimacy. As they disentangle the distinct registers, compliance is portrayed as resulting from a physical threat, not from the law or social order registers.

Police work everywhere can be conceptualised as an interplay of registers, with the law being only one of them. Practices such as friendly exchanges and politeness, which are described as the sociability register here, are another essential part of the repertoire. Switching from the law register gives civilians social reasons to conform and veils the inherent threats.[71] Luhmann writes that the judicial regulation is insufficient for dealing with the complexities at the interface of administration and clients and that therefore 'small additions of illegality' become necessary.[72] Ghanaian civilians did not criticise that police officers switched between various legitimating moral orders. Yet they criticised that the interplay of registers was dominated by market rationality and that the potential to use violence was so blatantly displayed. While Martin uses different categories, one of his main arguments is that seeking a compromise necessitates obscurity. '[K]eeping contradictions in order *requires* obscurity, a space in which conflicted "principles" can be compromised without causing further repercussion.'[73] Increasingly, this need for concealment is becoming important for Ghanaian police work.

Civilians all know that money changes hands at traffic checks. The fact that police officers use old newspapers to veil the handover of money is the worst kept secret in Ghana. But police officers are actually very good at hiding these exchanges. Over the course of several weeks, I saw the handover of money only two or three times. Police officers demand that civilians keep the handover of money secret, and become really angry if civilians hand money over visibly. Instead of unveiling the hidden exchanges and explaining the interaction in economic terms, it is perhaps more useful to ask why police officers bother to hide practices that are so obvious to all involved. According to this view, the secret of traffic checks is not money but legitimacy. Weber uses the term 'belief in legitimacy' (*Legitimitätsglaube*), and adds that this belief has to be raised and cultivated in accordance with the type of domination.[74] The established routines have become less and less sufficient because of civilians' varied responses and the new attitudes of senior officers. Accordingly, veiling the handover of money and lecturing about road safety can be seen as the police officers' attempt to maintain the belief that their practices are orientated towards law, social order, and sociability.[75]

Eckert writes that civilians in India expect state officials to follow written laws.[76] This is largely similar in Ghana, but civilians are more interested in knowing that the laws are not explicitly violated; or rather, civilians wish that registers were clearly distinguished. Salla, a teacher, said he knew a 'good policeman' who did not take money at the barrier. When the police officer finds a fault during his first traffic check, Salla explained, this policeman tells the civilian to bring his documents in order or to repair the vehicle. If this has not been done by their next encounter, he sends him to court. But the police officer would receive the civilian in his house to reach a compromise—never asking for gifts, but accepting them gratefully when offered. Similarly, a detective inspector of the CID complained that MTTU police officers collect money 'visibly'. 'Have you ever seen us handling money?', he asked. If he were attached to barrier duties, he would just send people to court. 'When they come to your house later, nobody will see it.' According to both the civilian and the inspector, the visibility, not the handover of money in itself, is the main problem. By separating the spaces in which the various moral orders are evoked, the inconsistency is less obvious. In the house, the interaction is more clearly informed by sociability. This also means that police officers can act more confidently during the interaction on the street. They then lecture and evoke the law without immediately suggesting a way out. In private conversations, senior officers likewise do not condemn the handover of money per se. Senior Officer Ndago elaborated that his assessment of corruption depended on 'the mood and the manner in which it is done'; in other words, on the specific way money is demanded and handed over. His guidelines to his officers were easy: 'If you do it, do it smart please.' They should not take money from everyone, they should conceal the handover, and they should be friendly. Smart, writing on corruption in China, argues that the handover of money is an 'art';[77] the relationship has to be presented as the primary concern, and instrumental reasons have to be presented as secondary. Handelman describes officials that switch roles in an interaction but have to convince the client that these roles are connected in a logical and beneficial way.[78] Following the register model, registration is the art of selecting and deselecting the guiding moral orders needed to resolve the situation without overtly subverting law or social order.

Conclusion

In police research, discretion has not been described as an art but as structured by informal rules: Ericson describes 'recipe rules' that are based on police culture;[79] Van Maanen writes about 'interpretative rules' that are based on the police officers' categorisation of civilians;[80] Waddington describes highly situational and contextualised 'working rules'.[81] Precisely because police practices in Ghana are so highly situational and because police officers are confronted with radical insecurities, the notion of rules does not really fit.[82] Ghanaian police officers have their own terminology. Constable Okletey stated: 'As a police officer, you have to use your number six, your discretion. You have five senses, but when you approach an unknown situation you have to rely on a sixth sense, your brains'. Police officers describe this 'number six' as the opposite of rule-based behaviour. In the face of immense insecurities and opaque moral orders at traffic checks, flexibility and adaptability to the situation are seen as key competencies. Police officers' practices are still part of organisational routines. In research on street-level bureaucrats, Lipsky argued that bureaucrats develop routines to reduce complexity, to control clients, and to organise limited resources.[83] Registers are such routines. The term registration, implying an art or craft, reflects the subtle complexities and verbal competence that police officers need to select and use them.[84] Selecting various registers in parallel is necessary to counter possible undesired civilian responses. But police officers have to avoid the dissonances that are created, if they select the registers market or violence mingled with other registers.

Many scholars of the African state apparatus argue that it has become enmeshed in market logic and new forms of sovereignty. At first glance, Ghanaian traffic checks seem to be another instance of this transformation. However, an analysis of everyday interactions shows that stateness is contrasted with the market and still highly relevant. This becomes apparent when stateness is analysed as emerging from interactions, not as a substantial essence of the police organisation or its members. Police officers tap several sources of legitimacy by their practices, evoking bureaucratic order and social order. According to Weber, the state is a social relationship that exists only insofar as mutual specific practices are realised.[85] Stateness emerges when police officers skilfully employ certain registers while maintaining a hierarchical interplay of the evoked moral orders and successfully concealing the inherent inconsistencies.

15

SOFT LAW ENFORCEMENT IN THE NIGERIEN GENDARMERIE

HOW A CASE IS BORN

Mirco Göpfert

Police work is often described as oscillating between law enforcement and peacekeeping, work by the book or inspired by practical norms depending on the police officers' discretionary use of the law. Egon Bittner, one of the first and most relevant social science police scholars, argued that police officers actually do enforce criminal law 'with the frequency located somewhere between virtually never and very rarely'.[1] But what about when they do?

Enforcing the law means working on a case; this is the same for the gendarmes in Niger. But several steps had to be taken before gendarmes could work a case. In the beginning, there needed to be, as Egon Bittner famously put it, 'something-that-ought-not-to-be-happening-and-about-which-somebody-had-better-do-something-now'.[2] '*Un événement s'est produit*'—'an event occurred'—was how the gendarmes put it. Then gendarmes needed to gain knowledge of such an event. There were three main ways of achieving this: they observed an offence on their own and *in flagranti*—which they rarely, if ever, did;[3] they received such information from informants, which also hardly ever happened (informants were more important when it came to investigating an offence); or, as in most cases, they were informed by complainants. Then the gendarmes still needed to accept the complaint and turn it into a case. This depended on how they qualified the alleged offence. Whether police officers or gendarmes enforce the law—that is, produce a case—has been discussed by scholars of policing in terms of police discretion, a necessary principle of police work everywhere.[4] Yet little has been said about the subtleties underlying this complex phenomenon. Remarkable exceptions are two articles by Jeffrey Martin and Jan Beek.[5] They both take a very close look at the police officers' decision-making process and reflect the complex rationalities involved therein. This chapter adopts a similar approach, but sets in a couple of steps prior to the gendarmes' decision-making: when people perceive 'something' as a problematic event and turn it into a complaint that is to be presented to the gendarmes. In other words, this chapter follows a chain of translation with the 'mutual enrollment and the interlocking of interests' of gendarmes and civilians: the translation of 'something' into a problematic event, then into a complaint and finally into a case.[6] I argue that there was no unique reference upon which the translation was based, and there was no unique reasoning by either civilians or the gendarmes when they engaged in this translation. However, the law was only of minor relevance to both.

When 'something' turns into a problematic event

It all has to start with 'someone seeing something, classifying it as problematic in some way, and noting that something must be done about it', as Joanna Shapland and Jon Vagg argue (quite remindful of Egon Bittner).[7] Somebody must recognise and isolate 'something' from the unremarkable and undifferentiated flow of time and classify it as problematic.[8] When the two girls in K.[9] went into the bush with a small flock of goats and sheep, there was nothing to recognise, contemplate, isolate or problematise. When they failed to return home that evening, their family started worrying that 'something' might have happened. When they found the girls' dead bodies two days later, the hollow 'something' turned into a concrete event namely two counts of murder.

It starts with an event, an act, a sequence of acts, also speech acts that are singled out, objectified, and given particular significance—in the case of problematic events, the feeling of harm. At the same time, the event lacks signification; something has happened, something in the form of a surprise that challenges our usual frames of reference.[10] Yet then we turn to other options of sense-making and thus responding to a given event.[11]

When people thus enter into what Laura Nader and Harry F. Todd describe as the 'grievance stage' of the disputing process, 'a circumstance or condition which one person (or group) perceives to be unjust, and the grounds for resentment or complaint', several possible responses are available.[12] The one most frequently used in Niger is to confront the person or group whose act caused the grievance; in Nader and Todd's terms, they enter the 'conflict stage'.[13] If this is not an option, for example when the author of the problematic event is unknown, as was the case in K., or if he is feared, the grieving party enters the 'dispute stage';[14] the matter is made public through the involvement of a third party.[15] In K., the first response to the perceived 'something' was the father sending a group of men to search for the girls. Only when the horror of the girls' killing was discovered, was the canton chief informed, the highest authority in K.

In many places, gendarmes were not an option like in K. This was because of either the distance to the next gendarmerie post or the gendarmes' unwillingness to respond. In K. the reason was that the canton chief had had his marabout *brandir le Coran*, literally, brandish the Qur'an: he made it publicly known that if any of his subjects went to or called the gendarmes without consulting him first, they would bring great suffering upon themselves and their families.[16] As a result, the gendarmes never received calls from people in K. except for the chief. According to the gendarmes, the canton chief had done this because he wanted absolute control over his subjects and his circumscription and because he wanted to 'eat' the money his subjects would bring to him.[17] The gendarmes were aware of that, but there was nothing they could do about it, they said. When they received the call from the canton chief of K., it was therefore clear to everybody that something terrible must have happened, something to which the canton chief had no response. This was also what Badji, my watchman and housemate suspected. He knew K. quite well, having spent a couple of years there as a teenager. 'Why did they call the gendarmes? They couldn't catch them on their own, could they?'[18]

The decision to report a problematic event to the police or the gendarmerie is only one of many options. As I described in an article on security and policing in Niamey,[19] responses to such events can be given by private security agents, vigilante groups, circles of young men gathering on the streets, the so-called *fada*—spontaneous gatherings often pejoratively called 'the mob'[20]— but also traditional authority figures like imams and chiefs, influential neighbours, or simply concerned individuals.[21] Who will eventually be called to respond to a given event—in Shapera's terms, who is 'entitled' to do so—depends on the type of transgression perceived, who committed it, and who the victims are.[22] Christian Lund shows how strategic the parties of land disputes in eastern Niger were in choosing the appropriate 'remedy agents'.[23] And the world of law and policing in its broadest sense is and has always been, in Niger and anywhere else, a pluralised one.[24]

When a problematic event turns into a complaint

A complaint was born as soon as people brought a problematic event to the gendarmes' attention, namely when they came to the brigade and told their story. According to widespread explanations, civilians only report an offence to the gendarmerie or police when alternative responses do not exist or have failed to achieve the desired results. This was, to some extent, true of what happened in K. And this is also represented in large portions of popular discourse about this issue in Niger. A Fulani *chef de groupement* explained in an interview: 'It's like, if you have a problem, you come and tell it to me. If he is a Fulani, we will arrange it here. If he's not a Fulani, we will go and tell his chief. But, you know, if his wrongdoing is small, we can arrange for him; if it is big, it is imperative that we bring him to the gendarmerie.'[25]

The explanation of the gendarmerie as the last resort gained accuracy the greater the chief's control (or that of other authorities) over his subjects and thus the flow of information to gendarmes. In places where the chief had no such power, more people came directly to the gendarmerie brigade without consulting their chiefs. There could be two major reasons for circumventing one's chief. One day a man in his sixties came to the brigade to file a complaint and the gendarmes asked him why he had not brought his neighbourhood chief with him. 'I am an ancient soldier', he replied in Hausa. 'What I do is none of the chief's business!'[26] He and many others did not recognise the chief's authority over him and thus circumvented him. Others came directly to the gendarmes because they were looking for something different than what their chief had to offer. They made a strategic evaluation of different options available to them—they engaged in the oft-cited 'forum shopping' (von Benda-Beckmann 1981)—and chose the gendarmes because they were looking not so much for uncertain and often indefinite reconciliation (which civil judges and chiefs were renowned for), but rather for a quick and decisive judgment.[27] They wanted, for example, that the opponent be forced to compensate the victim for the damages caused, thanks to the gendarmes' rigour, or that somebody receive an additional punishment for his wrongdoings.[28]

People who decided to call on the gendarmes' help came to the brigade alone or with their chief or one of his representatives, the so-called *baruma*, or any other supporting party. Those who came alone were usually inhabitants of the town or lived in villages where the gendarmerie brigade was installed. According to the gendarmes, these people who shared neighbourhoods with the gendarmes had no particular qualms about approaching them, as opposed to people from remote villages who only knew the repressive image of patrolling gendarmes and other uniformed state personnel. And yet, most of those who approached the brigade were extremely respectful and reticent: they laid their long sticks, swords or daggers beside the tree standing some fifteen metres in front of the brigade, men took off their turbans, they slackened their pace before they approached the gendarmes who were sitting on benches under the thatched roof. They took off their shoes, and then stopped a couple of metres in front of them and timidly greeted the gendarmes '*As-salamu alaykum*'. The gendarmes interrupted their conversation, greeted them in a friendly way, '*Wa alaykum as-salam*', and then generally continued their discussion. The complainants then either stood there and waited or sat down on a mat a couple of metres away from the gendarmes, where other complainants, suspects, witnesses, and detainees were sitting and lying in the shade, waiting for their turn.

Those who had at some point already had contact with the gendarmes were a bit more confident and addressed one of the gendarmes sitting there directly, and often they aimed at the most senior one. Since most civilians did not know the meaning of the stripes on the gendarmes' shoulders, and thus who the highest-ranking gendarme was, they often addressed the apparently oldest or most corpulent one. After the greetings, they said '*Ina son in kai kara*', 'I want to bring a complaint', or '*convocation nike so*', 'I want a summons', since they knew this was usually how gendarmes started a case—by handing the complainant a summons for the alleged wrongdoer. As the most corpulent or oldest one was not the highest ranking gendarme, often not even a non-commissioned officer, the complainants were usually asked to be patient and wait for a superior to listen to them.

Yet others wanted to speak directly to the brigade commander. Having met him before, they knew that he would decide whether to take over a case. They greeted the gendarmes and asked whether the brigade commander was around or whether he was with somebody in his office. Gendarmes usually told them that he was busy and would deal with them shortly. They would offer them a seat on a bench a bit away from the gendarmes, 'ka zamna, ka yi hankuri kadan', 'take a seat, have a little patience'. Others greeted the gendarmes only in passing and entered the brigade building; some merely threw a casual 'yana ciki?'—'Is he inside?'—in the gendarmes' direction. In this case, the gendarmes would call them back and rebuke them: they should greet them first, tell them what they wanted; then the gendarmes would inform the brigade commander, if necessary. However, you do not enter the office just like that. The complainants would then have to sit and wait on the bench or on the mat like everybody else.

When people had first gone to their chief with their problem and he could not find a solution to it, as was the case in K., the chief himself or, as in most cases, his representative or *baruma* would approach the gendarmes. The *baruma* are the chiefs' intermediaries between his own traditional office and state administrations, such as hospitals, the mayor's office, the prefect's office, forestry and custom services, and the gendarmerie. They knew where to go with what kind of problem, were experienced at negotiating with state officials, and they knew how to present a story to the gendarmes. When *baruma* came, the reception at the brigade was slightly different. Gado, a Fulani chief's representative, was a well-known guest at the gendarmerie brigade. He came there almost every other day. He greeted all the gendarmes with a handshake, knew everybody by name, and sat down on the gendarmes' benches, where no other civilians were allowed to sit. The reception was similarly warm-hearted, when the complainants were accompanied by other influential supporters such as local politicians, trade union leaders, members of the national guard or other state officials, even gendarmes.

Filing a complaint is the first step in the legal funnel described by Thomas Bierschenk.[29] Everybody tries to avoid falling into the funnel of the legal system, which, in most people's perspective, 'seems like a vacuum cleaner which functions on the basis of obscure mechanisms and which, once it aims its hose at the target group of a legal norm, threatens to suck it up in a vortex leading to the unknown', with the last step being unpredictable convictions and sanctions.[30] On the one hand, both legal professionals and gendarmes try to install filters to 'ensure that the funnel does not become blocked with too many cases'.[31] This means that gendarmes were often reluctant to take over new cases to limit their workload, and complainants had to make a strong case for themselves. On the other hand, most complainants did not want the opposing party to be sucked into the legal funnel either; they merely wanted compensation for the damages caused. In this ambivalent situation—wanting a case to be taken over by the gendarmes but not in the most rigorous way—having supporters was an important advantage. When accompanied by Gado or other supporters who knew how to talk to the gendarmes, for complainants the legal funnel seemed less threatening and the outcome less unpredictable. Their effect was to reduce the uncertainty in dealing with the gendarmes and the law, and to minimise the chances of being sent away. Those who came without any supporters did not enjoy this advantage. They minimised their uncertainty by maximising the gendarmes' sympathy and benevolence through extreme respectfulness and deference, rarely through in-advance gifts; thus grew the chance for a complaint to be accepted.[32]

In a few cases, civilians who had already reported their complaint to the public prosecutor came to the brigade. The prosecutor sent them to the gendarmes, with a small piece of paper indicating 'See Monsieur CB [*commandant de brigade*] of Godiya for compiling the procedure of...'[33] with a red stamp on the back: 'Tribunal d'Instances [district court] de Godiya, le Président', no signature. In this case, the gendarmes had little leeway; the case was already established. The prosecutor had already qualified the offence and as their superior in judicial matters, he tasked them with investigating the case and compiling the *procès-verbal*. The gendarmes themselves had to decide what to do with all other complaints.

When a complaint turns into a case

Whether an event was turned into a complaint depended on the willingness of the complainant; whether a complaint was turned into a case, an '*affaire*', as gendarmes called it, depended on the willingness of the gendarmes. Not all complaints turned into cases. The gendarmes first qualified what kind of a story the complainant had brought to them; and in order to do so, as banal as it may seem, gendarmes needed to listen to the complainant. As I mentioned earlier, the latter would be either standing or sitting a bit off from the gendarmes waiting to be addressed. When the gendarmes' conversation drew to an end, one of them would turn to the civilian and ask him or her, '*Lahiya?*' 'Are you alright?', '*Me ya faru?*' 'What happened?', '*Mine ne?*' 'What is it?', or simply '*Oui?*' Then the civilian would come a few steps closer, often squat down in front of the gendarme who had addressed him and begin explaining what brought him or her there. Rank-and-file gendarmes would then report this to one of the non-commissioned officers, the *chefs*, who were usually in one of the offices. These would then rehear the complainant. In cases they considered '*de grande envergure*' (very serious), like cases of fraud of several millions of Franc CFA, burglary under aggravated circumstances, homicides like those in K., they would report directly to the brigade commander, who would then listen to the complainant again and eventually, after consulting the public prosecutor over the phone, decide how to proceed.

As often happened during my stay at different brigades, complainants were forgotten on the mat.[34] And complainants would usually not insist on talking to the gendarmes and waited instead for somebody to approach them. Gendarmes chatted or drank tea, and occasionally the brigade commander would step out of his office and into the courtyard and see sometimes a good dozen of people sitting there, waiting to be addressed. 'Who are these people?' One brigade commander, Adjudant-Chef Souley, often harshly asked his gendarmes. 'Hey orderly, this woman, why is she here? Why do you look at her? What are you waiting for to listen to her? Do I always have to remind you?'[35] Then one of the gendarmes would stand up, walk towards the people on the mat and ask them what brought them here. Other complainants would directly get up and approach the brigade commander. '*Ni ne CB*', 'I am the brigade commander. But you haven't killed somebody, have you?' Souley jokingly replied. He knew that a lot of complainants were afraid of going to the gendarmes not to mention talk to them. His jokes often built on joking relationships between ethnic groups, he wanted to break the ice and make complainants feel a bit more at ease, he told me.

The second step was to check the validity of a complaint. Technically, for a story of complaint to turn into a case, gendarmes had to identify three elements constituting a criminal offence (*éléments constitutifs de l'infraction*): the legal, material and moral elements.[36] The legal element is the breach of a law. The material element is the materialisation of the offence through execution of an act or acts by its author. The moral element describes the offensive act or acts are the consequence of the authors' intention (or of a fault committed by a person aware of his or her acts). If only one of these elements was missing, there was no offence, there was no valid complaint, and the gendarmes had no legal mandate to engage, that is, turn it into a case. If all but the legal elements were found, it was a civil complaint, most of which were matters of land-conflict, heritage disputes, marriage disputes, adultery, issues of debt, and allegations of sorcery. Technically they had to be blocked and the complainants sent to the civil judge (or to traditional or religious authorities). However, whether a law of the *Code Pénal* had been broken or not, was at this point the gendarmes' least interest; this legal question was often unspoken and became important only when writing the final report.[37]

Yet the gendarmes treated such cases anyway, even though they knew that they had no protection whatsoever from their superiors, their officers and the prosecutor.[38] There were several reasons for this: first, gendarmes had financial interests. Both criminal and civil cases were potential sources of additional income, either through unofficial fees (for example for a summons) or through gifts from civilians in response to the gendarmes' having done a good job. And since the prosecutor was not involved and it resulted in an informal arrangement, perhaps accompanied by a mere fine, rather than a legal procedure, these cases presented greater opportunities for additional income. Second, gendarmes sincerely wanted to help people who had been caused harm, even if the codified state law, which they often felt inappropriate to local contexts, had no sanctions available for this type of wrongdoing. In the end, it was a question of how gendarmes qualified the gravity of the offence.

When gendarmes qualified the gravity of the harm caused, they paid particular attention to the material dimension of the alleged wrongdoing: the consequences of the offending act. Such an act could be physical with an impact on the complainant's body or property. In this case, it was rather simple for the gendarmes to measure the material gravity of an offence: How large is the field of crops that has been trampled down by a herder's cattle? How much are the stolen goods worth? How much did the treatment of injuries cost? How long is the victim's temporary disability?[39] But the offending act could also be a speech act that, through its social validity, had an immediate impact on the victim's social self.[40] Such acts were usually slanderous. When it came to such non-corporeal damage, the problem of defining the gravity of an act or in other words the problem of quantification was more complicated, since gendarmes could neither see nor put a precise figure on the damage. However, gendarmes were extremely cautious when it came to such soft damage. In one case, a woman filed a complaint against another woman who had spread a rumour that the former had HIV/Aids. For a non-commissioned officer, Chef Tahirou, at that time interim brigade commander, this was futile and he sent the woman away; his colleague Chef Boubacar, however, and all the other gendarmes did not agree with Tahirou and this led to a heated debate, almost to a brawl between Tahirou and Boubacar. Chef Boubacar explained afterwards: 'This is a very delicate affair. Everywhere in town, they sullied her name, and if you don't intervene in cases like this, soon there will be chaos! People will start tearing each other to pieces!'[41] The relevant category, also put forward by the prosecutor, was 'public disorder' (*trouble à l'ordre public*). 'Any offence', the prosecutor explained, 'is a societal problem. And any societal problem can incite societal disorder.'[42] The harm caused was always considered beyond the personal damages caused to the complainant and to pose a threat to peaceful coexistence at large.

The second aspect that the gendarmes paid attention to was the moral dimension. As an element of an offence, it refers to the motive behind the offensive act: was an act committed accidentally, by slight or gross negligence or by criminal intent? But when qualifying the gravity of an act, the gendarmes took the moral dimension beyond its textbook definition.[43] Adjudant-Chef Souley explained to me in an interview what the moral dimension was all about:

> You can commit a serious act in a tolerable situation. And you can commit a less serious act, a simple act, but in the spirit...in the spirit of a rogue. Or you can mock people, or show them that you are better than they are...or you want to show that you don't respect the law, or you want to show that you even refuse to admit that the law is there. ...In this case, even if it's a very small thing, I repress it even more than a serious fault in a spirit...without intention. This is what I find important. Because there are rogue people, there are people who are incorrigible. At worst they have—they think they have—somebody who can always protect them. Malicious spirits like that I do not tolerate. And whoever the guy is, in these cases I am stone cold. A thief, for example... You'll see somebody who steals four to five ewes. Among these five ewes is one that is somebody's only ewe. And the guy who stole it, when you go to his place you will see that his father has fifty, perhaps even 200 cows. And he, this guy, he comes into a village and steals somebody's only ewe? We will impose him a big ticket...to take or to leave and go to prison.[44]

Qualifying an offence was not only about what somebody did and whether it was intentional; it was also a deeply moral question. Who did it and in which spirit and in what kind of situation, or where did his intention to commit this act come from, what drove him to act in such a way? When a rich man stole from a poor man, when somebody showed no sign of remorse, or did not show any respect for the law (and those supposed to protect it), the wrong became even wronger in the gendarmes' eyes, and thus they were less inclined to find an alternative solution to the dispute.[45] Put another way, the chances of strict law enforcement grew with the alleged offender's disrespect for common social values, the law, and the gendarmes, regardless of whether he had actually broken the law. In cases where the material and moral dimensions of the offence were so striking, in cases where the harm caused was so obvious to the gendarmes, the legal element was secondary, and they took over the case. This was possible because of the softness of the different formal categories that qualify a case.

Qualifying a case: between civil and criminal matters

'Technically, this is a civil affair', gendarmes often said when they heard a complaint.[46] And technically gendarmes were not supposed to deal with civil cases. But the line between civil and criminal matters was a thin one, according to Adjudant-Chef Souley:

> Almost all civil affairs can turn into criminal affairs. For example in an affair about debt: how has he taken on this debt? And as soon as you penetrate just a little bit you will notice that there were some deceptive manoeuvres, or he has breached his confidence, or he defrauded him, and so on. So it's a breach of confidence [*abus de confiance*] or fraud [*escroquerie*]. So it's a criminal affair.[47]

In cases that involved some form of debt, like a simple loan, one could easily find some legal element in it, if it had not been repaid after the agreed period. Thus the civil matter turned into a criminal matter, a loan into a breach of trust, and allowed the gendarmes to become active. According to Chef Boubacar, the problem was that complainants had a clear interest in stressing, overemphasising or even inventing fraudulent manoeuvres in their stories to transform a civil affair into a criminal one and have the gendarmes take over the case, and have them work it in their favour. 'And this pushes us into ambiguity', Chef Boubacar explained.[48] And ambiguity was not only unacceptable in the gendarmes' work, it was also dangerous, he felt. If in the end it turned out that there was no legal reason whatsoever for the gendarmes' engagement, there could be negative repercussions like counter complaints, interventions by influential personalities, reprimands from their superiors, or even punishments. 'This is why you have to be very careful!' Chef Boubacar told his gendarmes again and again and again.[49]

To be on the safe side without pushing back complainants completely, gendarmes would in most cases send the complainants to the public prosecutor or simply call him and ask for his opinion. And there was no questioning what the prosecutor said. Even if affairs were obviously were civil matters, when somebody brought a note written by the prosecutor saying, 'See the CB...', gendarmes dealt with it. 'Without the piece of paper, it's civil. But with the piece of paper from the prosecutor it's criminal. BOOM! And we have our hands free', as Chef Boubacar put it. The note from the prosecutor not only defined the offence, it also protected the gendarmes from interventions by their superiors and politicians.

Due to the softness of the civil/criminal categories, civil cases could turn into criminal ones and vice versa. Adjudant-Chef Souley gave me one example: 'Take a breach of confidence (*abus de confiance*), for example. You can extract an element, one of the characteristic elements that constitute the breach of confidence, and you will directly say that it's a civil affair. It's the same for fraud. Because there is really nothing concrete in deceit.'[50] This practice was particularly relevant when gendarmes aimed for arrangement, an informal settlement.

If the gendarmes took over an affair and thus decided that it was a criminal case, they still had to define the type of offence. The corresponding legal categories were *crime*, *délit* and *contravention*.[51] A *crime* is a serious offence punishable by death or a minimum of ten years imprisonment, a *délit* a less serious offence punishable by a fine or a prison sentence of less than ten years, and a *contravention* a minor offence that is punished by a simple fine—a ticket.[52] The public prosecutor had to be involved in *crimes* and *délits* only; the gendarmes handed out tickets for a *contravention*. These categories reflect the distinction the gendarmes drew between '*grandes affaires*' on the one hand, and '*petites affaires*' or '*affaires courantes*' on the other.[53] Non-commissioned officers could decide *contraventions* and small *délits*, what they called 'everyday affairs'. Big affairs, important *délits* and *crimes*, had to be brought to the brigade commanders' attention, who would then inform the prosecutor.

However, these categories were—similar to 'civil' and 'criminal'—not neatly separated and could, except for serious crime, be transformed into the other. When a *délit* was transformed into a *contravention*, this meant that the prosecutor was not involved and the gendarmes had great leeway in terms of procedure. In the case of assault, for example, gendarmes made use of the dividing line between a *délit* and a *contravention*, which in their eyes was fixed at ten days of temporary disability of the victim (although the legal article gendarmes mentioned referred to unintentional harm);[54] and when consulting the medical doctor, who was a good friend of Adjudant-Chef Souley's, the number of days could be negotiated. The transformation of a *délit* into a *contravention* was usually part of the gendarmes' efforts to allow for an 'amicable arrangement'.

Most gendarmes were tired of working on such everyday affairs. Cases like the murder of the girls' in K. were a rupture in the unremarkable flow of routine activities.[55] Such cases stood out, were interesting, promising, and mobilised the gendarmes, whose, 'vocational ear is permanently and specifically attuned to such calls' as Bittner put it,[56] as opposed to the boring everyday *affaires courantes* like brawls and petty theft, which most gendarmes preferred not to deal with. In the case of a *crime*, a translation into a *délit* or even *contravention* was impossible. And the bigger the crime, the more restricted the gendarmes' leeway, particularly because of their superiors' rising interest in such cases. All homicides, like those in K., almost automatically turned into what David Simon, writing about the Baltimore Homicide Unit calls 'red ball-cases', that is, cases 'that matter' and that 'can mean twenty-four hour days and constant reports to the entire chain of command'.[57] This is exactly what happened with the case of the two girls murdered in K.

The translation of a complaint into a case was bureaucratically completed as soon as a radio message was sent to the superior officer, which happened only in severe cases, and when the prosecutor was informed. Like in France, judicial supervision is 'at the heart of the criminal procedure and in most cases it is the *procureur* who is responsible for overseeing the investigation'.[58] At what stage the *procureur* was informed depended on the gravity of the offence. In the case of a *crime*, a felony, the prosecutor was informed at once, as in the K. case. In the case of a *délit* or misdemeanour, when the prosecutor was informed depended on the gendarmes' discretion and the relationship of trust between the two. The later the call to the prosecutor, the longer the option of an informal arrangement persisted. And even when the prosecutor was informed, he could decide either way: '*faites la procédure*' (establish the procedure) or '*il faut les arranger*' (make them come to an arrangement). His decision depended particularly on the national or regional *politique pénale*, a 'policy relating to particular offences',[59] but also on his own workload and his relationship with the brigade commander. In the case of *contravention* or minor offences, the prosecutor was only informed after he received the copies of the tickets the gendarmes had handed out.

Conclusion

Law enforcement, the production of cases, is often described as a matter of police discretion. The complainants' discretion is neglected, or to put it differently the definition of a problematic event and its translation into a complaint to be brought to the attention of the police officers or gendarmes. Law enforcement depends, first of all, on the flow of information from civilians to those who are supposed to enforce the law. Whether a complaint was filed was always the result of somebody's strategic choice. That person felt that he had been harmed; it depended on the availability of different possible 'remedy agents';[60] and it depended on who controlled and to what extent the flow of information—or stories—to gendarmes. Then, whether a complaint was translated into a case depended on the gendarmes' strategic evaluation, particularly with regards to additional income and possible repercussions, on whether they were told to do so by their superiors or the prosecutor, but also, and decisively so, on whether their 'vocational ear' was attuned to a particular complainant's story.[61] And when qualifying a complaint and the problematic event it is based on, the gendarmes' ear—or, as Clifford Geertz calls it, 'legal sensibility'—was more attuned to the material and moral gravity of an offence than to the legal element in it.[62] Considering the invisibility of the law at this stage, it appears that the binary categories of state law—'civil' and 'criminal'—are not only problematic as analytical concepts;[63] they are, due to their softness, also subject to the law enforcers' interpretation. A crime was a crime not so much because it broke the law and thus offended the sovereignty of the state;[64] a crime was a crime because it undercut and imperilled what the gendarmes deemed fundamental values of social life.[65] In other words, gendarmes worked on the basis of a social rather than legal definition of crime.[66] According to John and Jean Comaroff, crime in this sense is something 'by means of whom, as *camera obscura*, a civil order may conceive itself'.[67] Problematic of course is that without a clear definition of a crime, thus what this civil order is, the gendarmes' actions can always be contested.[68]

At this stage of the law enforcement process, the gendarmes invoked the law only when the material and moral dimensions of an alleged offence were too weak for the gendarmes to appear as legitimate remedy agents or when their intervention was not launched by a complaint and a remedy was not sought. Typically this happened when the gendarmes were on traffic control duty and handed out tickets for breaches of the highway code (*code de la route*).[69] But in cases of theft, assault, murder or slander, social and moral norms were the reference, not the law, upon which depended the translation of an event into a case. Just as harm and crime have a 'contingent rather than necessary connection',[70] so do problematic events, complaints and cases. There was no unique reference upon which the translation was based, and there was no unique reasoning of both civilians and gendarmes when they engaged in this translation. However, law was only of minor relevance to both. This is why at this stage of law enforcement there was nearly always the option of an extra-legal settlement, or amicable arrangement.

EPILOGUE

Alice Hills

The detailed studies presented in this volume demonstrate how a new genera-tion of scholars is assessing the meaning of police and policing in contempo-rary sub-Saharan Africa. The chapters, which discuss cases ranging from Sierra Leone and Niger to Mozambique and South Africa via the DRC, emphasise different themes and issues, but all share one factor in common: that policing in Africa engages with elements of the Western canon while bringing out the fundamentals of policing in ways that are not otherwise obvious.[1] They show conclusively that ethnography can make a major contribution to police and area studies.

Police have long been notable actors in Africa's political and security land-scape, but were until recently neglected by both police and international studies. Most accounts of police and policing were biographical or historical in nature, and, while the work of political scientists such as Potholm, Lee, Enloe, and Marenin was groundbreaking, it failed to develop into a coherent research agenda.[2] If anything, the ending of the Cold War saw a new low in studies addressing police and policing in Africa, and investigations in the years imme-diately after the end of the Cold War revealed remarkably little relevant litera-ture.[3] This appeared to change with the end of Apartheid,[4] the emergence of security sector reform as a liberal project, and the implementation of multiple internationally-driven reform policies in the mid to late 1990s. However, the

POLICE IN AFRICA

literature associated with these developments was based on the assumption that liberal ideals and processes could, and should, be transferred to Africa.[5]

More recently, our understanding of policing has been informed by a greater awareness of the role played by informal providers such as vigilantes and associations representing market traders, okada riders or farmers.[6] Yet, regardless of this trend, remarkably few accounts of routine police work exist. Police and policing are seen primarily as targets for reform projects designed to break with the past, rather than a means to understand the rationalities shaping the activities of a significant state-based actor; there is remarkably little systematic research on the political economy of policing in Africa.[7] Most accounts address police in the light of the challenges associated with transitional societies, post-conflict reconstruction or security sector reform,[8] rather than as actors in their own right, and minimal attention is paid to the practices, pressures and power relations shaping everyday police work and culture. Further, many contemporary accounts of police practice focus on its brutal and predatory nature, with the most detailed provided by advocacy groups such as the New York-based Human Rights Watch.[9] More generally, the international community's approach to police and policing in the global South remains predicated on institutional ideals, practices and values based on or rooted in Anglo-American experience and research.

There is much to be said for approaching policing in Africa from this perspective. Africa's police share occupational commonalities with their peers in other regions (organisations such as Interpol and the Southern African Regional Police Chiefs Co-operation Organisation, SARPCCO, could not otherwise function), and anecdotal evidence suggests that many African officers regard western policing with respect because it is seen as representing 'modern', international, professional policing; the technical capacity (e.g. investigative skills) and resources (e.g. vehicles, computers and forensics) associated with it are highly desirable. Even so, debates about the commonalities shared by international and local police, and about policy transfers from the global North to the South, are essentially conducted in isolation because there is little material available on how southern police understand their job, rationalise their activities, and assess liberal ideals such as service and accountability.

It is only now that studies, such as those in this volume, address—and answer—such questions about the nature of police and policing in Africa, the ways in which officers articulate their role, and how they spend their days. It is not overstating the case to say that many of the chapters in this volume are groundbreaking. The reason is simple; with the exception of Marks (which,

264

significantly, concerned South Africa's police),[10] before the late 2000s there were few, if any, ethnographic studies of Africa's police; insights could be gained from accounts such as that of Heald,[11] but there was little research focused explicitly on police or policing.

A richer understanding

Police in Africa helps to rebalance research on police and policing in Africa while identifying new insights and potential research avenues. Its geographical and thematic scope is, inevitably limited in that of its twelve chapters, three focus on Francophone countries (DRC, Niger and Togo), three on Anglophone West Africa (Ghana, Nigeria and Sierra Leone) and five on southern Africa (one on Lusophone Mozambique and four on South Africa), but omit East Africa and the Horn. Also, there is nothing on, for example, south-south technical transfers, the daily routine of senior officers and headquarters' staff, or the role of officers operating in rule-based societies characterised by the legal pluralism of formal, customary, and Shari'a law; there is nothing to indicate what an Africa-based comparative policing might look like. Yet what is offered is notable for its richness and granularity. This owes much to the ethnographic methods used by the book's anthropologists, which in turn complement and enrich the chapters offered by contributors employing insights from, or the methodologies of, history, criminology and political science.

The book provides an overview of the trajectory of police work and policing trends in Southern, Central and West Africa in recent decades, and at its core is a series of detailed and empirically based accounts of police and the specifics of policing in the African environment. It offers insights into the role played by themes common in police studies, such as professionalisation, discretion and physical coercion, but, more importantly, it provides insights into African perspectives on what it means to be a police officer, rather than a soldier or a vigilante. For example, it explores how members of paramilitary police units distinguish themselves from soldiers and regular police officers, and how the military framework of such units affects their everyday interactions with civilians. Above all, the book shows how low ranking officers from across the continent understand, articulate and conduct their job; it identifies what motivates them, how they assess the risks and rewards of police work, and how they engage with the bureaucratic procedures characterising police organisations. The picture that emerges is of occupational commonalities, one of which is the banality of routine police work.

Some aspects of the Western canon are as a result confirmed. The use made of discretion by officers in Ghana, Mozambique and Niger is a case in point, as is the continuing influence of distinctions between high and low policing in the minds of those responsible for managing South Africa's security, while Sierra Leone's experience shows that trust between internationals and locals is an important determinant of whether reforms will succeed. Others aspects are rebutted. Thus professionalisation was not as significant in Togo's policing as western research suggests it should be, while the relationship between international and local actors can, as in Sierra Leone in the late 1990s and early 2002, be one of mutual understanding, rather than antagonism. In this way, the book's contributions provide a more balanced discussion of what it means to be police and do policework.

Change and continuity

Despite the arguably atypical experience of post-Apartheid South Africa, most of the studies offered here suggest that, while change happens in policing, much remains the same, especially at the most fundamental levels of coercive skills, political order and organisational resilience. Some of the changes identified by contributors are politically significant, as when the structure and culture of South Africa's police force is shaped by the task of managing conflict within the country's ruling party, rather than handling challenges to the regime. But it is equally clear that many commonly perceived changes reflect international perspectives, rather than local realities. The recognition now given to multi-choice policing by people looking for cheap and effective policing is a case in point.[12] Despite this, there is no sign that police are a threatened species or that policing has been fundamentally reconfigured;[13] the police analysed by Lee, Marenin and Potholm remain recognisable, as do those described by Schatzberg in 1988.

Africa's police forces will, no doubt, remain under-resourced, repressive and distrusted for the foreseeable future, just as its officers will accommodate regime change and their activities will be supplemented by those of community-based providers of informal security and justice. Further, police and police work will remain inaccessible to the inter-governmental organisations (IGOs) and donors who wish to mould their development and practice. IGOs, donors and international advisers may focus on reform (normative or technical) but it remains difficult for them to influence officers. This is partly because their advice is often ignored by international decision makers,[14] but, more importantly, it is because they cannot or, unlike this book's contributors, do not wish to access the world of African officers; they neglect the power relations, cultural imperatives and parallel networks that local police take for granted. Despite the attention now paid to local ownership, service and community-oriented policing, there is little evidence that IGOs, bilateral donors and international advisers have fundamentally reassessed their understanding of African police and police work; the continued promotion of police as a service to the community, and of projects intended to deliver the Millennium Development Goals in patriarchal, conservative or volatile societies suggests that realistic and accurate assessment remains lacking. Indeed, fundamental questions about the relationship between functionally effective policing of the sort employed in, say, Nigeria and democratic values remain unanswered. We do not, for example, know whether the current emphasis on representative recruitment and civilian accountability helps to explain why sustained reform is rare, and there are no rigorous assessments of the relative merits of technical assistance over appeals to democratic values.

However, change and continuity are, while critical, a distraction in this context because the book's focus is on the academy's understanding and knowledge of policing in Africa, and, specifically, on ethnography's contribution. The broader enquiry underpinning *Police in Africa* is whether an understanding rooted in Anglo-American experience and research can ever understand, let alone explain, police and police work in Africa. The question therefore arises of whether the contributors to this book have rethought police and policing, and, if so, what the analytical and empirical impact of their analysis might be. Does *Police in Africa* provide a persuasive account capable of sustaining a coherent analysis? Does it show what police studies might look like if it had originated in Abuja or Maputo, rather than London or Boston? Has African policing been rethought? The contributions here suggest that it has not been rethought so much as enhanced by a richer and more detailed understanding of everyday street-level police work.

Conclusion

Looking at trends in police studies, and in police and policing across Africa over the last three decades, it is clear that police practice has evolved significantly, albeit less than donors might wish. Whereas in the 2000s it was possible for IGOs, bilaterals and scholars to dismiss police as colonial relics, or to believe that police development would facilitate achieving Millennium

Development Goals such as poverty alleviation and gender equality, today's claims are in comparison muted. Admittedly, issues such as the fundamental purpose and remit of police, and of whether it has changed from regime policing to one of professional service to the populace, are controversial. To date, Africa's experience suggests that regimes may distrust their police but they find them useful, while police prefer to accommodate political change, rather than to mutiny. What is less open to question is the minimal level of knowledge and understanding displayed by most western commentators, with their awareness of the views and routine activities of low-level officers particularly poor. In practice, the knowledge needed for greater understanding was missing until approximately 2012 or 2013. Throughout the 2000s, there had been studies by African scholars addressing police from a political science perspective, but few—African or international—employed the ethnographic methods needed to produce detailed studies of routine street-level policing, let alone the views of low-ranking officers such as Beek's constable Betty.

That Africa's experience has been marginalised within police studies is, perhaps, unsurprising. It is partly explained by the withdrawal from Africa of international publishers, which meant that research by African scholars was effectively marginalised,[15] but it is mainly because policing in Africa is rarely seen internationally as a legitimate topic of inquiry. Further, comparative policing studies focusing on the global South have never been fashionable; Bayley's groundbreaking 1985 analysis of 'Patterns of policing' included Singapore and Sri Lanka, but his major reference points were France, India, Norway, the UK and the USA. *Police in Africa* suggests that the balance is gradually shifting. When combined with contemporary research on state-building and development, the studies conducted by this book's contributors show that an infinitely richer understanding of police and policing is possible.

In their introduction, the four editors suggest that ethnography makes three main contributions to the study of police work: it emphasises the banality of everyday police work, it makes the views of officers (and low-ranking officers in particular) accessible, and it allows for close comparisons. *Police in Africa's* contributors substantiate these claims. Contemporary police studies owes a substantial debt to anthropology.

NOTES

FOREWORD: TOWARDS WHAT KIND OF GLOBAL POLICING STUDIES?

1. Loader, Ian and A. Mulcahy, *Policing and the Condition of England: Memory, Politics and Culture*, Oxford: Oxford University Press, 2003, Ch. 2.
2. Murphy, C., 'Police Studies go Global: In Eastern Kentucky?', *Police Quarterly*, 8, 1 (2005), p. 137.
3. The recent upsurge of anthropological work on policing is, in my view, of much significance and likely to form an important element of the kind of global policing studies I have just briefly described (see also Fassin 2013; Garriott 2013).
4. Brodeur, Jean-Paul, *The Policing Web*, Oxford: Oxford University Press, 2010, p. 64.

INTRODUCTION: POLICING IN AFRICA RECONSIDERED

1. Iliffe, John, *Africans: The History of a Continent*, Cambridge: Cambridge University Press, 1995, pp. 263–4.
2. Iliffe, 1995, p. 263.
3. Bayart, Jean-François, Stephen Ellis and Béatrice Hibou, *The criminalisation of the state in Africa*, Oxford: International African Institute with James Currey, 1999.
4. Ferguson, James, *Expectations of Modernity: Myths and Meanings of Urban Life on the Zambian Copperbelt*, London: University of California Press, 1999.
5. Chabal, Patrick and Jean-Pascal Daloz, *Africa Works: Disorder as Political Instrument*, Oxford: James Currey, 1999; Reno, William, *Corruption and State Politics in Sierra Leone*, Cambridge: Cambridge University Press, 1995.
6. Bayart, Jean-Francois, *The State in Africa: The Politics of the Belly*, 2nd edition, Cambridge: Polity, 2010.
7. Herbst, Jeffrey, *States and Power in Africa: Comparative Lessons in Authority and Control*, Princeton: Princeton University Press, 2000.
8. Jackson, Robert H. and Carl G. Rosberg, 'Why Africa's Weak States Persist: The Empirical and the Juridical in Statehood', *World Politics*, 35, 1 (1982), pp. 1–24.

1

9. MacGaffey, Jane, *The Real Economy of Zaire: The Contribution of Smuggling and Other Unofficial Activities to National Wealth*, Oxford: James Currey, 1991.
10. Cruise O'Brien, Donal, 'A Lost Generation? Youth Identity and State Decay in West Africa,' in Werbner, Richard, and Terence Ranger (eds), *Postcolonial Identities in Africa*, London: Zed Books, 1996, pp. 55–74.
11. Jones, Will, Ricardo Soares D'Oliveira and Harry Verhoeven, 'Africa's Illiberal State-builders,' Refugee Studies Centre, Oxford University, *Working Paper Series*, No. 89, 2013.
12. DiNunzio, Marco, '"The Arada Have Been Eaten": Living Through Marginality in Addis Ababa's Inner City,' D. Phil Thesis, Oxford University, 2012.
13. Seekings, Jeremy, 'Are African Welfare States Distinctive? The Design and Politics of African Welfare-State Building in Comparative Perspective,' Keynote Address, Social Policy and Regimes of Social Welfare in Africa, University of Fribourg, 12 September 2014.
14. Among many examples, see Bates, Robert, *When Things Fell Apart: State Failure in Late-Century Africa*, Cambridge: Cambridge University Press, 2008; Anderson, David, 'Vigilantes, Violence and the Politics of Public Order in Kenya,' *African Affairs*, 101, 405 (2002), pp. 531–55.
15. See also Blundo, Giorgio and Joel Glasman (eds), *Bureaucrats in Uniform*, Special Issue of *Sociologus: Journal for Social Anthropology*, 63, 1 (2013).
16. Bayley, D. H. and Clifford Shearing, *The New Structure of Policing—Description, Conceptualisation and Research Agenda*, Washington DC: National Institute of Justice, 2001; Braithwaite, John, 'The New Regulatory State and the Transformation of Criminology,' *British Journal of Criminology*, 40, 2 (2000), pp. 222–38; Brogden, Mike, 'The emergence of the police—the colonial dimension', *British Journal of Criminology*, 27, 1 (1987), pp. 4–14.
17. For a recent example, see Baker, Bruce, 'Where Formal and Informal Justice Meet: Ethiopia's Justice Pluralism', *African Journal of International and Comparative Law*, 21, 2 (2013), pp. 202–18.
18. Miliband, Ralph, *The state in capitalist society*, New York: Basic Books, 1969, p. 117.
19. Abrams, Philip, 'Notes on the Difficulty of Studying the State', *Journal of Historical Sociology*, 1, 1 (1988), pp. 58–89.
20. Gupta, Akhil, 'Blurred boundaries: the discourse of corruption, the culture of politics and the imagined state', in Sharma, Aradhana and Akhil Gupta, *The anthropology of the state*, Oxford: Blackwell, 2006.
21. Roitman, Janet, *Fiscal disobedience: an anthropology of economic regulation in Central Africa*. Princeton: Princeton University Press, 2005; Chalfin, Brenda, *Neoliberal frontiers: an ethnography of sovereignty in West Africa*, Chicago: University of Chicago Press, 2011.
22. Blundo, Giorgio and Jean-Pierre Olivier de Sardan, *Everyday corruption and the state: Citizens and public officials in Africa*, London: Zed, 2006, p. 4.

23. Bierschenk, Thomas and Olivier de Sardan, Jean-Pierre (eds), *States at Work: dynamics of African bureaucracies*, Leiden: Brill, 2014; Blundo, Giorgio and Joël Glasman,'Introduction: Bureaucrats in Uniform', *Sociologus*, 63, 1 (2013), pp. 1–11.

24. Pratten, David and Atreyee Sen, 'Global vigilantes: perspectives on justice and violence', in Pratten, David and Atreyee Sen (eds), *Global Vigilantes*, London: Hurst, 2007, pp. 1–25.

25. See Davidson, Basil, *The Black Man's Burden: Africa and the curse of the nation-state*, London: James Currey, 1992; Ekeh, Peter, 'Colonialism and the Two Publics in Africa: A Theoretical Statement', *Comparative Studies in Society and History*, 17 (1975), pp. 91–112; Reno, W., *Warlord Politics and African States*, Boulder: Lynne Rienner, 1998 for these models respectively. This is not to say such models are invalid in their own terms, but that they do not provide explanations satisfactory for the historical juncture we observe.

26. For a more full explanation of layering of bureaucratic practices, see Bierschenk, Thomas, 'Sedimentation, fragmentation and normative double-binds in (West) African public services', in Thomas Bierschenk and Jean-Pierre Olivier de Sardan (eds), *States at Work: Dynamics of African Bureaucracies*, Leiden: Brill, 2014, pp. 221–49.

27. Bittner, Egon, 'The police on skid-row: a study of peace keeping', *American Sociological Review*, 32, 5 (1967), pp. 699–715; Bittner, Egon, 'Florence Nightingale in pursuit of Willie Sutton: a theory of the police', in Herbert Jacob (ed.), *Potential for Reform of Criminal Justice*, Beverly Hills: SAGE Publications, 1974, pp. 17–44.

28. Banton, Michael, *The Policeman in the Community*, London: Tavistock Publishers, 1964.

29. Westley, William A., *Violence and the Police: A Sociological Study of Law, Custom, and Morality*, Cambridge: MIT Press, 1970.

30. Holdaway, Simon, 'The police station', *Journal of Contemporary Ethnography*, 9, 1 (1980), pp. 79–100; Holdaway, Simon, *Inside the British Police: A Force at Work*, Oxford: Basil Blackwell, 1983; Young, Malcolm, *An Inside Job: Policing and Police Culture in Britain*, Oxford: Clarendon Press, 1991; Young, Malcolm, *In the Sticks: Cultural Identity in a Rural Police Force*, Oxford: Clarendon Press, 1993.

31. Manning, Peter K., *Police Work: The Social Organization of Policing*, Cambridge: MIT Press, 1977; Manning, Peter K., 'Producing drama: symbolic communication and the police', *Symbolic Interaction*, 5, 2 (1982), pp. 223–42. For a more detailed overview of British police research see Newburn, Tim and Robert Reiner, 'Policing and the police', in Maguire, Mike, Rodney Morgan and Robert Reiner (eds), *The Oxford Handbook of Criminology*, Oxford: Oxford University Press, 2007, pp. 910–52; for an overview of German police research, see Reichertz, Jo and Norbert Schröer, 'Hermeneutisch-wissenssoziologische Polizeiforschung', in Reichertz, Jo and Norbert Schröer (eds), *Hermeneutische Polizeiforschung*,

Opladen: Leske + Budrich, 2003, pp. 17–36; Ohlemacher, Thomas, 'Empirische Polizeiforschung: Auf dem Weg zum Pluralismus der Perspektiven, Disziplinen und Methoden', in Lange, Hans-Jürgen (ed.), *Die Polizei der Gesellschaft: Zur Soziologie der Inneren Sicherheit*, Opladen: Leske und Budrich, 2003, pp. 377–98.

32. Monjardet, Dominique, *Ce que fait la police: Sociologie de la force publique*, Paris: La Découverte, 1996.

33. Some of the ideological forerunners of this approach are the scholars in and around the research project 'States at work: public services and civil servants in West Africa' coordinated by Thomas Bierschenk and Mahaman Tidjani Alou. Bierschenk and Olivier de Sardan speak of a newly 'emerging research paradigm' with regards to research on state bureaucracies; see Bierschenk, Thomas and Jean-Pierre Olivier de Sardan, 'Ethnographies of public services in Africa: an emerging research paradigm', in Bierschenk, Thomas and Jean-Pierre Olivier de Sardan (eds), *States at Work: Dynamics of African Bureaucracies*, Leiden: Brill, 2014, pp. 35–65.

34. Marenin, Otwin, 'Policing African states: toward a critique', *Comparative Politics*, 14, 4 (1982), pp. 379–96.

35. Tamuno, T. N. 1970. *The police in modern Nigeria, 1861–1965: origins, development and role*. Ibadan: Ibadan University Press, 1970; Anderson, David and David Killingray (eds), *Policing the Empire: Government, Authority, and Control, 1830–1940*, Manchester: Manchester University Press, 1991; Anderson, David and David Killingray (eds), *Policing and Decolonisation: Politics, Nationalism, and the Police, 1917–65*, Manchester: Manchester University Press, 1992; Rotimi, K. 2001. *The police in a federal state: the Nigerian experience*. Ibadan: College Press, 2001; for current work, see Sinclair, Georgina, *At the End of the Line: Colonial Policing and the Imperial Endgame 1945–80*, Manchester: Manchester University Press, 2006.

36. Bat, Jean-Pierre and Nicolas Courtin (eds), *Maintenir l'ordre colonial: Afrique et Madagascar, XIXe-XXe siècles*, Rennes: PU Rennes, 2012; especially the contribution Blanchard, Emmanuel and Joël Glasman, 'Introduction générale: Le maintien de l'ordre dans l'empire français: une historiographie émergente', in Bat, Jean-Pierre and Nicolas Courtin (eds), *Maintenir l'ordre colonial. Afrique et Madagascar, XIXe-XXe siècles*, Rennes: PU Rennes, 2012, pp. 11–41.

37. Hills, Alice, *Policing Africa: Internal Security and the Limits of Liberalization*, Boulder: Lynne Rienner Publishers, 2000.

38. Buur, Lars, 'Reordering society: vigilantism and expressions of sovereignty in Port Elizabeth's townships', *Development and Change*, 37, 4 (2006), pp. 735–57; Comaroff, John L. and Jean Comaroff, 'Popular justice in the new South Africa: policing the boundaries of freedom', in Tyler, Tom R. (ed.), *Legitimacy and Criminal Justice: International Perspectives*, New York: Russell Sage Foundation, 2008, pp. 215–37; Fleischer, Michael L., '"Sungusungu": state-sponsored village

vigilante groups among the Kuria of Tanzania', *Africa*, 70, 2 (2000), pp. 209–28; Fourchard, Laurent, 'A new name for an old practice: vigilantism in south-western Nigeria', *Africa*, 78, 1 (2008), pp. 16–40; Heald, Suzette, 'State, law, and vigilantism in northern Tanzania', *African Affairs*, 105, 419 (2006), pp. 265–83; Jensen, Steffen, 'Policing Nkomazi: crime, masculinity and generational conflicts', in Pratten, David and Atreyee Sen (eds), *Global Vigilantes*, London: Hurst Publishers, 2007, pp. 47–68; Kirsch, Thomas G. and Tilo Grätz, 'Vigilantism, state ontologies and encompassment: an introductory essay', in Kirsch, Thomas G. and Tilo Grätz (eds), *Domesticating vigilantism in Africa*, Oxford: Currey, 2010, pp. 1–25; Last, Murray, 'The search for security in Muslim northern Nigeria', *Africa*, 78, 1 (2008), pp. 41–63; Meagher, Kate, 'Hijacking civil society: the inside story of the Bakassi Boys vigilante group of south-eastern Nigeria', *Journal of Modern African Studies*, 45, 1 (2007), pp. 89–115; Pratten, David, '"The thief eats his shame": practice and power in Nigerian vigilantism', *Africa*, 78, 1 (2008), pp. 64–83; Smith, Daniel J., 'The Bakassi Boys: vigilantism, violence, and political imagination in Nigeria', *Cultural Anthropology*, 19, 3 (2004), pp. 429–55.

39. Following John and Jean Comaroff this field could be called part of an 'anthropological criminology'; Comaroff, John L. and Jean Comaroff, 'Reflections on the anthropology of law, governance and sovereignty', in von Benda-Beckmann, Franz, Keebet von Benda-Beckmann and Julia M. Eckert (eds), *Rules of Law and Laws of Ruling: On the Governance of Law*, Farnham: Ashgate, 2009, p. 55.

40. Biecker, Sarah and Klaus Schlichte, 'Policing Uganda, policing the world', *Working Papers of the Priority Programme 1448 of the German Research Foundation*, 2 (2013).

41. Comaroff, Jean and John L. Comaroff, 'Criminal obsessions, after Foucault: postcoloniality, policing, and the metaphysics of disorder', in Comaroff, Jean and John L. Comaroff (eds), *Law and disorder in the postcolony*, Chicago: University of Chicago Press, 2006, pp. 273–98.

42. Klantschnig, Gernot, 'The politics of law enforcement in Nigeria: lessons from the war on drugs', *The Journal of Modern African Studies*, 47, 4 (2009), pp. 529–49.

43. Eckert, Julia, 'Work in progress: the state at work in urban India', in Schareika, Nikolaus, Eva Spies and Pierre-Yves Le Meur (eds), *Auf dem Boden der Tatsachen: Festschrift für Thomas Bierschenk*, Köln: Köppe, 2011, pp. 435–45; Jauregui, Beatrice, 'Provisional agency in India: jugaad and legitimation of corruption', *American Ethnologist*, 41, 1 (2014), pp. 76–91.

44. Fassin, Didier, *La force de l'ordre: une anthropologie de la police des quartiers*, Paris: Seuil, 2011.

45. Martin, Jeffrey, 'A reasonable balance of law and sentiment: social order in democratic Taiwan from the policeman's point of view', *Law & Society Review*, 41, 3 (2007), pp. 665–98.

46. Fassin, Didier, 'Scenes from urban life: a modest proposal for a critical perspectivist approach', *Social Anthropology/Anthropologie Sociale*, 21, 3 (2013), p. 372.

47. Pollock proposes such explicit comparison, see Pollock, Sheldon, 'Comparison without hegemony', in Joas, Hans and Barbro Klein (eds), *The Benefit of Broad Horizons: Intellectual and Institutional Preconditions for a Global Social Science*, Leiden: Brill, 2010, p. 202; see also Niewöhner, Jörg and Thomas Scheffer, 'Introduction', *Comparative Sociology*, 7 (2008), pp. 273–85.

48. See Bayart, Jean-François, 'Comparer par le bas', *Sociétés politiques comparées*, n°1 (2008), p. 25, URL: http://www.fasopo.org/reasopo/n1/comparerparlebas.pdf, last accessed 4 June 2014.

49. Glaeser, A. *Divided in Unity: Identity, Germany and the Berlin Police*. Chicago, University of Chicago Press, 2000.

50. For a first study of police work in Somalia see Hills, Alice, 'Somalia works: police development as State building', *African Affairs*, 113, 450 (2014b), pp. 88–107.

52. Comaroff, Jean and John L. Comaroff, *Theory from the South: Or, How Euro-America Is Evolving Toward Africa*, Boulder: Paradigm Publishers, 2012.

1. POLICING AFRICA: STRUCTURES AND PATHWAYS

1. Cf. Johnson, David R., *Policing the Urban Underworld. The Impact of Crime on the Development of the American Police, 1800–1887*, Philadelphia, Penn.: Temple University Press, 1979, and Monkkonen, Eric, 'The Organized Response to Crime in Nineteenth- and Twentieth-Century America', *Journal of Interdisciplinary History*, 16, 1 (1983), pp. 113–28.

2. On the debate concerning the convergence of police forces see Hoberg, George, 'Globalization and Policy Convergence: Symposium Overview', *Journal of Comparative Policy Analysis, Research and Practice*, 23 (2001), 127–32. On the discussion about diffusion of policy models cf. Börzel, Tanja and Thomas Risse, 'From Europeanisation to Diffusion: Introduction', *West European Politics*, 35, 1 (2012), pp. 1–17.

3. See Neocleus, Mark, *The Fabrication of Social Order. A critical theory of police power*, London: Pluto Press, 2000.

4. See Deflem, Mathieu, *Policing World Society*, Oxford: Oxford University Press, 2002.

5. Cf. Bigo, Didier, 'Security and Immigration: Toward a Critique of the Governmentality of Unease', *Alternatives* 27 (2002), pp. 63–92, and Bigo, Didier, *Polices en réseaux. L'expérience européenne*, Paris: Presses de Science Po, 1996.

6. See the title of Lüdtke, Alf, *Gemeinwohl' Polizei und ,Festungspraxis'. Staatliche Gewaltsamkeit und innere Verwaltung in Preußen, 1815–1850*, Göttingen: Vandenhoeckh & Ruprecht, 1982.

7. Cf. Migdal, J.S. and Schlichte, K., 'Rethinking the State', in: K. Schlichte (ed.), *The*

Dynamics of States. The formation and crisis of state domination outside the OECD, Aldershot: Ashgate, 2005, p. 1–40.

8. Honoré Antoine Frenier's book 'Des classes dangereuses de la population dans le grandes villes', published in 1839, became a European success for the justification of urban police forces, cf. Lütke *Gemeinwohl' Polizei*, p. 117.

9. Biecker, Sarah and Schlichte, Klaus, 'Between Governance and Domination: the Everyday Life of Uganda's Police Forces', in: Koechlin, Lucy; Förster, Till (ed.), *The Politics of Governance. The state in Africa reconsidered*, London: Taylor & Francis, 2014.

10. Cf. The contribution of E. Krogstad in this volume and Bachmann, Jan, 'The Danger of "Uncovered Spaces": the "War on Terror" and its Effects on the Sahel Region', in Eckert, Julia (ed.), *The Social Life of Anti-Terrorism Laws: The War on Terror and the Classification of the 'Dangerous Other'*, New Brunswick: Bielefeld, Transkript, 2008, pp. 131–62.

11. Cf. Fassin, Didier, *La raison humanitaire. Une histoire morale du temps présent*, Paris: Gallimard, 2010, and Barnett, Michael, *Empire of Humanity. A history of humanitarianism*, Ithaca, N.Y.: Cornell UP, 2011.

12. Migdal, Joel S., *State in Society. Studying how states and societies transform and constitute one another*, Princeton, NJ: Princeton University Press, 2001.

13. See for example Badie, Bertrand, *L'Etat importé. L'occidentalisation du politique*, Paris: Fayard, 1992.

14. Brogden, Mike, 'The Emergence of the Police: the colonial dimension', *British Journal of Criminology*, 27, 1 (1987), pp. 4–14.

15. Bhambra, Gurminder K., 'Historical Sociology, international relations and connected histories', *Cambridge Review of International Affairs*, 23, 1 (2010), pp. 127–43.

16. On bureaucratic elements in African police forces cf. Göpfert, Mirco, 'Bureaucratic aesthetics: Report writing in the Nigérien gendarmerie', *American Ethnologist*, 40, 2 (2013), pp. 324–34, and Biecker and Schlichte, 'Between governance and domination'. Weber's classical formulations are to be found in: Weber, Max, 'The Profession and Vocation of Politics', in: Lassman, Peter and Speirs, Ronald (eds.), *Weber: Political Writings*, Cambridge, Cambridge University Press, p. 328; on the irrationality of rational bureaucracies cf. Herzfeld, Michael, *The Social Production of Indifference. Exploring the symbolic roots of Western bureaucracy*, Chicago,Ill.: University of Chicago Press, 1992 and Gupta, Akhil, *Red Tape: Bureaucracy, Structural Violence, and Poverty in India*, Durham, NC: Duke University Press, 2012.

17. See for example Bowling, Ben and Sheptycki, James, *Global Policing*, London: Sage, 2012, and Mattelart, Armand, *La globalisation de la surveillance. Aux origins de l'ordre sécuritaire*, Paris: La Découverte, 2007.

2. WHAT IS THE CONCEPT OF PROFESSIONALIZATION GOOD FOR?
AN ARGUMENT FROM LATE COLONIALISM

1. This article reworks an argument made in my monograph on police history in Togo (Glasman, Joël, *Les Corps habillés. Genèse coloniale des métiers de police au Togo*, Paris: Karthala, 2014). I thank Carly McLaughlin, Caroline Schubert and Julia Eichenberg for their comments on this piece.

2. OCDE-CAD, *Lignes directrices et ouvrages de référence du CAD. Réforme des systèmes de sécurité et gouvernance. Principes et bonnes pratiques*, OCDE, 2005; CDD, *Security Sector Governance in Africa: a Handbook*, Lagos: CDD, 2005; Berlière, Jean-Marc, *Le monde des polices en France*, Bruxelles: Complexe, 1996; Berlière, Jean-Marc, Catherine Denys, Dominique Kalifa and Vincent Milliot (eds), *Métiers de police. Être policier en Europe, XVIIIe-XXe siècles*, Rennes: PUR, 2008. For a discussion of the research on colonial police history, see: Blanchard, Emmanuel, Quentin Deluermoz and Joël Glasman, 'La professionnalisation policière en situation coloniale: détour conceptuel et explorations historiographiques', *Crime, History & Society*, 15, 2 (2011), pp. 33–53.

3. Cooper, Frederick, 'What is the Concept of Globalization Good for? An African Historian's Perspective', *African Affairs*, 100 (2001), pp. 189–213.

4. A collection of thirty-two life-stories of former members of police forces compiled in 2007 and 2008.

5. Foucault, Michel, *Surveiller et Punir. Naissance de la Prison*, Paris: Gallimard, 1975.

6. On the reform of the 1930s, see: Glasman, Joël, 'Unruly Agents: Police Reform, Bureaucratization and Police Agents' Agency in Interwar Togo', *The Journal of African History*, 55 (2014), pp. 79–100.

7. Glasman, 2014.

8. These calculations are made on the basis of: *Rapport annuel du gouvernement français au Conseil de la Société des Nations sur l'administration du Togo sous mandat*, 1930, and *Rapport du gouvernement français à l'Assemblée Générale des Nations Unies sur l'administration du Togo placé sous la tutelle de la France*, 1952 and 1953.

9. The reforms of police institutions in Togo were explicitly linked to the general criticism of the role of Native Guards voiced in the National Assembly in Paris. ANT 2APA Kouto 94: Affaires militaires. Circulaire du Commissaire de la République aux commandants de cercle, 21 avril 1948.

10. Cf.: *Rapport du gouvernement français à l'Assemblée Générale des Nations Unies sur l'administration du Togo placé sous la tutelle de la France*, 1947 (pp. 35–9) and 1957 (pp. 35–40).

11. I analysed all files of policemen serving from the 1940s to the 1960s available at the Archive (N=114). On the methodology of the micro-statistical analysis of personal files, see: Béliard, Aude and Emilie Biland, 'Enquêter à partir de dossiers personnels. Une ethnographie des relations entre institutions et individus', *Genèses*,

70 (2008), pp. 106–19; Daviet-Vincent, Marie-Bénédicte, 'La prise en compte de plusieurs générations dans la méthode prosoprographique: l'exemple des hauts fonctionnaires prussiens sous l'Empire et la République de Weimar', *Genèses*, 56 (2004), pp. 117–30; Mbaye, Saliou, 'Personnel Files and the Role of Qadis and Interpreters in the Colonial Administration of Saint-Louis, Senegal, 1857–1911', in: Benjamin N. Lawrance, Emily L. Osborn and Richard L. Roberts (eds), *Intermediaries, Interpreters and Clerks: African Employees in the Making of Colonial Africa*, Madison: University of Wisconsin Press, 2006, pp. 289–95.

12. Reasons for leaving the police (N=114): retirement (36 per cent), dismissal (28 per cent), death (18 per cent), resignation (14 per cent), unknown (4 per cent) (source: data base on career files).

13. Number of institutions in which the policemen served (N=107): only in the police (22 per cent); in two different security institutions (that is at least two institutions noted in the file) (55 per cent); in three security institutions (15 per cent); in four security institutions or more (8 per cent) (source: date base on career files).

14. AMFP/ Personnal File Gnabodé A.

15. This amounts to around 9 per cent of the active population. However, we should approach this figure, taken from the reports of the Inspection générale du travail, with caution, since the definition of the working population was flawed by a result of the underestimation of work in West African societies (the institution's definition of the working population included only male individuals aged fifteen to fourty-five). See Fall, 2010: pp. 189–90 and pp. 205–6.

16. In the original sources: cadre local supérieur (commissaires, inspecteurs, assistants de police) and cadre subalterne (adjudants-chefs, adjudants, brigadiers, agents de police).

17. Remaining part: unknown (N=114) (source: date base on personal files).

18. Former policeman, born around 1938, interview in Lomé Tokoin-Tamé, 28 November 2008.

19. Former soldier, born in 1937, about his first year in 1957. Interview in Lomé Dogbéavou-Gbonvié, 23 December 2008.

20. Former policeman, born in 1938, interview in Lomé-Amoutivé, 2 December 2008.

21. Blanchard & Deluermoz & Glasman 2011, Bograh 2003, Tete-Adjalogo 2006

3. THE COLONIAL SUBTEXT OF BRITISH-LED POLICE REFORM IN SIERRA LEONE

1. Egnell, Robert and Peter Halden, 'Laudable, Ahistorical and Overambitious: Security Sector Reform Meets State Formation Theory', *Conflict, Security & Development*, 9, 1 (2009), pp. 27–54; Giustozzi, Antonio, *The Art of Coercion: The Primitive Accumulation and Management of Coercive Power*, New York: Colombia University Press, 2011.

2. Giustozzi, op. cit.

3. Peake, Gordon and Eric Scheye, 'Unknotting Local Ownership', in Anja H. Ebnother and Perito, Robert M. 'Afghanistan's police', *Special Report of the United States Institute of Peace*, August 2009, p. 236.

4. Peake, Gordon. and Marenin, Otwin, 'Their reports are not read and their recommendations are resisted' *Police Practice and Research*, 9, 1 (2008), p. 64.

5. Ayoob, M., 'Humanitarian Intervention and State Sovereignty', *The International Journal of Human Rights*, 6, 1 (2002), pp. 81–102.

6. Bayart, Jean-François, 'Africa in the world: a history of extraversion', 99, 395 (2000), p. 228.

7. Baker, Bruce, 'Community policing in Freetown, Sierra Leone: foreign import or local solution?', *Journal of Intervention and Statebuilding*, 2, 1 (2008), pp. 23–42.; Jackson, Paul and Peter Albrecht, *Reconstructing Security after Conflict: Security Sector Reform in Sierra Leone*, Basingstoke: Palgrave MacMillan, 2011; Denney, Lisa 'Reducing poverty with teargas and batons: the security-development nexus in Sierra Leone', *African Affairs*, 110, 439 (2011), pp. 275–94; Stone, C., 'Supporting security, justice and development: lessons for a new era' New York: Vera Institute of Justice, 2005.

8. Fakondo, Kadi, 'Reforming and building capacity of the Sierra Leone police, 1997–2007' (Paper no. 8, Security System Transformation in Sierra Leone, 1997–2007), Birmingham: University of Birmingham, 2008; Meek, Sarah, 'Policing Sierra Leone', in Mark Malan, Sarah Meek, Thokozani Thusi, Jeremy Ginifer and Patrick Coker (eds.), *Building the Road to Recovery*, Pretoria: Institute for Security Studies, 2004; Horn, Adrian, Funmi Olonisakin and Gordon Peake, 'United Kingdom-led security sector reform in Sierra Leone', *Civil Wars*, 8, 2 (2006), pp. 109–23.

9. Baker, Bruce, 'The African post-conflict agenda in Sierra Leone', *Conflict, Security & Development*, 6, 1 (2006), pp. 25–49.

10. Quoted in Albrecht, Peter and Paul Jackson, *Security System Transformation in Sierra Leone, 1997–2007*, Birmingham: University of Birmingham, 2009.

11. Jackson, Paul and Peter Albrecht, *Reconstructing Security after Conflict: Security Sector Reform in Sierra Leone*, Basingstoke: Palgrave Macmillan, 2011, p. 54.

12. Ball, Nicole, Piet Biesheuvel, Tom Hamilton-Baillie and 'Funmi Olonisakin, 'Security and justice sector reform programming in Africa', *Evaluation Working Paper 23, Department for International Development, London*, April 2007.

13. *Commonwealth Police Development Task Force Sierra Leone. 'Interim Report', September 1998.* Adrian Horn private document.

14. Ibid.

15. Baker, 2006, p. 25.

16. Krogstad, Erlend Grøner, *Enduring Challenges of Statebuilding: British-led Police Reforms in Sierra Leone, 1945–1961 and 1998–2007*. D.phil thesis, University of Oxford, 2012.

17. According to a Sierra Leone government report, the SSD consisted of 1,844 officers in 1996. *Report of the Dr. Banya Committee on The Republic of Sierra Leone Police Force. August, 1996.* Adrian Horn private document.

18. *The Situation in Sierra Leone, A Security and Operational Perspective: A 'Mismatch' of Policies and Reality, 8.8.2004.* Ray England private document.

19. Albrecht and Jackson, 2009, p. 184.

20. Clapham, Christopher, 'Sierra Leone: The global-local politics of state collapse and attempted reconstruction', Paper presented at the Failed State Conference in Florence, 10–14 April 2001.

21. Keith Biddle, personal interview, Crewe, 27.10.09.

22. Dave Thomas, personal interview, Freetown 28.5.2010.

23. F.O. Sesay, personal interview, Freetown, 7.4.2010.

24. Solomon Berewa, personal interview, Freetown 12.6.2010.

25. See Nexon, Daniel and Thomas Wright, 'What's at Stake in the American Empire Debate', *American Political Science Review*, 101, 2 (2007), pp. 253–71.

26. Chesterman, Simon, *You, The People: The United Nations, Transitional Administration, and State-Building*, Oxford: Oxford University Press, 2004.

27. Paris, Roland, 'International peacebuilding and the "mission civilisatrice"', *Review of International Studies*, 28, 4 (2002), pp. 637–56; Paris, Roland, *At War's End: Building Peace after Civil Conflict*, Cambridge: Cambridge University Press, 2004; Bain, William, *Between Anarchy and Society: Trusteeship and the Obligations of Power*, Oxford: Oxford University Press, 2003; Bhuta, Nehal, 'Against State-Building', *Constellations*, 15, 4 (2008), pp. 517–42.

28. Abrahamsen, Rita, 'African studies and the postcolonial challenge', *African Affairs*, 102, 407 (2003), p. 192.

29. Richmond, Oliver, *A Post-Liberal Peace*, New York: Routledge, 2011, p. 1.

30. Ibid., p. 4.

31. Wendt, Alexander and Daniel Friedheim, 'Hierarchy under anarchy: informal empire and the East German state', *International Organization*, 49, 4 (1995), p. 245.

32. Brysk, Alison, Craig Parsons and Wayne Sandholtz, 'After empire: national identity and post-colonial families of nations', *European Journal of International Relations*, 8, 2 (2002), p. 268.

33. Ibid., p. 296.

34. Dave Thomas, personal interview, Freetown, 28.5.2010.

35. Gary Horlacker, personal interview, Freetown, 27.5.2010

36. Kaifi, Belal, Wajma Aslami, Seleiman Noori and Danielle Korhummel, 'A Decade after the 9/11 attacks: the demand for leaders with emotional intelligence and counselling skills', *Journal of Business Studies Quarterly*, 2, 2 (2011), p. 59.

37. Ebnother, Anja H. and Perito, Robert M. 'Afghanistan's police', *Special Report of the United States Institute of Peace*, August 2009.

38. Brysk, Parsons and Sandholtz, 2002, p. 277.

39. Ibid.

40. *The Sierra Leone Telegraph*: '49 Years of Independence and Freedom—What Is There to Celebrate?' 30.4.2010.

41. *Awareness Times*: 'Celebrating 50 Years of What?' 15.4.11.

42. *Awareness Times*: 'What a 50th Independence Anniversary!' 8.3.2011.

43. *The Sierra Leone Telegraph*: 50 years of Independence: What Is There to Celebrate? 26.2.2011

44. *The Exclusive Press Newspaper*: '50 Years of Backward Progression.' 12.8.2010

45. *The Sierra Leone Telegraph*: '49 Years of Independence and Freedom—What Is There to Celebrate?' 30.4.2010.

46. *Salone Times*, 26.4.2011.

47. Quoted in *Focus on Sierra Leone:* 'A Desire to Be Re-Colonised or Simply a Case of Nostalgia and Popular Desperation?' 27.5.2000. http://www.focus-on sierra-leone.co.uk/Colonialist_Moral_Crusader1.html (accessed 24.10.2011).

48. Ibid.

49. *The Telegraph* (UK): 'British Troops Lead Independence Parade' 28.4.2001, (my emphasis).

50. *The Sierra Leone Telegraph*: 'Rebuilding Lives and Regenerating War Torn Communities: Sierra Leone's Finance Minister Welcomes the Return of Direct British Intervention in Governance.' 14.6.2010.

51. *Focus on Sierra Leone:* 'A Desire to Be Re-Colonised or Simply a Case of Nostalgia and Popular Desperation?' 27.5.2000.

52. Shaw, Rosalind, *Memories of the Slave Trade. Ritual and the Historical Imagination in Sierra Leone*, Chicago: The University of Chicago Press, 2002; see also Osagie, Iyunolu, 'Historical memory and a new national consciousness: the Amistad revolt revisited in Sierra Leone', *The Massachusetts Review*, 38, 1 (1997), pp. 63–83; Ferme, *The Underneath of Things: Violence, History, and the Everyday in Sierra Leone*, Berkeley, Los Angeles and London: University of California Press, 2001, p. 219.

53. Bayart, Jean-François, 'Africa in the world: a history of extraversion', 99, 395 (2000), pp. 217–67, p. 218; Bayart, Jean-François, *The State in Africa: The Politics of the Belly*, London: Longman, 1993.

54. Chabal, Patrick and Jean-Pascal Daloz, *Africa Works: Disorder as Political Instrument*, Oxford: James Currey, 1999.

55. Clapham, Christopher, 'Review article: the *longue durée* of the African State", *African Affairs*, 93, 372 (1994), pp. 433–9.

56. Taylor, Ian, *The International Relations of Sub-Saharan Africa*, New York: Continuum, 2011, p. 6.

57. *BBC Newsnight*: 'Can Britain Lift Sierra Leone Out of Poverty?' 23.6.2010.

58. This appears somewhat conceited given that he was made Paramount Chief and

was, by his own admission, 'wildly popular' in the country. In fact, Paramount Chiefs interviewed by the BBC were not slow to express their wishes to see Blair treated with the pomp and circumstance normally reserved for state leaders: 'We would like that the next time he visited, he would ride in a motorcade along the street'. *BBC Newsnight*: 'Can Britain lift Sierra Leone out of poverty?' 23.6.2010.

59. Wendt, Alexander and Daniel Friedheim, 'Hierarchy under anarchy: informal empire and the East German state', *International Organization*, 49, 4 (1995), pp. 689–721.

60. *BBC Newsnight*: 'Can Britain Lift Sierra Leone Out of Poverty?' 23.6.2010.

61. Jackson and Albrecht, 2011, p. 16.

62. Keith Biddle, personal interview, Crewe, 27.10.09. Peter Penfold, who was also firmly of the opinion that Britain needed 'executive authority to push advice through', recalled that Kabbah 'had meetings with Clare Short, [where] he made the point that he wanted a British person to head the police force'. Penfold, personal interview, Oxford 19.10.2010.

63. Hampson, Fen Osler, 'Can peacebuilding work?' *Cornell International Law Journal*, 30, 3 (1997), p. 708.

64. Paris, 2002, p. 645.

65. This position of Kabbah's was referred to by Peter Penfold. Penfold, personal interview, Oxford 19.10.2010.

66. *Address by President Ahmed Tejan Kabbah to the Nation*, 27.4.1999. http://www.sierra-leone.org/Speeches/kabbah-042799.html, last accessed 1 November 2011.

67. See Ayoob, 2002; Chandler, David, *Empire in Denial: The Politics of State Building*, London: Pluto Press, 2006; Bickerton, Bickerton, Christopher J., Philip Cunliffe and Alexander Gourevitch (eds.), *Politics without Sovereignty: A Critique of Contemporary International Relations*, London: UCL Press, 2007. Those who think it is necessary to suspend the sovereignty of 'weak' or 'rogue' states in order to solve global problems emanating from them also pay little attention to the agency of such states as they become the subject of neo-imperial statebuilding. See for example Ferguson, Niall, *Colossus: The Rise and Fall of the American Empire*, London: Penguin, 2004.

68. Krasner, Stephen, 'Sharing sovereignty: new institutions for collapsed and failing states', *International Security*, 29, 2 (2004), pp. 85–120.

69. Ibid., p. 108; see also Keohane, Robert, 'Political authority after intervention: gradations in sovereignty', in J. L. Holzgrefe and Robert Keohane (eds), *Humanitarian Intervention. Ethical, Legal and Political Dilemmas* Cambridge: Cambridge University Press, 2003.

70. Jackson and Albrecht, 2011, p. 66.

71. Ibid.

72. Wendt and Friedheim, 1995, p. 702f.

73. Wendt, Alexander and Michael Barnett, 'Dependent state formation and third world militarization", *Review of International Studies*, 19, 4 (1993), p. 322.

74. Krasner, 2004, p. 108.
75. Donais, Timothy, 'Empowerment or imposition? Dilemmas of local ownership in post-conflict peacebuilding processes', *Peace & Change*, 34, 1 (2009), p. 3.
76. Chesterman, 2004, p. 5.
77. United States Institute of Peace, 'Local Ownership of Security Sector Reform' (USIP, Washington DC, 2010).
78. Ginifer, Jeremy, 'Evaluation of the conflict prevention pools', *Department for International Development, Evaluation Report EV 647*, 2004, p. 2.
79. United States Institute of Peace, 'Local Ownership of Security Sector Reform'.
80. Richard Moigbe, personal interview, Freetown, 8.4.2010
81. Morie Lengor, personal interview, Freetown 1.12.2009.
82. Keith Biddle, personal interview, Crewe, 27.10.09.
83. Keith Biddle, personal interview, Crewe, 27.10.09.
84. Peake and Marenin, 2008, p. 65.
85. Dave Thomas, personal interview, Freetown 28.5.2010.
86. Keith Biddle, personal interview, Crewe, 27.10.09.
87. Ibid.
88. Brima Acha Kamara, personal interview, Freetown, 7.4.2010.
89. Desmond Buck, personal interview, Makeni, 12.4.2010.
90. Kellie Conteh, personal interview, Freetown, 2.6.2010.
91. Desmond Buck, personal interview, Makeni, 12.4.2010.
92. Kellie Conteh, personal interview, Freetown, 2.6.2010.
93. Peter Penfold, personal interview, Oxford 19.10.2010.
94. Lundestad, Geir, 'Empire by invitation? The United States and Western Europe, 1945–1952', *Journal of Peace Research*, 23, 3 (1985), p. 268.
95. Ibid.

4. POLICING DURING AND AFTER APARTHEID: A NEW PERSPECTIVE ON CONTINUITY AND CHANGE

1. A similar version of this essay was published in African Affairs 113/145, 173–191 2014.
2. Altbeker, Antony, *The Dirty Work of Democracy: A Year on the Streets with the SAPS*. Johannesburg: Jonathan Ball, 2005; Leggett, Ted, 'The State of Crime and Policing', in J. Daniel, R. Southall and J. Lutchman, eds, *State of the Nation: South Africa, 2004–2005*. Pretoria: HSRC Press, 2006, pp. 215–41; Brogden, Mike, '"Horses for courses" and "thin blue lines": Community policing in transitional society', *Police Quarterly* 8, 1 (2005), pp. 64–98; Steinberg, Jonny, 'Crime Prevention Goes Abroad: Policy Transfer and Policing in Post-Apartheid South Africa,' *Theoretical Criminology*, 15, 4 (2011), pp. 349–64.
3. For a book-length study of the failure of criminal justice transformation in South

Africa, Gordon, Diana *Transformation and Trouble: Crime, Justice and Participation in Democratic South Africa*. Ann Arbor: Michigan University Press, 2006.

4. See, for instance, Super, Gail, *Governing Through Crime in South Africa: The Politics of Race and Class In Neoliberalizing Regimes*. London: Ashgate, 2013. Super argues that in both the late apartheid and democratic periods, the commodification of more and more spheres of social life has resulted in the structural marginalization of the poor, requiring them to be governed coercively.

5. Hornberger, Julia, 'From General to Commissioner to General: On the popular state of policing in South Africa', *Law and Social Inquiry* 38(3) (2013), pp. 598–614; Steinberg, Jonny, 'Security and Disappointment: Policing, freedom and xenophobia in South Africa,' *British Journal of Criminology*, 52, 2 (2012) pp. 345–60.

6. Brodeur, Jean-Paul, 'High and Low Policing: Remarks about the policing of political activities', *Social Problems* 30, 5 (1983), pp. 507–20; Brodeur, Jean-Paul, *The Policing Web*. New York, Oxford University Press, 2010, pp. 223–54.

7. Brodeur, *The Policing Web*, p. 224.

8. See, famously, Garland, David, *The Culture of Control: Crime and social order in contemporary society*. Oxford, Oxford University Press, 2001.

9. O'Brien, Kevin, 'Counter-Intelligence for Counter-Revolutionary Warfare: the South African Police Security Branch 1979–1990, *Intelligence and National Security* 16, 3 (2001), p. 38.

10. With the notable exception of Altbeker, Antony, 'Solving crime: the state of the SAPS detective service' monograph, Institute for Security Studies, Pretoria, 1998; Altbeker, Antony, *A country at war with itself*. Johannesburg, Jonathan Ball, 2007.

11. Ellis, Stephen, *External Mission: the ANC in exile 1960–1990*. London, Hurst, 2012, pp. 60–64.

12. Giliomee, Hermann, *The Last Afrikaner Leaders: A supreme test of power*. Cape Town, Tafelberg, 2012, pp. 124–128.

13. For an account of Botha's disdain for the SAP's role in high policing, see Giliomee, *The Last Afrikaner Leaders*, pp. 118–38.

14. Seegers, Annette, 'South Africa's National Security Management System, 1972–1990,' *Journal of Modern African Studies*, 29, 2 (1991), pp. 253–273.

15. Seegers, Annette, *The Military in the Making of Modern South Africa*. London, I.B. Tauris, 1996, pp. 161–202.

16. Swilling, Mark, and Phillips, Mark, 'State Power in the 1980s: from "total strategy" to "counter-revolutionary warfare"', in J. Cock and L. Nathan (eds) *War and Society: the Militarization of South Africa*. New York, St Martin's Press, 1989, pp. 134–48.

17. Andre Roos, former security policeman, email to author, 24 August 2012.

18. Interview with former security policeman, Pretoria, 17 August 2012.

19. Interview with Johan Burger, Pretoria, 21 August 2012.

20. Interview with Johan Burger, Pretoria, 21 August 2012.

21. For a brief exploration of how variegated and complex the history of uniformed policing in urban South Africa was see Steinberg, Jonny, *Thin Blue: the unwritten rules of policing South Africa*. Johannesburg, Jonathan Ball, 2008, pp. 69–99.

22. For a good sense of what 'ordinary' policing looked like in black urban Johannesburg from the beginning of the 1930s until the end of the 1950s, see Goodhew, David, 'Between the Devil and the Deep Blue Sea: Crime, policing and the western areas of Johannesburg, c. 1930–1962,' Paper presented to the Wits History Workshop, Johannesburg, February 1990.

23. Brewer, John D, *Black and Blue: Policing in South Africa*. Oxford, Clarendon Press, 1994, p. 2.

24. Steinberg, *Thin Blue*, pp. 83–99.

25. Shaw, Mark, 'Point of Order: policing the compromise,' in S. Friedman and D. Atkinson (eds), *South African Review 7: Small Miracle—South Africa's negotiated settlement*. Johannesburg: Ravan Press, 1994, pp. 68–85.

26. Albeit in highly modified form because information gathered on organized crime is only useful if presentable as court evidence and thus requires something of a reinvention of how information is gathered.

27. While the new Police Commissioner, George Fivaz, once worked as a detective, he had risen through the ranks in the police's Efficiency Services department and was thus regarded as an organizational technocrat who knew the mechanics of uniformed policing well.

28. Dixon, William J, 'Globalising the local: A genealogy of sector policing in South Africa,' *International Relations* 21, 2 (2007), pp. 163–82.

29. This argument is stated most powerfully and originally in Altbeker, *A Country at War With Itself*.

30. Altbeker, 'Solving crime'.

31. Indeed, two of the departments that had done the lion's high policing since 1978, the police and the military, now barely did it at all. The question of who might spy upon politicians and bureaucrats was of course very sensitive. For now, the only organization entrusted with the task was the newly formed National Intelligence Agency which was flooded with trusted ANC personnel.

32. Steinberg, *Thin Blue*.

33. Leggett, 'The State of Crime'.

34. Leggett, ibid.; Hornberger, Julia, *Policing and Human Rights: the meaning of violence and justice in the everyday policing of Johannesburg*. London, Routledge, 2011.

35. Bittner, Egon, 'Florence Nightingale in Pursuit of Willie Sutton: a theory of the police,' in Idem, *Aspects of Police Work*, Boston: Northeastern University Press, 1990.

36. See especially Booysen, Susan, *The African National Congress and the Regeneration of Political Power*. Johannesburg: Wits University Press, 2011.

37. Gevisser, Mark, *Thabo Mbeki: The dream deferred*. Johannesburg: Jonathan Ball, 2007, pp. 653–795.
38. The best account is by Cargill, Jenny, *Trick or Treat: Rethinking black economic empowerment*. Cape Town: Jacana, 2010.
39. Holden, Paul and Van Vuuren, Hennie, *The Devil in the Detail: How the arms deal changed everything*. Johannesburg: Jonathan Ball, 2011.
40. Interview, senior police officer, Pretoria, 21 June 2000.
41. These included the Serious and Violent Crimes Unit, the Organized Crime Unit, the South African Narcotics Bureau, the Child Protection Unit, the Precious Metals Smuggling Unit, and Anti-Corruption Unit and others.
42. Burger, Johan, 'Reflections on Restructuring in the SAPS,' paper presented to the Conference of Policing in South Africa, Institute for Security Studies, Pretoria, 2007.
43. Interview with Rudolph Zinn, University of South Africa, 21 August 2012.
44. Interview with senior police official, Pretoria, 19 August 2012.
45. Basson, Adriaan, *Finish & Klaar: Selebi's fall from Interpol to the underworld*. Cape Town, Tafelberg, 2012.
46. Basson, *Finish and Klaar*; Basson, Adriaan, *Zuma Exposed*. Johannesburg, Jonathan Ball, 2012; Weiner, Mandy, *Killing Kebble: an underworld exposed*. Johannesburg, Pan Macmillan, 2011. Pikoli, Vusi and Weiner, Mandy, *My Second Initiation*. Johannesburg: Picador, 2013.
47. Pauw, Jacques, *Into the Heart of Darkness: Confessions of apartheid's assassins*. Johannesburg, Jonathan Ball, 2007.
48. Steinberg, Jonny, 'Living in fear of the day the attack dogs obey another master,' *Sunday Times*, 13 February 2011.
49. Bruce, David, 'The Road to Marikana: Abuses of force during public order policing operations,' South African Civil Society Information Service, 12 October 2012, at http://sacsis.org.za/site/article/1455, last accessed 20 January 2017.
50. For a fine analysis, see Von Holdt, Karl, *et al*, *The Smoke That Calls: Insurgent citizenship, collective violence and the struggle for a place in the new South Africa*. Johannesburg: Centre for the Study of Violence and Reconciliation, 2011.
51. Booysen, *The African National Congress*, pp. 126–73.
52. Bruce, David, 'Marikana and the Doctrine of Maximum Force, *Mampoer*, 2013, at http://www.marikanacomm.org.za/exhibits/Exhibit-FFF-14.pdf, last accessed 20 January 2017.

5. HISTORICISING VIGILANTE POLICING IN PLATEAU STATE, NIGERIA

1. Part of the primary data used for this chapter is from fieldwork conducted in Langtang North, Langtang South, Shendam, and Mikang Local Governments of Plateau State, Nigeria. This is part of a broader field research undertaken in pursuance of a doctorate degree at the University of Bayreuth, Germany.

2. Examples of such literature are Baker, B 'When the Bakassi Boys came: Eastern Nigeria Confronts Vigilantism', *Journal of Contemporary African Affairs*, 20, (2002) pp. 223–44. Pratten, David, 'The Thief eats his Shame: Practice and Power in Nigerian Vigilantism', *Africa* 78 (1), (2008) pp. 64–83. Meagher, Kate, Hijacking Civil Society: the Inside Story of the Bakassi Boys Vigilante Group of South-Eastern Nigeria, *Journal of Modern African Studies*, 45, 1, (2007), pp. 89–115. Fourchard, L. 'A New Name for an Old Practice: Vigilantes in South-Western Nigeria', *Africa* 78 (1) (2007) pp. 16–40. Akinleye, R.T. 'Ethnic Militancy and National Stability in Nigeria: A Case Study of the Oodua People's Congress', *African Affairs*, 100, 401, (2001), pp. 623–40.

3. See Murray Last, 'The Search for Security in Muslim Northern Nigerian', *Africa*, 78, 1, (2008) pp. 41–63. Adamu, F.L, 'Gender, Hisba and the Enforcement of Morality in Northern Nigeria', *Africa*, 78, 1 (2008) and Matusitz, J. and Repass, M 'Gangs in Nigeria: An Updated Examination', *Crime Law and Social Change*, Springer Science and Business Media (2009).

4. See Adam, Higazi, 'Social Mobilization and Collective Violence: Vigilantes and Militias in the Lowlands of Plateau State, Central Nigeria', *Africa* 78, 1, (2008) pp. 108–35.

5. Pratten, David, 'Singing thieves: History and practice in Nigerian popular justice,' in Artreye Sen and David Pratten (eds.), *Global Vigilantes*, Hurst, London, 2007 pp. 175–206; also see Pratten, David, 'Bodies of Power: Narratives of Selfhood and Security in Nigeria,' in Kirsch, Thomas and Tilo Gratz (eds.), *Domesticating Vigilantism in Africa*, London: James Currey, 2010, pp. 118–38; and Higazi, Adam, 'Social Mobilization and Collective Violence'.

6. Higazi, Adam, 'Social Mobilization and Collective Violence'.

7. Ray Abrahams, 'Sungusungu: village vigilante groups in Tanzania', *African Affairs*, 86 (1987), pp. 179–96, also see Ray Abrahams, *Vigilant Citizens: Vigilantism and the State*, Cambridge: Cambridge University Press, 1998.

8. It should be noted though that there are some exceptions. In some cases it is not the state making the attempt; some vigilantes have been anti-state. However in Anambra state around 1997–2000, the state passed a law to transform (co-opt) Bakassi Boys hired by traders' associations into Anambra Vigilante Services. The coexistence with formal police was not smooth.

9. Fourchard, Laurent, 'A new name for an old practice: Vigilantes in south western Nigeria' *Africa*, 78, 1, (2008) pp. 16–40.

10. Buur, Lars and Jensen, Steffen, 'Introduction: Vigilantism and the policing of everyday life in South Africa' *African Studies* 63, 2 (2004), p. 140

11. Fourchard, *A new name for an old practice*.

12. Gratz, Tilo, 'Devi and his Men: The Rise and Fall of a Vigilante Movement in Benin' in Kirsch and Gratz, *Domesticating Vigilantism in Africa*, p. 79–97.

13. This date marked Nigeria's return to civil rule after almost two decades of military rule.

14. B. F. Bawa 'Origin, Migrations and Early History of the Lowland Communities of Plateau State', Aliyu A. Idrees and Yakubu A. Ochefu (eds), *Studies in the History of Central Nigeria Area*, volume 1, Lagos: CSS, 2002, pp. 71–2.

15. Examples of such emirates in the Plateau Province were Wase and Kanam.

16. For a detailed and sustained analysis of this resistance see Moses E. Ochuno, *Colonialism By Proxy: Hausa Imperial Agents and Middle Belt Consciousness in Nigeria*, Bloomington and Indianapolis: Indiana University Press, 2014, pp. 77–85.

17. For more on this see Tamuno, T.N., *The Police in Modern Nigeria*, 1861–1965, Ibadan, University Press, 1960.

18. Tamuno, ibid., pp. 51–6.

19. Rotimi, Kemi, *The Police in a Federal State: the Nigerian Experience*, Ibadan: College Press, 2001.

20. Rotimi, ibid., p. 14.

21. Whitaker, C.S., *The Politics of Tradition: Continuity and Change in Northern Nigeria 1946–1969*, Princeton University Press, 1970, p. 31

22. Dudley, B.J., *Parties and Politics in Northern Nigeria*, London: Frank Cass, 1968, p. 63

23. Ibid., pp. 63–64

24. Yahaya, A.D., *The Native Authority System in Northern Nigeria, 1950–1970*, Zaria: Ahmadu Bello University Press, 1980, pp. 4–5.

25. Ibid., p. 5.

26. Ibid., p. 5.

27. Rotimi, *The Police in a Federal State*, p. 20, In interviews with former colonial officers who had served amongst the non-Muslim groups of the then northern Nigeria, this point was reiterated.

28. Rotimi, ibid., p. 20

29. NAK. 2/24/11/1932, Annual Report, Plateau Province 1931, 2 Mar 1932.

30. The exceptions were Jema'a, Shendam, and Wase where there was some semblance of a centralised paramount chieftaincy when indirect rule was introduced in the Plateau Province.

31. Mangvwat, M, 'Warfare on the Jos Plateau in the Nineteenth Century' in Falola, Toyin and Law, Robin (eds), *Warfare and Diplomacy in Precolonial Nigeria: Essays in Honor of Robert Smith*, African Studies Program: University of Wisconsin-Madison, 1992, p. 115.

32. Ibid., p. 115.

33. Originally Dogarai were personal security staff of the chiefly authorities of the Hausa ruling aristocracy (*Habe Sarki Sarauta System*) in pre-colonial times.

34. Mamdani, Mahmood, *Citizen and Subject: Contemporary Africa and the Legacy of Late Colonialism*, Princeton: Princeton University Press, 1996.

35. Ibeanu, Okechukwu and Momoh, Abubakar, 'State Responsiveness to Public Security Needs: The Politics of Security Decision-Making, Nigeria Country Study,' *CSDG Papers*, No. 14, (2008) p. 8.

36. Ibeanu and Momoh, ibid., p. 8.
37. Baker, Bruce, *Multi-Choice Policing in Africa*, Uppsala: Nordic Africa Institute, 2008, p. 6.
38. The colonial Native Authority Police were colloquially referred to as 'Yandoka'. This was a reference to the Native Authority constables as enforcers of the law.
39. NAK. SNP 147/1937, Memo to all Residents, Yandoka, 14 Aug 1937.
40. NAK. No. 149/231, D.O. Shendam to R.O. PlaProf, Yandoka, 20 Mar 1944.
41. Officer Administering the Government (O.A.G) to the Secretary of State for Colonies (S.O.S), 10 Apr 1929, TNA: PRO, CO583, p. 8.
42. This was usually a temporary appointment for periods which the Governor of the Colony is outside the territory or indisposed and unable to perform his duties—Interview with Mr. John Smith, Cheltenham, UK, 17 Aug 2013.
43. O.A.G, to the S.O.S, 10 Apr 1929, TNA: PRO, CO583, P9.
44. Interview with Mr Robin Mitchell, Kent, United Kingdom, 23 Aug 2013.
45. In the 70s and 80s vigilante groups in Plateau state were known as Yanbanga, a corruption of the English word 'vanguard'—instead of 'Yan-vanguard' (the prefix 'Yan'denotes literally 'sons of' and is used to label a collective) it quickly became Yanbanga in colloquial Hausa. This should not be confused with the other usage of Yanbanga in the late 1970s and early 1980s in the northern Nigerian city of Kano, which refers to political party thugs recruited to unsettle political rivals. In recent times amongst the Hausa speaking areas of Plateau State the name Yan-Sintiri—which means watchmen or the official legal title Vigilante Group of Nigeria (VGN) are the preferred terms.
46. NAK. JosProf, 1/1/6451, Annual Report Lowland Division, 1953, p. 4 and 1955, p. 4
47. Op. cit., Mangvwat, *A History of Class Formation in the Plateau Province*, 2014, p. 43.
48. Ibid., p. 44.
49. Once the name of the particular chief is mentioned, it is easy to establish the period when the events being recounted occurred.
50. Alhaji Ali Dakshang, interviewed by Jimam Lar, Dadur, Langtang North, 12.08.2012
51. Op. cit., Mangvwat, *A History of Class Formation on the Plateau*, 2014, p. 44.
52. Ibid., p. 45.
53. Alhaji Ali Dakshang, interviewed by Jimam Lar, Dadur, Langtang North, 12.08.2012
54. In this context, Yanbanga refers to community and neighbourhood policing structures.
55. Group interview with four former *Yanbanga*, Dadur, Langtang North, 13.08.2012, and interview with a former Vigilante, Shendam, Plateau state, 11.11.2012.
56. Isichei, E., *Studies in the History of Plateau State, Nigeria*, London: Macmillan Press, 1982, p. 25.

57. Group interview, former *Yanbanga*, Dadur, Langtang North, Plateau State, 13.08.2012.

58. Comparatively see Pratten, *The Thief eats his Shame*.

59. Group Interview Dadur, Langtang North LGA, 10.08.2012 and Group Interview Shimankar, Shendam LGA, 14.11.2012.

60. For more on this argument see Pratten, '"The Thief Eats His Shame": Practice and Power in Nigerian Vigilantism'. *Africa*, 78, pp. 64–83; also see Fourchard, Laurent, 'A new name for an old practice: Vigilantes in south western Nigeria'.

61. Olukoshi, Adebayo, ed., *Crisis and Adjustment in the Nigerian Economy*, Lagos: JAD, (1991) pp. 28–33.

62. Hausa name for Ward Head, adopted by ethnic groups in central Nigeria.

63. Interview with Chairman Vigilante Group of Nigeria, Langtang North, at his residence Langtang, 14.08.2012.

64. The '*yansandan* NA' referred to was another colloquial term for the Native Authority Police.

65. DPM is an abbreviation for Director of Personnel Management, usually the head of administration, and normally the most senior career civil servant at the local government level.

66. The typology of these suspects ranged from armed robbers to petty thieves and even delinquent youths.

67. The dance of shame refers to a practice of punishment that entailed parading the individual found guilty of an offence around the village or the market square in larger towns, the objective being to humiliate but also to deter.

68. In this context armed robbery refers to robbery armed with machetes and small axes, not guns.

69. It is hard to verify the extent to which this network of vigilantes is organised and structured across the landscape of the country. I can however confirm that for states which I visited, mainly Plateau and neighbouring Nassarawa, Kaduna, and Bauchi, there were vigilante groups on the ground which recognised Alhaji Ali Sokoto as the national leader.

70. There are however, exceptions where monthly stipends and allowances are paid.

71. Gratz, 'Devi and his Men'.

72. Ownership here refers not to land title but to which community should be recognised as customary proprietors of the area, with corresponding primary citizenship rights and political entitlements.

73. Higazi, *Social Mobilization and Collective Violence*, 2008.

74. Hüsken, Thomas and Klute, Georg, 'Emerging Forms of Power in Contemporary Africa—a Theoretical and Empirical Research Outline', *Diskussionspapiere 101*, Berlin: Klaus Schwarz Verlag, 2008.

75. Group Interview, Vigilante Group of Nigeria, Yelwa Town Branch held at Local office, Yelwa 15.11.2012.

76. Abrams, Philip, 'Notes on the difficulty of studying the state', *Journal of Historical Sociology* 1, 1, (1988) pp. 58–89.

77. Harnischfeger, Johannes, 'Ethnicity, Religion and the Failure of "Common Law" in Nigeria', in Thomas G. Kirsch and Tilo Gratz (eds), James Currey, Suffolk and Rochester, 2010, pp. 51–78.

78. For more on this see Fourchard, *A new name for an old practice*, and also Abrahamsen, Rita and Williams, Michael C., *Security Beyond the State: Private Security in International Politics*, Cambridge: Cambridge University, Press, 2011.

79. Mbembe, Achille, *On the Postcolony*, Berkeley: University of California Press, 2001, p. 110.

6. WHO ARE THE POLICE IN AFRICA?

1. See Bayley, David, *Patterns of Policing: A Comparative International Analysis*, New Brunswick: Rutgers University Press, 1985; Brodeur, Jean-Paul (ed.), *Comparisons in Policing: An International Perspective*, Aldershot: Avebury, 1995; Dennis, Norman and George Erdos, *Cultures and Crimes: Policing in Four Nations*, London: The Institute for the Study of Civil Society, 2005. For one of the rare comparative studies, see Owen, Olly and Sarah-Jane Cooper-Knock, 'Between vigilantism and bureaucracy: improving our understanding of police work in Nigeria and South Africa', *Theoretical Criminology* (published online before print 19 November 2014).

2. This text was inspired by the research carried out by Mainz anthropologists on the police in Benin, Ghana and Niger (Badou, Agnes, *Socialisation professionnelle et gestion des carrières des agents de sécurité publique au Bénin*, Dr. phil. dissertation, Mainz, 2013; Beek, Jan, *Boundary Work: The Police in Ghana*, Dr. phil. dissertation, Mainz, 2014; Göpfert, Mirco, 'Enforcing the Law, Restoring Peace: An Ethnography of the Nigerian Gendarmerie', Dr. phil. dissertation, Mainz, 2014; Hofferberth, Elena, 'La justice au village: Akteure und Dynamiken der Konfliktregelung im ländlichen Bénin (Boukombé)', Magister thesis, Mainz, 2013; Peth, Lisa, 'C'est le terrain qui commande: Normenpluralismus im Alltag von Polizisten in Parakou, Benin', *Working Paper of the Department of Anthropology and African Studies* 151 (2014); Thurmann, Laura, '"We are the best of the best": Self-images of Congolese special police officers', BA thesis, Mainz, 2014; Witte, Annika, 'Grauzonen: Funktionsweisen der Beniner Polizei und ihr Verhältnis zur Bevölkerung', *Working Paper of the Department of Anthropology and African Studies* 133 (2012). This text was also inspired by the Mainz studies on States at Work (Bierschenk, Thomas, and Jean-Pierre Olivier de Sardan (eds), *States at Work: Dynamics of African Bureaucracies*, Leiden: Brill, 2014a), which included research on the legal system (Budniok, Jan, 'The Politics of Integrity: Becoming and Being a Judge in Ghana,' Dr. phil. dissertation, Mainz, 2014; Kolloch, Annalena, '"Il faut être un modèle": Richterinnen und Staatsanwältinnen in der Republik Benin zwischen Berufsidealen und

Anpassungsstrategien', Magister thesis, Mainz, 2013; Schütz, Elisa, *Schlichtungsgerichte in Benin: Graswurzeljustiz oder der verlängerte Arm des Leviathan?*, Magister thesis, Mainz, 2013) and the education sector, particularly the teaching profession (Bierschenk, Thomas, *Doing the State, en attendant: Ethnographic Explorations among Primary School Teachers in the Republic of Benin*, manuscript, 2009; Tama, Clarisse, *Etre enseignant au Bénin: Les mutations d'un groupe professionnel*, Köln: Köppe, 2014; Fichtner, Sarah, *The NGOisation of Education: Case Studies from Benin*, Köppe: Köln, 2012), provided an additional context. Thus the reader will have no difficulty in identifying a strong West African bias in the following account, if not an overt focus on Benin. I would like to thank Jan Beek, Mirco Göpfert and Laura Thurmann for their detailed comments on earlier versions of this text, and Susan Cox for translation into English.

3. Gluckman, Max, 'Concepts in the comparative study of tribal law', in Nader, Laura (ed.), *Law in Culture and Society*, Chicago: Aldine, 1969, pp. 349–73.

4. Bohannan, Paul, 'Ethnography and comparison in legal anthropology', in Nader, Laura (ed.), *Law in Culture and Society*, Chicago: Aldine, 1969, pp. 401–18.

5. Espagne, Michel, *Comparison and Transfer: A Question of Method*, in Midell, Matthias and Lluis Roura Aulinas (eds), *Transnational Challenges to National History Writing*, London: Palgrave Macmillan, 2012, pp. 36–53.

6. Behrends, Andrea, Sung-Joon Park, and Richard Rottenburg, *Travelling Models in African Conflict Resolution: Translating Technologies of Social Ordering*, Leiden: Brill, 2014. See also Bierschenk, Thomas, 'From the anthropology of development to the anthropology of global social engineering', *Zeitschrift für Ethnologie* 139, 1 (2014a), pp. 73–98.

7. Paramilitary *gendarmerie*-like police organizations are also found, however, in Lusophone Africa, e.g. the Policia Nacional in Guinea Bissau which was only established a few years ago (Kohl, Christoph, 'Translationsprobleme bei der Reform des Polizeisektors in Guinea Bissau', *Peace Research Institute Frankfurt Report* 6/2014 (2014), p. 6). The (Belgian) Congo had a *gendarmerie* for a long time; however, it was abolished or integrated into the current police force in the course of various police reforms (Nlandu, Thierry Mayamba, *Mapping Police Services in the Democratic Republic of Congo: Institutional Interactions at Central, Provincial and Local Levels*, Brighton: Institute of Development Studies, 2012).

8. Communication by Klaus Schlichte, Police in West Africa workshop, Mainz, 15.6.2013.

9. On this point, see Beek, Jan, and Mirco Göpfert, 'Travelling Police: The potential for change in the wake of police reform in West Africa', *Social Anthropology* 23, 4 (2015), pp. 465–79.

10. See Anderson, David and David Killingray, Consent, coercion and colonial control: policing the empire, 1830–1940, in Anderson, David and David Killingray (eds), *Policing the Empire: Government, Authority, and Control, 1830–1940*,

Manchester: Manchester University Press, 1991, pp. 1–15; Sinclair, Georgina, *At the End of the Line: Colonial Policing and the Imperial Endgame 1945–80*, Manchester: Manchester University Press, 2006; Williams, Chris A., 'Expendiency, authority and duplicity: reforming Sheffield's police 1832–1840', in Trainor, Richard and Robert Morris (eds), Urban Governance: Britain and Beyond since 1750, Ashgate: Aldershot, 2000, pp. 115–27; for the Gold Coast/Ghana, see Beek, 2014.

11. Bierschenk, 2014a.

12. Glasman, Joel and Giorgio Blundo (eds), 'Bureaucrats in Uniform', Thematic issue of *Sociologus* 63, 1–2 (2013).

13. Bierschenk, Thomas, and Jean-Pierre Olivier de Sardan, 'Ethnographies of public services in Africa: an Emerging research paradigm', in Bierschenk, Thomas, and Jean-Pierre Olivier de Sardan (eds), *States at Work: Dynamics of African Bureaucracies*, Leiden: Brill, 2014b, pp. 35–65.

14. For an initial attempt of this nature, see Olivier de Sardan, Jean-Pierre, 'La sage femme et le douanier: Cultures professionnelles locales et culture professionnelle privatisée en Afrique de l'Ouest', *Autrepart* 20 (2001), pp. 61–73.

15. Brodeur, 1995; Williams, 2000.

16. Glasman, Joël, *Les corps habillés au Togo: Genèse coloniale des métiers de police*, Paris: Karthala, 2014.

17. Witte, 2012.

18. Badou, 2013.

19. Oral communication Laura Thurmann.

20. Migdal, Joel S. and Klaus Schlichte, 'Rethinking the state', in Schlichte, Klaus (ed.), *The Dynamics of States: The Formation and Crises of State Domination*, Aldershot: Ashgate, 2005, pp. 1–40. See also Bierschenk, Thomas, and Jean-Pierre Olivier de Sardan, 'Studying the dynamics of African bureaucracies: an introduction to states at work', in Bierschenk, Thomas, and Jean-Pierre Olivier de Sardan (eds), *States at Work: Dynamics of African Bureaucracies*, Leiden: Brill, 2014c, pp. 3–33.

21. Abrams, Philip, 'Notes on the difficulty of studying the state', *Journal of Historical Sociology* 1, 1 (1988), pp. 58–89; Althusser, Louis, *Ideology and ideological state apparatuses, notes towards an investigation*, in Sharma, Aradhana and Akhil Gupta (eds), *The Anthropology of the State: A Reader*, London, Blackwell, 2007, pp. 86–111.

22. For example in the sense of retrospective bureaucratic rationalization, Hilbert, Richard A., 'Bureaucracy as belief, rationalization as repair: Max Weber in a post-functionalist age', *Sociological Theory* 5,1 (1987), pp. 70–86.

23. Weber, Max, 'Wesen, Voraussetzungen und Entfaltung der bürokratischen Herrschaft', in Weber, Max, *Wirtschaft und Gesellschaft*, Studienausgabe, Tübingen: Mohr (Siebeck), 1972, pp. 551–79.

24. See, for example, Beek, 2014; Bittner, Egon, 'The police on skid-row: a study of

peace keeping', *American Sociological Review* 32, 5 (1967), pp. 699–715; Göpfert, 2014; Martin, Jeffrey, 'A Reasonable Balance of Law and Sentiment: Social Order in Democratic Taiwan from the Policemen's Point of View', *Law & Society Review* 41, 3 (2007), pp. 665–98; Schröer, Norbert, 'Interkulturelles Patt', in Reichertz, Jo and Norbert Schröer (eds), *Hermeneutische Polizeiforschung*, Opladen: Leske + Budrich, 2003, pp. 73–5.

25. Olivier de Sardan, Jean-Pierre, 'Researching the practical norms of real governance in Africa', *Discussion Paper* 5 (2009).

26. Spittler, Gerd, 'Streitregelung im Schatten des Leviathan: Eine Darstellung und Kritik rechtsethnologischer Untersuchungen', *Zeitschrift für Rechtssoziologie* 1 (1980), pp. 4–32.

27. Beek, 2014; Göpfert, 2014; Schröer, 2003.

28. Beek, 2014.

29. Reiner, Robert, *The Politics of the Police*, 3rd ed., Oxford: Oxford University Press, 2000.

30. See Beek, Jan, '"Every car has an offence on it": Register polizeilichen Handelns bei Verkehrskontrollen in Nordghana', *Sociologus* 61, 2 (2011), pp. 197–222.

31. On the private equipping of the police in Benin, see Bierschenk, Thomas, 'Sedimentations, fragmentations and normative double-binds in (West) African public services', in Bierschenk, Thomas, and Jean-Pierre Olivier de Sardan (eds), *States at Work: Dynamics of African Bureaucracies*, Leiden: Brill, 2014b, pp. 221–45; on police buildings in Uganda, see Biecker, Sarah and Klaus Schlichte, 'Policing Uganda, Policing the World', *SPP 1448 Working Paper Series*, 2013; on moonlighting by police officers see Diphorn (this volume).

32. Bierschenk, 2014b.

33. Hartmann, Sarah, 'The informal market of education in Egypt: private tutoring and its implications', *Working Paper of the Department of Anthropology and African Studies* 88 (2008).

34. Kurian, George T. (ed), *World Encyclopedia of Police Forces and Correctional Systems*, 2nd ed., Detroit: Thomson Gale, 2006, p. 427, p. 630.

35. http://www.auswaertiges-amt.de/DE/Aussenpolitik/Laender/Laenderinfos/Mali/Wirtschaftsdatenblatt_node.html, last accessed 10 Feb. 2015.

36. For an example, see Bierschenk, 2014b.

37. Copans, Jean, 'Afrique noire: un état sans fonctionnaires?', *Autrepart* 20 (2001), pp. 11–27.

38. Weick, Karl E., 'Educational organizations as loosely coupled systems', *Administrative Science Quarterly* 21 (1976), pp. 1–19.

39. Luhmann, Niklas, *Soziologische Aufklärung 3: Soziales System, Gesellschaft, Organisation*, Wiesbaden: Verlag für Sozialwissenschaften, 1975, p. 351.

40. The fact that a similar situation prevails in other sectors is demonstrated by Bierschenk (Bierschenk, Thomas, 'The everyday functioning of an African pub-

lic service: informalization, privatization and corruption in Benin's legal system', *Journal of Legal Pluralism* 57 (2008), pp. 101–39) for justice and Tama, 2014 for education.

41. Tama, 2014 for the education sector.

42. Based on Badou, 2013; Peth, 2014 for Benin; see also Beek, 2014 for Ghana. The additional advantage of this example is that it concerns the back office, which has been the focus of far less research up to now than the police front office. Other sectors can also be referred to here. For example, remuneration practices are a notorious 'black box' in the public service of many African countries.

43. Olivier de Sardan, Jean-Pierre and Yannick Jaffré, *La construction sociale des maladies: Les entités nosologiques populaires en Afrique de l'Ouest*, Paris: PUF, 1999.

44. Thurmann, oral communication, 28.3.2015

45. For similar circumstances among teachers in Benin, see Tama, 2014.

46. Osborne, Thomas, 'Bureaucracy as a vocation: governmentality and administration in nineteenth-century Britain', *Journal of Historical Sociology* 7, 3 (1994), p. 309.

47. Beek, 2014; Bierschenk, 2009; Lentz, 2014; Peth, 2014.

48. Bierschenk, 2009.

49. Peth, 2014.

50. Beek, 2011; see also his contribution to this volume; Peth, 2014.

51. Elguezabal, Eleonora, 'De la division morale du travail de contrôle dans le métro parisien', *Déviance et société* 34, 2 (2010), pp. 189–200.

52. Weick, 1976.

53. Olivier de Sardan, Jean-Pierre, 'A moral economy of corruption in Africa?', *The Journal of Modern African Studies* 37, 1 (1999), pp. 25–52; Weick, 1976.

54. Espagne, 2012.

55. Latour, Bruno, *We Have Never Been Modern*, Cambridge: Harvard University Press, 1993.

7. SOMEWHERE BETWEEN GREEN AND BLUE: A SPECIAL POLICE UNIT IN THE DEMOCRATIC REPUBLIC OF THE CONGO

1. When writing about the police in Western countries, I mean all state organizations that conduct civil police work. Also, it is possible to find police forces that are not clearly separated from the military. Especially with regards to the actual fighting of terrorist attacks, the boundaries between the police and the military apparently vanish, as noted in regard to Germany (Die Zeit, 7 May 2013). Yet these cases are exceptional and do not form part of police officers' or soldiers' daily duties in which they still work strictly separated from each other.

2. Lefever, Ernest W., *Spear and Scepter: Army, police, and politics in tropical Africa*. Washington DC: Brookings Institution, 1970.

3. Olivier de Sardan, Jean-Pierre, 'Etat, bureaucratie et gouvernance en Afrique de l'Ouest francophone', *Politique africaine*, 96 (2004), pp. 139–62.

4. Justaert, Arnout, 'The Governance of Police Reform in the DR Congo: Reform Without Alignment?' Presentation in the Panel: 'Bureaucrats in Uniform: Historical and Anthropological Explorations of an African Professional Field' at *European Conference on African Studies*, Uppsala, June 2011.

5. Kraska, Peter B. and Kappler, Victor E., 'Militarizing American Police: The Rise and Normalization of Paramilitary Units', *Social Problems* 44, 1 (1997), p. 2.

6. Beek, Jan and Göpfert, Mirco, 'State violence specialists in West Africa', *Sociologus*, 63, 1–2 (2013), p. 104.

7. Nlandu, Thierry Mayamba, *Mapping Police Services in the Democratic Republic of Congo: Institutional Interactions at Central, Provincial and Local Levels*. Brighton: Institute of Development Studies, 2012., p. 21.

8. Kraska and Kappler, 'Militarizing American Police', p. 1.

9. GFN-SSR, *A Beginner's Guide to Security Sector Reform (SSR)*, Birmingham: Birmingham University Press, 2007, p. 8.

10. Bundeswehr Homepage, *Bildung, Ausbildung, Tugenden*, 2013.

11. South African Army Homepage 2013: http://www.army.mil.za/aboutus/values. htm, last accessed 5 May 2013.

12. Martin, Jeffrey, 'A Reasonable Balance of Law and Sentiment: Social Order in Democratic Taiwan from the Policemen's Point of View', *Law and Society Review*, 41, 3 (2007), p. 674.

13. Bayley, David H., *Patterns of Policing: A Comparative International Analysis*. New Brunswick: Rutgers University Press, 1990, p. 104.

14. Bayley, *Patterns of Policing*, p. 104.

15. As the co-workers of the unit wished to stay anonymous, I do not name the development aid organisations that financed and trained the unit.

16. Hills, Alice, 'Towards a Critique of Policing and National Development in Africa', *Journal of Modern African Studies*, 34, 2 (1996), p. 297.

17. Lefever, Ernest W., *Spear and Scepter: Army, police, and politics in tropical Africa*. Washington: Brookings Institution, 1970, p. 126; Shaw, Bryant P., *Force Publique, Force Unique: The military in the Belgian Congo, 1914–1939*. Michigan: University of Michigan Press, 1984, p. 2.

18. Zolberg, Aristide R., 'A view from the Congo', *World Politics*, 19, 1 (1966), pp. 137–49.

19. Zolberg, 'A view', p. 127.

20. Lefever, Spear and Scepter, p. 127; Nlandu, *Mapping Police Services*; Strizek, Helmut, „Das Autoritäre Regime unter General Joseph Désiré Mobutu: Ein Symbol des Kalten Krieges", in Chiari, Bernhard, Kollmer, Dieter H., and Pahl, Magnus (eds), *Wegweiser zur Geschichte. Demokratische Republik Kongo*. Paderborn: Schöning, 2008, pp. 49–64.

21. Nlandu, *Mapping Police Services*, p. 23.

22. Nlandu, *Mapping Police Services*, p. 25; Ebenga, Jacques, and Nlandu, Thierry, 'The Congolese National Army: In Search of an Identity', in Rupiya, Martin, (ed.): *Evolutions and Revolutions, a Contemporary Africa*. Cape Town: Institute for Security Studies, 2005, p. 68.

23. Nlandu, *Mapping Police Services*, p. 25.

24. Dahrendorf, Nicola, 'MONUC and the Relevance of Coherent Mandates: The Case of the DRC', in: Hänggi, Heiner and Scherrer, Voncenza (eds): *Security Sector Reform and UN Integrated Missions*. London: LIT, 2008, p. 69.

25. Constitutionnet, *Constitution of the DR Congo*, 2013.

26. Dahrendorf, 'MONUC', p. 69.

27. GFN-SSR, *A Beginner's Guide to Security Sector Reform (SSR)*, Birmingham: Birmingham University Press, 2007, p. 8.

28. Nlandu, *Mapping Police Services*.

29. Martin, 'A Reasonable Balance', p. 674.

30. Loader, Ian, 'Policing and the social: Questions of symbolic power', *The British Journal of Sociology*, 48, 1 (1997), pp. 1–18.

31. Eriksson-Baaz, Eriksson-Baaz, Maria, 'Not enough to add women and stir', *Nordiska AfrikaInstitutet*. http://urn.kb.se/resolve?urn=urn:nbn:se:nai:diva-1384, 2011, last accessed 2. April 2013, p. 1.

32. Dahrendorf, 'MONUC' p. 72; Bureau of Democracy, *Democratic Republic of the Congo 2012*. Human Rights Report, 2012. http://www.state.gov/j/drl/rls/hrrpt/humanrightsreport/index.htm?year=2012anddlid=204107#wrapper, last accessed on 24 November 2013.

33. The Congolese *Police Judiciaire* is comparable to Criminal Investigation Departments (CID) in Western countries.

34. Revised field notes.

35. Bourdieu, Pierre, *Die verborgenen Mechanismen der Macht. Schriften zu Politik und Kultur 1*. Hamburg: VSA, 2005. p. 82.

36. See Loader, 'Policing and the social'.

37. Constitutionnet, *Constitution of the DR Congo*; GNF-SSR, *A Beginner's Guide*, p. 8.

38. Hendriks, Hendriks, Maarten, *Straatkinderen (bashege) in Kinshasa. Structureel geweld versus agency*. Antwerpen: Maklu, 2012, p. 47.

39. Jermier, John M. and Leslie J. Berkes, 'Leader behaviour in a police command bureaucracy: a closer look at the quasi-military model', *Administrative Science Quarterly*, 24 (1979), p. 2.

40. Jörgel, Magnus, 'Security Sector Reform in Sub-Saharan Africa: A New Playground, Different Rules, New Players?', in Ekengrenand, Magnus, and Simons, Greg, (eds) *The Politics of Security Sector Reform: Challenges and Opportunities for the European Union's Global Role*, Farnham: Ashgate, 2011, pp. 243–58.

41. Hills, Alice, *Policing Post-Conflict Cities*. London: Zed Books, 2009, p. 46.
42. Hills, *Policing Post-Conflict Cities*, p. 47.
43. Jörgel, 'Security Sector Reform'.

8. MOONLIGHTING: CROSSING THE PUBLIC-PRIVATE POLICING DIVIDE IN DURBAN, SOUTH AFRICA

1. Abrahamsen, Rita and Michael Williams, *Security Beyond the State: Private Security in International Politics*, Cambridge: Cambridge University Press, 2011.
2. PSIRA Annual Report, 2010–11, see www.psira.co.za.
3. Loader, Ian, 'Consumer Culture and the Commodification of Policing and Security', *Sociology*, 33, 2 (1999), pp. 373–92.
4. Garland, David, 'The Limits of the Sovereign State: Strategies of Crime Control in Contemporary Society', *The British Journal of Criminology*, 36, 4 (1996), p. 455.
5. See: Berg, Julie, 'Seeing like private security: Evolving mentalities of public space protection in South Africa', *Criminology and Criminal Justice*, 10, 3 (2010), pp. 287–301; Rigakos, George S., *The New Parapolice. Risk Markets and Commodified Social Control*, London: University of Toronto Press, 2002.
6. Button, Mark, *Private Policing*, Devon: Willan Publishing, 2002.
7. Button, 2002, p. 12.
8. This is based on the concept of twilight institutions, which was introduced and explored in a special issue of *Development and Change* in 2006.
9. Lund, Christian, 'Twilight Institutions: An Introduction', *Development and Change*, 37, 4 (2006), p. 677.
10. Moonlighting is a worldwide phenomenon that is defined differently per context (See Ayling, Julie and Clifford Shearing, 'Taking care of business: public police as commercial security vendors', *Criminology and Criminal Justice*, 8, 1 (2008), pp. 27–50; Crawford, Adam and Stuart Lister, 'Additionally Security Patrols in Residential Areas: Notes from the Marketplace', *Policing and Society*, 16, 2 (2006), pp. 164–88; Davis, Diane E., 'Non-State Armed Actors, New Imagined Communities, and Shifting Patterns of Sovereignty and Insecurity in the Modern World', *Contemporary Security Policy*, 30, 2 (2009), pp. 221–45; Grabosky, Peter, 2004, 'Toward a Theory of Public/Private Interaction in Policing', in McCord, Joan (ed.), *Beyond Empiricism: Institutions and Intentions in the Study of Crime. Advances in Criminological Theory*, Transaction Books, Piscataway, 2004, pp. 69–82; Jones, Trevor and Tim Newburn, 'The Transformation of Policing? Understanding Current Trends in Policing Systems', *British Journal of Criminology*, 42 (2002), pp. 129–46; Reiss, Albert, *Private Employment of Public Police*, Washington: National Institute of Justice, 1987; Rigakos 2002).
11. Gans, Jeremy, 'Privately Paid Public Policing: Law and Practice', *Policing and Society*, 10 (2000), pp. 183–206.

12. Ayling and Shearing, 2008.
13. In fact, Reiss (1987) states that privately-paid public policing was implemented through official channels to combat moonlighting.
14. See: Beinart, William, *Twentieth-Century South Africa*, Oxford: Oxford University Press, 2001; Brogden, Mike and Clifford Shearing, *Policing for a New South Africa*, London and New York: Routledge, 1993; Philip, Kate, 'The private sector and the security establishment', in Cock, J. and L. Nathan (eds), *War and Society. The Militarisation of South Africa*, Cape Town/Johannesburg: David Philip Publisher, 1989, pp. 202–16. Security in the mining industry was primarily provided through in-house security: guards were employed and trained by the mining houses (Philip 1989: 214). This is in contrast to contract security, which involves 'contracting' a third party, such as a company, to provide the security services. Contract security is more common in contemporary South Africa.
15. Shearing, Clifford and Julie Berg, 'South Africa', in Jones, Trevor and Tim Newburn (eds), *Plural Policing. A comparative perspective*, London/New York: Routledge, 2006, p. 201.
16. Shaw, Mark, *Crime and Policing in Post-Apartheid South Africa: Transforming under Fire*, Indianapolis: Indiana University Press, 2002.
17. See Brogden and Shearing, 1993; Grant, 1989; Irish, Jenny, *Policing for Profit: The Future of South Africa's Private Security Industry*, Pretoria: Institute for Security Studies, 1999; Singh, Anne-Marie, *Policing and Crime Control in Post-apartheid South Africa*, Aldershot: Ashgate Publishing Limited, 2008.
18. A national key point was defined as "any place or area that is of such national importance that its loss, damage, disruption, or immobilization may prejudice the Republic, or any place or area which the Minister (of Defence) considers necessary or expedient for the safety of the Republic or in the public interest" (Jackson, 1987, p. 37, in Philip, 1989, p. 213). The Minister of Defence determined which sites were labelled as a National Key Point.
19. Singh, 2008, p. 44.
20. Ibid.
21. Grant, 1989.
22. Brogden and Shearing, 1993, p. 71.
23. The security officers of a national key point site fell under government authority, either the SAP or a commanding officer of the Defence Force (Grant, Evadne, 'Private Policing', *Acta Juridica, 1989*, p. 108). Additionally, the Minister of Defence could determine the meticulous details of a site (such as the amount of officers on each site) and control the entire spectrum of security provision (Grant, 1989, p. 107). The Minister thus had the power to decide which private security company would provide the security for a particular site.
24. Although passed in October 1987, the Act was promulgated in April 1989 (Grant, 1989, p. 103).

25. Dom passes refer to passes implemented by the apartheid state to control the movement of Blacks.
26. Watchman refers to a security officer. It is currently regarded as a derogatory term.
27. Interview: 13 March 2009.
28. Berg, Julie, 'The private security industry in South Africa: a review of applicable legislation', *South African Journal of Criminal Justice*,16 (2003), p. 179.
29. Singh, 2008.
30. Ibid., p. 43.
31. Shaw, 2002.
32. Brogden and Shearing, 1993.
33. Goold, Benjamin, Loader, Ian, and Angelica Thumala, A., 'Consuming security? Tools for a sociology of security consumption', *Theoretical Criminology*, 14, 1 (2010), p. 15.
34. These individuals are also referred to as the '*bakkie* brigade', as these men primarily operated from bakkies, a South African term for a pick-up truck.
35. The armed response sector also emerged through 'techies', companies that installed alarms for commercial businesses.
36. Interview: 21 April 2010.
37. 1993, p. 72–3.
38. Ibid.
39. Philip, 1989.
40. Interview: former police officer, 26 April 2010.
41. Cock, 2005.
42. Singh, 2008.
43. Taxi violence refers to violence between taxi owners over transport routes during this period. In KwaZulu-Natal, the taxi violence was strongly affiliated to the political violence between the ANC and IFP (Beinart, 2001).
44. Interview: security consultant, 26 April 2010.
45. Interview: police officer, 30 April 2010.
46. Minnaar, Anthony, 'Private-Public Partnerships: Private Security, Crime Prevention and Policing in South Africa', *Acta Criminologica*, 18, 1 (2005), p. 95.
47. The Act came into operation on 14 February 2002.
48. Berg, 2003.
49. The Security Officers Board (SOB) consisted of ten members: six officials from the private security industry, a commissioned officer of the SAP, an officer aligned to the minister, and two other persons assigned by the then Minister of Law and Order. The current Council consists of a chairperson, vice-chairperson, and three councillors that are appointed by the Minister of Safety and Security. The council members do therefore not have a 'direct or indirect financial or personal interests in the private security industry or represent in any way the interests of those within the industry' (PSIRA, 2001).

50. Interview: police reservist, 6 May 2010.
51. I primarily retrieved my data from former police officers, of which many are currently working in the industry.
52. Interview: joint interview with two owners of private security companies, 22 April 2010.
53. Interview: former police officer, 16 August 2010.
54. Interview: police reservist, 6 May 2010.
55. Interview: PSIRA employee, 17 August 2010.
56. Interview: 6 August 2010.
57. Berg, Julie, 'Private Policing in South Africa: The Cape Town city improvement district—pluralisation in practice', *Society in Transition*, 35, 2 (2004), p. 227.
58. Singh, 2008, p. 14.
59. Hornberger, Julia, *Policing and Human Rights: The Meaning of Violence and Justice in the Everyday Policing of Johannesburg*. New York: Routledge, 2011, p. 4, italics in original.
60. Minnaar, 2005, p. 89.
61. See McManus, Michael, *From Fate to Choice: Private Bobbies, Public Beats*, Aldershot: Avebury, 1995; Rigakos, 2002; Wakefield, Alison, *Selling Security. The private policing of public space*, Devon: Willan Publishing, 2003.
62. Stenning, Philip C., 'Private Police and Public Police: Toward a Redefinition of the Police Role', in Loree, Donald J. (ed.), *Future Issues in Policing: Symposium Proceedings*, Ottawa: Canadian Police College, 1989, p. 180, emphasis in original.
63. Minnaar, Anthony and P. Ngoveni, 'The relationship between the South African Police Service and the private security industry: Any role for outsourcing in the prevention of crime?', *Acta Criminologica*, 17, 1 (2004), p. 55.
64. Minnaar 2005, p. 99.
65. These are also known as Extended Station Crime Combating Forum (ESCCF) meetings or SCCF meetings.
66. Lippert, Randy and Daniel O'Connor, 'Security Intelligence Networks and the Transformation of Contract Private Security', *Policing and Society*, 16, 1 (2006), p. 53.
67. Interview: police reservist, 31 August 2010.
68. Interview: owner of private security company, ex-police officer, 30 July 2010.
69. Interview: police reservist, 6 August 2010.
70. Interview: former police officer, 26 April 2010.
71. Interview: former police officer, 1 July 2010.
72. Interview: police officer, 30 April 2010.
73. Interview: security consultant, 26 April 2010.
74. Interview: former police officer, 30 July 2010.
75. It is common to put the company on a family name. The received money from the profit can be interpreted as a 'family gift'.

76. Interview: former member of PSiRA council, 26 August 2008.
77. Interview: police officer, 30 April 2010.
78. Interview: former member of PSIRA council, 25 May 2010.
79. Lippert and O'Connor, 2006.
80. Interview: police officer, 30 April 2010.
81. Interview: owner of private security company, 2 August 2010.
82. Interview: police officer, 30 April 3010.
83. Interview: police officer, 30 April 2010.
84. Interview: owner of a private security company, 6 August 2010.
85. Interview: owner of an armed response company, 1 September 2010.
86. Interview: joint interview with two owners of private security companies, 22 April 2010.
87. Davis, 2009, p. 240.
88. Interview: police reservist, 6 May 2010.

9. RISK AND MOTIVATION IN POLICE WORK IN NIGERIA

1. This paper is based on fieldwork conducted for doctoral research between 2009 and 2011 in 'B' Division, a police formation of around 170 officers which covers urban and rural areas in and around the town of Dutsin Bature, Gida State in Nigeria's savannah middle-belt. These names, and names of all other local places, persons and ethnic groups in this chapter, have been pseudonymised.
2. Owen, O., An Institutional Ethnography of the Nigeria Police Force. Unpublished DPhil thesis, Institute of Social and Cultural Anthropology, Oxford University, 2013.
3. http://www.unicef.org/infobycountry/nigeria_statistics.html, last accessed 21 June 2012.
4. Sometimes fatalities themselves arise from the consequences of police practice— prior to my arrival a popular deputy superintendent in Gida State had bled to death on the floor of a clinic whose doctors refused to treat him without a police report. This is because, incredibly, at a point it became routine for hospitals in Nigeria to refuse to treat emergency cases of wounding without first obtaining a police report, lest the doctors themselves became suspects. Despite plentiful orders to reverse the process from successive inspectors-general, the practice remained widespread and thus hugely increased the likelihood of a person dying even if they did reach hospital.
5. It is even starker in the big city: Lagos State's Governor Fashola stated that in the-four years to end-2011, 603 police officers were killed while on duty in the city. Joke Kujenya 'Idle hands, devil's workshop' in *The Nation* newspaper, http://www.the nationonlineng.net/2011/index.php/news/30265-%E2%80%98idle-hands,-devil%E2%80%99s-workshop%E2%80%99.html, last accessed 19 December 2011.
6. Fieldnotes, 9 June 2010.

7. A paramilitary public order force, hereafter referred to as 'MOPOL'.

8. He alleged that the bus owner paid compensation to the State Police Command but that 'one naira did not reach me'. To the hardships related in this testimony must be factored in the sergeant's additional loss of earnings by being unavailable for deployment during the three-year period and since. Note also that the testimony above comes from an injured officer continuing to serve with a mobile unit seven years after being rendered unfit, showing that sympathetic commanders and colleagues do improvise to provide job security and welfare for those without alternative safety nets.

9. In Ibadan, a constable tells me of the competition not to be the driver when responding to a bank robbery, as the robbers usually shoot the driver first.

10. DPO stands for Divisional Police Officer, the commanding officer of a Division (equivalent to a US Precinct).

11. Less than 20 per cent of 'B' division's personnel establishment.

12. That is, a voluntary act of charity.

13. In fact the militant potential of youth in Gida State is even felt to be a risk by the same local politicians who empower them; a state-wide community policing programme to engage in dialogue with youth groups was suspended after complaints from the state's Local Government Chairmen, who were extremely nervous of the potential consequences of any such gatherings.

14. Owen, *Institutional Ethnography of the Nigeria Police Force*, 2012.

15. Sometimes, however, the fuckup is much less complex in origin; for instance the officer tricked out of their weapon by a car full of people who stopped to ask for directions; when he drew close, they grabbed his gun. This serious matter, which has of course to be kept as quiet as possible, is reputed to be punishable with a N300,000 fine, nearly a year's pay for an early-career constable.

16. Sometimes the officers deemed responsible for an error such as this, will be given responsibility for remedying it, and a grace period in which to do so. When a pair of prisoners escaped from 'B' Division's cells overnight, the duty CRO and station guard, on whose watch it had happened, were given a week (until one of the escapees' scheduled court appearance) to recapture them or face disciplinary procedures.

17. This echoes the primacy of quickly producing an arrested suspect as the central and *a priori* aim of criminal investigations.

18. The mobile commander talks with feeling of his friend, demoted from deputy superintendent to assistant superintendent, while his classmates are assistant commissioners by now, because someone was killed by an officer under his command, asking me rhetorically 'is it fair?'

19. A passenger transport depot, where 'bush taxi' shared cars to set destinations load passengers.

20. Nigeria's most senior police officer, hereafter, as in vernacular conversation, abbreviated to 'IG'.

21. In a competitive professional milieu of limited trust and plentiful suspicion, it is also temping for officers to connect such misfortunes with the work of unseen enemies; thus an inspector detained at HQ on suspicion of allowing theft from detained cement trucks confides in me that he believes this has happened at the behest of his former boss in the State CID, who hates him and has been waiting for a chance to get him in trouble.

22. Young, M. *An Inside Job: Policing and Police Culture in Britain.* Oxford: Clarendon Press, 1991.

23. A query is a disciplinary procedure common to most government bureaucracies in Nigeria, asking the person queried to give a satisfactory explanation for their actions or face sanction.

24. Fieldnotes, 9 June 2010.

25. And equally in hope of the lucky coincidence which helps them, for example, to come to the notice of an influential senior officer or public figure.

26. Assistant Superintendent, Dutsin Bature Traffic Division, 16 February 2010. The ASP, an old man nearing retirement, uses the evocative archaic pidgin expression to describe an arduous and stressful experience.

27. They may unfortunately however have forgotten the (approximately three hours in total) marksmanship and safe weapon handling they learned at the training school, but that is another story.

28. Station Officer, senior administrative officer responsible for personnel in a division.

29. Special Anti-Robbery Squad, a widely-feared armed reaction detective and intervention squad.

30. *Oga* is a Yoruba word meaning boss which has entered vernacular English usage. Bown observes that junior police officers in Ethiopia are also reluctant to take decisions, which he attributes as common to party-states where decision-making was reserved in party officials and 'wrong decisions were severely punished' (Bown, J., 'UK Policing influence overseas: a practitioner perspective'. Unpublished paper presented at conference on policing and the policed in the postcolonial state, Institute of Commonwealth Studies, London, 2010). Sometimes, too, in an institution where the dealings of seniors and colleagues may be opaque and tied to unseen and personal agendas, sticking to procedure, rather than deviating from it, may equally be a route to downfall. Consider this true story: a senior officer working at national headquarters is detailed to research a particular procurement requirement. He researches and recommends a particular product, available from a range of suppliers. He is then directed from above to use a certain preferred bidder. The products arrive, he inspects them, finds them unsatisfactory for purpose, and makes a report to that effect to his superiors, upon which he finds himself transferred to head border patrol (a minor command and career backwater), where he must wait for a change of IG before he is rehabilitated into an operational post.

31. Such exercises also have the convenient attribute of allowing extraordinary capital expenditure. Equally, the fact that supposedly routine promotion is done as an occasional exercise means that when such long-awaited events occur, subordinates tend to attribute them to the munificence of the particular IG, rather than as a procedural function of the institution, thus re-personalising supposedly bureaucratic institutional power.

32. And some too are notoriously slovenly, lazy, greedy or weak, and all these reputations spread quickly through the intimate institutional world.

33. Jauregui, B. *Shadows of the State, Subalterns of the State: Police and "Law and Order" in postcolonial India*. Unpublished PhD thesis, Department of Anthropology, University of Chicago, 2010, p. 227.

34. Ibid., p. 226.

35. Remember too that Nigeria has a long history of hierarchical social relations using ideologies of kinship, servitude and fealty within which labour relations are embedded and by which labour freedom is constrained, so to possess and exploit the labour of a subordinate beyond the bounds of formal rules is a habituated practice.

36. To the Deputy Inspector-General for Operations in Abuja, as well as to the Commissioner of the state.

37. Fieldnotes, 18 February 2010.

38. The stock phrase when instructing a managing officer to find their own resources to carry out a task is 'you should know how to look after your men'.

39. Ibid., 18 February 2010.

40. Ibid. 'Fire' means to shoot.

41. Jauregui, Shadows of the state, pp. 227–8.

42. Notably parts of the South-East, Rivers State and Lagos. For instance http://www.nigeriapolicewatch.com/2012/03/police-in-river-state-disregard-ig-keeps-extortion-road-blocks/, last accessed 6 June 2012.

43. Note the discrepancy in punishment, despite the ASP's presumed greater responsibility. This may be another product of the relationship between hierarchy and discipline—the softer treatment meted out to 'officers and gentlemen' than to rank and file in the institution's internal class system—or lenience towards a long-serving officer near retirement (an ASP in a small division near retirement usually suggests someone recently promoted from inspector in a final 'reward' posting).

44. Christian Morgenstern's 1910 poem tells the story of an old man who is run over by a car, but on examining the traffic bylaws and finding that cars were banned from the area, concludes that he is therefore not dead, 'for, he reasons pointedly, that which must not, cannot be.' Morgenstern, C., *The Gallows songs* (Translated, with an introduction by Max Knight). Berkeley: University of California Press, 1964.

45. That is, to join the paramilitary Police Mobile Force.

46. 18 February, Ibid. Compare the commander's disposition with that of the second-in-command who later succeeds him, and whom I met three times: First when I interview him in his office and he offers me cold drinks and gives me pat, by-the-book and completely disingenuous answers; secondly, six months later when I met him again in his office he appeared to misrecognise me as the sales representative from Globacom telecoms; and thirdly when I am trying to leave Dutsin Bature stuck in market day traffic, and the arrival of the new commander's convoy behind me was heralded by MOPOL officers loping through the go-slow like the Wizard of Oz's winged monkeys, rifles up, yelling orders and whipping cars with their *koboko* whips to clear the road for Oga's gold-coloured 4WD.

47. The interaction has the ring of truth since I have heard it from the other side; a friend, a young professional highly conscious of his legal rights, had an argument with a constable at a roadblock who rudely demanded the papers of the foreign anthropologist with whom he was travelling. The older inspector called him over and advised him never to argue with a man with a gun, since if anything happens, 'we can discipline him, but it won't bring you back to life'.

48. Bierschenk, T., 'Sedimentation, Fragmentation and Normative Double-Binds in (West) African Public Services', in Bierschenk, Thomas and Olivier de Sardan, Jean–Pierre (eds), *States at Work: Dynamics of African Bureaucracies*, Leiden: Brill, 2014. And not only West African bureaucrats. A Greek civil servant friend describes the public service social contract in Greece as 'Like the old communist countries. I pretend to work and they pretend to pay me'.

49. And of course, an awareness that the superior themselves may have something to hide can make the enforcement of discipline even more problematic, as we shall see in the closing section.

50. Fieldnotes, 9 June 2010, The reference is to Commissioner of Police Nuhu Ribadu, who was head of the anti-corruption Economic and Financial Crimes Commission (EFCC) between 2003 and December 2007. Ribadu was publicly acclaimed for his impact in fighting high-level corruption, but became a victim of his own success when one of his prime suspects, former Delta State Governor James Ibori, used generous campaign contributions to the election of late President Yar'Adua to buy the political influence and force Ribadu out, using rules on police training and promotion as a pretext.

51. Maier, K., *This house has fallen: Nigeria in crisis.* London: Allen Lane, The Penguin Press, 2000.

52. Fieldnotes, 9 July 2010.

53. Note that this direct risk and police responses to it are historically contingent, and in some places grew noticeably even during my research. As I completed fieldwork, the incipient Boko Haram insurgency meant that many police station compounds in vulnerable areas were being adorned with sandbagged firing points. Even in inner-city Lagos, a DPO showing me round his new station pointed out the upstairs vantage-point for a sentry.

54. The colonial 'strangers-to-police-strangers' logic of avoiding divided loyalties.

55. Sometimes risk-mitigation strategies are overt and central in police officers' inter-actions with the public. I accompanied a friend to report a street robbery at Maitama police station in Abuja. The (plainclothes) IPO assigned to us gave his phone contacts and first name, but refused to give his surname—'just put officer Kayode'. In this way he hoped to preserve his anonymity, and thus deflect his accountability within the overall opacity of the institution to the outsider.

56. That is in the hope that he would give them money.

57. That is 'shot them, and ended it'. 18 February 2010, ibid.

58. As tanker drivers are employed by fuel marketing companies with heavy economic and political muscle, my friend took the constable's readiness to stand up to them as an indicator of moral courage.

59. See Owen, O. 'Positions of Security and the Security of Position: Bureaucratic Prebendalism Inside the State' in Adebanwi, W. and Obadare, E. (eds) *Democracy and Prebendalism in Nigeria: Critical Interpretations*. Basingstoke: Palgrave Macmillan, 2013.

60. Albeit usually only with the power to moderate, but not to neutralise entirely, institutional disciplinary power.

61. Scott, J.C. Domination and the arts of resistance: hidden transcripts. New Haven, CT: Yale University Press, 1990.

62. Mbembe, A., Provisional Notes on the Postcolony. *Africa* 62 (1) 1992, pp. 3–37.

63. Mbembe, *Provisional Notes on the Postcolony*, p. 8.

64. Ibid., p. 10.

65. Ibid., p. 26.

10. FIGHTING FOR RESPECT: VIOLENCE, MASCULINITY AND LEGITIMACY IN THE SOUTH AFRICAN POLICE SERVICE

1. Sapa, 'Mido Macia died from hypoxia—autopsy', *City Press*, 11 March 2013, avail-able at: http://www.citypress.co.za/news/mido-macia-died-from-hypoxia-autopsy/ (last accessed 14 March 2013).

2. BBC, 'Mido Macia: South Africa police accused denied bail', 12 March 2013, *BBC News* Africa, available at: http://www.bbc.co.uk/news/world-africa-21761515 (last accessed 14 March 2013).

3. Mokati, Noni, 'Murder-accused cops' urgent bail bid', *IOL News*, 9 March 2013, available at http://www.iol.co.za/news/south-africa/murder-accused-cops-urgent-bail-bid-1.1483589.... (last accessed 9 March 2013).

4. Gilligan, James, *Preventing Violence*, Thames & Hudson: London, 2001.

5. Goffman, Irvin, *The presentation of self in everyday life*, Garden City, New York: Doubleday, Anchor Books, 1959.

6. Reiner, Robert, *The Politics of Police*, 4th edition, Oxford: Oxford University Press, 2010, pp. 122–31.

7. Reiner, 2010.
8. Lipsky, Michael, *Street-level bureaucrats: dilemmas of the individual in public service*, New York: Russell Sage Foundation, 2010, p. xv.
9. Chan, Janet, 'Changing police culture', *British Journal of Criminology*, 36, 1 (1996), pp. 109–33.
10. Loftus, Bethan, *Police Culture in a changing World*, Clarendon Studies in Criminology, Oxford & New York: Oxford University Press, 2009.
11. Steinberg, Jonny, *Thin Blue: the unwritten rules of policing South Africa*, Jeppestown: Jonathan Ball Publishers, 2008; Marks, Monique, *Transforming the robocops: changing police in South Africa*. Scottsville: University of Kwazulu-Natal Press, 2005; Altbeker, Antony, *The dirty work of democracy: a year on the streets with the SAPS*, Jeppestown: Jonathan Ball Publishers, 2005; Hornberger, Julia, *Policing and Human Rights: the meaning of violence and justice in the everyday policing of Johannesburg*, Abingdon: Routledge, 2011.
12. Goffman, 1959.
13. Young, Malcolm, *An Inside Job: policing and police culture in Britain*, Oxford Press: Clarendon, 1991.
14. 'Pushing back the frontiers of evil' was an official SAPS slogan used on posters, billboards and other paraphernalia in 2010. Then Deputy Minister of Police, Susan Shabungu first suggested police should 'Kill the bastards' in 2008, a sentiment echoed by her successors in later years.
15. Von Holdt, Karl, 'Nationalism, bureaucracy and the developmental state: the South African Case', *South African Review of Sociology*, 41, 1 (2010), pp. 4–27.
16. Reiner, 2010.
17. Once, while on patrol in a street lined with busy taverns, the van I was driving in was hit by a stone hurled by a reveller. On another occasion we were called to assist a patrol van in our group after a stone was thrown through its passenger window near a dark railway crossing. So there appeared to be some truth to the stories at the station. However, there were far more times when we left police cars unattended, or walked through communities to hand out leaflets, when cars were not vandalised and there appeared to be little threat to our personal safety.
18. 'Crime Prevention' units at the station worked eight and ten-hour shifts based on an analysis of crime trends. They were not expected to attend to complaints regarding crimes that have already taken place ('bravo crimes'), but rather stop and search young men, respond to crimes in progress, and increase the visible presence of police in key locations.
19. 3rd Degree, *amaBerete Terrorise Townships*, 23 August 2012, available at: http://www.youtube.com/watch?v=rBehRHqQiy4 (Accessed 14 March 2013).
20. All quotes are extracts from my fieldwork diary. I have done my best to record the wording of police officials as accurately as possible.
21. A reference to an apartheid era form of torture akin to waterboarding.

22. Shearing, Clifford and Richard Ericson, 'Culture as figurative action', *British Journal of Sociology*, 42, 1991, pp. 481–506.
23. Holdaway, Simon, *Inside the British police: A force at work*, Oxford: Basil Blackwell Publishers, 1983, p. 62.
24. Marks, 2005, p. 172.
25. Holdaway, 1983, p. 139.
26. Loftus, 2009, p. 195; Waddington, Pat, 'Police (canteen) sub-culture: an appreciation', *British Journal of Criminology*, 39, 2 (1999), pp. 287–309.
27. Loftus, Bethan, 'Police occupational culture: classic themes, altered times', *Policing and Society: An International Journal of Research and Policy*, 20, 1 (2010), p. 10.
29. Peddie is a small town in the Eastern Cape Province of South Africa.
30. I have never known any South African police official to formally state the reason for arrest when forcing someone into the back of a van, and this remained true during these eight months of research.
31. Von Holdt, 2010.
32. Manning, Peter K., 'The police: mandate, strategies and appearances', 1978, reprinted in Newburn, Tim (ed.), *Policing: key readings*, Cullompton: Willan Publishing, 2005.
33. Collins, Anthony, 'Violence is not a crime: a broader view of interventions for social safety', *South African Crime Quarterly*, 43 (2013), p. 30.
34. Centre for the Study of Violence and Reconciliation (CSVR), *Why South Africa is so violent and what should be done about it: statement by the Centre for the Study of Violence and Reconciliation*, Tuesday 9 November 2010, available online at: http://www.csvr.org.za/docs/study/CSVRstatement091110.pdf (last accessed 28 May 2014).
35. Seedat, Mohamed, Ashley van Niekerk, Rachel Jewkes, Shahnaaz a Suffl and Kopano Ratel, 'Violence and injuries in South Africa: prioritising an agenda for prevention', *The Lancet* 374, September 19 (2009), pp. 1011–22.
36. Ratel, Kopano, 'Masculinity and male mortality in South Africa', *African Safety Promotion: A journal of inquiry*, 6, 22 (2008), p. 35.
37. Letsela, Lebohang and Kopano Ratele, *Masculinity and perceptions of risk: factors to premature male mortality in South Africa*, 2009, available at: http://www.brothersforlife.org/sites/default/files/docs/Men_and_their_perceptions_of_Risks.pdf (accessed 21 March 2013).
38. Reiner, 2010, pp. 127–128.
39. See for example: Holtmann, Barbara, *What it looks like when it's fixed: A case study in developing a systemic model to transform a fragile social system*, Johannesburg: PWC, 2011, pp. 28–43.
40. See for example 'Mixed Messages' in Faull, Andrew and Brian Rose, *Professionalism and the Police Occupation in South Africa: what is it and how can it help build safer communities?* ISS Occasional Paper No. 240, Pretoria: Institute for Security Studies, 2012, pp. 8–11.

41. Sapa, 'South Africa is not violent—says Zuma', *Mail & Guardian*, 7 March 2013, available at: http://mg.co.za/article/2013-03-07-south-africa-not-a-violent-country-says-zuma (last accessed 14 March 2013).

42. Sapa, 'Zuma invokes gay wrath', *News24*, 26 September 2006, available at: http://www.news24.com/SouthAfrica/News/Zuma-invokes-gay-wrath-20060926 (last accessed 28 May 2014).

43. Staff Reporter, 'Don't hold your breath for action on Cele findings', *Mail & Guardian*, 11 March 2011, available at: http://mg.co.za/article/2011-03-11-dont-hold-your-breath-for-action-on-cele-findings (last accessed 14 March 2013).

44. Nini, Asanda 'You're not entitled to any rights, MEC tells pupils', *DispatchOnline*, 12 March 2013, available at: http://www.dispatch.co.za/youre-not-entitled-to-any-rights-mec-tells-pupils/ (last accessed 16 March 2013).

45. Carlisle, Adrienne, 'Rights groups take on education MEC', *Dispatch Online*, 14 March 2013, available at: http://www.dispatch.co.za/rights-groups-take-on-education-mec/ (last accessed 17 March 2013).

46. The Afrobarometer Survey's 2012 results suggest South Africans think crime is the second most pressing concern facing the country, and which government should address. The only matter considered more important for government intervention is unemployment (Afrobarometer, *Public Agenda and Evaluation of Government*, 2012, available at: http://www.afrobarometer.org/files/documents/media_briefing/saf_r5_presentation1.pdf (accessed 15 April 2014)). Julia Hornberger (2011) has suggested that the ability to control crime has become a barometer by which the effectiveness of South Africa's government is measured.

47. Hornberger, 2011.

48. Hornberger, 2011, p. 126.

49. Ben Bradford, Aziz Huq, Jonathan Jackson and Benjamin Roberts, 2013 "What price fairness when security is at stake? Antecedents of Police Legitimacy in South Africa" in *Regulation and Governance*, pp. 1–24; Faull, Andrew *Corruption in the South African Police Service: civilian perceptions and experiences*, ISS Occasional Paper No. 226, Pretoria: Institute for Security Studies, 2011.

50. Whitehead, Antony, 'Man to Man Violence: How Masculinity May Work as a Dynamic Risk Factor', *The Howard Journal*, 44, 4 (2005), p. 415.

51. Connell, R.W. and James W. Messerschmidt, 'Hegemonic Masculinity: Rethinking the Concept', *Gender & Society*, 19 (2005), p. 832.

52. Morrell, Robert, Rachel Jewkes, Graham Lindegger and Vijay Hamlall, 'Hegemonic Masculinity: Reviewing the Gendered Analysis of Men's Power in South Africa', *South African Review of Sociology*, 44, 1 (2013), p. 5.

53. Faull, Andrew, *Behind the badge: the untold stories of South Africa's Police Service Members*, Cape Town: Zebra Press, 2010, pp. 117–18.

54. Steinberg, 2008.

55. Steinberg, Jonny, 'Establishing police authority and civilian compliance in post-

apartheid Johannesburg: an argument from the work of Egon Bittner', *Policing and Society: an international journal of research and policy*, 22, 4 (2012), pp. 1–15.

56. Faull, 2010, pp. 177–8.
57. Faull, Andrew, *Corruption and the South African Police Service: a review and its implications*, ISS Occasional Paper No. 150, Pretoria: Institute for Security Studies, 2007, p. 8.
58. Visagie, Justin *Who are the middle class in South Africa? Does it matter for policy?* Available at: http://www.econ3x3.org/article/who-are-middle-class-south-africa-does-it-matter-policy, 2013 (accessed 16 April 2014).
59. Faull, 2006, p. 8.
60. SSSBC (Safety and Security Bargaining Council), 2011. *Agreement No. 2/2011: Agreement on the South African Police Service Rank Structure, revised rank structure and matters relating thereto*, p. 4
61. Statistics South Africa, 2011. Statistical Release (revised) Census 2011, available at: http://www.statssa.gov.za/Publications/P03014/P030142011.pdf (last accessed 16 March 2013), p. 41.
62. South African Police Service, *Annual Report 2012/13*, 2013, p. 175.
63. Statistics South Africa, 2011, p. 42.
64. South African Police Service, 2013, p. 175.
65. Visagie, 2013, p. 8.
66. Bruce, David, 'Racism, self-esteem and violence in SA: Gaps in the NCPS' explanation?', *SA Crime Quarterly*, 17 (2006), pp. 34–5.
67. Gilligan, 2001.
68. Giddens, Anthony, *Modernity and Self-Identity: Self and Society in the Late Modern Age*, Polity Press: Cambridge, 1991, p. 65.
69. Giddens, 1991, p. 69.
70. Schiff, Kerry-Gaye, 'Discourse of workplace violence: painting a picture of the South African Police Service', unpublished doctoral thesis, Unisa, 2010, p. 370.
71. For an overview of literature on masculinity and violence see: Muntingh, Lukas and Chandré Gould, *Towards an understanding of repeat violent offending: A review of the literature*, ISS Occassional Paper No. 213, Pretoria: Institute for Security Studies, 2010.
72. Morrell, Robert, 'Of boys and men: masculinity and gender', *Journal of Southern African Studies*, 24, 4 (1998), pp. 605–30; Breckenridge, Keith, 'The allure of violence: men, race and masculinity on the South African goldmines, 1900–1950', *Journal of Southern African Studies*, 24, 4 (1998), pp. 669–93.
73. Gilligan, 2001.
74. Young, *An Inside Job*; Bittner, Egon, *The functions of the police in modern society: a review of background factors, current practices, and possible role models*, Rockville: National Institute of Mental Health, Center for Studies of Crime and Delinquency, 1970.
75. Gilligan, 2001, p. 80.

11. POLICING BOUNDARIES: THE CULTURAL WORK OF AFRICAN POLICING

1. I am adapting Peel's conception as given here: '… "culture" must not be seen as a mere precipitate or bequest of the past. Rather it is an active reflection on the past, a cultural *work*.' Peel, J. D. Y. 'The cultural work of Yoruba ethnogenesis', in Tonkin, E., M. McDonald & M. Chapman (eds) *History and Ethnicity*. London: Routledge, 1999, p. 199.

2. Bayley, David and Shearing, Clifford, 'The New Structure of Policing: Description, Conceptualization and Research Agenda', Research Report, National Institute of Justice: U.S. Department of Justice (2001).

3. Baker, Bruce. 'Protection from crime: what is on offer for Africans?', *Journal of Contemporary African Studies* 22, 2 (2004), pp. 165–88.

4. Loader, Ian, 'Plural policing and democratic governance', *Social & Legal Studies* 9, 3, (2000), pp. 323–45.

5. Bayley and Shearing, 'The New Structure…' p. 8.

6. Chanock, Martin, *Law, Custom and Social Order: The Colonial Experience in Malawi and Zambia*. Cambridge: Cambridge University Press, 1985; Moore, Sally Falk, *Social Facts and fabrications: Customary law on Kilimanjaro, 1880–1980*. New York: Cambridge University Press, 1986; Roberts, Richard and Mann, Kristin (eds), *Law in Colonial Africa*, London: James Currey, 1991.

7. Olivier de Sardan, Jean Pierre. 'A moral economy of corruption in Africa?', *Journal of Modern African Studies* 37, 1, (1999), pp. 25–52.

8. Fisiy, Cyprian, 'Containing Occult Practices: Witchcraft Trials in Cameroon', *African Studies Review* 41, 3 (1998), pp. 143–63; Rowlands, Michael, and Warnier, Jean Pierre, 'Sorcery, Power and the Modern State in Cameroon', *Man* 23 (1988), pp. 118–32.

9. Fields, Karen E, (1982) 'Political Contingencies of Witchcraft in Colonial Central Africa: Culture and the State in Marxist Theory', *Canadian Journal of African Studies* 16, 3 (1982), pp. 567–93.

10. Das, Veena, and Poole, Deborah 'Introduction', in Das and Poole (eds.), *Anthropology in the margins of the state*. Oxford: James Currey, 2004, pp. 2–32.

11. Douglas, Mary, *Purity and danger: an analysis of concepts of pollution and taboo*. New York: Routledge, 2002.

12. Comaroff, Jean, & John L. Comaroff, 'Criminal obsessions, after Foucault. Postcoloniality, Policing and the Metaphysics of Disorder', in Comaroff, J. & J.L. Comaroff (eds) *Law and disorder in the postcolony*. Chicago: University of Chicago Press, 2006, pp. 273–98.

13. Mbembe, Achille, 'Aesthetics of superfluity', *Public Culture* 16, 3 (2004) pp. 373–405.

14. Pratten, David, (2008) '"The thief eats his shame": Practice and power in Nigerian vigilantism', *Africa* 78, 1 (2008), pp. 64–83.

15. Malkki, Lisa H, *Purity and exile: violence, memory, and national cosmology among Hutu refugees in Tanzania*. Chicago: University of Chicago Press, 1995, pp. 55–6.
16. Ferme, Mariane. C. *The underneath of things: violence, history, and the everyday in Sierra Leone*. Berkeley: University of California Press, 2001, p. 181.

12. THE BELLY OF THE POLICE

1. South Africa has eleven official languages.
2. Zelizer, Vivian, *The Social Meaning of Money*, Princeton Paperbacks. Princeton University Press, 1997.
3. Bayart, Jean–François, *The State in Africa: The Politics of the Belly*, London: Longman, 1993.
4. Freud, Sigmund, *Totem und Tabu. Einige Uebereinstimmungen im Seelenleben der Wilden und der Neurotiker*, 3rd ed, Leipzig: Internationaler Psychoanalytischer Verlag, 1922.
5. Marshall, Lorna, 'Sharing, talking and giving: relief of social tensions among !Kung bushmen', *Africa*, 31 (1961), pp. 231–49.
6. Bloch, Maurice, *Prey into Hunter: The Politics of Religious Experience*, Cambridge: Cambridge University Press, 1992.
7. Lévi-Strauss, Claude, *The Raw and the Cooked. Mythologiques Volume One*, Chicago: University of Chicago Press, 1969.
8. Levis-Strauss, Claude, 'The culinary triangle', *Partisan Review*, 33, 4 (1966), pp. 586–95.
9. Douglas, Mary, *Implicit Meaning*, 2nd ed, London: Routledge, 1999.
10. Manning, Paul, *Semiotics of Drink and Drinking*, New York: Continuum, 2012.
11. Ibid., pp. 14–17.
12. Landecker, Hannah, 'Food as exposure: nutritional epigenetics and the new metabolism', *BioSocieties*, 6, 2 (2011), pp. 167–94.
13. Beck, Stefan and Jörg Niewoehner, 'Somatographic Investigations Across Levels of Complexity', *Biosocieties*, 1, 2 (2006), p. 224; Landecker, 2011, p. 179.
14. White, Hylton, 'Beastly whiteness: animal kinds and the social imagination in South Africa', *Anthropology Southern Africa*, 34, 3–4 (2011), pp. 104–12.
15. Mol, Annemarie, 'Moderation or satisfaction? Food ethics and food facts', in Sofie Vandamme, Suzanne van de Vathorst and Inez de Beaufort (eds.), *Whose Weight Is It Anyway? Essays on Ethics and Eating*, Leuven: Acco Academic Publishers, 2010, pp. 121–32.
16. Ibid., p. 9.
17. Simmel, Georg, 'Soziologie der Mahlzeit', *Der Zeitgeist, Beiblatt zum Berliner Tageblatt*, 41 (1910), p. 1 (my translation).
18. Bruce, David, 'Marikana not Ramaphosa's finest moment.' *M&G*, January 18, 2013. http://mg.co.za/print/2013-01-18-00-marikana-not-ramaphosas-finest-moment.

19. Brewer, John, *Black and Blue. Policing in South Africa*, New York: Oxford University Press, 1994.

20. Tait, Sean, and Monique Marks, 'You Strike a Gathering, You Strike a Rock: Current Debates in the Policing of Public Order in South Africa', *South African Crime Quarterly*, 38 (2014), pp. 15–22.

21. Soske, John, 'Marikana and the New Politics of Grief', 2012, http://abahlali.org/taxonomy/term/jon_soske/jon_soske/ (accessed on 1 September 2014).

22. Comaroff, John, and Jean Comaroff, *Ethnography and the Historical Imagination*, Boulder, CO: Westview Press, 1992, p. 84.

23. White, Hylton, 'A post-fordist ethnicity: insecurity, authority, and identity in South Africa', *Anthropological Quarterly*, 85, 2 (2012), pp. 397–427; Hornberger, Julia, *Policing and Human Rights: The Meaning of Violence and Justice in the Everyday Policing of Johannesburg*. London, Routledge, 2013.[0]

24. Hornberger, Julia, 'Ma-Slaan-Pa docketse: negotiations at the boundary between the private and the public', in Gorgio Blundo and Pierre-Yves Le Meur (eds.), *Governance of Daily Life in Africa*, Leiden: Brill Press, 2009, pp. 171–204.

25. Comaroff and Comaroff, 1992, p. 82.

26. Simmel, 1910; Fischler, C., 'Commensality, society and culture', *Social Science Information*, 50, 3–4 (2011), pp. 528–48.

27. Fischler, 2011, p. 534.

28. Fischler, 2011, p. 533.

29. Hornberger, Julia, *Policing and Human Rights: The Meaning of Violence and Justice in Everyday Policing in Johannesburg. Law, Development and Globalization*, London: Routledge, 2011.

30. Mauss, Marcel, *The Gift: The Form and Reason for Exchange in Archaic Societies*, London: Routledge, 2002 [1950].

31. Mol, 2010.

32. Mintz, S.W., *Sweetness and Power: The Place of Sugar in Modern History*, Elisabeth Sifton Books. Penguin Books, 1986.

13. INSIDE THE POLICE STATIONS IN MAPUTO CITY: BETWEEN LEGALITY AND LEGITIMACY

1. Hornberger, Julia, 'From General to Commissioner to General—On the Popular State of Policing in South Africa', *Law and Social Inquiry*, 38, 3 (2013), pp. 598–614; Comaroff, Jean L. and John Comaroff, J. (eds). *Law and Disorder in the Postcolony*, Chicago and London: University of Chicago Press, 2006.

2. Araújo, Sara, 'Toward an Ecology of Justices: An urban and Rural Study of Mozambican Plurality', in Kyed et al. (eds), *The Dynamics of Legal Pluralism in Mozambique*, Maputo: Kapicua, (2012) pp. 109–29

3. For a much more detailed account of this plural landscape see Kyed, Helene M.,

João C. B. Coelho, Amelia N. de Souto and Sara Araújo (eds), *The Dynamics of Legal Pluralism in Mozambique*, Maputo: Kapicua, 2012.

4. As in other African contexts there are very few ethnographic studies of the police in Maputo, and so far none of them have been published academically, apart from one master thesis by Dela Widenmann from 2007 (Dela Widenmann, Christina, 'Police Corruption—a Study of corruption in the Police of Maputo', Masters Thesis, International Development Studies, Roskilde University and Center for African Studies, Copenhagen University, 2007). There are a number of publications about the corruption and human rights violations of the police in the 1990s reform period, with the latter being explained as a lack of sufficient human rights training and as influenced by the paramilitary history of the police force in Mozambique (see Baker, Bruce, *Taking the law into their own hands. Lawless law enforcers in Africa*. Burlington and Hampshire: Ashgate, 2002). Another core area of study has been the increase in mob-justice and lynching, pointing to the inadequacies of the police and justice system in the poorer neighbourhoods of Maputo (see Papadakis, Vitalina. C. Vigilante 'Justice' and Collective Violence', in Kyed et al, *The Dynamics of Legal Pluralism in Mozambique*, 2012, pp. 186–95; Serra, Carlos (ed.), *Linchamento em Moçambique I (Uma desordem que apela à ordem)*, Maputo: Imprensa Universitária, 2008.)

5. Service conflicts were very common, with at least one a day during fieldwork. Mechanics were the main professional group accused of cheating and letting down customers, who claimed their money back or used the police to pressure the mechanic to repair their car properly, after having been paid or given spare parts. Many of these mechanics operated without formal licenses, yet this was not included in case handling, although, legally speaking, the police could charge them for illegal business.

6. Araújo, Sara and José A. Cristiano, *Pluralismo jurídico, legitimidade e acesso à justiça. Instâncias comunitárias de resolução de conflitos no Bairro de Inhagoia 'B'-Maputo*. Oficina do CES [CES Working Paper], 284, 2007; Kyed, Helene M., 'State Recognition of Traditional Authority. Authority, Citizenship and State Formation in Rural Post-War Mozambique', PhD dissertation, Roskilde University, 2007.

7. Fieldnote transcript, 02.06.2010.

8. *Circulo* is the name for the central governance site of a *bairro* (neighborhood), which houses the *secretário do bairro* (lowest administrative head approved by the population), the sector police officer and the Frelimo party branch. In some neighborhoods you also find here the headquarters for the community court and/or the community police, but this varies from place to place.

9. Fieldnote transcript, 24.05.2010.

10. Hornberger, 'From General to Commissioner to General', p. 11.

11. Fieldnote transcripts, 27.05.2010.

12. Fieldnote transcripts, 31.05.2010.

13. That the use of the cell was educational, yet also used with some caution was evident in a case where a thirteen-year-old boy was released after two days in the cell after he had been caught pick pocketing on the street. Before he left the station, the officer in charge of the weaponry sat down and had a chat with him, as a father to son: 'You should not grow up in prison, my son. You should go to school...and help make things clean and nice at home'. He smiled at the boy and shook his hands before he left the station and then he said to me: 'This is very early to go to prison. The danger now is that he is no longer afraid of the cell, because he can see that you can leave it again. It's like when parents beat their children too much, then they stop fearing the beating' (Fieldnote transcript, 28.05.2010).

14. In this particular case from 25.05.2010 the woman had already received two instalments from the thief's family, but for some reason, apparently without her knowing, the court case had ended while the thief was in the cell, which was a mistake, according to the officer who had initially dealt with the case, also as we heard it. He had only been in the cell, I was told, to make sure that the family paid out all the money that was missing.

15. On the latter see also Dela Widenmann, *Police Corruption—a Study of corruption in the Police of Maputo*, p. 37

16. That this notion of negotiation was strong among the criminals frequenting the station was evident in that at Police Station Nine it was common to see arrestees, as they were dragged towards the door of the cell, pleading to be heard one last time or to be set free.

17. Dela Widenmann, *Police Corruption—a Study of corruption in the Police of Maputo*, p. 56.

18. Dela Widenmann, *Police Corruption—a Study of corruption in the Police of Maputo*, p. 40.

19. Station Commander, 25.05.2010.

20. Kyed, Helene M., 'Community policing in post-war Mozambique', *Policing and Society*, 9, 4 (2009), pp. 354–71; Kyed, Helene M. 'The Contested Role of Community Policing. "New" non-state actors in the plural legal landscape of Mozambique', *DIIS Working Paper*, 26 (2010).

21. Sector police are the Police Station representatives in the neighborhoods, and form part of the community policing concept, where plainclothes officers collaborate closely with members of the population and the local leadership structures. Commonly they worked with civilian community policing groups selected by the local leadership, and comprising mainly young unemployed men (see Kyed, 'Community policing in post-war Mozambique'; Kyed, 'The Contested Role of Community Policing', 2010).

22. Pedro, Community Police, 12.06.2009.

23. Kyed, 'The Contested Role of Community Policing', 2010.

24. Lalá, Anicia and Laudemiro Francisco, 'The Difficulties of Donor Coordination: Police and Judicial Reform in Mozambique', *Civil Wars*, 8, 2 (2006), pp. 166.
25. Hornberger, 'From General to Commissioner to General', p. 10.

14. MONEY, MORALS AND LAW: THE LEGITIMACY OF POLICE TRAFFIC CHECKS IN GHANA

1. Waddington, P. A. J., *Policing Citizens: Authority and Rights*, London: University College London Press, 1999, p. 5.; see also Reiner, Robert, *The Politics of the Police*, 3rd edition, Oxford: Oxford University Press, 2000, p. 19.
2. Revised field notes, Akansa, 2010. Names and locations have been changed. The article is based on sixteen months of fieldwork in the Ghanaian police, beginning in 2008.
3. See Kemp, Charles, Clive Norris and Nigel Fielding, *Negotiating Nothing. Police Decision-Making in Disputes*, Aldershot: Avebury, 1992, p. 86; Waddington, 1999, p. 38. When the early police researcher Goldstein discovered police discretion, he problematized the issue that discretionary decisions were not visible and based on the 'private value system of individual officers' (Goldstein, Joseph, 'Police discretion not to invoke the criminal process: low-visibility decisions in the administration of justice', *The Yale Law Journal*, 69, 4 (1960), p. 575).
4. Bittner, Egon, 'The police on skid-row: a study of peace keeping', *American Sociological Review*, 32, 5 (1967), p. 711; see also Reiss, Albert J., *The Police and the Public*, New Haven: Yale University Press, 1977, p. 134.
5. Martin, Jeffrey, 'A reasonable balance of law and sentiment: social order in democratic Taiwan from the policeman's point of view', *Law & Society Review*, 41, 3 (2007), p. 694.
6. Weber, Max, *Wirtschaft und Gesellschaft*, Tübingen: Mohr, 1980 [1922], p. 16.
7. von Benda-Beckmann, Franz, Keebet von Benda-Beckmann and Julia Eckert, 'Rules of law and laws of ruling: law and governance between past and future', in von Benda-Beckmann, Franz, Keebet von Benda-Beckmann and Julia Eckert (eds), *Rules of Law and Laws of Ruling: on the Governance of Law*, Farnham: Ashgate, 2009, p. 4.
8. Muir's description of police officers' defensive responses is quite similar, though he argues that the response depends on the police officer's personality, and that only one response is selected in an interaction (Muir, William Ker, *Police: Streetcorner Politicians*, Chicago: University of Chicago Press, 1977, pp. 145–6).
9. See Schielke, Samuli, 'Being good in Ramadan: ambivalence, fragmentation, and the moral self in the lives of young Egyptians', *Journal of the Royal Anthropological Institute*, 15, issue supplement s1 (2009), p. 15.
10. Waddington, 1999, pp. 15–16; see also Bittner, Egon, 'Florence Nightingale in pursuit of Willie Sutton: a theory of the police', in Herbert Jacob (ed.), *Potential*

for Reform of Criminal Justice, Beverly Hills: SAGE Publications, 1974, pp. 17–44; Reiner, 2000, p. 7.

11. Weber, 1980, p. 29, own translation.

12. See Shon, Phillip Chong Ho, "'I'd grab the S-O-B by his hair and yank him out the window": the fraternal order of warnings and threats in police-citizen encounters', *Discourse & Society*, 16, 6 (2005), p. 837–8.

13. Waddington, 1999, p. 20.

14. This comment resembles a similar one by a German police officer in the 1960s: 'There is no moped without fault' (Feest, Johannes and Erhard Blankenburg, *Die Definitionsmacht der Polizei: Strategien der Strafverfolgung und soziale Selektion*, Düsseldorf: Bertelsmann Universitäts-Verlag, 1972, p. 26, own translation). In both cases, referring to the law is just the first step and then enables police officers to select other registers.

15. After Rawling's second coup in 1984, police officers were authorised to issue on the spot fines. This was discontinued in 1985 following complaints of increased corruption (see Government of Ghana, *Report of the Presidential Commission into the Ghana Police Service* [Archer Report], volume 1, 1997, p. 98).

16. Luhmann, Niklas, *Die Politik der Gesellschaft*, with assistance of André Kieserling, Frankfurt am Main: Suhrkamp, 2000, p. 262; see also Ericson, Richard, *Reproducing Order: Study of Police Patrol Work*, Toronto: University of Toronto Press, 1982, p. 13; Kemp et al., 1992, p. 86)

17. Arifari, Nassirou, "'We don't eat the paper": corruption in transport, customs and the civil forces', in Blundo, Giorgio and Jean-Pierre Olivier de Sardan (eds), *Everyday Corruption and the State: Citizens and Public Officials in Africa*, London: Zed Books, 2006, p. 196.

18. Bierschenk, Thomas, 'The everyday functioning of an African public service: informalization, privatization and corruption in Benin's legal system', *Journal of Legal Pluralism*, 57 (2008), pp. 101–39.

19. See Dixon, David, Clive Coleman and Keith Bottomley, 'Consent and the legal regulation of policing', *Journal of Law and Society*, 17, 3 (1990), pp. 345–62.

20. Paperman, Patricia, 'Surveillance underground: the uniform as an interaction device', in *Ethnography*, 4, 3 (2003), p. 411.

21. See Waddington, 1999, p. 39; Martin, 2007, p. 666.

22. Police officers also use coded language to conceal their activities from civilians. A police officer will ask a colleague to 'roger' a civilian (ROGER designates the letter R in radio communications and stands for 'receive'). Similarly, police officers call work at the barriers 'baker duty' (BAKER designates the letter B in radio communications).

23. See Martin, 2007, p. 691.

24. In a questionnaire issued by Tankebe, most Ghanaians claimed they had never paid a police officer for advantages (Tankebe, Justice, 'Public confidence in the

police: testing the effects of public experiences of police corruption in Ghana', *British Journal of Criminology*, 50, 2 (2010), p. 307). This probably means they often do not see the handover of money as corruption.

25. Jauregui, Beatrice, 'Provisional agency in India: jugaad and legitimation of corruption', *American Ethnologist*, 41, 1 (2014), p. 80.
26. Schielke, 2009, p. 31.
27. Hasty, Jennifer, 'The pleasures of corruption: desire and discipline in Ghanaian political culture', *Cultural Anthropology*, 20, 2 (2005), pp. 271–301; Olivier de Sardan, Jean-Pierre, 'A moral economy of corruption in Africa?', *Journal of Modern African Studies*, 37, 1 (1999), p. 26.
28. The vocabulary itself hints at these histories. *Dash* (gift) is a Ghanaian word whose current meaning emerged from the first encounters between European trade vessels and Fanti traders (Sarbah, John M. and Hollis R. Lynch, *Fanti National Constitution: A Short Treatise on the Constitution and Government of the Fanti Asanti and Other Akan Tribes of West Africa*, 2nd edition, London: Thomas Nelson, 1968, p. 30). It may be an appropriated Portuguese word (*das-me*) (Huber, Magnus, *Ghanaian Pidgin English in its West African Context: A Sociohistorical and Structural Analysis*, Amsterdam: John Benjamins Publishing, 1999, p. 100).
29. Twumasi, Paul K., *Criminal Law in Ghana*, Tema: Ghana Publishing Corporation, 1985, p. 517. According to the Police Service Instruction, police officers are only allowed to take gifts if their superior permits it (see Government of Ghana, *Ghana Police Service Instructions*, Accra, 1992, pp. 63–4). This regulation does not forbid the handover of money but structures internal money distribution.
30. Mensa-Bonsu, Henrietta J. A. N., *The Annotated Criminal Offences Act of Ghana*, 5th edition, Accra: Black Mask Limited, 2008, p. 201–3.
31. Clark, Gracia, *Onions are My Husband: Survival and Accumulation by West African Market Women*, Chicago: The University of Chicago Press, 1994, p. 132. She categorises these practices as 'quantity bargaining' and differentiates these from 'price bargaining', though she adds that both are not clearly separated.
32. Though this rule only extended to the police division in Akansa. Drivers had to pay again beyond this jurisdiction.
33. Martin, 2007, p. 675.
34. Bierschenk, 2008, p. 132.
35. These responses are evocative of Scott's 'weapons of the weak' as most are individual actions (Scott, James C., *Weapons of the Weak: Everyday Forms of Peasant Resistance*, New Haven: Yale University Press, 1985, p. 29). However, many civilians are neither ideologically nor factually weak. These responses are therefore not acts of resistance in Scott's sense (Scott, 1985, p. 290).
36. Particularly at night, lorry drivers often ignore police officers and drive past them.
37. During fieldwork, civilians stabbed a police officer, who was trying to make an arrest, twice. Civilians threw stones at a detective driving through town. Several other assaults on police officers occurred.

38. See Beek, Jan and Mirco Göpfert, 'Police violence in West Africa: perpetrators' and ethnographers' dilemmas', *Ethnography*, 14, 4 (2013), pp. 477–500.

39. Even if police officers managed to arrest the attackers, such cases were ultimately settled. This does not mean that Ghanaians are unafraid of the police. 'Fear government' is an oft-repeated warning, pointing out the long arm of the police.

40. Adinkrah, Mensah, 'Vigilante homicides in contemporary Ghana', *Journal of Criminal Justice*, 33, 5 (2005), p. 418.

41. Lofthouse, Michael, 'The core mandate of policing', in Critcher, Chas and David Waddington (eds), *Policing Public Order: Theoretical and Practical Issues*, Aldershot: Avebury, 1996, p. 45; Muir, 1977, p. 263; Reiner, 2000, p. 8.

42. In the Global North, civilians can avoid law enforcement at traffic checks by appearing respectable and co-operative (Ericson, 1982, p. 144–6). In Ghana, civilians can avoid handing over money through similar practices.

43. See Arifari, 2006, p. 192.

44. There are some limits to this use of connections. Many actors have only connections to local politicians and low ranking police officers. Police officers can resist orders from such people in other jurisdictions. Still, police officers will more readily 'consider' a civilian in such cases but not let him pass immediately. Furthermore, some senior officers are reluctant to protect civilians, as it undermines their reputation within the police service.

45. See Feest and Blankenburg, 1972, p. 76.

46. This reflects the classical Marxist discourse on the control of the state by the dominant classes. Yet the fact that it is expressed by a state official shows his aspiration towards organisational autonomy.

47. Feest and Blankenburg, 1972, p. 11; Skolnick, Jerome H., *Justice Without Trial: Law Enforcement in Democratic Society*, New York: Wiley, 1975 [1966], p. 206.

48. A police officer explained that he had 'planted' his own acquaintances to call the radio station in the event of someone calling about him. His acquaintances would then give contrary accounts of the incident and act as character witnesses.

49. Scott, 1985, p. 282.

50. See Owen in this volume.

51. Chatterjee, Partha, *The Politics of the Governed: Reflections on Popular Politics in most of the World*, New York: Columbia University Press, 2004, p. 60.

52. Politicians are not the only group pressuring the police (see Arifari, 2006, p. 183–5). In Ashaiman, a suburb of greater Accra, the commercial drivers' unions had protested violently against police traffic checks. After negotiations between union representatives and senior police officers, some of the traffic laws were not enforced afterwards.

54. Daily Graphic, 'Four MTTU men held over extortion', 28 Jan 2010.

55. By simultaneously informing the press, the police administration made certain that the case goes to court. Police officers later complained that the IGP had tar-

geted the lower ranks. But they also complained that such overt handover of money at traffic checks undermines the image of the police.

56. Olivier de Sardan, 1999, p. 29.
57. For a comprehensive study on the perspective of road users in Ghana see Klaeger, Gabriel, 'Dwelling on the road: routines, rituals and roadblocks in southern Ghana', *Africa* 83, 3 (2013), pp. 446–69.
58. Tyler, Tom R., Anthony Braga, Jeffry Fagan, Tracey Meares, Robert Sampson, Chris Winship, 'Legitimacy and criminal justice: international perspectives', in Tyler, Tom R. (ed.), *Legitimacy and Criminal Justice: A Comparative Perspective*, New York: Russell Sage Foundation, 2008, p. 10–13.
59. Weber, 1980, p. 123.
60. Ericson, 1982, p. 3; Lofthouse, 1996, p. 42; Reiner, 2000, p. 34; Reiss, 1977, p. 46.
61. See Lentz, Carola, 'The chief, the mine captain and the politician: legitimating power in northern Ghana', *Africa*, 68 (1998), p. 47.
62. Ibrahim, Ahmed, *Flamingo social studies for junior secondary schools: pupil's book three*, Accra, n.d., p. 72.
63. Chesshyre, Robert, *The Force: Inside the Police*, London: Sidgwick & Jackson, 1989, p. 168.
64. Hough argues that scholarly interest in police legitimacy surfaces only, if it is endangered (Hough, Mike, 'Policing, new public management and legitimacy in Britain', in Tom R. Tyler (ed.), *Legitimacy and Criminal Justice: A Comparative Perspective*, New York: Russell Sage Foundation, 2008, p. 65; see Júnior, Domício P. and Jacqueline Muniz, '"Stop or I'll call the police!": the idea of police, or the effects of police encounters over time', *British Journal of Criminology*, 46, 2 (2006), p. 244).
65. Pendleton, Michael R., 'Policing the park: understanding soft enforcement', *Journal of Leisure Research*, 30, 4 (1998), p. 567.
66. See Blundo, Giorgio and Jean-Pierre Olivier de Sardan, 'The popular semiology of corruption', in Blundo, Giorgio and Jean-Pierre Olivier de Sardan (eds), *Everyday Corruption and the State: Citizens and Public Officials in Africa*, London: Zed Books, 2006, pp. 133–4. Boubacar relayed an interesting rumour about the four arrested MTTU police officers. They had had demanded 2 cedis instead of one, explaining to civilians that other government fees had also risen. Accordingly, police management had only arrested these police officers because their demands were unreasonable.
67. Detective Lance Corporal Christian also relayed this perception but qualified it weakly: 'They will say the police are only interested in money. But this is not always true.'
68. See Olivier de Sardan, Jean-Pierre, 'State bureaucracy and governance in west francophone Africa: an empirical diagnosis and historical perspective', in Blundo, Giorgio and Pierre-Yves Le Meur (eds), *The Governance of Daily Life in Africa:*

Ethnographic Explorations of Public and Collective Services, Leiden: Brill, 2009, p. 47.

69. At another traffic check, Moses wanted to show me how to stop a vehicle correctly, but the lorry driver surprised him by giving him 2 cedis (approx. 1 €) immediately and saying: 'Happy New Year! Take this for coco (British English: porridge)'. Perplexed, Moses took the money and let the lorry pass. He then looked at me and said it would have been 'wicked' to refuse the older man's gift. But he still seemed ashamed, and then said we had to share the gift. I refused, but he stuffed the one cedi bill into my trouser pocket. Before I went with him to the traffic check, he had joked about his earnings. But to be seen accepting money embarrassed him. He therefore seemed to attempt to justify it and to implicate me.

70. Luhmann, 2000, p. 45–6.

71. See Dixon et al., 1990, p. 353; Shon, 2005, p. 843.

72. Luhmann, 2000, p. 261, own translation.

73. Martin, 2007, p. 692, italics in the original.

74. Weber, 1980, p. 122.

75. In other words, these concealing practices are forms of boundary work, see Beek, Jan, '"There should be no open doors in the police": criminal investigations in northern Ghana as boundary work', *The Journal of Modern African Studies*, 50, 4 (2012), pp. 551–72.

76. Eckert, Julia, 'From subjects to citizens: legalism from below and the homogenisation of the legal sphere', *Journal of Legal Pluralism*, 53, 3 (2006), p. 45.

77. Smart, Alan, 'Expressions of interest: friendship and guanxi in Chinese societies', in Bell, Sandra and Simon Coleman (eds), *The Anthropology of Friendship*, Oxford: Berg Publishers, 1999, p. 139.

78. Handelman, Don, 'Bureaucratic interpretation: the perception of child abuse in urban Newfoundland', in Handelman, Don and Elliott Leyton (eds), *Bureaucracy and World View: Studies in the Logic of Official Interpretation*, St. John's Newfoundland: University of Newfoundland, 1978, p. 29.

79. Ericson, 1982, p. 14; see O'Neill, Megan, *Policing Football: Social Interaction and Negotiated Disorder*, Houndmills: Palgrave Macmillan, 2005, pp. 74–5; Skolnick, 1975.

80. Van Maanen, John, 'The asshole', in Manning, Peter K. and John Van Maanen (eds), *Policing: A View from the Street*, Santa Monica: Goodyear Publishing, 1978, p. 234–5.

81. Waddington, 1999, p. 128.

82. See Holdaway, Simon, 'Discovering structure: studies of the British police occupational culture', in Mollie Weatheritt (ed.), *Police Research: Some Future Prospects*, Aldershot: Avebury, 1989, pp. 68–9.

83. Lipsky, Michael, *Street-Level Bureaucracy: Dilemmas of the Individual in Public Services*, New York: Russell Sage Foundation, 1980, p. 86.

84. The concept of police work as an art or craft, depending on personal competence, was emphasised in the early works some police researchers (see Muir, 1977; Bittner 1967).
85. Weber, 1980, p. 13.

15. SOFT LAW ENFORCEMENT IN THE NIGERIEN GENDARMERIE; HOW A CASE IS BORN

1. Bittner, Egon, 'Florence Nightingale in pursuit of Willie Sutton: a theory of the police', in Herbert Jacob (ed.), *Potential for Reform of Criminal Justice*, Beverly Hills: SAGE Publications, 1974, p. 23.
2. Bittner, 1974, p. 31.
3. Only those gendarmes on traffic control duty who were out on the streets checking vehicles, drivers, cargo and passengers regularly observed offences, but most were mere breaches of the highway code (*Code de la Route*).
4. See Feest and Blankenburg, 1972, p. 19; Goldstein, 1960, pp. 543–94; Ignatieff, 1979, p. 445; Monjardet, 1996, p. 38; Reiner, 2000, p. 19; Waddington, P. A. J., *Policing Citizens: Authority and Rights*, London: University College London Press, 1999, p. 38.
5. Martin, Jeffrey, 'A reasonable balance of law and sentiment: social order in democratic Taiwan from the policeman's point of view', *Law & Society Review*, 41, 3 (2007), pp. 665–98; Beek, Jan, '"Every car has an offence on it": Register polizeilichen Handelns bei Verkehrskontrollen in Nordghana', *Sociologus*, 61, 2 (2011), pp. 197–222.
6. Mosse, David and David T. Lewis, 'Theoretical approaches to brokerage and translation in development', in David Lewis and David Mosse (eds), *Development Brokers and Translators: The Ethnography of Aid and Agencies*, Bloomfield, CT: Kumarian Press, 2006, p. 13.
7. Shapland, Joanna and Jon Vagg, *Policing by the Public*, London: Routledge, 1988, p. 66.
8. See also Wender, Jonathan M., *Policing and the Poetics of Everyday Life*, Urbana, Chicago: University of Illinois Press, 2008, p. 3.
9. I withhold the names of the places and change all names of the gendarmes mentioned in this text in order to ensure their anonymity.
10. Bensa, Alban and Eric Fassin, 'Les sciences sociales face à l'événement', *Terrain*, 38 (2002), p. 11. Their reflections are mostly based on Deleuze, Gilles, *Logique du sens*, Paris: Editions de Minuit, 1969.
11. Ibid., p. 19; Weick, Karl E., *Sensemaking in Organizations*, Thousand Oaks: SAGE, 1995, p. 2.
12. Nader, Laura and Harry F. Todd, 'Introduction', in Laura Nader and Harry F. Todd (eds), *The Disputing Process: Law in Ten Societies*, New York: Columbia University Press, 1978, p. 14.

13. Ibid., p. 15.
14. Ibid.
15. See Blankenburg, Erhard, 'Recht als gradualisiertes Konzept: Begriffsdimensionen der Diskussion um Verrechtlichung und Entrechtlichung', in Erhard Blankenburg, Ekkehard Klausa and Hubert Rottleuthner (eds), *Alternative Rechtsformen und Alternativen zum Recht*, Opladen: Westdeutscher Verlag, 1980, p. 86.
16. Rijk van Dijk describes a similar practice called a 'voodoo oath' that Nigerian prostitutes in the Netherlands had taken. See van Dijk, Rijk, '"Voodoo" on the doorstep: young Nigerian prostitutes and magic policing in the Netherlands', *Africa*, 71, 4 (2001), pp. 565–6.
17. On the popular semiology of money transactions, particularly in terms of manducation, see Blundo, Giorgio and Jean-Pierre Olivier de Sardan, 'The Popular Semiology of Corruption', in Giorgio Blundo and Jean-Pierre Olivier de Sardan (eds), *Everyday Corruption and the State: Citizens and Public Officials in Africa*, Cape Town: Philip, 2006, pp. 121–2.
18. Hausa: 'Dommi sun kira jendarmomi? Basu iya kama musu, ko?' (Field notes)
19. Göpfert, Mirco, 'Security in Niamey: an anthropological perspective on policing and an act of terrorism in Niger', *Journal of Modern African Studies*, 50, 1 (2012), pp. 53–74.
20. See Baker, Bruce, 'Multi–choice policing in Uganda', *Policing and Society*, 15, 1 (2005), pp. 35–6.
21. See Jensen, Steffen, 'Policing Nkomazi: crime, masculinity and generational conflicts', in David Pratten and Atreyee Sen (eds), *Global Vigilantes*, London: Hurst, 2007, pp. 51–2.
22. Shapera, I., 'Some anthropological concepts of "crime": The Hobhouse Memorial Lecture', *The British Journal of Sociology*, 23, 4 (1972), p. 390; see also Kirsch, Thomas G. and Tilo Grätz (eds), *Domesticating Vigilantism in Africa*, Oxford: Currey, 2010, p. 1.
23. Lund, Christian, *Law, Power and Politics in Niger: Land Struggles and the Rural Code*, Hamburg: LIT, 1998.
24. See von Benda-Beckmann, Franz, and Keebet von Benda–Beckmann, 'The dynamics of change and continuity in plural legal orders', *Journal of Legal Pluralism*, 53–54 (2006), pp. 1–44; von Benda-Beckmann, Franz, Keebet von Benda–Beckmann and Julia M. Eckert (eds), *Rules of Law and Laws of Ruling: On the Governance of Law*, Farnham: Ashgate, 2009, p. 4; Hills, Alice, *Policing Post-Conflict Cities*. London: Zed Books, 2009, p. 19; Hills, 2013, pp. 81–102; Jensen, 2007, p. 49; Loader, Ian, 'Plural policing and democratic governance', *Social and Legal Studies*, 9, 3 (2000), pp. 323–45; Pratten, David, 'Introduction. The politics of protection: perspectives on vigilantism in Nigeria', *Africa*, 78, 1 (2008), p. 4; Reiner, Robert, *The Politics of the Police*, 3rd edition, Oxford: Oxford University Press, 2000, pp. 4–6.

25. Hausa: 'Kaman, aka samu wane massala. Zaa zo a gaya mini. In aka samu da wane fulani, zaa gyara nan. In ba fulani ba ne, muna tahi mun gaya ma sarkinshi. Amma, ka sani, in laihinshi yana karami, muna iya mun gyara shi. In ya yi girma, dole an kaishi gendarmerie.' (Interview)

26. Hausa: 'Sohon soja ne! Abinda nike yi, ba ruwan sarki ba ne!' (Field notes)

27. See Roberts, Richard, *Litigants and Households: African Disputes and Colonial Courts in the French Soudan, 1895–1912*, Portsmouth, NH: Heinemann, 2005, pp. 16–7, 232

28. See Eckert, Julia, 'Work in progress: the state at work in urban India', in Nikolaus Schareika, Eva Spies and Pierre–Yves Le Meur (eds), *Auf dem Boden der Tatsachen: Festschrift für Thomas Bierschenk*, Köln: Köppe, 2011, p. 437; Merry, 1979, p. 919.

29. Bierschenk, Thomas, 'The everyday functioning of an African public service: informalization, privatization and corruption in Benin's legal system', *Journal of Legal Pluralism*, 57 (2008), pp. 118–19.

30. Ibid., p. 119.

31. Ibid.

32. See Black, Donald J., 'Production of crime rates', *American Sociological Review*, 35 (1970), pp. 742–4.

33. 'Voir M. le CB de Godiya pour dresser procédure de...', *d'arrestation*, for example.

34. Jan Beek describes a similar routine in the Ghanaian police as a discretionary strategy to not produce cases. See Beek, Jan, '"There should be no open doors in the police": criminal investigations in northern Ghana as boundary work', *The Journal of Modern African Studies*, 50, 4 (2012), p. 556.

35. French: 'Qui sont les gens-là? Hé planton! La femme-là, elle fait quoi? Pourquoi vous la regardez? Qu'est-ce que vous attendez pour l'écouter?! Est-ce qu'il faut toujours qu'on vous rappelle?' (Field notes).

36. Bauer, Alain and Émile Pérez, *Les 100 mots de la police et du crime*, Paris: Presses universitaires de France, 2009, p. 97.

37. See Göpfert, Mirco, 'Bureaucratic aesthetics: report writing in the Nigérien gendarmerie', *American Ethnologist*, 40, 2 (2013), pp. 324–34.

38. A key incident often referred to by gendarmes occurred in the early 2000s, when a handcuffed detainee lost his hand after a wound on his wrist had become infected. He was detained illegally but legitimately, according to all gendarmes who told me this story. But it was not a criminal case. Human rights' associations then filed a complaint at the public prosecutor's office, and the gendarme on duty was severely punished and put on trial. Superior officers of the gendarmerie then explicitly forbade engagement in civil matters.

39. French: incapacité temporaire de travail

40. See Searle, John R., *Speech Acts: An Essay in the Philosophy of Language*, Cambridge: Cambridge University Press, 1969 and Searle, John R., *Expression and Meaning: Studies in the Theory of Speech Acts*, Cambridge: Cambridge University Press, 1979.

41. French: 'C'est une affaire très délicate. Partout dans la ville on a sali son nom, et si on n'intervient pas dans des cas pareils, bientôt ça serait le chaos! Les gens vont se taper dessus!' (Field notes)

42. French: 'Toute infraction est un problème sociétal. Et tout problème sociétal peut provoquer du trouble à l'ordre public.' (Interview)

43. See Bauer and Pérez, 2009, p. 97.

44. French: 'Vous pouvez commettre un acte grave dans une situation tolérable. Et vous pouvez commettre un acte moins grave, un acte simple, mais dans un esprit... un esprit de voyou. Ou tu peux te moquer des gens ou montrer aux gens que tu es meilleur...ou tu veux montrer que tu ne respectes pas la loi, ou tu veux montrer que tu refuses même d'admettre que la loi est là. ...Là, que ça soit minime, moi je le réprime plus que celui qui a fait une faute grave dans un esprit...sans intention. C'est ça qui importe chez moi. Parce qu'il y a des gens qui sont voyou, il y a des gens qui sont...incorrigible. Au pire ils ont, ils pensent qu'ils ont quelqu'un qui peut toujours les protéger. Ça, des esprits malins comme ça-là, je ne tolère pas. Et qui que le gars soit, je suis caillé là-dessus. Un voleur par exemple... Vous allez voir quelqu'un qui va voler quatre à cinq brebis. Parmi les cinq brebis il y a une brebis qui est la seule brebis de quelqu'un. Et le gars qui a volé ça, quand on va chez lui, on voit que son père peut avoir 50 vaches, même 200 vaches. Et lui le gars, il vient dans un village voler l'unique brebis de quelqu'un? On lui inflige une forte amende... à prendre ou aller partir en prison.' (Interview)

45. See also Nader, Laura, 'Crime as a category: domestic and globalized', in Philip C. Parnell and Stephanie C. Kane (eds), *Crime's Power: Anthropologists and the Ethnography of Crime*, New York: Palgrave Macmillan, 2003, p. 65.

46. French: 'En principe c'est une affaire civile...' (Field notes)

47. French: 'Presque toutes les affaires civiles se transforment en affaire pénale. Par exemple dans une affaire de dette: comment est-ce qu'il a pris la dette? Et dès qu'on pénètre un tout petit peu, tout suite on constate qu'il y avait des manœuvres fraud-uleux, ou il a abusé de sa confiance, ou bien il l'a escroqué ainsi de suite. Donc c'est abus de confiance ou escroquerie. Donc c'est une affaire pénale.' (Interview)

48. French: 'Et cela nous rentre dans l'ambiguïté' (Field notes)

49. French: 'C'est pour ça qu'il faut être très, très vigilant!' (Field notes)

50. French: 'L'abus de confiance, par exemple. On peut soutirer un élément, un des éléments caractéristiques qui forment l'abus de confiance, et directement on va dire que c'est une affaire civile. Pour l'escroquerie c'est la même chose. Parce que dans la tromperie il n'y a pas vraiment du concret.' (Interview)

51. Since these categories can only inappropriately be translated into felony, misde-meanor, and minor offences, I will stick to the French terminology.

52. République du Niger, *Code Pénal (last modification)*, Niamey: République du Niger, 2003, Art. 1 and 5; Bauer & Pérez, 2009, pp. 97–9.

53. See Jeanjean, Marc, 'La "culture policière" et l'"affaire": une approche eth-nographique de la police', *Ethnologie française*, 21, 1 (1991), pp. 84–5.

54. See République du Niger, 2003, Art. 272.
55. See Jeanjean, 1991.
56. Bittner, 1974, p. 28.
57. Simon, David, *Homicide: A Year on the Killing Streets*, Edinburgh: Canongate, 2009 [1991], pp. 20–1.
58. Hodgson, Jacqueline, 'Hierarchy, bureaucracy, and ideology in French criminal justice: some empirical observations', *Journal of Law and Society*, 29, 2 (2002), pp. 229, 255.
59. Hodgson, 2002, p. 236, FN 39.
60. Nader, Laura and Harry F. Todd, 'Introduction', in Laura Nader and Harry F. Todd (eds), *The Disputing Process: Law in Ten Societies*, New York: Columbia University Press, 1978, p. 1.
61. In an article on police violence, Jan Beek and I (2013) describe this as a framework of multiple and often conflicting moral discourses, of which the legal discourse is but one, and in which police officers and gendarmes have to position themselves and their actions. Continuing in this vein, the question here is: to which discourse was the gendarmes' vocational ear attuned? See Beek, Jan and Mirco Göpfert, 'Police violence in West Africa: perpetrators' and ethnographers' dilemmas', *Ethnography*, 14, 4 (2013)
62. Geertz, 1983, p. 175.
63. See Comaroff, John L. and Jean Comaroff, 'Criminal justice, cultural justice: the limits of liberalism and the pragmatics of difference in the new South Africa', *American Ethnologist*, 31, 2 (2004), p. 189; Nader, 2003, p. 58.
64. See Dubber, Markus D., 'The new police science and the police power model of the criminal process', in Markus D. Dubber and Mariana Valverde (eds), *The New Police Science: The Police Power in Domestic and International Governance*, Stanford, CA: Stanford University Press, 2006, pp. 118, 128–9.
65. See Buur, Lars, 'Reordering society: vigilantism and expressions of sovereignty in Port Elizabeth's townships', *Development and Change*, 37, 4 (2006), p. 754. Thus, I do not fully agree with Satnam Choongh's pessimistic vision of police work according to which 'the language of "crime" … is used as a cover to validate an illegal system in which individuals are harassed and punished' (1998, pp. 237–8).
66. See Jensen, 2007, p. 49; Nader, 2003, p. 65.
67. Comaroff, John L. and Jean Comaroff, 'Reflections on the anthropology of law, governance and sovereignty', in von Benda-Beckmann, Franz, Keebet von Benda-Beckmann and Julia Eckert (eds), *Rules of Law and Laws of Ruling: On the Governance of Law*, Farnham: Ashgate, 2009, p. 55.
68. See Ruteere, Mutuma and Marie–Emmanuelle Pommerolle, 'Democratizing security or decentralizing repression? The ambiguities of community policing in Kenya', *African Affairs*, 102 (2003), p. 588.
69. Aee Beek 2011, pp. 210–11.

70. Lasslett, Kristian, 'Crime or social harm? A dialectical perspective', *Crime, Law & Social Change*, 54 (2010), p. 2.

EPILOGUE

1. Lentz, Carola, Jan Beek and Mirco Göpfert (workshop); 'Just police work: ethnographic research on the police in Africa', Johannes Gutenberg University, Mainz, Germany, 2013, available at http://www.ifeas.uni-mainz.de/1105.php.

2. For a biographical account see Imray, Colin, *Policeman in Africa*, Sussex: Book Guild, 1997; for a historical account Anderson, David and David Killingray (eds), *Policing and Decolonisation: Politics, Nationalism, and the Police, 1917–65*, Manchester: Manchester University Press, 1992; for political science accounts Potholm, Christian, 'The multiple roles of the police as seen in the African context', *Journal of Developing Areas*, 3 (1969), pp. 139–58; Lee, J., *African Armies and Civil Order*, London: Chatto & Windus, 1969; Enloe, Cynthia, 'Ethnicity and militarization: factors shaping the roles of police in third world nations', *Studies in Comparative International Development*, 11 (1976), pp. 25–38.; Marenin, Otwin, 'Policing African states: toward a critique', *Comparative Politics*, 14, 4 (1982), pp. 379–94.

3. Hills, Alice, *Policing Africa: Internal Security and the Limits of Liberalization*, Boulder, CO: Lynne Rienner, 2000.

4. Brogden, Mike, and Clifford Shearing, *Policing for a New South Africa*, London: Routledge, 1993.

5. Bayley, David, Changing *the Guard: Developing Democratic Police Abroad*, Oxford: OUP, 2006; Downie, Richard, 'Building police institutions in fragile states: case studies from Africa', Washington, 2013, DC: CSIS. Available at http:// csis.org/files/publication/130115_Downie_BuildPoliceInstitutions_web.pdf, last accessed 20 January 2017

6. Olaniyi, Rashid, 'Community vigilantes in metropolitan Kano', Ibadan: French Institute for Research in Africa, IFRA, 2005; Baker, Bruce, *Security in Post-conflict Africa: The Role of Non-State Policing*, Boca Raton: CRC Press, 2010.

7. Contrast Giustozzi, Antonio and Mohammed Isaqzadeh, *Policing Afghanistan: The Politics of the Lame Leviathan*, London: Hurst, 2013.

8. Frances, David (ed.), *Policing in Africa*, Basingstoke: Palgrave Macmillan, 2012.

9. HRW, 2005.

10. Marks, Monique, *Transforming the Robocops: changing Police in South Africa*, Scottsville, SA: University of KwaZulu-Natal Press, 2005.

11. Heald, Suzette, *Controlling Anger: The Sociology of Gisu Violence*, Manchester: MUP, 1989.

12. Baker, 2010.

13. Biecker, Sarah and Schlichte, Klaus, 'Between governance and domination: the everyday life of Uganda's police forces', in: Koechlin, Lucy; Förster, Till (ed.), *The*

Politics of Governance. The State in Africa reconsidered, London: Taylor & Francis, 2014; Hills, Alice, 'Partnership policing: is it relevant in Kano, Nigeria? *Criminology & Criminal Justice*, 14, 1 (2014), pp. 8–24.

14. Peake, Gordon and Otwin Marenin, 'Their reports are not read and their recommendations are resisted: the challenge for the global police policy community', *Police Practice and Research* 19, 1 (2008), pp. 59–69.

15. E.g. Radda, Sadiq Isah, Bello Ibrahim, and Aminu Sabo Danbazau, 'A study of the nature of police patrol in Kano metropolis', Bayero University, Kano, unpublished report, 2010, on the views of more than 160 street-level officers.

BIBLIOGRAPHY

3rd Degree, *amaBerete Terrorise Townships*, 23 August 2012, available at http://www.youtube.com/watch?v=rBehRHqQiy4, last accessed 14 Mar. 2013.

Abrahams, Ray, Sungusungu: village vigilante groups in Tanzania, *African Affairs*, 86, (1987), pp. 179–96.

Abrahams, Ray, *Vigilant Citizens: Vigilantism and the State*, Oxford: Polity Press, 1998.

Abrahamsen, Rita, 'African studies and the postcolonial challenge', *African Affairs*, 102, 407 (2003), pp. 189–210.

Abrahamsen, Rita and Michael C. Williams, *Security Beyond the State: Private Security in International Politics*, Cambridge: Cambridge University Press, 2011.

Abrams, Philip, 'Notes on the Difficulty of Studying the State', *Journal of Historical Sociology*, 1, 1 (1988), pp. 58–89.

Adamu, F.L, 'Gender, Hisba and the Enforcement of Morality in Northern Nigeria', *Africa*, 78, 1 (2008) pp. 136–152.

Adinkrah, Mensah, 'Vigilante homicides in contemporary Ghana', *Journal of Criminal Justice*, 33, 5 (2005), pp. 413–27.

Afrobarometer, *Public Agenda and Evaluation of Government*, 2012, available at: http://www.afrobarometer.org/files/documents/media_briefing/saf_r5_presentation1.pdf, last accessed 15 Apr. 2014.

Akinleye, R.T. 'Ethnic Militancy and National Stability in Nigeria: A Case Study of the Oodua People's Congress', *African Affairs*, 100, 401, (2001), pp. 623–640.

Albrecht, Peter and Paul Jackson, *Security System Transformation in Sierra Leone, 1997–2007*, Birmingham: University of Birmingham, 2009.

Altbeker, Antony, 'Solving crime: the state of the SAPS detective service' monograph, Institute for Security Studies, Pretoria, 1998.

———, *A Country at War with Itself*, Johannesburg: Jonathan Ball, 2007.

———, *The Dirty Work of Democracy: A Year on the Streets with the SAPS*, Jeppestown: Jonathan Ball Publishers, 2005.

BIBLIOGRAPHY

Anderson, David, 'Vigilantes, violence and the politics of public order in Kenya', *African Affairs*, 101, 405 (2002), pp. 531–555.

Anderson, David and David Killingray (eds), *Policing the Empire: Government, Authority, and Control, 1830–1940*, Manchester: Manchester University Press, 1991.

—— (eds), *Policing and Decolonisation: Politics, Nationalism, and the Police, 1917–65*, Manchester: Manchester University Press, 1992.

Araújo, Sara, 'Toward an ecology of justices: an urban and rural study of Mozambican plurality', in Kyed et al. (eds), *The Dynamics of Legal Pluralism in Mozambique*, Maputo: Kapicua, (2012) pp. 109–129.

Araújo, Sara and José A. Cristiano, *Pluralismo jurídico, legitimidade e acesso à justiça. Instâncias comunitárias de resolução de conflitos no Bairro de Inhagoia 'B'—Maputo*. Oficina do CES [CES Working Paper], 284, 2007.

Arifari, Nassirou, '"We don't eat the paper": corruption in transport, customs and the civil forces', in Blundo, Giorgio and Jean–Pierre Olivier de Sardan (eds), *Everyday Corruption and the State: Citizens and Public Officials in Africa*, London: Zed Books, 2006, pp. 177–224.

Ayling, Julie and Clifford Shearing, 'Taking care of business: public police as commercial security vendors', *Criminology and Criminal Justice*, 8, 1 (2008), pp. 27–50.

Ayoob, M., 'Humanitarian intervention and state sovereignty', *The International Journal of Human Rights*, 6, 1 (2002), pp. 81–102.

Bachmann, Jan, 'The danger of "uncovered spaces": the "war on terror" and its effects on the Sahel Region', in Eckert, Julia (ed.), *The Social Life of Anti-Terrorism Laws: The War on Terror and the Classification of the 'Dangerous Other'*, Bielefeld, Transkript, pp. 131–62.

Badie, Bertrand, *L'Etat importé: l'occidentalisation du politique*, Paris: Fayard, 1992.

Bain, William, *Between Anarchy and Society: Trusteeship and the Obligations of Power*, Oxford: Oxford University Press, 2003.

Baker, Bruce, 'When the Bakassi Boys came: eastern Nigeria confronts vigilantism', *Journal of Contemporary African Affairs*, 20, (2002), pp. 223–44.

——, *Taking the Law into Their Own Hands. Lawless Law Enforcers in Africa*. Burlington and Hampshire: Ashgate, 2002.

——. 'Protection from crime: what is on offer for Africans?', *Journal of Contemporary African Studies* 22, 2, (2004), pp. 165–88.

——, 'Multi–choice policing in Uganda', *Policing and Society*, 15, 1 (2005), pp 19–41.

——, 'The African post–conflict agenda in Sierra Leone', *Conflict, Security & Development*, 6, 1 (2006), pp. 25–49.

——, 'Community policing in Freetown, Sierra Leone: foreign import or local solution?', *Journal of Intervention and Statebuilding*, 2, 1 (2008), pp. 23–42.

——, *Multi-Choice Policing in Africa*, Uppsala: Nordic Africa Institute, 2008.

——, *Security in Post-conflict Africa: The Role of Non-State Policing*, Boca Raton: CRC Press, 2010.

——, 'Where Formal and Informal Justice Meet: Ethiopia's Justice Pluralism', *African Journal of International and Comparative Law*, 21, 2 (2013), pp. 202–18.

Ball, Nicole, Piet Biesheuvel, Tom Hamilton–Baillie and 'Funmi Olonisakin, 'Security and justice sector reform programming in Africa', *Evaluation Working Paper 23, Department for International Development, London*, April 2007.

Banton, Michael, *The Policeman in the Community*, London: Tavistock Publishers, 1964.

Barnett, Michael, *Empire of Humanity. A History of Humanitarianism*, Ithaca, N. Y.: Cornell UP, 2011.

Basson, Adriaan, *Finish & Klaar: Selebi's Fall from Interpol to the Underworld*. Cape Town, Tafelberg, 2012.

——, *Zuma Exposed*. Johannesburg, Jonathan Ball, 2012.

Bat, Jean-Pierre and Nicolas Courtin (eds), *Maintenir l'ordre colonial: Afrique et Madagascar, XIXe–XXe siècles*, Rennes: PU Rennes, 2012.

Bates, Robert, *When Things Fell Apart: State Failure in Late–Century Africa*, Cambridge: Cambridge University Press, 2008.

Bauer, Alain and Émile Pérez, *Les 100 mots de la police et du crime*, Paris: Presses universitaires de France, 2009.

Bayart, Jean-François, 'Africa in the world: a history of extraversion', 99, 395 (2000), pp. 217–67.

——, 'Comparer par le bas', *Sociétés politiques comparées*, n°1 (2008), p. 25, URL: http://www.fasopo.org/reasopo/n1/comparerparlebas.pdf [2014–06–04].

——, Stephen Ellis and Béatrice Hibou, *The Criminalisation of the State in Africa*, Oxford: International African Institute with James Currey, 1999.

——, *The State in Africa: The Politics of the Belly*, 2nd edition, Cambridge: Polity, 2010 [1993].

Bayley, David H., *Patterns of Policing: A Comparative International Analysis*, New Brunswick, NJ: Rutgers, 1985.

——, *Patterns of Policing. A Comparative International Analysis*. New Brunswick: Rutgers University Press, 1990.

——, *Changing the Guard: Developing Democratic Police Abroad*, Oxford: OUP, 2006.

——. and Clifford Shearing, *The New Structure of Policing—Description, Conceptualisation and Research Agenda*, Washington: National Institute of Justice, 2001.

Bazenguissa, Rémy, *Les voies du politique au Congo. Essai de sociologie historique du champ politique congolais*, Paris: Karthala, 1997.

BBC, 'Mido Macia: South Africa police accused denied bail', 12 March 2013, *BBC News* Africa, available at: http://www.bbc.co.uk/news/world–africa–21761515, last accessed 14 Mar. 2013.

Beck, Stefan and Jörg Niewoehner, 'Somatographic investigations across levels of complexity', *Biosocieties*, 1, 2 (2006), pp. 219–27.

Becker, Howard S., 'Biographie et mosaïque scientifique', *Actes de la Recherche en Sciences sociales*, 62–63 (1986), pp. 105–110.

Beek, Jan, *Producing Stateness*. *Police Work in Ghana*, Leiden: Brill, forthcoming.

———, '"Every car has an offence on it": Register polizeilichen Handelns bei Verkehrskontrollen in Nordghana', *Sociologus*, 61, 2 (2011), pp. 197–222.

———, '"There should be no open doors in the police": criminal investigations in northern Ghana as boundary work', *The Journal of Modern African Studies*, 50, 4 (2012), pp. 551–72.

Beek, Jan and Mirco Göpfert, 'Police violence in West Africa: perpetrators' and ethnographers' dilemmas', *Ethnography*, 14, 4 (2013), pp. 477–500.

———, 'State violence specialists in West Africa', *Sociologus*, 63, 1–2 (2013), pp. 103–24.

Beinart, William, *Twentieth-Century South Africa*, Oxford: Oxford University Press, 2001.

Beliard, Aude and Emilie Biland, 'Enquêter à partir de dossiers personnels: une ethnographie des relations entre institutions et individus', *Genèses*, 70 (2008), pp. 106–19.

von Benda-Beckmann and Keebet von Benda Beckmann, 'Forum shopping and shopping forums: dispute settlement in a Minangkabau village in West Sumatra', *Journal of Legal Pluralism*, 19 (1981), pp. 117–59.

———, and Franz von Benda-Beckmann, 'The dynamics of change and continuity in plural legal orders', *Journal of Legal Pluralism*, 53–54 (2006), pp. 1–44.

———, and Franz von Benda-Beckmann and Julia M. Eckert (eds), *Rules of Law and Laws of Ruling: On the Governance of Law*, Farnham: Ashgate, 2009.

———, Franz von, Keebet von Benda-Beckmann and Julia Eckert, 'Rules of law and laws of ruling: law and governance between past and future', in Franz von Benda-Beckmann, Keebet von Benda-Beckmann and Julia Eckert (eds), *Rules of Law and Laws of Ruling: On the Governance of Law*, Farnham: Ashgate, 2009, pp. 1–30.

Bensa, Alban and Eric Fassin, 'Les sciences sociales face à l'événement', *Terrain*, 38 (2002): pp. 5–20.

Berg, Julie, 'The private security industry in South Africa: a review of applicable legislation', *South African Journal of Criminal Justice*,16 (2003), pp. 178–96.

———, 'Private policing in South Africa: the Cape Town city improvement district—pluralisation in practice', *Society in Transition*, 35, 2 (2004), pp. 224–50.

———, 'Seeing like private security: evolving mentalities of public space protection in South Africa', *Criminology and Criminal Justice*, 10, 3 (2010), pp. 287–301.

Berlière, Jean-Marc, 'La professionnalisation: revendication des policiers et objectifs des pouvoirs au début de la IIIᵉ République', *Revue d'Histoire Moderne et Contemporaine*, 3 (1990), pp. 398–428.

———, *Le monde des polices en France*, Bruxelles: Complexe, 1996.

Berliere, Jean-Marc, Catherine Denys, Dominique Kalifa and Vincent Milliot, *Métiers de police. Être policier en Europe, XVIIIe–XXe siècles*, Rennes: PUR, 2008.

Bhambra, Gurminder K., 'Historical sociology, international relations and connected histories', *Cambridge Review of International Affairs*, 23, 1 (2010), pp. 127–43.

Bhuta, Nehal, 'Against state-building', *Constellations*, 15, 4 (2008), pp. 517–42.

Bickerton, Christopher J., Philip Cunliffe and Alexander Gourevitch (eds), *Politics without Sovereignty: A Critique of Contemporary International Relations*, London: UCL Press, 2007.

Biecker, Sarah and Klaus Schlichte, 'Policing Uganda, policing the world', *Working Papers of the Priority Programme 1448 of the German Research Foundation*, 2 (2013).

Biecker, Sarah and Schlichte, Klaus, 'Between governance and domination: the everyday life of Uganda's police forces', in: Koechlin, Lucy; Förster, Till (eds), *The Politics of Governance. The State in Africa reconsidered*, London: Taylor & Francis, 2014.

Bierschenk, Thomas, 'The everyday functioning of an African public service: informalization, privatization and corruption in Benin's legal system', *Journal of Legal Pluralism*, 57 (2008), pp. 101–39.

Bierschenk, T., 'Sedimentation, Fragmentation and Normative Double-Binds in (West) African Public Services', in Bierschenk, Thomas and Olivier de Sardan, Jean-Pierre (eds), *States at Work: Dynamics of African Bureaucracies*, Leiden: Brill, 2014, pp. 221–45.

Bierschenk, Thomas and Olivier de Sardan, Jean-Pierre (eds), *States at Work: Dynamics of African Bureaucracies*, Leiden: Brill, 2014.

Bigo, Didier, *Polices en réseaux: l'expérience européenne*, Paris: Presses de Science Po, 1996.

———, 'Security and immigration: toward a critique of the governmentality of unease', *Alternatives* 27 (2002), pp. 63–92.

Bittner, Egon, 'The police on skid-row: a study of peace keeping', *American Sociological Review*, 32, 5 (1967), pp. 699–715.

———, *The Functions of the Police in Modern Society: A Review of Background Factors, Current Practices, and Possible Role Models*, Rockville: National Institute of Mental Health, Center for Studies of Crime and Delinquency, 1970.

———, 'Florence Nightingale in pursuit of Willie Sutton: a theory of the police', in Herbert Jacob (ed.), *Potential for Reform of Criminal Justice*, Beverly Hills: SAGE Publications, 1974, pp. 17–44.

———, *Aspects of Police Work*, Boston: Northeastern University Press, 1990.

Black, Donald J., 'Production of crime rates', *American Sociological Review*, 35 (1970), pp. 733–48.

Blanchard, Emmanuel, Quentin Deluermoz and Joël Glasman, 'La professionnalisation policière en situation coloniale: détour conceptuel et explorations historiographiques', *Crime, Histoire, Société*, 15, 2 (2011), pp. 33–53.

Blankenburg, Erhard, 'Recht als gradualisiertes Konzept: Begriffsdimensionen der

Diskussion um Verrechtlichung und Entrechtlichung', in Erhard Blankenburg, Ekkehard Klausa and Hubert Rottleuthner (eds), *Alternative Rechtsformen und Alternativen zum Recht*, Opladen: Westdeutscher Verlag, 1980, pp. 83–98.

Bloch, Maurice, *Prey into Hunter: The Politics of Religious Experience*, Cambridge: Cambridge University Press, 1992.

Blundo, Giorgio, '"Comme un ballon de foot": la gestion quotidienne des ressources humaines dans les services forestiers en Afrique de l'Ouest', in: Schareika, Nikolaus, Eva Spies and Pierre–Yves Le Meur (eds), *Auf dem Boden der Tatsachen: Festschrift für Thomas Bierschenk*, Köln: Köppe Verlag, 2011, pp. 377–94.

Blundo, Giorgio and Jean–Pierre Olivier de Sardan, 'The popular semiology of corruption', in Blundo, Giorgio and Jean–Pierre Olivier de Sardan (eds), *Everyday Corruption and the State: Citizens and Public Officials in Africa*, London: Zed Books, 2006, pp. 110–34.

Blundo, Giorgio and Jean-Pierre Olivier de Sardan (eds), *Everyday Corruption and the State: Citizens and Public Officials in Africa*, London: Zed, 2006.

Blundo, Giorgio and Joel Glasman (eds), *Bureaucrats in Uniform*, Special Issue of *Sociologus: Journal for Social Anthropology*, 63, 1 (2013).

Blundo, Giorgio and Joël Glasman, 'Introduction: Bureaucrats in uniform', *Sociologus*, 63, 1 (2013).

Bograh, Badjaglana Fonto, 'Le Nord Togo dans la vie politique togolaise de 1944 à 1960', master thesis, University of Lomé, 2003.

Boltanski, Luc, *De la critique: précis de sociologie de l'émancipation*, Paris: Gallimard, 2009.

Booysen, Susan, *The African National Congress and the Regeneration of Political Power*. Johannesburg: Wits University Press, 2011.

Börzel, Tanja and Thomas Risse, 'From europeanisation to diffusion: introduction', *West European Politics*, 35, 1 (2012), pp. 1–17.

Bourdieu, Pierre, 'Le langage autorisé: les conditions sociales de l'efficacité du discours rituel', *Actes de la recherche en sciences sociales*, 5–6 (1975), pp. 183–90.

———, *La distinction: Critique sociale du jugement*, Paris: Les Editions de minuit, 1979.

———, 'L'illusion biographique', *Actes de la Recherche en Sciences sociales*, 62–63 (1986), pp. 69–72.

———, *Die verborgenen Mechanismen der Macht. Schriften zu Politik und Kultur 1*. Hamburg: VSA, 2005.

Bowling, Ben and Sheptycki, James, *Global Policing*, London: SAGE, 2012.

Bown, J., 'UK policing influence overseas: a practitioner perspective', Unpublished paper presented at conference on policing and the policed in the postcolonial state, Institute of Commonwealth Studies, London, 2010.

Braithwaite, John, 'The new regulatory state and the transformation of criminology', *British Journal of Criminology*, 40, 2 (2000), pp. 222–38.

Breckenridge, Keith, 'The allure of violence: men, race and masculinity on the South

African goldmines, 1900–1950', *Journal of Southern African Studies*, 24, 4 (1998), pp. 669–93.

Brewer, John D, *Black and Blue: Policing in South Africa*. New York, Oxford: Clarendon Press, Oxford University Press, 1994.

Brodeur, Jean–Paul, 'High and low policing: remarks about the policing of political activities', *Social Problems* 30, 5 (1983), pp. 507–520.

Brodeur, Jean–Paul, *The Policing Web*, Oxford: Oxford University Press, 2010.

Brogden, Mike, 'The emergence of the police: the colonial dimension', *British Journal of Criminology*, 27, 1 (1987), pp. 4–14.

———, '"Horses for courses" and "thin blue lines": Community policing in transitional society', *Police Quarterly* 8, 1 (2005), pp. 64–98.

Brogden, Mike and Clifford Shearing, *Policing for a New South Africa*, London and New York: Routledge, 1993.

Bruce, David, 'Marikana and the doctrine of maximum force', *Mampoer*, 2013, http://www.marikanacomm.org.za/exhibits/Exhibit-FFF-14.pdf, last accessed 27 Oct. 2014.

———, 'Marikana not Ramaphosa's finest moment.' *M&G*, January 18, 2013, http://mg.co.za/article/2013-01-18-00-marikana-not-ramaphosas-finest-moment, last accessed 27 Oct. 2014.

———, 'Racism, self–esteem and violence in SA: Gaps in the NCPS' explanation?', *SA Crime Quarterly*, 17 (2006), pp. 34–5.

———, 'The road to Marikana: abuses of force during public order policing operations', South African Civil Society Information Service, 12 October 2012, at http://sacsis.org.za/site/article/1455, last accessed 27 Oct. 2014.

Brysk, Alison, Craig Parsons and Wayne Sandholtz, 'After empire: national identity and post–colonial families of nations', *European Journal of International Relations*, 8, 2 (2002), pp. 267–305.

Bundeswehr Homepage, *Bildung, Ausbildung, Tugenden.* www.bmvg.de/portal/a/bmvg/!ut/p/c4/Dce7EYAgEAXAWmyAy83s QkOcwBPegAfDz_ ZlNlo6aRI94 94HRDEh1pp8NiNZ8y73CqwnountFqThENQZkuN9e PfVEQ4cLX02e 6O Mph 35PddAM/, last accessed 03 Apr. 2013.

Bureau of Democracy, *Democratic Republic of the Congo 2012*. Human Rights Report, 2012. http://www.state.gov/j/drl/rls/hrrpt/humanrightsreport/index.htm?year= 2012anddlid=204107#wrapper, last accessed 24 Nov. 2013.

Burger, Johan, 'Reflections on restructuring in the SAPS', paper presented to the Conference of Policing in South Africa, Institute for Security Studies, Pretoria, 2007.

Button, Mark, *Private Policing*, Devon: Willan Publishing, 2002.

Buur, Lars, 'Reordering society: vigilantism and expressions of sovereignty in Port Elizabeth's townships', *Development and Change*, 37, 4 (2006), pp. 735–57.

Buur, Lars and Jensen, Steffen, 'Introduction: Vigilantism and the policing of everyday life in South Africa' *African Studies* 63, 2 (2004), pp. 139–52.

Cargill, Jenny, *Trick or Treat: Rethinking Black Economic Empowerment*. Cape Town: Jacana, 2010.

Carlisle, Adrienne, 'Rights groups take on education MEC', *Dispatch Online*, 14 March 2013, available at: http://www.dispatch.co.za/rights–groups–take–on–education–mec/, last accessed 17 Mar. 2013.

Cartier, Marie, 'La petite fonction publique, monde stable et séparé? L'exemple des facteurs des PTT des trente glorieuses', *Sociétés contemporaines*, 58 (2005), pp. 19–39.

Centre for the Study of Violence and Reconciliation (CSVR), *Why South Africa is so violent and what should be done about it: statement by the Centre for the Study of Violence and Reconciliation*, Tuesday 9 November 2010, available online at: http://www.csvr.org.za/docs/study/CSVRstatement091110.pdf, last accessed 28 May 2014.

Chabal, Patrick and Jean–Pascal Daloz, *Africa Works: Disorder as Political Instrument*, Oxford, James Currey, 1999.

Chalfin, Brenda, *Neoliberal Frontiers: An Ethnography of Sovereignty in West Africa*, Chicago: University of Chicago Press, 2011.

Chan, Janet, 'Changing police culture', *British Journal of Criminology*, 36, 1 (1996), pp. 109–33.

Chandler, David, *Empire in Denial: The Politics of State Building*, London: Pluto Press, 2006.

Chanock, Martin, *Law, Custom and Social Order: The Colonial Experience in Malawi and Zambia*. Cambridge: Cambridge University Press, 1985.

Chatterjee, Partha, *The Politics of the Governed: Reflections on Popular Politics in most of the World*, New York: Columbia University Press, 2004.

Chesshyre, Robert, *The Force: Inside the Police*, London: Sidgwick & Jackson, 1989.

Chesterman, Simon, *You, The People: The United Nations, Transitional Administration, and State–Building*, Oxford: Oxford University Press, 2004.

Clapham, Christopher, 'Review article: the *longue durée* of the African State", *African Affairs*, 93, 372 (1994), pp. 433–439.

———, 'Sierra Leone: The global–local politics of state collapse and attempted reconstruction', paper presented at the Failed State Conference in Florence, 10–14 April 2001.

Clark, Gracia, *Onions are My Husband: Survival and Accumulation by West African Market Women*, Chicago: The University of Chicago Press, 1994.

Clayton, Anthony, *Histoire de l'armée française en Afrique: 1830–1962*, Paris: Albin Michel, 1994.

Clive, Emsley, 'The policeman as worker: a comparative survey', *International Review of Social History*, 45 (2000), pp. 89–110.

Collins, Anthony, 'Violence is not a crime: a broader view of interventions for social safety', *South African Crime Quarterly*, 43 (2013), pp. 29–38.

Comaroff, Jean and John L. Comaroff (eds), *Law and Disorder in the Postcolony*, Chicago: University of Chicago Press, 2006.

Comaroff, Jean, & John L. Comaroff, 'Criminal obsessions, after Foucault. postcoloniality, policing and the metaphysics of disorder', in Comaroff, J. & J.L. Comaroff (eds), *Law and Disorder in the Postcolony*. Chicago: University of Chicago Press, 2006, pp. 273–98.

Comaroff, Jean and John L. Comaroff, *Theory from the South: Or, How Euro–America Is Evolving Toward Africa*, Boulder: Paradigm Publishers, 2012.

Comaroff, John, and Jean Comaroff, *Ethnography and the Historical Imagination*, Boulder, CO: Westview Press, 1992.

Comaroff, John L. and Jean Comaroff, 'Criminal justice, cultural justice: the limits of liberalism and the pragmatics of difference in the new South Africa', *American Ethnologist*, 31, 2 (2004), pp. 188–204.

——, 'Reflections on the anthropology of law, governance and sovereignty', in Franz von Benda-Beckmann, Keebet von Benda-Beckmann and Julia Eckert (eds), *Rules of Law and Laws of Ruling: On the Governance of Law*, Farnham: Ashgate, 2009, pp. 31–59.

Connell, R.W. and James W. Messerschmidt, 'Hegemonic masculinity: rethinking the concept', *Gender & Society* 19 (2005), pp. 829–59.

Constitutionnet, *Constitution of the DR Congo*, 2013. http://www.constitutionnet. org/files/DRC%20-%20Congo%20Constitution.pdf, last accessed 3 Apr. 2013.

Cooper, Frederick, 'What is the concept of globalization good for? An African historian's perspective', *African Affairs*, 100 (2001), pp. 189–213.

Crawford, Adam and Stuart Lister, 'Additionally security patrols in residential areas: notes from the marketplace', *Policing and Society*, 16, 2 (2006), pp. 164–88.

Dahrendorf, Nicola, 'MONUC and the relevance of coherent mandates: the case of the DRC', in: Hänggi, Heiner and Scherrer, Voncenza (eds),: *Security Sector Reform and UN Integrated Missions*. London: LIT, 2008, pp. 67–113.

Daily Graphic, 'Four MTTU men held over extortion', 28.01.2010.

Darmon, Muriel, 'La notion de carrière: un instrument interactionniste d'objectivation', *Politix*, 82 (2008), pp. 149–67.

Das, Veena, and Poole, Deborah 'Introduction', in Das and Poole (eds), *Anthropology in the Margins of the State*. Oxford: James Currey, 2004, pp. 2–32.

Davidson, Basil, *The Black Man's Burden: Africa and the Curse of the Nation-State*, London: James Currey, 1992.

Daviet-Vincent, Marie–Bénédicte, 'La prise en compte de plusieurs générations dans la méthode prosopographique: l'exemple des hauts fonctionnaires prussiens sous l'Empire et la République de Weimar', *Genèses*, 56 (2004), pp. 117–30.

Davis, Diane E., 'Non-state armed actors, new imagined communities, and shifting patterns of sovereignty and insecurity in the modern world', *Contemporary Security Policy*, 30, 2 (2009), pp. 221–45.

BIBLIOGRAPHY

Deflem, Mathieu, *Policing World Society*, Oxford: Oxford University Press, 2002.

Dela Widenmann, Christina, *Police Corruption: A Study of corruption in the Police of Maputo*, Master Thesis, International Development Studies, Roskilde University and Center for African Studies, Copenhagen University, 2007.

Deleuze, Gilles, *Logique du sens*, Paris: Editions de Minuit, 1969.

Denney, Lisa, 'Reducing poverty with teargas and batons: the security–development nexus in Sierra Leone', *African Affairs*, 110, 439 (2011), pp. 275–94.

Denys, Catherine, *Police et sécurité au XVIIIe siècle dans les villes de la frontière franco-belge*, Paris: L'Harmattan, 2002.

DiNunzio, Marco, '"The Arada have been eaten": living through marginality in Addis Ababa's inner city', D. Phil Thesis, Oxford University, 2012.

Dixon, David, Clive Coleman and Keith Bottomley, 'Consent and the legal regulation of policing', *Journal of Law and Society*, 17, 3 (1990), pp. 345–62.

Dixon, William J, 'Globalising the local: A genealogy of sector policing in South Africa', *International Relations* 21, 2 (2007), pp. 163–82.

Donais, Timothy, 'Empowerment or imposition? Dilemmas of local ownership in post-conflict peacebuilding processes', *Peace & Change*, 34, 1 (2009), pp. 3–26.

Douglas, Mary, *Implicit Meaning*, 2nd ed, London: Routledge, 1999.

——, *Purity and Danger: An Analysis of Concepts of Pollution and Taboo*. New York: Routledge, 2002.

Downie, Richard, 'Building police institutions in fragile states: case studies from Africa', Washington, 2013, DC: CSIS. Available at http://csis.org/files/publication/130115_Downie_BuildPoliceInstitutions_web.pdf, last accessed 27 Oct. 2014.

Dubber, Markus D., 'The new police science and the police power model of the criminal process', in Markus D. Dubber and Mariana Valverde (eds), *The New Police Science: The Police Power in Domestic and International Governance*, Stanford, CA: Stanford University Press, 2006, pp. 107–44.

Dudley, Billy J., *Parties and Politics in Northern Nigeria*, London: Frank Cass, 1968.

Ebenga, Jacques, and Nlandu, Thierry, 'The Congolese national army: in search of an identity', in Rupiya, Martin, (ed.), *Evolutions and Revolutions, a Contemporary Africa*. Cape Town: Institute for Security Studies, 2005.

Echenberg, Myron, *Colonial Conscripts: The Tirailleurs Sénégalais in French West Africa, 1857–1960*, London, Portsmouth: Heinemann, 1991.

Eckert, Julia, 'From subjects to citizens: legalism from below and the homogenisation of the legal sphere', *Journal of Legal Pluralism*, 53, 3 (2006), pp. 45–75.

——, 'Work in progress: the state at work in urban India', in Nikolaus Schareika, Eva Spies and Pierre–Yves Le Meur (eds), *Auf dem Boden der Tatsachen: Festschrift für Thomas Bierschenk*, Köln: Köppe, 2011, pp. 435–45.

Egnell, Robert and Peter Halden, 'Laudable, ahistorical and overambitious: security sector reform meets state formation theory', *Conflict, Security & Development*, 9, 1 (2009), pp. 27–54.

Ekeh, Peter, 'Colonialism and the two publics in Africa: a theoretical statement', *Comparative Studies in Society and History*, 17 (1975), pp. 91–112.

Ellis, Stephen, *External Mission: the ANC in exile 1960–1990*. London, Hurst, 2012.

Enloe, Cynthia, 'Ethnicity and militarization: factors shaping the roles of police in third world nations', *Studies in Comparative International Development*, 11 (1976), pp. 25–38.

Ericson, Richard, *Reproducing Order: Study of Police Patrol Work*, Toronto: University of Toronto Press, 1982.

Eriksson–Baaz, Maria, 'Not enough to add women and stir'. *Nordiska AfrikaInstitutet*. http://urn.kb.se/resolve?urn=urn:nbn:se:nai:diva–1384, 2011, last accessed 2 Apr. 2013.

Fakondo, Kadi, 'Reforming and building capacity of the Sierra Leone police, 1997–2007' (Paper no. 8, Security System Transformation in Sierra Leone, 1997–2007), Birmingham: University of Birmingham, 2008.

Fall, Babacar, *Sénégal: le travail au XXième siècle*, thesis, University of Amsterdam, 2010.

Falola, Toyin and Robin Law (eds), *Warfare and Diplomacy in Precolonial Nigeria: Essays in Honor of Robert Smith*, Madison: University of Wisconsin Press, 1992.

Fassin, Didier, *La raison humanitaire: une histoire morale du temps présent*, Paris: Gallimard, 2010.

———, *La force de l'ordre: une anthropologie de la police des quartiers*, Paris: Seuil, 2011.

———, *Enforcing Order: An Ethnography of Urban Policing*, Cambridge: Polity, 2013.

———, 'Scenes from urban life: a modest proposal for a critical perspectivist approach', *Social Anthropology/Anthropologie Sociale*, 21, 3 (2013), pp. 371–7.

Faull, Andrew, *Corruption and the South African Police Service: A Review and its Implications*, ISS Occasional Paper No. 150, Pretoria: Institute for Security Studies, 2007.

———, *Behind the Badge: The Untold Stories of South Africa's Police Service Members*, Cape Town: Zebra Press, 2010.

Faull, Andrew and Brian Rose, *Professionalism and the Police Occupation in South Africa: What Is It and How Can It Help Build Safer Communities?*, ISS Occasional Paper No. 240, Pretoria: Institute for Security Studies, 2012.

Feest, Johannes and Erhard Blankenburg, *Die Definitionsmacht der Polizei: Strategien der Strafverfolgung und soziale Selektion*, Düsseldorf: Bertelsmann Universitäts–Verlag, 1972.

Ferguson, James, *Expectations of Modernity: Myths and Meanings of Urban Life on the Zambian Copperbelt*, London: University of California Press, 1999.

Ferguson, Niall, *Colossus: The Rise and Fall of the American Empire*, London: Penguin, 2004.

Ferme, Mariane, *The Underneath of Things: Violence, History, and the Everyday in*

BIBLIOGRAPHY

Sierra Leone, Berkeley, Los Angeles and London: The University of California Press, 2001.

Fields, Karen E, 'Political contingencies of witchcraft in colonial Central Africa: culture and the state in Marxist theory', *Canadian Journal of African Studies* 16, 3 (1982), pp. 567–93.

Fischler, C., 'Commensality, society and culture', *Social Science Information*, 50, 3–4 (2011), pp. 528–48.

Fisiy, Cyprian, 'Containing occult practices: witchcraft trials in Cameroon', *African Studies Review* 41, 3 (1998), pp. 143–63.

Fleischer, Michael L., '"Sungusungu": state–sponsored village vigilante groups among the Kuria of Tanzania', *Africa*, 70, 2 (2000), pp. 209–28.

Foucault, Michel, *Surveiller et Punir. Naissance de la Prison*, Paris: Gallimard, 1975.

Fourchard, Laurent, 'A new name for an old practice: vigilantism in south–western Nigeria', *Africa*, 78, 1 (2008), pp. 16–40.

Frances, David (ed.), *Policing in Africa*, Basingstoke: Palgrave/Macmillan, 2012.

Freud, Sigmund, *Totem und Tabu. Einige Uebereinstimmungen im Seelenleben der Wilden und der Neurotiker*, 3rd ed, Leipzig: Internationaler Psychoanalytischer Verlag, 1922.

Gans, Jeremy, 'Privately paid public policing: law and practice', *Policing and Society*, 10 (2000), pp. 183–206.

Garland, David, 'The limits of the sovereign state: strategies of crime control in contemporary society', *The British Journal of Criminology*, 36, 4 (1996), pp. 445–71.

———, *The Culture of Control: Crime and Social Order in Contemporary Society*, Oxford, Oxford University Press, 2001.

Garriott, William, (ed.) *Policing and Contemporary Governance: The Anthropology of Police in Practice*, Basingstoke: Palgrave, 2013.

Geertz, Clifford, *Local Knowledge: Further Essays in Interpretive Anthropology*. New York: Basic Books, 1983.

Gevisser, Mark, *Thabo Mbeki: The Dream Deferred*. Johannesburg: Jonathan Ball, 2007.

GFN–SSR, *A Beginner's Guide to Security Sector Reform (SSR)*, Birmingham: Birmingham University Press, 2007.

Giddens, Anthony, *Modernity and Self–Identity: Self and Society in the Late Modern Age*, Polity Press: Cambridge, 1991.

Giliomee, Hermann, *The Last Afrikaner Leaders: A Supreme Test of Power*. Cape Town, Tafelberg, 2012.

Gilligan, James, *Preventing Violence*, Thames & Hudson: London, 2001.

Ginifer, Jeremy, 'Evaluation of the conflict prevention pools', *Department for International Development, Evaluation Report EV 647*, 2004.

Giustozzi, Antonio, *The Art of Coercion: The Primitive Accumulation and Management of Coercive Power*, New York: Colombia University Press, 2011.

Giustozzi, Antonio and Mohammed Isaqzadeh, *Policing Afghanistan: The Politics of the Lame Leviathan*, London: Hurst, 2013.

Glaeser, A. *Divided in Unity: Identity, Germany and the Berlin Police*. Chicago: University of Chicago Press, 2000.

Glasman, Joël, 'Penser les intermédiaires coloniaux: note sur les dossiers de carrière de la police du Togo', *History in Africa*, 37 (2010), pp. 51–81.

———, 'Les Corps habillés. Genèse des métiers de police au Togo (1885–1963)', PhD thesis, Université Paris 7, Denis–Diderot and Universität Leipzig, 2011.

———, 'Unruly agents: police reform, bureaucratization and police agents' agency in interwar Togo', *The Journal of African History*, 55 (2014), pp. 79–100.

Goffman, Erving, *The Presentation of Self in Everyday Life*, Garden City, New York: Doubleday, Anchor Books, 1959.

Goldstein, Joseph, 'Police discretion not to invoke the criminal process: low–visibility decisions in the administration of justice', *The Yale Law Journal*, 69, 4 (1960), pp. 543–94.

———, *Report of the Presidential Commission into the Ghana Police Service* [Archer Report], volume 1, 1997.

Goodhew, David, 'Between the devil and the deep blue sea: crime, policing and the western areas of Johannesburg, c. 1930–1962,' Paper presented to the Wits History Workshop, Johannesburg, February 1990.

Goody, Jack, *La Raison graphique. La domestication de la pensée sauvage*, Paris: Éditions de Minuit, 1979 [1977].

Goold, Benjamin, Loader, Ian, and Angelica Thumala, A., 'Consuming security? Tools for a sociology of security consumption', *Theoretical Criminology*, 14, 1 (2010), pp. 3–30.

Göpfert, Mirco, 'Security in Niamey: an anthropological perspective on policing and an act of terrorism in Niger', *Journal of Modern African Studies*, 50, 1 (2012), pp. 53–74.

———, 'Bureaucratic aesthetics: report writing in the Nigérien gendarmerie', *American Ethnologist*, 40, 2 (2013), pp. 324–34.

Gordon, Diana, *Transformation and Trouble: Crime, Justice and Participation in Democratic South Africa*. Ann Arbor: Michigan University Press, 2006.

Government of Ghana, *Ghana Police Service Instructions*, Accra, 1992.

Grabosky, Peter, 2004, 'Toward a theory of public/private interaction in policing', in McCord, Joan (ed.), *Beyond Empiricism: Institutions and Intentions in the Study of Crime. Advances in Criminological Theory*, Transaction Books, Piscataway, 2004, pp. 69–82.

Grant, Evadne, 'Private policing', *Acta Juridica*, 92 (1989), pp. 92–117.

Grätz, Tilo, 'Devi and his men: the rise and fall of a vigilante movement in Benin' in Thomas Kirsch and Tilo Grätz, (eds) *Domesticating Vigilantism in Africa*, London: James Currey, 2010. pp. 79–97.

Gupta, Akhil, *Red Tape: Bureaucracy, Structural Violence, and Poverty in India*, Durham, NC: Duke University Press, 2012.

Hampson, Fen Osler, 'Can peacebuilding work?' *Cornell International Law Journal*, 30, 3 (1997), pp. 701–16.

Handelman, Don, 'Bureaucratic interpretation: the perception of child abuse in urban Newfoundland', in Handelman, Don and Elliott Leyton (eds), *Bureaucracy and World View: Studies in the Logic of Official Interpretation*, St. John's Newfoundland: University of Newfoundland, 1978, pp. 15–70.

Harnischfeger, Johannes, 'Ethnicity, religion and the failure of "common law" in Nigeria', in Thomas G. Kirsch and Tilo Gratz (eds), *Domesticating Vigilantism in Africa*, London: James Currey, 2010. pp. 51–78.

Hasty, Jennifer, 'The pleasures of corruption: desire and discipline in Ghanaian political culture', *Cultural Anthropology*, 20, 2 (2005), pp. 271–301.

Heald, Suzette, *Controlling Anger: The Sociology of Gisu Violence*, Manchester: MUP, 1989.

———, 'State, law, and vigilantism in northern Tanzania', *African Affairs*, 105, 419 (2006), pp. 265–83.

Hendriks, Maarten, *Straatkinderen (bashege) in Kinshasa. Structureel geweld versus agency*. Antwerpen: Maklu, 2012.

Herbert Jacob (ed.), *Potential for Reform of Criminal Justice*, Beverly Hills: SAGE Publications, 1974.

Herbst, Jeffrey, *States and Power in Africa: Comparative Lessons in Authority and Control*, Princeton: Princeton University Press, 2000.

Herzfeld, Michael, *The Social Production of Indifference. Exploring the symbolic roots of Western bureaucracy*, Chicago,Ill.: University of Chicago Press, 1992.

Higazi, Adam, 'Social mobilization and collective violence: vigilantes and militias in the lowlands of Plateau State, central Nigeria', *Africa* 78, 1, (2008) pp. 108–35.

Hills, Alice, 'Towards a critique of policing and national development in Africa', *Journal of Modern African Studies*, 34, 2 (1996), pp. 217–91.

———, *Policing Africa: Internal Security and the Limits of Liberalization*, Boulder, CO: Lynne Rienner, 2000.

———, *Policing Post–Conflict Cities*. London: Zed Books, 2009.

———, 'On being a professional police officer in Kano', *Sociologus* 63, 1–2 (2013), pp. 81–102.

———, 'Partnership policing: is it relevant in Kano, Nigeria? *Criminology & Criminal Justice*, 14, 1 (2014a), pp. 8–24.

Hills, Alice, 'Somalia works: police development as State building', *African Affairs*, 113, 450 (2014b), pp. 88–107.

Hoberg, George, 'Globalization and policy convergence: symposium overview', *Journal of Comparative Policy Analysis, Research and Practice*, 23 (2001), 127–32.

Hodgson, Jacqueline, 'Hierarchy, bureaucracy, and ideology in French criminal justice:

some empirical observations', *Journal of Law and Society*, 29, 2 (2002), pp. 227–57.

Holdaway, Simon, 'The police station', *Journal of Contemporary Ethnography*, 9, 1 (1980), pp. 79–100.

——, *Inside the British Police: A Force at Work*, Oxford: Basil Blackwell, 1983.

——, 'Discovering structure: studies of the British police occupational culture', in Mollie Weatheritt (ed.), *Police Research: Some Future Prospects*, Aldershot: Avebury, 1989, pp. 55–76.

Holden, Paul and Van Vuuren, Hennie, *The Devil in the Detail: How the arms deal changed everything*. Johannesburg: Jonathan Ball, 2011.

Holtmann, Barbara, *What It Looks Like When It's Fixed: A Case Study in Developing a Systemic Model to Transform a Fragile Social System*, Johannesburg: PWC, 2011.

Horn, Adrian, Funmi Olonisakin and Gordon Peake, 'United Kingdom-led security sector reform in Sierra Leone', *Civil Wars*, 8, 2 (2006), pp. 109–23.

Hornberger, Julia, 'Ma–Slaan–Pa docketse: negotiations at the boundary between the private and the public', in Gorgio Blundo and Pierre-Yves Le Meur (eds), *Governance of Daily Life in Africa*, Leiden: Brill Press, 2009, pp. 171–204.

——, 'From general to commissioner to general: on the popular state of policing in South Africa', *Law and Social Inquiry*, 38, 3 (2013), pp. 598–614.

——, *Policing and Human Rights: The Meaning of Violence and Justice in the Everyday Policing of Johannesburg*. New York: Routledge, 2011.

Hough, Mike, 'Policing, new public management and legitimacy in Britain', in Tom R. Tyler (ed.), *Legitimacy and Criminal Justice: A Comparative Perspective*, New York: Russell Sage Foundation, 2008, pp. 63–83.

Huber, Magnus, *Ghanaian Pidgin English in its West African Context: A Sociohistorical and Structural Analysis*, Amsterdam: John Benjamins Publishing, 1999.

Human Rights Watch (HRW), '"Rest in pieces": police torture and deaths in custody in Nigeria', New York, 2005, Available at http://www.hrw.org/reports/2005/07/26/rest-pieces.

Hüsken, Thomas and Georg Klute, *Emerging Forms of Power in Contemporary Africa: a Theoretical and Empirical Research Outline*, Diskussionspapiere 101, Berlin: Klaus Schwarz Verlag, 2008.

Ibeanu, Okechukwu and Abubakar Momoh, 'State responsiveness to public security needs: the politics of security decision–making, Nigeria country study', *CSDG Papers*, No. 14, (2008).

Ibrahim, Ahmed, *Flamingo Social Studies for Junior Secondary Schools: Pupil's Book Three*, Accra, n.d.

Ignatieff, Michael, 'Police and the people: the birth of Mr Peel's "Blue Locusts"', *New Society*, 49 (1979), pp. 443–5.

Iliffe, John, *Africans: The History of a Continent*, Cambridge: Cambridge University Press, 1995.

Imray, Colin, *Policeman in Africa*, Sussex: Book Guild, 1997.

Irish, Jenny, *Policing for Profit: The Future of South Africa's Private Security Industry*, Pretoria: Institute for Security Studies, 1999.

Isichei, E., *Studies in the History of Plateau State*, Nigeria, London: Macmillan Press, 1982.

Jackson, Paul and Peter Albrecht, *Reconstructing Security after Conflict: Security Sector Reform in Sierra Leone*, Basingstoke: Palgrave Macmillan, 2011.

Jackson, Robert H. and Carl G. Rosberg, 'Why Africa's weak states persist: the empirical and the juridical in statehood', *World Politics*, 35, 1 (1982).

Jauregui, Beatrice, 'Shadows of the State, Subalterns of the State: Police and "Law and Order" in Postcolonial India'. Unpublished PhD thesis, Department of Anthropology, University of Chicago, 2010.

———, 'Provisional agency in India: jugaad and legitimation of corruption', *American Ethnologist*, 41, 1 (2014), pp. 76–91.

Jeanjean, Marc, 'La "culture policière" et l'"affaire": une approche ethnographique de la police', *Ethnologie française*, 21, 1 (1991), pp. 79–87.

Jensen, Steffen, 'Policing Nkomazi: crime, masculinity and generational conflicts', in David Pratten and Atreyee Sen (eds), *Global Vigilantes*, London: Hurst, 2007, pp. 47–68.

Jermier, John M. and Leslie J. Berkes, 'Leader behaviour in a police command bureaucracy: a closer look at the quasi–military model', *Administrative Science Quarterly*, 24 (1979), pp. 1–23.

Joas, Hans and Barbro Klein (eds), *The Benefit of Broad Horizons: Intellectual and Institutional Preconditions for a Global Social Science*, Leiden: Brill, 2010.

Johnson, David R., *Policing the Urban Underworld: The Impact of Crime on the Development of the American Police, 1800–1887*, Philadelphia, Penn.: Temple University Press.

Join–Lambert, Odile, *Le receveur des Postes, entre l'État et l'usager (1944–1973)*, Paris: Belin, 2001.

Jones, Trevor and Tim Newburn, 'The transformation of policing? Understanding current trends in policing systems', *British Journal of Criminology*, 42 (2002), pp. 129–46.

Jones, Will, Ricardo Soares D'Oliveira and Harry Verhoeven, 'Africa's Illiberal state-builders', Refugee Studies Centre, Oxford University, *Working Paper Series*, No. 89, 2013.

Jörgel, Magnus, 'Security Sector Reform in Sub-Saharan Africa: a new playground, different rules, new players?', in Ekengrenand, Magnus, and Simons, Greg, (eds): *The Politics of Security Sector Reform: Challenges and Opportunities for the European Union's Global Role*, Farnham: Ashgate, 2011, pp. 243–58.

Júnior, Domício P. and Jacqueline Muniz, '"Stop or I'll call the police!": the idea of police, or the effects of police encounters over time', *British Journal of Criminology*, 46, 2 (2006), pp. 234–57.

Justaert, Arnout, 'The governance of police reform in the DR Congo: reform without alignment?' Presentation in the Panel: 'Bureaucrats in Uniform: Historical and Anthropological Explorations of an African Professional Field' at *European Conference on African Studies*, Uppsala, June 2011.

Kaifi, Belal, Wajma Aslami, Seleiman Noori and Danielle Korhummel, 'A Decade after the 9/11 attacks: the demand for leaders with emotional intelligence and counselling skills', *Journal of Business Studies Quarterly*, 2, 2 (2011), pp. 54–67.

Kemp, Charles, Clive Norris and Nigel Fielding, *Negotiating Nothing: Police Decision-Making in Disputes*, Aldershot: Avebury, 1992.

Keohane, Robert, 'Political authority after intervention: gradations in sovereignty', in J.L Holzgrefe and Robert Keohane (eds), *Humanitarian Intervention. Ethical, Legal and Political Dilemmas* Cambridge: Cambridge University Press, 2003.

Kirsch, Thomas G. and Tilo Grätz (eds), *Domesticating Vigilantism in Africa*, Oxford: Currey, 2010.

———, 'Vigilantism, state ontologies & encompassment: an introductory essay', in Thomas G. Kirsch and Tilo Grätz (eds), *Domesticating Vigilantism in Africa*, Oxford: Currey, 2010, pp. 1–25.

Klaeger, Gabriel, 'Dwelling on the road: routines, rituals and roadblocks in southern Ghana', *Africa* 83, 3 (2013), pp. 446–69.

Klantschnig, Gernot, 'The politics of law enforcement in Nigeria: lessons from the war on drugs', *The Journal of Modern African Studies*, 47, 4 (2009), pp. 529–49.

Kraska, Peter B. and Victor E. Kappler, 'Militarizing American police: the rise and normalization of paramilitary units', *Social Problems* 44, 1 (1997), pp. 1–18.

Krasner, Stephen, 'Sharing sovereignty: new institutions for collapsed and failing states', *International Security*, 29, 2 (2004), pp. 85–120.

Krogstad, Erlend Grøner, *Enduring Challenges of Statebuilding: British-led Police Reforms in Sierra Leone, 1945–1961 and 1998–2007*. Dphil thesis, University of Oxford, 2012.

Kyed, Helene M., *State Recognition of Traditional Authority. Authority, Citizenship and State Formation in Rural Post-War Mozambique*, PhD dissertation, Roskilde University, 2007.

———, 'Community policing in post–war Mozambique', *Policing and Society*, 9, 4 (2009), pp. 354–71.

——— 'The contested role of community policing: 'new' non-state actors in the plural legal landscape of Mozambique', *DIIS Working Paper*, 26 (2010).

———, João C. B. Coelho, Amelia N. de Souto and Sara Araújo (eds), *The Dynamics of Legal Pluralism in Mozambique*, Maputo: Kapicua, 2012.

Lalá, Anicia and Laudemiro Francisco, 'The difficulties of donor coordination: police and judicial reform in mozambique', *Civil Wars*, 8, 2 (2006), pp. 166.

Landecker, Hannah, 'Food as exposure: nutritional epigenetics and the new metabolism', *BioSocieties*, 6, 2 (2011), pp. 167–94.

Lange, Marie-France, *L'Ecole au Togo: processus de scolarisation et institution de l'école en Afrique*, Paris: Karthala, 2000.

Lange, Hans-Jürgen (ed.), *Die Polizei der Gesellschaft: Zur Soziologie der Inneren Sicherheit*, Opladen: Leske und Budrich, 2003.

Lasslett, Kristian, 'Crime or social harm? A dialectical perspective', *Crime, Law & Social Change*, 54 (2010), pp. 1–19.

Last, Murray, 'The search for security in Muslim northern Nigeria', *Africa*, 78, 1 (2008), pp. 41–63.

Lawler, Nancy E., *Soldiers of Misfortune: Ivoirien Tirailleurs of World War II*, Athens: Ohio University Press, 1992.

Lee, J.M., *African Armies and Civil Order*. London: Chatto and Windus, 1969.

Lefever, Ernest W., *Spear and Scepter: Army, police, and politics in tropical Africa*. Washington: Brookings Institution, 1970.

Leggett, Ted, 'The state of crime and policing', in J. Daniel, R. Southall and J. Lutchman (eds), *State of the Nation: South Africa, 2004–2005*. Pretoria: HSRC Press, 2006, pp. 215–41.

Lentz, Carola, 'The chief, the mine captain and the politician: legitimating power in northern Ghana', *Africa*, 68 (1998), pp. 46–67.

——, Jan Beek and Mirco Göpfert (workshop); 'Just police work: ethnographic research on the police in Africa', Johannes Gutenberg University, Mainz, Germany, 2013, available at http://www.ifeas.uni-mainz.de/1105.php, last accessed 27 Oct. 2014.

Letsela, Lebohang and Kopano Ratele, *Masculinity and perceptions of risk: factors to premature male mortality in South Africa*, 2009, available at: http://www.brothersforlife.org/sites/default/files/docs/Men_and_their_perceptions_of_Risks.pdf, accessed 21 Mar. 2013.

Levis–Strauss, Claude, 'The culinary triangle', *Partisan Review*, 33, 4 (1966), pp. 586–95.

Lévi-Strauss, Claude, *The Raw and the Cooked. Mythologiques, Volume One*, Chicago: University of Chicago Press, 1969.

Lippert, Randy and Daniel O'Connor, 'Security intelligence networks and the transformation of contract private security', *Policing and Society*, 16, 1 (2006), pp. 50–66.

Lipsky, Michael, *Street-Level Bureaucracy: Dilemmas of the Individual in Public Services*, New York: Russell Sage Foundation, 2010[1980].

Loader, Ian, 'Policing and the social: questions of symbolic power', *The British Journal of Sociology*, 48, 1 (1997), pp. 1–18.

——, 'Consumer culture and the commodification of policing and security', *Sociology*, 33, 2 (1999), pp. 373–92.

——, 'Plural policing and democratic governance', *Social and Legal Studies*, 9, 3 (2000), pp. 323–45.

Loader, Ian. and A. Mulcahy, *Policing and the Condition of England: Memory, Politics and Culture*, Oxford: Oxford University Press, 2003.

Lofthouse, Michael, 'The core mandate of policing', in Critcher, Chas and David

Waddington (eds), *Policing Public Order: Theoretical and Practical Issues*, Aldershot: Avebury, 1996, pp. 39–51.

Loftus, Bethan, *Police Culture in a Changing World*, Clarendon Studies in Criminology, Oxford & New York: Oxford University Press, 2009.

———, 'Police occupational culture: classic themes, altered times,' *Policing and Society: An International Journal of Research and Policy*, 20, 1 (2010), pp. 1–20.

Lüdtke, Alf, *Gemeinwohl' Polizei und 'Festungspraxis'. Staatliche Gewaltsamkeit und innere Verwaltung in Preußen, 1815–1850*, Göttingen: Vandenhoeckh & Ruprecht, 1982.

Luhmann, Niklas, *Die Politik der Gesellschaft*, with assistance of André Kieserling, Frankfurt am Main: Suhrkamp, 2000.

Lund, Christian, *Law, Power and Politics in Niger: Land Struggles and the Rural Code*, Hamburg: LIT, 1998.

———, 'Twilight institutions: an introduction', *Development and Change*, 37, 4 (2006), pp. 673–84.

Lundestad, Geir, 'Empire by invitation? The United States and Western Europe, 1945–1952', *Journal of Peace Research*, 23, 3 (1985), pp. 263–277.

Lunn, Joe, *Memoirs of the Maelstrom: A Senegalese Oral History of the First World War*, Portsmouth/ London: Heinemann, 1999.

MacGaffey, Jane, *The Real Economy of Zaire: The Contribution of Smuggling and Other Unofficial Activities to National Wealth*, Oxford: James Currey, 1991.

Maguire, Mike, Rodney Morgan and Robert Reiner (eds), *The Oxford Handbook of Criminology*, Oxford: Oxford University Press, 2007.

Maier, K., *This House Has Fallen: Nigeria in Crisis*. London: Allen Lane, The Penguin Press, 2000.

Malkki, Lisa H, *Purity and Exile: Violence, Memory, and National Cosmology among Hutu Refugees in Tanzania*. Chicago: University of Chicago Press, 1995.

Mamdani, Mahmood. *Citizen and Subject: Contemporary Africa and the Legacy of Late Colonialism*, Princeton: Princeton University Press, 1996.

Mangvwat, M., "Warfare on the Jos Plateau in the Nineteenth Century" in Falola, Toyin and Robin Law (eds), *Warfare and Diplomacy in Precolonial Nigeria: Essays in Honor of Robert Smith*, Madison: University of Wisconsin Press, 1992.

———, *A History of Class Formation in the Plateau Province of Nigeria, 1902–1960*, Durham: Carolina Academic Press, 2013.

Mann, Gregory, *Native Sons: West African Veterans and France in the 20th Century*, Durham: Duke University Press, 2006.

Mann, Gregory, 'What was the *indigénat*? The "Empire of Law" in French West Africa', *Journal of African History*, 50 (2009), pp. 331–53.

Manning, Paul, *Semiotics of Drink and Drinking*, New York: Continuum, 2012.

———, *Police Work: The Social Organization of Policing*, Cambridge: MIT Press, 1977.

———, 'Producing drama: symbolic communication and the police', *Symbolic Interaction*, 5, 2 (1982), pp. 223–42.

————, 'The police: mandate, strategies and appearances', 1978, reprinted in Newburn, Tim (ed.), *Policing: Key Readings*, Cullompton: Willan Publishing, 2005.

Marenin, Otwin, 'Policing African states: toward a critique', *Comparative Politics*, 14, 4 (1982), pp. 379–96.

Marks, Monique, *Transforming the Robocops: Changing Police in South Africa*, Scottsville, SA: University of KwaZulu-Natal Press, 2005.

Marshall, Lorna, 'Sharing, talking and giving: relief of social tensions among !Kung bushmen', *Africa*, 31 (1961), pp. 231–49.

Martin, Jeffrey, 'A reasonable balance of law and sentiment: social order in democratic Taiwan from the policeman's point of view', *Law & Society Review*, 41, 3 (2007), pp. 665–98.

Mattelart, Armand, *La globalisation de la surveillance. Aux origins de l'ordre sécuritaire*, Paris: La Découverte, 2007.

Matusitz, J. and M. Repass, 'Gangs in Nigeria: an updated examination', *Crime Law and Social Change*, Springer Science and Business Media, 2009.

Mauss, Marcel, *The Gift: The Form and Reason for Exchange in Archaic Societies*, London: Routledge, 2002 [1950].

Mbaye, Saliou, 'Personnel files and the role of qadis and interpreters in the colonial administration of Saint–Louis, Senegal, 1857–1911', in: Benjamin N. Lawrance, Emily L. Osborn and Richard L. Roberts (eds), *Intermediaries, Interpreters and Clerks: African Employees in the Making of Colonial Africa*, Madison: University of Wisconsin Press, 2006, pp. 289–95.

Mbembe, Achille, 'Provisional notes on the postcolony', *Africa* 62 (1) 1992, pp. 3–37.

————, *On the Postcolony*, Berkeley: University of California Press, 2001.

————, 'Aesthetics of superfluity', *Public Culture* 16, 3 (2004) pp. 373–405.

McManus, Michael, *From Fate to Choice: Private Bobbies, Public Beats*, Aldershot: Avebury, 1995.

Meagher, Kate, 'Hijacking civil society: the inside story of the Bakassi Boys vigilante group of south-eastern Nigeria', *Journal of Modern African Studies*, 45, 1 (2007), pp. 89–115.

Meek, Sarah, 'Policing Sierra Leone', in Mark Malan, Sarah Meek, Thokozani Thusi, Jeremy Ginifer and Patrick Coker (eds), *Building the Road to Recovery*, Pretoria: Institute for Security Studies, 2004.

Mensa-Bonsu, Henrietta J. A. N., *The Annotated Criminal Offences Act of Ghana*, 5th edition, Accra: Black Mask Limited, 2008.

Merry, Sally E., 'Going to court: strategies of dispute management in an American urban neighborhood', *Law & Society Review*, 14, 4 (1979), pp. 891–925.

Michel, Marc, *Les Africains et la Grande Guerre: L'Appel à l'Afrique 1914–1918*, Paris: Karthala, 2003 [1983].

Migdal, Joel S., *State in Society. Studying How States and Societies Transform and Constitute One Another*, Princeton, NJ: Princeton University Press, 2001.

Migdal, J.S. and Schlichte, K., 'Rethinking the State', in: K. Schlichte (ed.), *The Dynamics of States. The formation and crisis of state domination outside the OECD*, Aldershot: Ashgate, p. 1–40.

Miliband, Ralph, *The State in Capitalist Society*, New York: Basic Books, 1969.

Minnaar, Anthony and P. Ngoveni, 'The relationship between the South African Police Service and the private security industry: any role for outsourcing in the prevention of crime?', *Acta Criminologica*, 17, 1 (2004), pp. 42–65.

Minnaar, Anthony, 'Private-Public Partnerships: Private Security, Crime Prevention and Policing in South Africa', *Acta Criminologica*, 18, 1 (2005), pp. 85–114.

Mintz, S.W., *Sweetness and Power: The Place of Sugar in Modern History*, Elisabeth Sifton Books. Penguin Books, 1986.

Mokati, Noni, 'Murder-accused cops' urgent bail bid', *IOL News*, 9 March 2013, available at http://www.iol.co.za/news/south–africa/murder–accused–cops–urgent–bail–bid–1.1483589, last accessed 9 Mar. 2013.

Mol, Annemarie, 'Moderation or satisfaction? Food ethics and food facts', in Sofie Vandamme, Suzanne van de Vathorst and Inez de Beaufort (eds), *Whose Weight Is It Anyway? Essays on Ethics and Eating*, Leuven: Acco Academic Publishers, 2010, pp. 121–32.

Monjardet, Dominique, 'La culture professionnelle des policiers'. *Revue Française de Sociologie*, 35, 3 (1994), pp. 393–411.

———, *Ce que fait la police: Sociologie de la force publique*, Paris: La Découverte, 1996.

Monkkonen, Eric, 'The organized response to crime in nineteenth- and twentieth-century America', *Journal of Interdisciplinary History*, 16, 1 (1983), pp. 113–28.

Moore, Sally Falk, *Social Facts and Fabrications: Customary Law on Kilimanjaro, 1880–1980*. New York: Cambridge University Press, 1986.

Morgenstern, C., *The Gallows Songs* (Translated, with an introduction by Max Knight), Berkeley: University of California Press, 1964.

Morrell, Robert, 'Of boys and men: masculinity and gender', *Journal of Southern African Studies*, 24, 4 (1998), pp. 605–30.

Morrell, Robert, Rachel Jewkes, Graham Lindegger and Vijay Hamlall, 'Hegemonic masculinity: reviewing the gendered analysis of men's power in South Africa', *South African Review of Sociology*, 44, 1 (2013), pp. 4–21.

Mosse, David and David T. Lewis, 'Theoretical approaches to brokerage and translation in development', in David Lewis and David Mosse (eds), *Development Brokers and Translators: The Ethnography of Aid and Agencies*, Bloomfield, CT: Kumarian Press, 2006, pp. 1–26.

Muir, William Ker, *Police: Streetcorner Politicians*, Chicago: University of Chicago Press, 1977.

Muntingh, Lukas and Chandré Gould, *Towards an understanding of repeat violent offending: A review of the literature*, ISS Occasional Paper No. 213, Pretoria: Institute for Security Studies, 2010.

Murphy, C., 'Police studies go global: in eastern Kentucky?', *Police Quarterly*, 8, 1 (2005), pp. 137–45.

Nader, Laura, 'Crime as a category: domestic and globalized', in Philip C. Parnell and Stephanie C. Kane (eds), *Crime's Power: Anthropologists and the Ethnography of Crime*, New York: Palgrave Macmillan, 2003, pp. 55–76.

Nader, Laura and Harry F. Todd, 'Introduction', in Laura Nader and Harry F. Todd (eds), *The Disputing Process: Law in Ten Societies*, New York: Columbia University Press, 1978, 1–40.

Neocleus, Mark, *The Fabrication of Social Order. A Critical Theory of Police Power*, London: Pluto Press, 2000.

Nexon, Daniel and Thomas Wright, 'What's at Stake in the American Empire Debate', *American Political Science Review*, 101, 2 (2007), pp. 253–71.

Niewöhner, Jörg and Thomas Scheffer, 'Introduction', *Comparative Sociology*, 7 (2008), pp. 273–85.

Nini, Asanda 'You're not entitled to any rights, MEC tells pupils', *DispatchOnline*, 12 March 2013, available at: http://www.dispatch.co.za/youre-not-entitled-to-any-rights-mec-tells-pupils/, last accessed 16 Mar. 2013.

Nlandu, Thierry Mayamba, *Mapping Police Services in the Democratic Republic of Congo: Institutional Interactions at Central, Provincial and Local Levels*. Brighton: Institute of Development Studies, 2012.

O'Brien, Kevin, 'Counter-intelligence for counter-revolutionary warfare: the South African police security branch 1979–1990, *Intelligence and National Security* 16, 3 (2001), pp. 27–59.

O'Neill, Megan, *Policing Football: Social Interaction and Negotiated Disorder*, Houndmills: Palgrave Macmillan, 2005.

Olaniyi, Rashid, 'Community vigilantes in metropolitan Kano', Ibadan: French Institute for Research in Africa, IFRA, 2005.

Olivier de Sardan, Jean-Pierre, 'A moral economy of corruption in Africa?', *Journal of Modern African Studies*, 37, 1 (1999), pp. 25–52.

———, 'Etat, bureaucratie et gouvernance en Afrique de l'Ouest francophone', *Politique africaine*, 96 (2004), pp. 139–62.

———, 'A la recherche des normes pratiques de la gouvernance réelle en Afrique', *Discussion Paper*, 5 (2008), Africa Power and Politics (APPP), Oversea Development Institut (ODI).

Olivier de Sardan, Jean-Pierre, 'State bureaucracy and governance in west francophone Africa: an empirical diagnosis and historical perspective', in Blundo, Giorgio and Pierre–Yves Le Meur (eds), *The Governance of Daily Life in Africa: Ethnographic Explorations of Public and Collective Services*, Leiden: Brill, 2009, pp. 39–72.

Olukoshi, Adebayo, (ed) *Crisis and Adjustment in the Nigerian Economy*. Lagos: JAD, 1991.

Osagie, Iyunolu, 'Historical memory and a new national consciousness: the Amistad revolt revisited in Sierra Leone', *The Massachusetts Review*, 38, 1 (1997), pp. 63–83.

Owen, Olly, 'Positions of security and the security of position: bureaucratic preben-dalism inside the state' in Adebanwi, W. and Obadare, E. (eds) *Democracy and Prebendalism in Nigeria: Critical Interpretations*. Basingstoke: Palgrave Macmillan, 2013.

———, 'An Institutional Ethnography of the Nigeria Police Force', Unpublished DPhil thesis, Institute of Social and Cultural Anthropology, Oxford University, 2013.

Papadakis, Vitalina. C. Vigilante 'Justice' and Collective Violence', in Kyed et al, *The Dynamics of Legal Pluralism in Mozambique*, 2012, pp. 186–195; Serra, Carlos (ed.), *Linchamento em Moçambique I (Uma desordem que apela à ordem)*, Maputo: Imprensa Universitária, 2008.

Paperman, Patricia, 'Surveillance underground: the uniform as an interaction device', in *Ethnography*, 4, 3 (2003), pp. 397–419.

Paris, Roland, 'International peacebuilding and the "mission civilisatrice"', *Review of International Studies*, 28, 4 (2002), pp. 637–56.

———, *At War's End: Building Peace after Civil Conflict*, Cambridge: Cambridge University Press, 2004.

Passeron, Jean-Claude. 1989. 'Biographies, flux, itinéraires, trajectoires', *Revue française de sociologie*, 31 (1989), pp. 3–22.

Pauw, Jacques, *Into the Heart of Darkness: Confessions of Apartheid's Assassins*. Johannesburg, Jonathan Ball, 2007.

Peake, Gordon and Eric Scheye, 'Unknotting Local Ownership', in Anja H. Ebnother and Perito, Robert M. 'Afghanistan's police', *Special Report of the United States Institute of Peace*, August 2009.

Peake, Gordon and Otwin Marenin, 'Their reports are not read and their recom-mendations are resisted: the challenge for the global police policy community', *Police Practice and Research* 19, 1 (2008), pp. 59–69.

———, 'Their reports are not read and their recommendations are resisted' *Police Practice and Research*, 9, 1 (2008), pp. 59–69.

Peel, J. D. Y. 'The cultural work of Yoruba ethnogenesis', in Tonkin, E., M. McDonald & M. Chapman (eds) *History and Ethnicity*. London: Routledge, 1999, pp. 198–215.

Pendleton, Michael R., 'Policing the park: understanding soft enforcement', *Journal of Leisure Research*, 30, 4 (1998), pp. 552–71.

Philip Fluri (eds), *After Intervention: Public Security Management in Post–Conflict Societies*, Vienna and Geneva: Bureau for Security Policy at the Austrian Ministry of Defence, 2005.

Philip, Kate, 'The private sector and the security establishment', in Cock, J. and L. Nathan (eds), *War and Society. The Militarisation of South Africa*, Cape Town/Johannesburg: David Philip Publisher, 1989, pp. 202–16.

Pikoli, Vusi and Weiner, Mandy, *My Second Initiation*. Johannesburg: Picador, 2013.

BIBLIOGRAPHY

Potholm, Christian, 'The multiple roles of the police as seen in the African context', *Journal of Developing Areas*, 3 (1969), pp. 139–58.

Pratten, David, 'Singing thieves: history and practice in Nigerian popular justice,' in Artreye Sen and David Pratten (eds), *Global Vigilantes*, Hurst and Company, London, 2007, pp. 175–206.

———, '"The thief eats his shame": practice and power in Nigerian vigilantism', *Africa*, 78, 1 (2008), pp. 64–83.

———, 'Introduction. The politics of protection: perspectives on vigilantism in Nigeria', *Africa*, 78, 1 (2008), pp. 1–15.

———. 'Bodies of power: narratives of selfhood and security in Nigeria,' in Thomas Kirsch and Tilo Gratz (eds), *Domesticating Vigilantism in Africa*, London: James Currey, 2010, pp. 118–138.

Pratten, David and Atreyee Sen (eds), *Global Vigilantes*, London: Hurst, 2007.

Proteau, Laurence and Geneviève Pruvost, 'Se distinguer dans les métiers d'ordre (armée, police, prison, sécurité privée)', *Sociétés contemporaines*, 72 (2008), pp. 7–13.

Radda, Sadiq Isah, Bello Ibrahim, and Aminu Sabo Danbazau, 'A study of the nature of police patrol in Kano metropolis', Bayero University, Kano, unpublished report, 2010.

Ratel, Kopano, 'Masculinity and male mortality in South Africa', *African Safety Promotion: A journal of inquiry*, 6, 22 (2008), pp. 19–41.

Reichertz, Jo and Norbert Schröer (eds), *Hermeneutische Polizeiforschung*, Opladen: Leske + Budrich, 2003.

Reiner, Robert, *The Politics of the Police*, 3rd edition, Oxford: Oxford University Press, 2000.

Reinwald, Brigitte, *Reisen durch den Krieg: Erfahrungen und Lebensstrategien westafrikanischer Weltkriegsveteranen der französischen Kolonialarmee*, Berlin: Schwarz, 2005.

Reiss, Albert J., *The Police and the Public*, New Haven: Yale University Press, 1977.

———, *Private Employment of Public Police*, Washington DC: National Institute of Justice, 1987.

Reno, William, *Corruption and State Politics in Sierra Leone*, Cambridge: Cambridge University Press, 1995.

———, *Warlord Politics and African States*, Boulder: Lynne Rienner, 1998.

République du Niger, *Code Pénal (last modification)*, Niamey: République du Niger, 2003.

Richmond, Oliver, *A Post-Liberal Peace*, New York: Routledge, 2011.

Rigakos, George S., *The New Parapolice. Risk Markets and Commodified Social Control*, London: University of Toronto Press, 2002.

Roberts, Richard and Mann, Kristin (eds), *Law in Colonial Africa*, London: James Currey, 1991.

Roberts, Richard, *Litigants and Households: African Disputes and Colonial Courts in the French Soudan, 1895—1912*, Portsmouth, NH: Heinemann, 2005.

Roitman, Janet, *Fiscal Disobedience: An Anthropology of Economic Regulation in Central Africa*. Princeton: Princeton University Press, 2005.

Rotimi, Kemi, *The Police in a Federal State: the Nigerian Experience*, Ibadan: College Press, 2001.

Rowlands, Michael, and Warnier, Jean Pierre, 'Sorcery, power and the modern state in Cameroon', *Man* 23 (1988), pp. 118–32.

Russian Army Homepage, 2013, http://eng.mil.ru/en/career/conscription.htm, last accessed 5 May 2013.

Ruteere, Mutuma and Marie–Emmanuelle Pommerolle, 'Democratizing security or decentralizing repression? The ambiguities of community policing in Kenya', *African Affairs*, 102 (2003), pp. 587–604.

Saada, Emmanuelle, 'The empire of law: dignity, prestige, and domination in the "colonial situation"', *French Politics, Culture and Society*, 20 (2002), pp. 98–120.

Sapa, 'Zuma invokes gay wrath', *News24*, 26 September 2006, available at: http://www.news24.com/SouthAfrica/News/Zuma-invokes-gay-wrath-20060926, last accessed 28 May 2014.

———, 'South Africa is not violent—says Zuma', *Mail & Guardian*, 7 March 2013, available at: http://mg.co.za/article/2013-03-07-south-africa-not-a-violent-country-says-zuma, last accessed 14 Mar. 2013.

———, 'Mido Macia died from hypoxia—autopsy', *City Press*, 11 March 2013, available at: http://www.citypress.co.za/news/mido-macia-died-from-hypoxia-autopsy/, last accessed 14 Mar. 2013.

Sarbah, John M. and Hollis R. Lynch, *Fanti National Constitution: A Short Treatise on the Constitution and Government of the Fanti Asanti and Other Akan Tribes of West Africa*, 2nd edition, London: Thomas Nelson, 1968.

Schareika, Nikolaus, Eva Spies and Pierre-Yves Le Meur (eds), *Auf dem Boden der Tatsachen: Festschrift für Thomas Bierschenk*, Köln: Köppe, 2011.

Schatzberg, Michael, *The Dialectics of Oppression in Zaire*, Bloomington and Indianapolis: Indiana University Press, 1988.

Schielke, Samuli, 'Being good in Ramadan: ambivalence, fragmentation, and the moral self in the lives of young Egyptians', *Journal of the Royal Anthropological Institute*, 15, issue supplement s1 (2009), pp. 24–40.

Schiff, Kerry-Gaye, 'Discourse of workplace violence: painting a picture of the South African Police Service', unpublished doctoral thesis, Unisa, 2010.

Scott, James C., *Weapons of the Weak: Everyday Forms of Peasant Resistance*, New Haven: Yale University Press, 1985.

———, *Domination and the Arts of Resistance: Hidden Transcripts*. New Haven, CT: Yale University Press, 1990.

———, *Seeing like a State. How Certain Schemes to Improve the Human Condition Have Failed*, New Haven: Yale University Press, 1998.

Searle, John R., *Expression and Meaning: Studies in the Theory of Speech Acts*, Cambridge: Cambridge University Press, 1979.

————, *Speech Acts: An Essay in the Philosophy of Language*, Cambridge: Cambridge University Press, 1969.

Seedat, Mohamed, Ashley van Niekerk, Rachel Jewkes, Shahnaaz a Suffl and Kopano Ratel, 'Violence and injuries in South Africa: prioritising an agenda for prevention', *The Lancet* 374, September 19 (2009), pp. 1011–22.

Seegers, Annette, 'South Africa's National Security Management System, 1972–1990', *Journal of Modern African Studies*, 29, 2 (1991), pp. 253–73.

————, *The Military in the Making of Modern South Africa*. London, IB Tauris, 1996.

Seekings, Jeremy, 'Are African welfare states distinctive? The design and politics of African welfare-state building in comparative perspective', Keynote Address, Social Policy and Regimes of Social Welfare in Africa, University of Fribourg, 12 September 2014.

Shapera, I., 'Some anthropological concepts of "crime": The Hobhouse Memorial Lecture', *The British Journal of Sociology*, 23, 4 (1972), pp. 381–94.

Shapland, Joanna and Jon Vagg, *Policing by the Public*, London: Routledge, 1988.

Sharma, Aradhana and Akhil Gupta, *The Anthropology of the State*, Oxford: Blackwell, 2006.

Shaw, Bryant P., *Force Publique, Force Unique: The military in the Belgian Congo, 1914–1939*. Michigan: University of Michigan Press, 1984.

Shaw, Mark, 'Point of Order: policing the compromise', in S. Friedman and D. Atkinson (eds), *South African Review 7: Small Miracle—South Africa's negotiated settlement*. Johannesburg: Ravan Press, 1994, pp. 68–85.

————, *Crime and Policing in Post-Apartheid South Africa: Transforming under Fire*, Indianapolis: Indiana University Press, 2002.

Shaw, Rosalind, *Memories of the Slave Trade. Ritual and the Historical Imagination in Sierra Leone*, Chicago: University of Chicago Press, 2002.

Shearing, Clifford and Julie Berg, 'South Africa', in Jones, Trevor and Tim Newburn (eds), *Plural Policing. A Comparative Perspective*, London/New York: Routledge, 2006, pp. 190–221.

Shearing, Clifford and Richard Ericson, 'Culture as figurative action', *British Journal of Sociology*, 42 (1991), pp. 481–506.

Shon, Phillip Chong Ho, '"I'd grab the S-O-B by his hair and yank him out the window": the fraternal order of warnings and threats in police–citizen encounters', *Discourse & Society*, 16, 6 (2005), pp. 829–45.

Simmel, Georg, 'Soziologie der Mahlzeit', *Der Zeitgeist, Beiblatt zum Berliner Tageblatt*, 41 (1910), pp. 1–2.

Simon, David, *Homicide: A Year on the Killing Streets*, Edinburgh: Canongate, 2009 [1991].

Sinclair, Georgina, *At the End of the Line: Colonial Policing and the Imperial Endgame 1945–80*, Manchester: Manchester University Press, 2006.

Singh, Anne-Marie, *Policing and Crime Control in Post-apartheid South Africa*, Aldershot: Ashgate Publishing Limited, 2008.

Skolnick, Jerome H., *Justice Without Trial: Law Enforcement in Democratic Society*, New York: Wiley, 1975 [1966].

Smart, Alan, 'Expressions of interest: friendship and guanxi in Chinese societies', in Bell, Sandra and Simon Coleman (eds), *The Anthropology of Friendship*, Oxford: Berg Publishers, 1999, pp. 119–36.

Smith, Daniel J., 'The Bakassi Boys: vigilantism, violence, and political imagination in Nigeria', *Cultural Anthropology*, 19, 3 (2004), pp. 429–55.

Soske, John, 'Marikana and the New Politics of Grief', 2012, http://abahlali.org/taxonomy/term/jon_soske/jon_soske/, last accessed 1 Sep. 2014.

South African Army Homepage 2013: http://www.army.mil.za/aboutus/values.htm, last accessed 5 May 2013.

South African Police Service, *Annual Report 2012/13*, 2013.

Staff Reporter, 'Don't hold your breath for action on Cele findings', *Mail & Guardian*, 11 March 2011, available at: http://mg.co.za/article/2011-03-11-dont-hold-your-breath-for-action-on-cele-findings, last accessed 14 Mar. 2013.

Statistics South Africa, 2011. *Statistical Release (revised) Census 2011*, available at: http://www.statssa.gov.za/Publications/P03014/P030142011.pdf, last accessed 16 Mar. 2013.

Steinberg, Jonny, *Thin Blue: The Unwritten Rules of Policing South Africa*, Jeppestown: Jonathan Ball Publishers, 2008.

——, 'Crime prevention goes abroad: policy transfer and policing in post–apartheid South Africa', *Theoretical Criminology*, 15, 4 (2011), pp. 349–64.

——, 'Living in fear of the day the attack dogs obey another master', *Sunday Times*, 13 February 2011.

——, 'Security and disappointment: policing, freedom and xenophobia in South Africa', *British Journal of Criminology*, 52, 2 (2012) pp. 345–60.

——, 'Establishing police authority and civilian compliance in post–apartheid Johannesburg: an argument from the work of Egon Bittner', *Policing and Society: an international journal of research and policy*, 22, 4 (2012), pp. 1–15.

Stenning, Philip C., 'Private police and public police: toward a redefinition of the police role', in Loree, Donald J. (ed.), *Future Issues in Policing: Symposium Proceedings*, Ottawa: Canadian Police College, 1989, pp. 169–92.

Stone, C., 'Supporting security, justice and development: lessons for a new era' New York: Vera Institute of Justice, 2005.

Strizek, Helmut, ,Das Autoritäre Regime unter General Joseph Désiré Mobutu: Ein Symbol des Kalten Krieges', in Chiari, Bernhard, Kollmer, Dieter H., and Pahl, Magnus (eds), *Wegweiser zur Geschichte. Demokratische Republik Kongo*. Paderborn: Schöning, 2008, pp. 49–64.

Super, Gail, *Governing Through Crime in South Africa: The Politics of Race and Class in Neoliberalizing Regimes*. London: Ashgate, 2013.

Swilling, Mark, and Phillips, Mark, 'State power in the 1980s: from "total strategy" to "counter-revolutionary warfare", in J. Cock and L. Nathan (eds) *War and Society: The Militarization of South Africa*. New York, St Martin's Press, 1989, pp. 134–48.

Tait, Sean, and Monique Marks, 'You strike a gathering, you strike a rock: current debates in the policing of public order in South Africa', *South African Crime Quarterly*, 38 (2014), pp. 15–22.

Tamuno, T.N., *The Police in Modern Nigeria, 1861–1965*, Ibadan, University Press, 1960.

Tankebe, Justice, 'Public confidence in the police: testing the effects of public experiences of police corruption in Ghana', *British Journal of Criminology*, 50, 2 (2010), pp. 296–319.

Taylor, Ian, *The International Relations of Sub-Saharan Africa*, New York: Continuum, 2011.

Tete-Adjalogo Têtêvi Godwin, *Histoire du Togo. La palpitante quête de l'ablodé (1940–1960)*, Editions Auteurs du Monde, Paris: NM7, 2006.

Twumasi, Paul K., *Criminal Law in Ghana*, Tema: Ghana Publishing Corporation, 1985.

Tyler, Tom R. (ed.), *Legitimacy and Criminal Justice: International Perspectives*, New York: Russell Sage Foundation, 2008.

Tyler, Tom R., Anthony Braga, Jeffry Fagan, Tracey Meares, Robert Sampson, Chris Winship, 'Legitimacy and criminal justice: international perspectives', in Tyler, Tom R. (ed.), *Legitimacy and Criminal Justice: A Comparative Perspective*, New York: Russell Sage Foundation, 2008, pp. 9–29.

United States Institute of Peace, *Local Ownership of Security Sector Reform*, Washington DC, USIP, 2010.

van Dijk, Rijk, '"Voodoo" on the doorstep: young Nigerian prostitutes and magic policing in the Netherlands', *Africa*, 71, 4 (2001), pp. 558–86.

van Maanen, John, 'The asshole', in Manning, Peter K. and John Van Maanen (eds), *Policing: A View from the Street*, Santa Monica: Goodyear Publishing, 1978, pp. 221–38.

Visagie, Justin, *Who are the middle class in South Africa? Does it matter for policy?* Available at: http://www.econ3x3.org/article/who-are-middle-class-south-africa-does-it-matter-policy, 2013, last accessed 16 Apr. 2014.

von Holdt, Karl, 'Nationalism, bureaucracy and the developmental state: the South African Case', *South African Review of Sociology*, 41, 1 (2010), pp. 4–27.

———, et al, *The Smoke That Calls: Insurgent Citizenship, Collective Violence and the Struggle for a Place in the New South Africa*. Johannesburg: Centre for the Study of Violence and Reconciliation, 2011.

Waddington, P. A. J., *Policing Citizens: Authority and Rights*, London: University College London Press, 1999.

———, 'Police (canteen) sub-culture: an appreciation', *British Journal of Criminology*, 39, 2 (1999), pp. 287–309.

Wakefield, Alison, *Selling Security. The Private Policing of Public Space*, Devon: Willan Publishing, 2003.

Weber, Max, *Wirtschaft und Gesellschaft*, Tübingen: Mohr, 1980 [1922].

———, 'The profession and vocation of politics', in Peter Lassman and Ronald Speirs (eds), *Weber: Political Writings*, Cambridge, Cambridge University Press, 1994.

Weick, Karl E., *Sensemaking in Organizations*, Thousand Oaks: Sage, 1995.

Weiner, Mandy, *Killing Kebble: An Underworld Exposed*. Johannesburg, Pan MacMillan, 2011.

Wender, Jonathan M., *Policing and the Poetics of Everyday Life*, Urbana, Chicago: University of Illinois Press, 2008.

Wendt, Alexander and Daniel Friedheim, 'Hierarchy under anarchy: informal empire and the East German state', *International Organization*, 49, 4 (1995), pp. 689–721.

Wendt, Alexander and Michael Barnett, 'Dependent state formation and third world militarization", *Review of International Studies*, 19, 4 (1993), pp. 321–47.

Werbner, Richard, and Terence Ranger (eds), *Postcolonial Identities in Africa*, London: Zed Books, 1996.

Westley, William A., *Violence and the Police: A Sociological Study of Law, Custom, and Morality*, Cambridge: MIT Press, 1970.

Whitaker, C.S., *The Politics of Tradition: Continuity and Change in Northern Nigeria 1946–1969*, Princeton: Princeton University Press, 1970.

White, Hylton, 'Beastly whiteness: animal kinds and the social imagination in South Africa', *Anthropology Southern Africa*, 34, 3–4 (2011), pp. 104–12.

White, Hylton, 'A post-fordist ethnicity: insecurity, authority, and identity in South Africa', *Anthropological Quarterly*, 85, 2 (2012), pp. 397–427.

Whitehead, Antony, 'Man to man violence: how masculinity may work as a dynamic risk factor', *The Howard Journal*, 44, 4 (2005), pp. 411–22.

Yahaya, A.D., *The Native Authority System in Northern Nigeria, 1950–1970*, Zaria: Ahmadu Bello University Press, 1980.

Young, Malcolm, *An Inside Job: Policing and Police Culture in Britain*. Oxford: Clarendon Press, 1991.

———, *In the Sticks: Cultural Identity in a Rural Police Force*, Oxford: Clarendon Press, 1993.

Zeit Online, 2012: *Karlsruhe erlaubt bewaffneten Einsatz der Bundeswehr im Innern* http://www.zeit.de/politik/deutschland/201208/bundesverfassungsgericht–militaer–inland, last accessed 5 May 2013.

Zelizer, Vivian, *The Social Meaning of Money*, Princeton Paperbacks. Princeton University Press, 1997.

Zolberg, Aristide R., 'A view from the Congo', *World Politics*, 19, 1 (1966), 137–49.

INDEX

Abidjan, Côte d'Ivoire, 2
Abrahamsen, Rita, 43
Abrams, Philip, 5, 98
Abuja, Nigeria, 155, 157
accidents, 33, 151, 155
Accra, Ghana, 3, 319
Addis Ababa, Ethiopia, 3
Afghanistan, 25, 45
Africa Conflict Prevention Pool, 42
African Corps, Togo, 35
African National Congress (ANC),
    12, 64–8, 70–73, 75–6, 137, 138,
    204, 210
African Spring, 106
Africans: The History of a Continent
    (Iliffe), 1
Afrobarometer Survey, 309
AK-47s, 121, 131, 167, 213, 234, 239
Akansa, Ghana, 231–48
Akpai people, 165
alcohol, 212
Algeria, 35
Alliance des Forces Démocratiques
    (AFDL), 125
Anambra Vigilante Services, 286
ancestral cults, 92, 93
Anderson, David, 7

Anglo-American models, xiii, xiv, xv,
    172, 264, 267
Angola, 3, 65
animals
    criminals as, 196
    ethnic identity of, 202
Annang people, 92
anthropology, 119, 201, 268, 269
apartheid, 12, 61–7, 69, 74, 137–40,
    181, 183, 188, 204, 263, 266
Araújo, Sara, 215
armed robbery, 94, 152
austerity, 93
autonomy, 29
Awareness Times, 45

Bakassi Boys, 99, 286
Baker, Bruce, 42, 87
bakkie brigade, 299
Baltimore Homicide Unit, 261
Bambara people, 37
banditry, 10
Bangladeshis, 209–10
Banton, Michael, xiii, 7
Barnett, Michael, 52
Bat, Jean-Pierre, 7
Bauchi Province, Nigeria, 82, 83

Bavaria, Germany, 105
Bayart, Jean-Francois, 2, 14, 41, 48, 200
Bayelsa, Nigeria, 166
Bayley, David, 123, 268
Beek, Jan, 1–15, 110, 231–48, 250, 268
Behrends, Andrea, 105
Belgian Congo (1908–60), 124, 291
von Benda-Beckmann, Franz and
    Keebet, 252
Benin, 107–8, 112, 113, 115, 116, 290
Benjamin, Walter, 230
Benue-Plateau, Nigeria, 82
Berlin, Germany, 9
Berom people, 85–6
Bhambra, Gurminder, 24
Biddle, Keith, 41–3, 50, 52, 54–7
Bieker, Sarah, 8
Bierschenk, Thomas, 12, 103–19, 164,
    238, 254, 272
Bittner, Egon, 7, 9, 69, 233, 249, 260
Blair, Anthony 'Tony', 44, 49, 281
Blundo, Giorgio, 6
Bohannan, Paul, 104
Boko Haram, 151
Borno, Nigeria, 151
Bosnia, 50
Botha, Pieter Willem, 64–5
boundary-making, 193–7
Bourdieu, Pierre, 128
braais, 212
bricolage, 12
Bridges, Billy, 46
Brodeur, John-Paul, xvi, 63, 74
Brogden, Mike, 139
Bruce, David, 76, 186
Bureau of Democracy, 126
bureaucracy, 4, 10, 65, 74, 109–10, 112
bureaucratic ceremonies, 196
bureaucratisation, 24–5, 28, 31–8
bureaucrats in uniform, 106
Buur, Lars, 81

buy-in, 42, 53

Canada, 25, 144
capacity building, 21
Cape Town, South Africa, 69, 172,
    174–89
Cape Verde, 108
capital punishment, 93, 227
capitalism, 20, 24, 71, 86, 108
Cele, Bheki, 75, 181
Central Intelligence Agency (CIA), 63
Centre for the Study of Violence and
    Reconciliation (CSVR), 179
Chalfin, Brenda, 5
Chan, Janet, 173
Chatterjee, Partha, 241
Chesterman, Simon, 43, 53
chiefs
    Mozambique, 194, 195, 215
    Niger, 194, 251, 252
    Nigeria, 84–96
China, 246
cholera, 2
Christianity, 91–2, 97, 165
citizen education, 223, 235
citizenship
    Nigeria, 86
    South Africa, 69
civil police work, 123–4, 126, 128, 294
Clapham, Christopher, 48
Clark, Gracia, 237
coffee, 201–2
Cold War, 59, 263
Collins, Anthony, 179
colonialism, 21–5, 105–7, 118–19,
    194
    British Nigeria (1861–1960), 83–9,
        159
    British Sierra Leone (1808–1961),
        40, 41, 43, 44, 45–8, 53–59
    French Togoland (1916–60), 29–38

and intervention, 43–4
subtext, 44–5, 49, 55–8
Comaroff, Jean and John, 8, 10, 206, 214, 262, 273
Comité de Suivi de la Réforme de Police (CSRP), 125
Commonwealth, 41, 44, 45, 53
communism, 65
community policing, 11
  Mozambique, 215, 228–9
  Niger, 251
  Nigeria, 81, 94
  Sierra Leone, 54, 55
  South Africa, 142
  and vigilantism, 81
complaints, 14, 33, 215–28, 250–62
Congo, Democratic Republic of the, 8, 9, 13, 108, 121–33, 263
connected history, 24–5
conviviality, 99, 167, 196, 197, 205, 208, 211
'cool drink talk', 199–200, 203, 212
copper, 2
corporal punishment, 93, 94, 177, 178, 221
corruption, 5, 8, 14, 106, 117, 118
  causes of, 118
  DR Congo, 125
  and food, 196–7, 199–212
  Ghana, 231–48
  gifts, 117, 214, 226, 236–7, 244–6
  and informality, 226–8
  and language of friendship, 117
  Mozambique, 213, 222, 223, 226–8, 230
  Nigeria, 160–64
  and registers, 231–48
  Sierra Leone, 41
  South Africa, 65, 71, 73–6, 144–5, 184, 199–212
Côte d'Ivoire, 2

Coulibaly, 37
Courtin, Nicolas, 7
critical perspectivism, 8
cultural work, 194–7
culture of negotiation, 226
customary law, 33, 86, 89–90, 91
cybercrime, xiv
Cyrildene, Johannesburg, 208

Dadur, Nigeria, 90
Dahomey, 107–8
Dahrendorf, Nicola, 126
Dakshang, Ali, 90
dance of shame, 92–3, 94
Daveyton, South Africa, 171
Dawn, The, 152
debt, 139, 143, 195, 216, 217, 219, 222–4, 228, 256
decentralised despotism, 86
decline, 2
Dela Widenmann, Christina, 215, 226, 314
demilitarisation, 13, 122, 125, 127, 132
democracy, 9, 12, 188
  DR Congo, 125
  Ghana, 241
  Nigeria, 153, 165, 267
  Sierra Leone, 42
  South Africa, 61–4, 173
demonstrations, *see* protests
Department for International Development (DfID), 42
dependency, 22, 51, 58
Diphoorn, Tessa, 13, 135–47
discipline, 23
  and corruption, 160–64
  and dissimulation, 149, 150, 160, 162, 166–9
  and drills, 196
  and education, 37
  and professionalism, 29, 36–7

and proximity to population, 23, 29, 126, 132
and punishment, 158–9, 164, 178, 181, 183, 220
and symbolic power, 129, 130, 131, 133
and uniforms, 28, 29, 36–7, 128–9, 133
disease, 1–2, 151
dissimulation, 149, 150, 160, 162, 166–9
divide and rule, 57
Dogarai, 84, 85, 86, 90, 287
domestic violence, 216, 222
Douglas, Mary, 195, 201
'drama', 7
drills, 196
Driver and Vehicle Licensing Authority (DVLA), 232
Dudley, Billy Joseph, 84
Durban, South Africa, 135–47, 209
Dutsin Bature, Nigeria, 149–69
dyadic relationships, 166, 168

East Germany (1949–90), 9
East Timor, 50
Eastern Cape, South Africa, 172, 178, 182
Eckert, Julia, 8, 246
education, 2
  citizen education, 223, 235
  Nigeria, 87
  shadow education system, 111
  South Africa, 66, 182, 184
  Togo, 35–7
Edward, Duke of Kent, 46
Eggon people, 85
Enloe, Cynthia, 263
entrance tests, 114
equality before the law, 107
Ericson, Richard, 175, 247

Espagne, Michel, 119
esprit de corps, 115
État major, 127
Ethiopia, 3, 5, 303
ethno-nationalism, 89
ethnography, xv–xvi, 1–4, 7–10, 15, 104–19
Eurocentrism, 11, 28, 132, 133
European Union (EU), 108
Europeanisation, 20, 24
Europol, xiv
extortion, 126, 153, 160, 213, 237
extraversion, 2, 22, 41, 48–9, 52–3, 58–9

face saving, 177
failing states, 52
Fassin, Didier, 8
Faull, Andrew, 171–89
Federal Bureau of Investigation (FBI), 63
Ferguson, James, 2
Festival for African Arts and Culture (FESTAC), 93
Fischler, Claude, 206
Fivaz, George, 70
food, 196–7, 199–212
force and domination, 123
force multipliers, 142, 175
Force Publique, 124
forced labour, 32
forum shopping, 253
Foucault, Michel, 20, 29
Fourchard, Laurent, 81
Françafrique, la, 22
France, 7, 8, 44, 45, 49, 261, 268
  Dahomey (1904–58), 107–8
  gendarmeries, 105, 108
  Togoland (1916–60), 29–38
Francisco, Laudemiro, 230
fraud, 216–17, 223, 256

Freetown, Sierra Leone, 41
Friedheim, Daniel, 52
Frontex, xiv
Fulani people, 82–3, 153, 156, 252, 254
functionalism, 19

G4S, 221
Gada Biu, Nigeria, 156
gangs, 4, 10, 75, 126, 130, 132
Garba, Alhaji Dahiru, 97
Garde Civile, Congo 125
gatekeeper institutions, 5
Geertz, Clifford, 262
gendarmeries, 105, 108
  Belgian Congo (1908–60), 124, 291
  French Togoland (1916–60), 30, 31, 34, 37
  Niger, 249–62
  Zaire (1971–97), 125
gender roles, 186
Germany, 9, 25, 108
  and Afghanistan, 45
  Armed Forces, 123
  police density, 112
  Togoland Protectorate (1884–1916), 29
  and Uganda, 105
Ghana, 1, 3, 4, 8, 112, 115, 193, 196, 231–48, 266, 290
Gida, Nigeria, 149–69, 301
Giddens, Anthony, 187
gifts, 117, 214, 226, 236–7, 244
Gilligan, James, 172, 186, 189
Glaeser, Andreas, 9
Glasman, Joël, 11, 24, 27–38
global dangers, 25
Global North and South, xiv, xvi, 9, 10, 103–19, 240, 264, 268
Gluckman, Max, 104
Gnabodé, A., 34

Goemai people, 85
Goffman, Irvin, 172–3
Goldie, George, 83
Göpfert, Mirco, 1–15, 122, 249–62
governance, xvii
Grätz, Tilo, 81
guardians of the law, 109
Guinea-Bissau, 291
Gupta, Akhil, 5

Haiti, 25
Handelman, Don, 246
Hausa people, 82–3, 85, 90
Heald, Suzette, 265
Hegel, Georg Wilhelm Friedrich, 23
Herbst, Jeffrey, 2
heterogeneity, 112–15
hierarchies, 13, 24
  Nigeria Police Force, 149, 152, 154, 156, 158
  Police Nationale Congolaise, 130
  South African Police Service 'partnership policing', 142
  Togolese institutions, 30
  Vigilante Group of Nigeria, 95
Higazi, Adam, 97
high policing, 63–7, 68, 70–76, 266
Hills, Alice, 7, 124, 133, 263–8
Hisbah, 99
HIV/AIDS, 3–4, 257
Hobbes, Thomas, 169
Holdaway, Simon, 7, 175
von Holdt, Karl, 174, 177
homosexuality, 181
Hornberger, Julia, 14, 182, 199–212, 214, 230
hot and cold social transactions, 205–6
human rights, 182–3, 203, 209, 213–15, 227, 230, 314
Human Rights Watch, 264
humanitarianism, 22
hybrid policing bodies, 136

Ibeanu, Okechukwu, 87
Iliffe, John, 1
illegal businesses, 224, 227
illiberal states, 3
Ilorin, Nigeria, 88
immediate justice, 214, 219, 227
imperialism, 43, 57
imported state, 24
Impossible Fact (Morgenstern), 162,
    304
India, 5, 8, 158, 236, 246, 268
indirect rule, 83, 85
Indochina, 35
informalisation, 214–30
insecurity, 4, 9, 10, 151
institutional theory, 20
inter-governmental organisations
    (IGOs), 266–8
interaction formats, 116–17
International Monetary Fund (IMF),
    82, 93
internationalisation, 20, 22, 24–5
Interpol, 264
intervention, 43–4, 46–59
Islam, 83, 86, 97, 99, 165, 251, 265
isomorphism, 20, 21, 24, 105, 106

Jackson, Robert, 3
Jauregui, Beatrice, 8, 158, 160, 236
Jema'a, Nigeria, 83
Jensen, Steffen, 81
Johannesburg, South Africa, 69, 137,
    143, 184, 196–7, 203–12
Jonathan, Goodluck, 166
Jörgel, Magnus, 132
Jos, Nigeria, 82, 88, 96
juju, 238, 241
Justaert, Arnout, 122

Kabbah, Ahmed Tejan, 42, 50–51,
    53–5, 281

Kaduna, Nigeria, 88, 95
Kamara, Samura, 49
Kano, Nigeria, 84, 88
Kappler, Victor, 123
Kebble, Brett, 73–4
Keystone Cops, 167
Killingray, David, 7
Kinshasa, DR Congo, 13, 121–33
Kivu, Congo, 126
Klantschnig, Gernot, 8
Koroma, Salia, 46
Kosovo, 50
Kraska, Peter, 123
Krasner, Stephen, 51
Krogstad, Erlend Grøner, 11, 12, 22,
    39–59
Kuluna, 130
Kumasi, Ghana, 3
Kwararafa, Nigeria, 165
KwaZulu-Natal, South Africa, 202
Kyed, Helene Maria, 14, 213–30

Lagos, Nigeria, 157, 166, 301
Lalá, Anicia, 230
Landecker, Hannah, 202
Langtang, Nigeria, 90, 91, 94
Lar, Jimam, 12, 22–3, 79–99
law register, 233, 234–6, 238, 240, 243
League of Nations, 31
Lee, John Michael, 263, 266
Leggett, Ted, 69
legitimacy, 6, 10, 11, 14
    belief in (*Legitimitätsglaube*), 246
    and colonialism, 87, 89
    competition for, 10, 14
    and informality, 213–15, 226–8
    and monopoly of violence, 3, 4–5,
        234
    and public morality, 23
    and registers, 14, 242–8
    and stateness, 6, 14, 196, 247

and vigilantism, 6, 10, 14, 23, 97
Letsela, Lebohang, 179
Lévi-Strauss, Claude, 201
liberal peace, 43–4
liberal political theory, 19
Liberia, 44–5
Lippert, Randy, 144
Lipsky, Michael, 173, 247
literacy, 35–7, 87
Loader, Ian, xiii–xvii, 128
lobbying, 115
Local Needs Policing, 42
local ownership, 52–3, 55
Loftus, Bethan, 173, 175, 177
Lomé, Togo, 30, 31, 34
Lonmin, 204
low police density, 112
low policing, 63–4, 67–70, 266
Lowland Division, Nigeria, 82, 87
Luhmann, Niklas, 235, 245
Lund, Christian, 136, 252
Lundestad, Geir, 58

Macia, Mido, 171–2, 189
Maintenir l'ordre colonial, 7
Makupula, Mandla, 182
Mali, 5, 108, 112
Mamdani, Mahmood, 86
Mandela, Nelson, 140
Mangvwat, Monday, 90
Manning, Peter, 7, 179, 201
Maputo, Mozambique, 14, 213–30
Marenin, Otwin, 7, 40, 56, 263, 266
Marikana massacre (2012), 13, 76, 174,
    183, 204, 211
market register, 237–8
Marks, Monique, 175, 264
martial races, 31
Martin, Jeffrey, 8, 123, 125, 233, 238,
    245, 250
Marxism, 20, 108

masculinity, 13, 31, 97, 172, 179–89
Mbeki, Thabo, 70–71, 75
Mbembe, Achille, 99, 167–8, 169
mega-events, xiv
Mende people, 46
MI5/MI6, 63
Middle Belt, Nigeria, 80, 82, 83
middle class, 3, 172, 182, 185–6, 188
Miliband, Ralph, 5
Milice, Togo, 30, 34, 37
militaries, 11, 28
    DR Congo, 13, 108, 121–33
    Germany, 123
    Russia, 123
    Sierra Leone, 39, 42, 50
    South Africa, 123, 138
    Togo, 29, 30, 31, 32, 35–6
militias, 80, 97, 165
Millennium Development Goals,
    267–8
Minna, Nigeria, 88
mob justice, 228, 251
Mobutu, Joseph-Désiré, 124
modernisation, 28, 31
Mol, Annemarie, 202
Momoh, Abubakar, 87
Monjardet, Dominique, 7
monopoly of violence, 3, 4–5, 109–10,
    194, 234
moonlighting, 13, 135–47, 299
moral orders, 14, 110, 115, 164, 219,
    233–48
Morgenstern, Christian, 162, 304
Morrell, Robert, 183
Mozambique, 8, 14, 171, 193–5,
    213–30, 263, 266
multiple modernities, 24
murder, 70, 73, 90, 176, 180, 250,
    260–62
    Macia murder (2013), 171–2, 189
    Steenkamp murder (2013), 181

Muri Province, Nigeria, 82
Murphy, Christopher, xiv
Mwaghavul people, 85–6

Nader, Laura, 251
Namibia, 50
Nasarawa State, Nigeria, 82
National Party, South Africa, 65
Native Authority (NA) system, 84–91, 288
Native Authority System in Northern Nigeria, The (Yahaya), 84–5
Native Guard, Togo, 32, 34, 37
neocolonialism, 43, 48–9, 52
neoliberalism, 106, 107
neopatrimonialism, 106, 118
Ngas people, 85–6
Niamey, Niger, 251
Niger, 8, 14–15, 193, 194–5, 249–62, 263, 266, 290
Niger Delta, Nigeria, 80, 156
Nigeria, 4, 5, 8, 12, 79–99, 149–69
  ancestral cults, 92, 93
  Bakassi Boys, 99, 286
  Berom people, 85–6
  Boko Haram, 151
  Christianity, 91–2, 97
  citizenship, 86
  Civil War (1967–70), 82, 91
  colonial era (1861–1960), 83–9, 159
  Corporate Affairs Commission, 80
  Dogarai, 84, 85, 86, 90, 287
  ethno-nationalism, 89
  Festival for African Arts and Culture (1977), 93
  Fulani people, 82–3, 153, 156
  general elections (2007), 153
  Hausa people, 82–3, 85, 90
  Hisbah (Sharia Police), 99
  Independent Corrupt Practices Commission, 163
  Independent National Electoral Commission (INEC), 153
  Islam, 83, 86, 97, 99
  Mwaghavul people, 85–6
  National Orientation Agency, 163
  Native Authority (NA) system, 84–9, 91, 98
  Native Authority Police Force (NAPF), 82, 84, 86–9, 91, 98, 288
  Ngas people, 85–6
  officer administering the government (OAG), 88
  Oga-ism, 158, 303
  oil boom (1970–78), 93
  Oodu'a People's Congress (OPC), 99
  People's Democratic Party (PDP), 165
  Plateau State, 12, 79–99
  plural policing, 79–99
  Protectorate Ordinance (1924), 84
  Royal Niger Constabulary (RNC), 83
  sectarian violence, 82, 97
  slavery, 83
  Sokoto Jihad (1809), 83
  Structural Adjustment Programme (1986–1994), 82, 93
  Tarok people, 86, 91, 92, 94
  vigilantism, 12, 13, 79–82, 90–99, 288
  Yanbanga, 90–94, 97, 288
  Yandoka system, 87–8, 90, 288
Nigeria Police Force (NPF), 89, 149–69
  Mechanised Salary Scheme, 162
  Mobile Police (MOPOL), 159, 160, 163–5, 305
  Public Relations Officer (PPRO), 166

risk and motivation, 13, 149–69, 301
roadblocks, 153, 160–62
Special Anti-Robbery Squad (SARS), 158
Noble, Debbie, 46
non-contributory welfare transfers, 3
non-state actors, 4, 5, 6, 7, 10, 12, 80
  community policing, 228–9
  militias, 80, 97, 165
  private security firms, 13, 111, 135–47, 228
  vigilantes, 4, 6, 7, 12, 79–99, 111, 196, 251, 286, 288
norm pluralism, 113
Norway, 268
Nyanga, Cape Town, 174–5, 177

O'Connor, Daniel, 144
Ochuno, Moses, 83
officer administering the government (OAG), 88
Oga-ism, 158
Oga-ism, 158, 303
Ogidi, Nigeria, 153
oil, 1, 93
old boys' network, 138–40, 145, 146
Olivier de Sardan, Jean-Pierre, 6, 122, 194, 242, 272
Olukoshi, Adebayo, 93
Olympio, Sylvanus, 31
one-man shows, 138–9
Ontario, Canada, 144
Oodu'a People's Congress (OPC), 99
opacity, 112–15
orders of life, 115
Organisation for Economic Co-operation and Development (OECD), 45
organised crime, xiv, 13, 25
  DR Congo, 126
  South Africa, 67

othering, 105, 119, 203
Owen, Olly, 1–15, 149–69

palace guards, 84, 85
Pankshin Division, Nigeria, 82
Paperman, Patricia, 235
Park, Sung-Joon, 105
partnership policing, 141–2
party states, 5, 9
path-dependency, 106–8
patriotism, 123, 130
peace building, 43, 50
peacekeeping operations, xiv, 124
Peake, Gordon, 40, 56
'peanuts' narrative, 184–6
Peddie, South Africa, 177, 308
Penfold, Peter, 281
People's Democratic Party (PDP), 165
performances, 172, 173
petty corruption, 14, 199–212
Pistorius, Oscar, 181
Plateau State, Nigeria, 12, 79–99
plural policing, 79–99
poaching, 138–9
police consultation, 225
police idea vs practices, 109
Police Judiciaire, 126, 128, 296
Police Nationale Congolaise (PNC), 124–33
police-free areas, 112
Policing Africa (Hill), 7
policing cultures, xiv
political order, xvii
politics of the belly, 14, 200
politics of unease, 20
polyvalence, 132
Portugal, 22
post-conflict reconstruction, xiv, 9, 43
  DR Congo, 123
  Sierra Leone, 40, 53
Potholm, Christian, 263, 266

poverty, 1
Pratten, David, 13, 92, 193–7
private investigators, 143
private security firms, 111, 135–47,
    228–9, 251
Private Security Industry Regulatory
    Authority (PSIRA), 140–41, 144
private sphere, 110–11, 135–47, 228–9
Professional Intelligence and Profes-
    sional Standards Bureau (PIBS), 242
professionalisation, 11, 24–5, 27–38,
    266
professionalism, xvi, 28–38
    autonomy, 29
    discipline, 29, 36–7
    norms, 113
    proximity to population, 23, 29,
        126, 132
    report writing, 28, 29, 32, 38
    self-image, 115
property rights, 20
prostitution, 33
protests, xiv, 13, 38, 75–6, 93, 137
    Marikana massacre (2012), 13, 76,
        174, 183, 204, 211
proxy governance, 50–51
public morality, 23
public vs private sphere, 110–11,
    135–47
punishment
    capital, 93, 227
    corporal, 93, 94, 177, 178, 181, 183,
        221
    dance of shame, 92–3, 94
    disciplinary, 158–9, 164, 178, 181,
        183, 220, 315
    postings, 150, 156–7, 303
    privatised, 228–9
    tangible, 214, 219, 227, 228–30
    violence, 189

Qur'an, 251

racism, xiii, 107, 173
radical insecurity, 10, 151, 196, 247
Ramaphosa, Cyril, 204
rapid mobilisation, 132
Ratele, Kopano, 179
Raw and the Cooked, The (Lévi-
    Strauss), 201
reciprocal comparison, 119–20
reconstruction relationships, 40, 41
recruitment requirements, 114, 126
red ball-cases, 261
registers, 14, 110, 115, 156, 164, 219,
    233–48
Reiner, Robert, 172
report writing, 28, 29, 32, 38
repression, 20, 21, 107
resources, lack of, 111–12, 116
respect violence, 13, 117, 129, 163,
    172, 174–89
Rhodesia (1965–79), 65
Richards, David, 50
Richmond, Oliver, 43–4
Ringim, Hafiz, 166
risk and motivation, 13, 149–69, 301
roadblocks, 81, 96, 153, 160–62
Roitman, Janet, 5
Rosberg, Carl, 3
Rotimi, Kemi, 7, 84, 85
Rottenburg, Richard, 105
Royal Niger Company, 83
Royal Niger Constabulary (RNC), 83
rule of law, 213, 224, 230
Rwanda, 3, 5

Schapera, Isaac, 252
Schatzberg, Michael, 266
Schiff, Kerry-Gaye, 187
Schlichte, Klaus, 8, 19–25
Scotland, 7
sectarian violence, 82, 97
Security Officers Act (1987), 137

Security Sector Reform (SSR), 11, 21, 27, 28, 29, 106, 263
DR Congo, 122, 124, 126, 130, 132, 133
Sierra Leone, 39–59
sedimentation, 6, 10, 106–8, 194
Seedat, Mohamed, 179
Selebi, Jackie, 70–75, 211
self-esteem, 186–8
self-perception, 13, 115–16, 122, 124, 129–33, 245
separation of powers, 107, 125
Service de Sûreté, Togo, 29, 32
sexism, xiii
sexualised violence, 126
Shabungu, Susan, 307
shadow education system, 111
shame, 67, 172, 184, 186–8
Shangana, 217
Shapland, Joanna, 250
Shari'a law, 99, 265
Shearing, Clifford, 139, 175
Shendam, Nigeria, 82, 87, 91
Short, Clare, 281
Sierra Leone, 8, 9, 11–12, 39–59, 263, 266, 281
Sierra Leone Telegraph, 45
Simmel, Georg, 203
Simon, David, 261
simulacre, 167, 169
Singapore, 268
Singh, Anne-Marie, 138
slave mentality, 57
slavery, 83, 188
sleeping sickness, 2
Smart, Alan, 246
Snakes and Ladders, 157
Soares de Oliveira, Ricardo, 3
sociability register, 233, 236, 237
social capital, 115, 154, 166
social cases, 195, 215–30

social order register, 235, 236, 239, 240, 244
soft power, 44
Sokoto, Nigeria, 83, 88
Sokoto, Alhaji Ali, 95
Somalia, 9
Sophiatown, Johannesburg, 205–12
Soske, John, 204
South Africa, 4, 8, 12, 13, 61–77, 135–47, 171–89, 193, 196–7, 199–212, 263, 266
African National Congress (ANC), 12, 64–8, 70–73, 75–6, 137, 138, 204, 210
Angolan War (1975–89), 65
apartheid era, 12, 61–7, 69, 74, 137–40, 181, 183, 188, 204, 263, 266
Bangladeshi community, 209–10
citizenship, 69
Civil Co-operation Bureau, 74
community policing forums (CPFs), 142
democratic era, 61–4, 67–77, 141–7, 171–89
gross national product (GNP), 108
Ground Operational Co-Oordinating Committee (GOCOC), 142
hot and cold social transactions, 205–6
internal regime competition, 23
Justice Department, 71
Kebble assassination (2005), 73–4
Macia murder (2013), 171–2, 189
Marikana massacre (2012), 13, 76, 174, 183, 204, 211
masculinity, 13, 172, 179–89
middle class, 172, 182, 185–6
moonlighting, 13, 135–47, 299
murder rate, 70
National Crime Prevention Strategy (NCPS), 61, 142

National Director of Public Prosecutions, 71–2
National Intelligence Service, 63, 71
National Key Points Act (1980), 137, 298
National Party, 65
National Security Management System (NSMS), 65
partnership policing, 141–2
Police Act (1995), 140–41
Private Security Industry Regulatory Authority (PSIRA), 140–41, 144
Security Officers Act (1987), 137, 140, 298
State Security Council, 65
Steenkamp murder (2013), 181
taxi violence, 140
trade unions, 71
Umkhonto we Sizwe, 65
Wankie campaign (1967), 65
White Paper on Safety and Security (1998), 142
South African Defence Force (SADF), 138–9
South African National Defence Force (SANDF), 123
South African Police (SAP), 61–8, 137–9
Crime Information Service, 67
Detective Branch, 63, 66, 67, 68
high policing, 63–7, 68
kitskonstabel, 67
moonlighting, 137–9, 299
old boys' network, 138–40, 145, 146
Security Branch, 63–4, 66, 68, 74
Uniformed Branch, 63, 66, 67, 68
South African Police Service (SAPS), 61–4, 68–77, 141–7, 171–89, 199–212
Commercial Crime Unit, 210
cool drink talk, 199–200, 203, 212

Crime Intelligence, 72
Detective Branch, 68, 72–4, 76
food, 196–7, 199–212
high policing, 70–76
low policing, 64, 67–70
Macia murder (2013), 171–2, 189
Marikana massacre (2012), 13, 76, 174, 183, 204, 211
moonlighting, 141–7
peanuts' narrative, 184–6
Security Branch, 74
Serious and Violent Crimes Unit, 73
Tactical Response Teams, 75–6, 175
Uniformed Branch, 68–70, 75–6
violence, 171–89
Southern African Regional Police Chiefs Co-operation Organisation (SARPCCO), 264
sovereignty, 40–41, 48–59
Spain, 22, 44, 45
spheres of influence, 43
Sri Lanka, 268
state at work, 106
state building, 21, 43, 52, 268
state failure, 25
state in society, 23
state police forces, xvii
statehood, 110
stateness, 6, 14, 196, 247
States at Work, 6, 272
Steenkamp, Riva, 181
Steinberg, Jonny, 1–15, 23, 61–77, 184
stop and search, 177
street-level bureaucrats, 173
structural adjustment programmes, 1, 82, 93
subtext, 44–5, 49, 55–8
Sudan, 3
suivre le dossier, 115
SWAT (Special Weapons And Tactics), 132

symbolic interactionism, 173
symbolic power, 127–8, 133

Taiwan, 8, 233
Tamuno, Tekena Nitonye, 7
tangible punishment, 214, 219, 227, 228–30
Tarok people, 86, 91, 92, 94
taxation, 33, 87, 90, 126
taxi violence, 140
Taylor, Ian, 48
ten commandments of the good policeman, 115
terminology, 127–8
terrorism, xiv, 25, 151
theft, 92–3, 216, 217, 219–21, 223, 225, 258
Theory from the South (Comaroff), 10
Thurmann, Laura, 13, 121–33
Tirailleurs, 37
toasts, 201
Todd, Harry, 251
Togo, 8, 11, 28–38, 266
totalitarianism, 21
totems, 201
trade unions, 71
traffic checks, 116–17, 231–48
training, 28, 114, 115, 126, 131–2
 National Police of Benin, 115
 Native Authority Police Force (Nigeria), 87
 Nigeria Police Force, 94, 163
 Police Nationale Congolaise, 126–7, 131–2
 Sierra Leone Police, 41
 South African Police Service, 72
 South African Police, 67
transparency, 113
transversal objects, 105, 119–20
travelling models, 105–6
tribalism, 163

tuberculosis, 2
twilight policing, 12, 136–47
Tyler, Tom, 242

Uganda, 8, 21, 105
Umkhonto we Sizwe, 65
uncovered spaces, 21
under-applying the law, 117
unemployment
 Mozambique, 215
 Nigeria, 93, 153
 self-esteem, 186–8
 South Africa, 186
 Togo, 34
uniforms, 28, 29, 36–7, 128–9, 133
United Kingdom, 7, 20, 44, 105–6, 156, 173, 177, 268
 Commonwealth, 41, 44, 45, 53
 Department for International Development (DfID), 42
 MI5/MI6, 63
 and Nigeria, 83–9, 159
 and Sierra Leone, 12, 39–59, 281
 United States, extraversion towards, 58–9
United Nations, 31, 124
 Civilian Police (CIVPOL), 53
 Development Programme (UNDP), 54, 230
 Millennium Development Goals, 267–8
United States, xiii, 7, 20, 116, 268
 Bureau of Democracy, 126
 Central Intelligence Agency (CIA), 63
 European extraversion, 58–9
 Federal Bureau of Investigation (FBI), 63
 SWAT (Special Weapons And Tactics), 132
universalism, 119

urbanisation, 19
Uttar Pradesh, India, 158

Vagg, Jon, 250
vagrancy, 33
Van Maanen, John, 247
vertical encompassment, 81
Vigilante Group of Nigeria (VGN), 12,
   80, 95–7, 99, 288
vigilantism, 4, 6, 7, 12, 79–99, 111,
   196, 251, 286, 288
   boundary-making, 196
   community policing, 81
   Niger, 251
   Nigeria, 12, 13, 79–99, 286, 288
violence, 8, 118, 163, 171–89, 203
   code of silence, 177
   and masculinity, 172, 179–89
   monopoly of, 3, 4–5, 109–10, 194,
      234
   and privatised policing, 228–9
   and registers, 234, 239
   and respect, 13, 163, 172, 174–89
   sexualised, 126
   and shame, 172, 184, 186–8
Visagie, Justin, 185–6
vocational ear, 14, 260, 262
Vongbut, Chenvong, 94

Waddington, Pat, 175, 231, 234
Wankie campaign (1967), 65

Wase District, Nigeria, 82
Weber, Max, 20, 35, 109, 115, 233,
   243, 245–6, 247
Wendt, Alexander, 52
Westdene, Johannesburg, 205
Westley, William, xiii, 7
White, Hylton, 202
Whitehead, Antony, 183
witchcraft, 195, 200, 233, 238, 241,
   256
women, police, 126, 179
World Bank, 93
World War I (1914–18), 88
World War II (1939–45), 35, 88

Yahaya, A.D., 84–5
Yanbanga, 90–94, 97, 288
Yandoka system, 87–8, 90, 288
yaws, 1
yellow fever, 2
Yelwa, Nigeria, 97
Yeoville, Johannesburg, 207
Young, Malcolm, 7, 156

Zaire (1971–97), 125
Zambia, 2
Zaria, Nigeria, 83
Zimbabwe, 223
Zulu people, 202
Zuma, Jacob, 73, 181